the Comprehensive Guide to Microsoft Office 97

the Comprehensive Guide to Microsoft Office 97

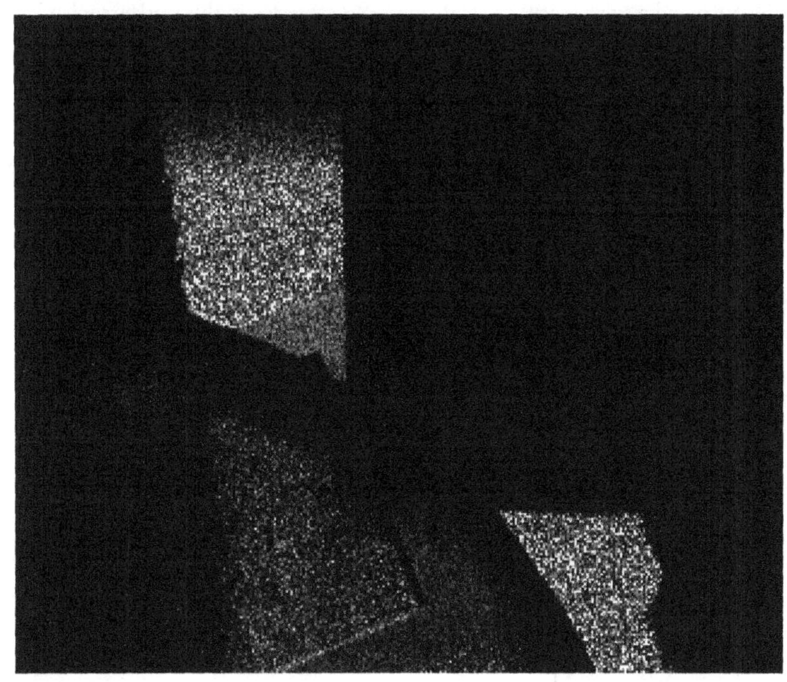

Ned Snell

VENTANA

toExcel

San Jose New York Lincoln Shanghai

THE COMPREHENSIVE GUIDE TO MICROSOFT OFFICE 97 VOL. I

This edition republished by arrangement with toExcel,
a strategic unit of Kaleidoscope Software, Inc.

iUniverse books may be ordered through booksellers or by contacting:

iUniverse
1663 Liberty Drive
Bloomington, IN 47403
www.iuniverse.com
844-349-9409

ISBN: 978-1-5834-8220-9 (sc)
ISBN: 978-1-4697-4097-3 (e)

Library of Congress Control Number: 9961422

Print information available on the last page.

iUniverse rev. date: 08/07/2025

About the Author

Before stumbling innocently into the software industry 11 years ago, Ned Snell had at one time or another been an unemployed actor, a public school teacher, a writer of S.A.T. preparation courseware, and a VCR tape-changer at Bloomingdales in Manhattan—all when not occupied in lesser careers.

Within two of the most successful software firms of the mid-eighties, Snell rose to become a senior editor, and later a documentation and training specialist. He eventually moved from industry participant to observer, becoming an award-winning computer journalist. Snell has written hundreds of articles for *Datamation* (for which he served as a contributing editor), *Software Magazine*, and others, and has served as editor-in-chief for several national publications, including *Edge* magazine and *Art & Design News*. He is the author of seven books (and co-author of several more), and his books have been translated into eight languages, including French, German, Japanese, Chinese, and Indonesian.

Between books, Snell enjoys acting in regional theatre, commercials, and industrial films. He lives with his wife and their two sons in Florida.

Contributing Author

Michael Groh, contributor of the section on Access (Chapters 17-20), is an author, writer, and consultant specializing in Windows database systems. His company, PC Productivity Solutions, provides information management applications and training to companies across the country. Mike is the editor of *Access/Visual Basic Advisor*, a publication of Advisor Communications. He has authored parts of more than 25 computer books, including *Microsoft Access 97 Power Toolkit* (Ventana, 1997), and is a frequent speaker at the Advisor database conferences around the United States.

Acknowledgments

This book is the happy result of the combined inspiration, persistence, wisdom, and plain hard work of a lot of good people. Chief among them are:

- Lisa Swayne and Neweleen Trebnik, who put the ball in motion.
- Diane Haugen, who early on steered the ball in a better direction.
- Jennifer Huntley, who followed the ball, pushed obstacles out of its way, and said encouraging things to keep it rolling.
- Marie Dobson, who made sure the ball went where it was supposed to go.
- Russ Mullen, who made sure the ball's rates of rotation and deceleration conformed to known laws of the universe.
- And Scott Hosa and Laura Stalzer, who made sure that, after the many months of rolling and bouncing, it was still a nice-looking ball.

My gratitude to all.

Dedication

Oh, the people I owe for this book. I dedicate it with gratitude to my family, who patiently permitted this book to borrow me for a third of a year.

Contents

Section II: Word

Section VI: Access

Section VII: Getting It Together

Introduction

Welcome to Office 97! Come in, relax, have a snack. If you want to, kick off your shoes. It's always dress-down day here.

This is *The Comprehensive Guide to Office 97*, and while that sounds terribly lofty, the book you've picked up is lofty only when you count its pages. But if you're like most people, you won't use every page—you'll use just the parts you need. And the parts, my friend, are simple, clear, and—when nobody's looking—fun.

Fun notwithstanding, this book is very serious about helping you accomplish whatever it is you plan to do in Office 97. To meet that end, the book follows a time-tested educational axiom: People learn best when you empower them with a little background and a few important skills, and then get the heck out of their way. As you'll learn if you take a quick read through this Introduction, this comprehensive guide aims to empower you, to give you skills and understanding to take you confidently in whatever direction that your own personal Office projects lead.

If I've done my job right, you shouldn't need this book for very long. You'll be much too busy working productively in Office to be flipping pages here. If you follow the approach outlined in this Introduction, you should be able to quickly acquire all the Office skills you need without wading through a lot of stuff that does not contribute directly to the skill set you seek. After that, you may want to keep the book around for reference or to one day explore any programs or features you skipped the first time around.

Ready to get started? Then read on. I'll start the countdown to the day you go solo.

Who This Book Is For

This book is for real people. And real people have work to do.

Real people don't set out to learn Office for its own sake. They want to learn Word because somebody put them in charge of the newsletter, or learn PowerPoint to prepare for a speech at an upcoming conference, or learn Outlook to find more time in a day, or learn Excel or Access to make straight sense of seemingly random information. They don't want to learn every tiny technical detail, nor do they want to be treated like "dummies" and taught too little. They want to learn enough to get the job done and done right. And because real people all have too much to do, they want the time they invest in learning a new skill to pay long-term returns by laying a foundation from which they can grow, easily adding to their skill set later as their needs evolve.

This book is written for real people who want to learn to use Office at a beginning-to-intermediate level, whether they're newcomers to Office or upgraders from a previous version. It is designed and organized to make you productive in your chosen Office applications as quickly as possible, while at the same time grounding you in essential concepts that equip you to build upon what you learn. Here and there, the book also contains a little humor, since real people have to laugh sometimes or else they'll get crusty.

To achieve all that, of course, the book has to leave something out. What you won't find here are advanced Office techniques that have less to do with getting something done and more to do with programming and with the administration of Office on a network. But even if you're a PC guru, you'll find this book a useful guide to the general operation of Office. This book places no limits on the reader—it just limits the discussion to intermediate ambitions.

Which Office 97 Does This Book Cover?

At this writing, Office is available in four flavors. This book covers all of the programs available in the two principal Office versions:

- The Standard Edition (Word, Outlook, PowerPoint, and Excel)
- The Professional Edition (The Standard Edition plus Access)

In addition to those, there is a Small Business Edition that contains Word, Excel, and Outlook, plus several other Microsoft applications; while this book does not cover all of that edition, users of that edition may benefit from this book's coverage of Word, Excel, and Outlook. The fourth favor, the Office Developer's Edition, contains the Professional Edition programs plus a suite of programming tools—which are not addressed in this book.

Whichever version you use, you may run Office on either Windows 95 or Windows NT. This book covers Office on either system; at the beginning/intermediate level, using Windows 95 and Windows NT is virtually the same, since they share a common user interface. In the few spots where performing an activity differs in the two systems, I'll alert you to the difference. Otherwise, trust that the instructions you find here work identically in Windows 95 and Windows NT. Just think of Windows as Windows—as long as it's not Windows 3.1, which Office no longer supports.

How to Use This Book Productively

The organization of this book is based on a fact of nature: Nobody will actually read it beginning to end, in order. In fact, virtually no one besides me and the copy editors will read the whole book, in any order. And frankly, I can't even make any promises about me.

That's because everyone comes to Office with a different agenda. Few Office users really use all of Office, at least not right away—so there's little incentive to approach the whole bailiwick start-to-finish. Every Office user has a primary application he or she wants to explore first. With a majority of users, that's Word—but with many others, it's something else. Also, folks upgrading from a previous Office version may want to go first to what's completely new—Outlook—before learning what's changed in their favorite Office programs.

With all of those different needs in mind, this book is designed so that you may jump directly to any section to learn about any program—after first taking your Office orientation by reading the two short chapters in Section I. The book is really divided into three chunks:

- **Section I.** A quick orientation to Office, which all readers should visit before moving on to any other section.
- **Sections II through VI.** Program sections, each covering one of the main Office 97 application programs: Word, PowerPoint, Outlook, Excel, and Access.

- **Section VII.** Semi-advanced material showing how you can use Office 97 programs collaboratively, integrate them together, and use them in concert with corporate networks and the Internet.

The two short, easy chapters in Section I orient you by showing you what's in Office and how to do important stuff that pertains to all of Office, such as opening programs or using Help. After reading Section I, feel free to jump directly to any of the program sections. The final section, Section VII, is best left until you've already become familiar with whichever Office programs you will use regularly.

Each of the five program sections is self-contained; it doesn't require you to have read any of the other program sections. For example, after reading Section I, you may jump straight to Section IV to begin learning about Outlook, then jump back to Section II to learn about Word.

You should be aware, however, that if you happen to be interested in learning all of Office, there are rewards to following the sections in order. The order is designed to make the transition from one program to another simple. For example, Word comes first because it's the most used—and most intensively used—Office program for most folks. PowerPoint is the most "Word-like" of the other programs, so it comes hot on Word's heels, while Word is fresh in the reader's mind. Similarly, Excel introduces data management concepts—concepts later expanded upon by Access, which follows Excel. (Okay, so why is Outlook smack in the middle of the book? Simple: Outlook makes it own rules.)

While you needn't follow the order of the program sections, the chapters within each section do build upon one another, so it's best to read the chapters within a section in order. The first chapter in each program section is always "Getting Started," and grounds you in the absolute basics of using the program—creating and saving files, getting around in the program, important terms and concepts, and so on. As the chapters progress, they cover ever-more sophisticated activities; the most advanced (and least used) parts of a program are always covered in the final chapter of a section. Depending upon your needs, you may find that you've learned everything you want to learn before reaching the end of a section. That's OK—learn what you want, and leave the rest for a time when your needs expand.

If You're an Upgrader From Office 95...

If you're moving up from Office 95, you'll find much in Office 97 that feels familiar, and a lot of other stuff that's new. Even such basic activities as saving a file work a little differently in Office 97 from the way they worked in Office 95. So although Office is not new to you, it's a good idea to read Chapter 1, "Discovering Office 97," and Chapter 2, "Getting to Know the Office 97 Environment," to become familiar with general changes to the Office 97 interface and other new Office-wide features before moving on to the program sections.

In the program sections, pay special attention to the "Getting Started" chapter that begins each section. There you'll find not only new features governing the overall use of the program but also essential upgrading information, such as instructions for converting your existing document or data files to Office 97 format.

Stuff You'll See Along the Way

As you go, you'll notice a variety of helpful sidebars, blurbs set aside from the body of the page by a box or shading. You'll quickly see that all of this stuff is self-explanatory, just like the sidebars you'd see in a magazine. But it is a longtime law of computer book publishing that anything self-explanatory be explained anyway, in the Introduction. (That's okay—for the rest of the book, I'll let the self-explanatory explain itself.)

You'll see four kinds of sidebars:

Fast Track

A Fast Track tip describes a faster way to get something done, or offers semi-advanced tips for performing the task at hand. Nothing you'll find in a Fast Track is essential, so you can skip 'em when you're not feeling ambitious.

FYI: For Your Information

Interesting, practical stuff—an FYI box offers expanded information related to the topic at hand—special considerations, problems to watch out for, ideas to muse upon. Atop every FYI, a title summarizes the FYI's main point, so you can easily decide at a glance whether to read the FYI or skip it.

Net-Savvy

A Net-Savvy tip describes Internet-related activities involving the task at hand, or tells where you can find related information and resources on the Internet. Like Fast Tracks, Net-Savvys are never essential—they're just handy if you use the Internet.

Walk-Through

Step-by-step practice—you'll find most explanations in this book clear and simple, so you should have no trouble going directly to Office and applying your new knowledge there. Again, the goal of this book is to empower you with skills you can apply in your own way, not to force you to memorize step-by-step procedures. However, when you work through a lot of new information, the stuff sometimes sinks in better if you take a quick, hands-on practice run. That's what a Walk-Through offers.

Completely voluntary, a Walk-Through gives you a step-by-step, guided tour of the most important activities covered in the general vicinity where the Walk-Through appears. Every chapter in the program sections has two or three Walk-Throughs, each of which leads you through a series of practice steps to accomplish one or more important goals: formatting text, inserting pictures, sending messages, and so on.

Not everything you can learn from this book is covered in a Walk-Through—if it were, the book would cover Office only superficially, or it would have to be three times as long as it is. But the Walk-Throughs provided will give you enough hands-on practice to crystallize the rest of what you discover.

What You Need to Get Started

Starting with Chapter 1, this book assumes that Office 97 has already been installed (by you or someone else) on your PC or local area network. If Office has not yet been installed on your PC, skip to the Appendix to install Office 97 before proceeding with the program sections. (You may want to visit Chapter 1, "Discovering Office 97," before installing, to learn which programs may be valuable to you.)

Note that the various CD files that make up Office—programs, add-ins, accessories, and so on—may be installed in different combinations. During the installation process, the installer can select from among three different installation scenarios, each of which copies a different set of programs and files to the hard disk: Typical, Run from CD-ROM (a space-saving minimum configuration), and Custom (any set of files the installer chooses). At any time after installation, you may open the Office Setup program to add or remove Office programs and files or to customize your personal Office setup. (You learn how to do this in the Appendix.)

The Typical installation scenario has been designed to install all of the programs and files the beginning or intermediate user will need, while leaving advanced stuff on the CD to be installed later, if and when the user needs it. (If you purchased a PC with Office pre-installed, it probably has the Typical installation.)

Throughout the book, the explanations assume that your PC has been equipped with the Typical installation (or with a Custom installation that nonetheless includes at least all of the Typical set's files). Here and there, I cover a file or program that is not included in the Typical installation; when I do, I remind you that you may have to run Office Setup (as described in the Appendix) to add the file or program if you want to use it.

What You Need to Run Office 97

If you have not yet purchased Office 97 (or purchased a PC on which Office is pre-installed), it's important to know Office's system requirements:

- **Operating System.** Office 97 requires Windows 95 (any version) or Windows NT (version 3.51 and up with Service Packs; see the Appendix). At this writing, a Macintosh version is imminent; however, this book covers only the Windows 95/NT version.

- **PC.** Office will not run in the minimum Windows 95 system configuration (4MB of RAM, 386 processor), which is okay, since virtually nothing else runs in that setup either. Officially, Office 97 requires a 486 or Pentium PC with 8 MB for Windows 95 (12 MB for using Access), or 16 MB for Windows NT Workstation. However, for best all-around performance, the recommended minimum is a Pentium PC with 16 MB for Windows 95, 24 MB for Windows NT.
- **Hard Disk Space.** The amount of disk space you need for Office depends upon which edition of Office you purchase and on which installation scenario (Typical, Custom, and so on) you select. You probably need at least 100MB to 120MB of free space on your hard disk for the Typical installation, and require roughly 200MB if you installed all of the Office 97 Professional Edition. If you have Office 95 on your PC, the Office Setup program can optionally delete your old Office 95 program files (but not the document or data files you've created) to recover some space.

  Note, however, that you should never allow your hard disk to come anywhere near full. For one thing, you'd have no room on the disk for your creations. But more important, Windows 95 and NT use hard disk space as a cache to run programs that demand more memory on the PC than is available. Even on a PC with 16MB of memory, the Office programs will perform well only when Windows has plenty of free hard disk space available for caching. For good Office performance, your hard disk should always be at least 10% empty, or have at least 80MB of free space, whichever is greater.
- **Peripherals.** The Office 97 package includes a coupon you can use to order the Office Standard Edition on 45 diskettes, in case you don't have a CD-ROM drive. But realistically, a CD-ROM drive is required for installing Office. A CD-ROM drive is also useful for later adding programs and accessories, when needed, that may have been left out of the installation, or to take advantage of other files included on the Office CD-ROM, such as the Valupack (see Chapter 1, "Discovering Office 97").
- **A Pointing Device.** A Windows pointing device, such as a mouse or trackball, isn't technically required to use Office; you can perform most activities with the keyboard alone. But a pointing device is highly recommended. Finally, you'll need a sound card and a modem to take advantage of the audio and communications features in some Office programs, such as PowerPoint and Outlook.

Online Updates

As we all know, software, technology and the Internet are constantly changing. As hard as I've tried to make the information in this book current, the truth is that some of it may need updating soon after the book goes to press. Ventana provides an easy way to meet this challenge: *The Comprehensive Guide to Microsoft Office 97* Online Updates. You can access this valuable resource via Ventana's World Wide Web site at http://www.vmedia.com/updates. Once there, you'll find updated material relevant to this book.

What If I'm New to Windows 95/NT?

The explanations in this book do not assume you have any prior experience with Office or its programs, but do assume you know the basics of getting around in Windows. To get started you need to be able to perform the basic actions listed below:

- Start up your PC and Windows.
- Locate the Windows taskbar (it's usually at the bottom of the screen).
- Use your mouse (or other pointing device) to move the pointer to an object on the screen.
- Use your mouse buttons. You can perform most activities by pointing to an object, clicking the left mouse button once, and releasing it immediately. (That's called single-clicking.)

  Note: If you're left-handed, you can configure Windows to swap the actions of the left and right mouse buttons to make using the mouse more natural. If you have reconfigured Windows in this way, remember to click right when I say left, and vice-versa.
- Open a program from the Windows Start menu by clicking the Start button on the taskbar and then clicking an item in the menu that appears. Most items on the Start menu display other menus, whose items you may click to start programs or open still further menus.
- Open My Computer, or Windows Explorer, and navigate among the files on your hard disk and/or network by clicking on folders and drive letters.

If you can do just these six things, I'll take you the rest of the way, beginning in Chapter 2, "Getting to Know the Office 97 Environment," where a number of other Windows skills are covered. If you feel you should strengthen your Windows skills before proceeding with Office, see if you can get Windows open (on most PCs, Windows 95 or NT opens automatically shortly after you switch on the PC). With Windows open, press the F1 key to open Windows Help. Click on the word Contents to open the Contents tab, then click the top item in the Contents tab: "Tour: Ten Minutes to Using Windows." Windows will lead you through a short tour which will give you a solid enough footing to proceed with this book.

Also, if you consider yourself a real newcomer and you're not sure where to start your Office education, I highly recommend beginning with Word (after reading Section I, of course). Of all Office programs, Word is the one that a true newcomer will most likely visit first. I have therefore provided in the Word chapters a little extra beginner's detail, such as how to type and make corrections on a PC keyboard.

Enough introducing already—go to Chapter 1, begin your own Office journey. And by the way—thanks for taking me along.

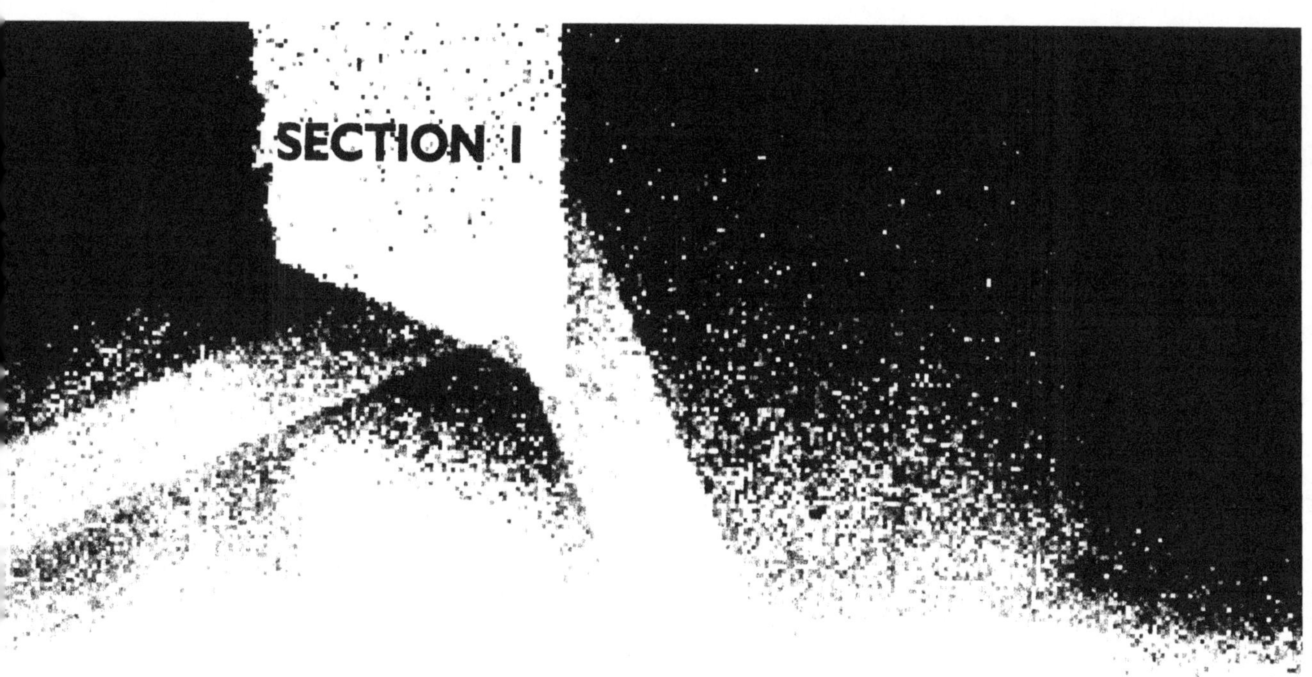

The Office Environment

1

Discovering Office 97

Office? Hmmm...

In naming its all-purpose program suite, Microsoft implies that Office 97 is a traditional business tool, a one-piece replacement for the cubicle typewriter, meeting-room blackboard, mailroom, ledger book, and file cabinet. Maybe that's just a marketing thing—I don't see Office quite that way.

People use their PCs for an astonishing variety of jobs. I once knew a guy who used his PC solely to look for Biblical references in Shakespeare. In practice, no matter where and why people use computers, and whether they use them at work or at home, most people spend most of their time on PCs doing any of the following: writing and formatting documents, drawing pictures, adding up numbers, managing files of information (recipes, baseball cards, stock portfolios), exchanging e-mail, browsing the Internet, and playing games. Office 97 does all of that—except the game playing, of course—and adds just one largely business-specific activity, presentation-making.

The bottom line is that Office is about more than the bottom line. It's a great tool to use around the office, no question. But truly, it's more flexible than that, more universal. Office is really an effort to package together the programs that most people need most often and to give those programs a common look and feel so that users can apply experience with one program to learning another. That's it.

In this chapter, you get a quick overview of the Office 97 programs and their suggested uses. What I hope you'll see in this chapter is that choosing an Office program for any particular project has more to do with your goals than with the traditional "business" role of a program. Office 97 is a tool. How and where you use it is entirely up to you.

What's Office 97, Anyhow?

Office 97 is an *application suite*, a family of programs each of which does a different job, but which together share a common appearance, some features, and the ability to exchange information with one another.

First and foremost, the Office applications are five separate programs which, 90% of the time or more, you will use separately. Each does something different, and for any given job you will open up the program that's best suited to the task at hand. The family relationship among the Office programs does have a benefit—consistency—even when you use the programs one at a time.

As much as possible, the programs have been designed to look and act alike in many respects—with one important exception, Outlook. The use of Outlook is so different from that of the other Office programs that it simply can't fit the mold that Word, Excel, PowerPoint, and Access share, although it tries. Among the other Office 97 programs, however, you will find the following level of consistency:

- **Appearance.** The applications have similarly styled windows, menu text, toolbars, and other aesthetics (see Figure 1-1). This makes all Office programs feel familiar once you've learned one, providing you with the confidence to explore new programs more easily.
- **Menus.** The organization of the menus is very similar from program to program. While each program has its own unique menus, the File, Edit, Window, and Help menus have the same positions on the menu bar in each program and contain many of the same choices. (Some of this synergy exists in all Windows applications, but the Office programs observe it to a high degree.)

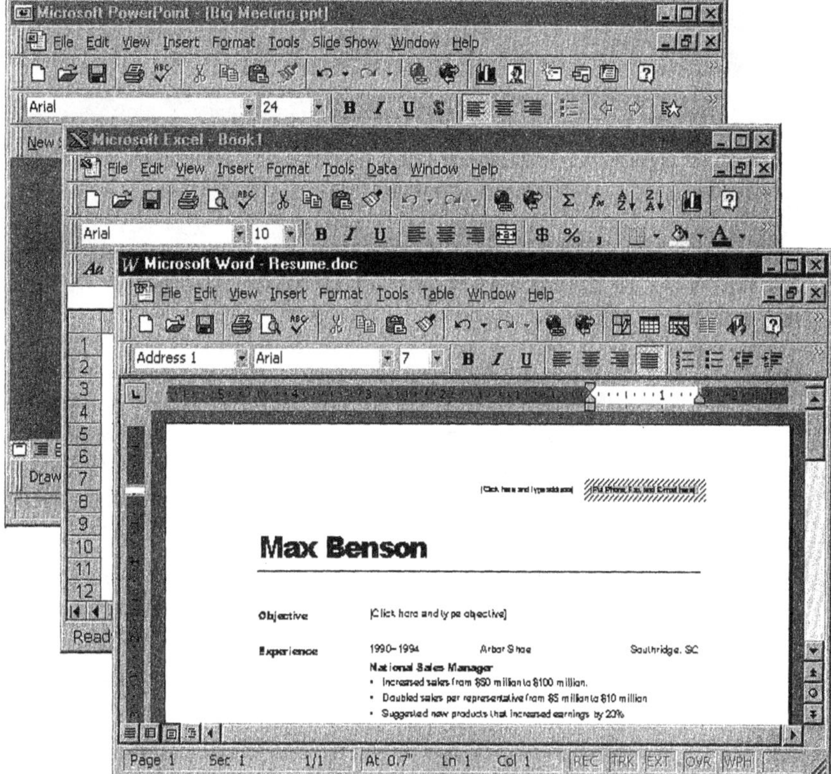

Figure 1-1: Office programs share a strong family resemblance, which makes learning multiple programs easier.

- **Dialog boxes.** The dialogs on which you perform common tasks, such as saving or opening files, are nearly identical among the programs. Although there are subtle differences and unique options among the programs, by and large, once you know how to open, save, or print files in one Office program, you know how to open and save files in them all.
- **Standard toolbar.** Each application has a Standard toolbar (see Figure 1-2), which appears right below the menu bar. While the Standard toolbars differ by program, they all contain buttons for performing common activities such as opening and saving files, and printing. Those buttons are in the same position on every Standard toolbar, and look the same, as well.

Figure 1-2: Notice the similarities (and differences) among these Standard toolbars, each of which is from a different Office program.

- **Formatting toolbar.** Each application also has a Formatting toolbar for formatting text. The buttons on the Formatting toolbars are almost identical, program to program—so when you know how to pick a font from a toolbar in Word, you know how to pick a font anywhere.
- **Office Shortcut bar.** All Office applications are available from the Office Shortcut bar, an optional accessory that hangs out on your Windows desktop to give you quick access to Office programs and files. (You learn more about the Shortcut bar in Chapter 2, "Getting to Know the Office 97 Environment.")
- **Help options.** The Help facilities in all Office programs (including Outlook) work exactly the same way. In particular, each of the programs features Web Help (for finding help and resources on the Internet) and the Office Assistant, a friendly, animated helper that butts in with advice related to what you're doing, while you're doing it. (You learn more about Help and the Office Assistant in Chapter 2.)

In addition to these shared family traits, the Office 97 programs are designed to share information with one another. They do this in the traditional ways all Windows applications share information, by allowing you to cut or copy information from one program and paste it into another or by linking information in one program to a file in another. The Office programs have their own, special level of integration. For example, you can generate form letters by merging a Word document with a list of addresses managed by Outlook, and you can click a button on Word's toolbar to import a table or chart from Excel. You can also use the Office Binder to group together files from different Office programs and treat them as a single project.

You'll learn how to use some of these integration features as you work through the program sections, and about others in Chapter 21, "Collaborating & Integrating With Office 97."

FYI: Is Office 97 "Built for the Internet?"

Office 97 is "built for the Internet," according to Microsoft. But what exactly does that mean?

Well, it means a few things. First, it means that you can use all of the Office applications—except Outlook—in the creation of Web pages that you can publish online. Word is the principal Web-authoring tool, but the other programs can play a part.

Next, it means that you can configure all Internet addresses you see in Office files—whether in a Word document, a PowerPoint show, Excel worksheet, Access database, or Outlook message—as "live" hyperlinks. Click on the address and Windows attempts to connect to it online.

Third, it means that the Help menus of all Office programs include "Web Help," a group of choices which, when you click them, connect to Web pages at Microsoft to display extra help and resources.

Finally, it means that Office includes two programs for interacting with the Internet: Outlook for exchanging e-mail and Internet Explorer for browsing the Web. (Internet Explorer isn't really part of the suite, but it's thrown in to the Office CD anyway, to strengthen Microsoft's claim.)

You'll learn about Outlook's e-mail capabilities in Section IV and about all of Office's other Internet capabilities in Section VII.

About the Programs

The next several pages describe the major Office 97 application programs, their important features, and the types of projects to which you may want to apply them.

Word 97

The most widely used and versatile of the Office programs, the word processor Word provides a space in which you freely type text, edit that text, format the text to customize its appearance, and organize it into attractively designed pages. A true WYSIWYG (What You See Is What You Get) word processor, Word formats your work on the screen just as it will appear in print, so you can easily evaluate the appearance of your document as you work on it.

Word's main gig is producing attractive printed documents, such as letters, memos, resumes, reports, screenplays, and books. In keeping with the times, however, Word is evolving into an equally effective tool for formatting and editing text that you may never print, text that you may instead present online. In particular, Word's ability to help you write better—by correcting spelling, suggesting grammar and style improvements, and supplying alternative word choices (synonyms)—enhances your words no matter where you publish them.

Word's document formatting prowess extends to a level that was once the exclusive domain of desktop publishing programs. Word gives you precise typographic control of text, not only enabling you to choose the font (typeface) and size of your text, but also to control character spacing, line spacing, and the printing of kerning pairs. You can also easily incorporate pictures into pages, controlling the pictures' position, size, and appearance in various ways. The ability to incorporate pictures—along with such desktop-publishing capabilities as newspaper-style columns, borders, and shading—gives Word the formatting versatility to produce newsletters, advertisements, and magazine pages.

Of course, another beauty of Word is that the program's design makes ignoring its complexity easy. When you want a place to bang out a quick, good-looking document—and you couldn't care less about kerning or columns—Word lets you get in, get the job done, and get out.

When Does a Job Call for Word?

Word is your program of choice when the most important aspect of your project is the effectiveness, accuracy, and appearance of the text it contains, and also the layout and appearance of the page as a whole.

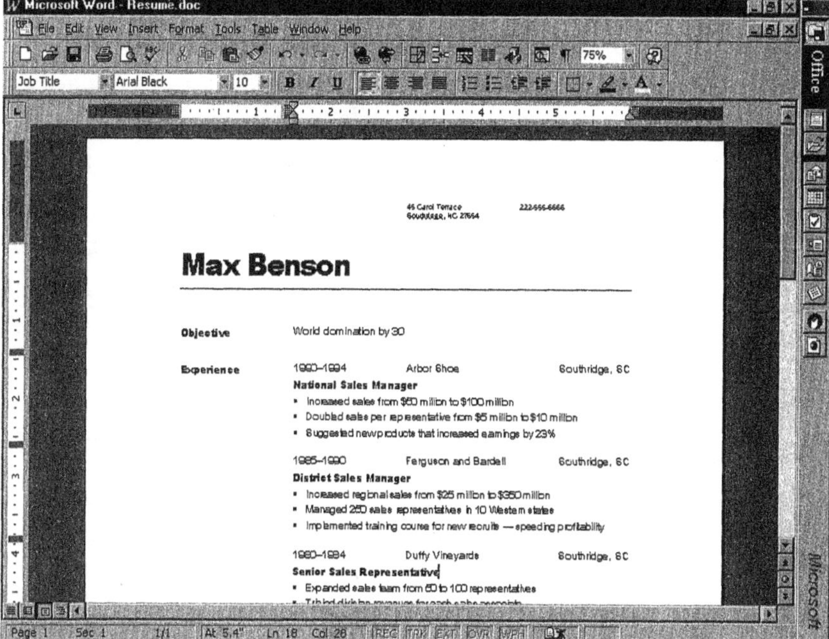

Figure 1-3: With Word, you may produce a limitless variety of formatted documents.

Key Word 97 Features

Among Word 97's most powerful, convenient, or surprising features are:

- Multiple view options that tailor the display to the kind of work you want to do.
- Templates and Wizards that preformat various types of documents to give you a head start.
- Easy text and paragraph formatting—including fonts, automatic numbered and bulleted lists, bold and italic text, and paragraph alignment and indentation—all accessible from buttons on the Formatting toolbar.
- Copy and paste, cut and paste, format copying, and other productivity tools to save you time and typing.

- Powerful tools for adding graphical impact to documents, including pictures, rules, borders, shading, and color.
- Automatic, as-you-go spelling and grammar checking, plus checking on-demand.
- Instant, automatic correction of common typing mistakes.
- Automatic completion of words or phrases you type often, after you type only a few letters of the word or phrase.
- Mail merge capabilities that you can integrate with Outlook's Contacts folder.

PowerPoint 97

Like Word, PowerPoint is about producing documents. But unlike the versatile Word, PowerPoint produces documents with a narrower purpose: to make a point, succinctly. (PowerPoint, get it?) PowerPoint organizes small dollops of text—usually just a title and a short paragraph or list of points—into dynamic, eye-catching slides. The slides are ideal as visual aids to accompany a speech or presentation, or the slides can serve as a self-running presentation, making their point without the aid of a speaker.

Often, people who must make presentations are not day-to-day PC users, or even if they are, they're folks who must squeeze their presentation creation into a day otherwise filled with meetings, travel, and other commitments. Perhaps in recognition of that, PowerPoint is amazingly easy to use. You can put together a great-looking presentation of a dozen slides in an hour or two. Of course, when time and ambition allow, PowerPoint also gives you access to a host of advanced features for controlling and enhancing every aspect of the show.

PowerPoint can send its slides to any Windows printer, which you may load with transparency film to produce great-looking overheads. PowerPoint can also package its output for computer service bureaus that can quickly print your work on 35mm slides (for use in a regular slide projector) or on high-quality overheads.

Additionally, in the age of multimedia notebook PCs, LCD overhead panels, and big-screen monitors, many presenters never bother to "output" their slides to any medium, preferring instead to have a PC show the slides electronically—and that's when PowerPoint really shines. Not only does PowerPoint help you easily create, prepare, and display an electronic show, it also enables you to add exciting dimensions to your slides possible only in an electronic show, such as sound clips and music, recorded voice narration, animated text and transitions between slides, and even video clips.

When Does a Job Call for PowerPoint?

PowerPoint is your program of choice when your project must communicate through an eye-catching series of slides or pages, each containing only a small amount of text and (optionally) pictures.

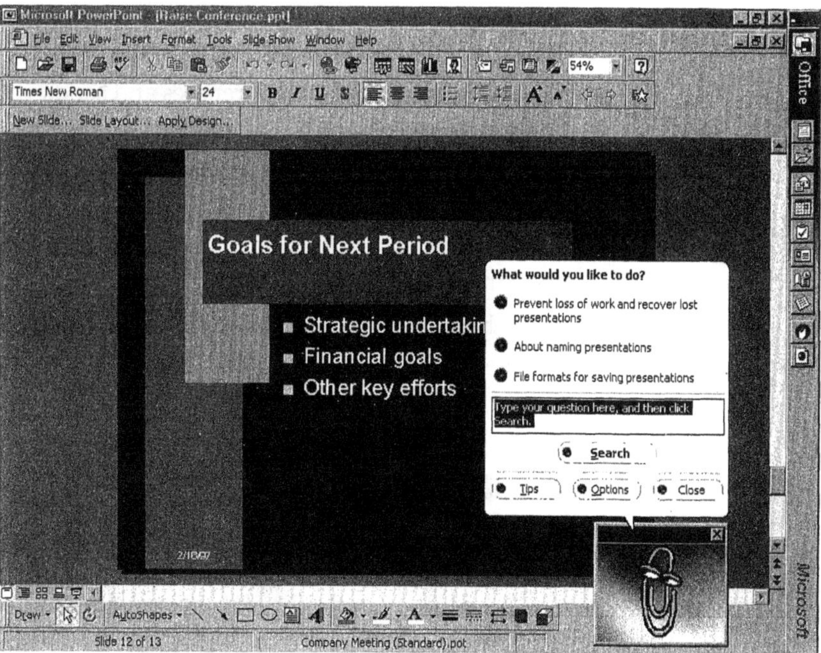

Figure 1-4: With PowerPoint, slides can back up a presentation—or give the presentation on their own.

Key PowerPoint 97 Features

PowerPoint 97's most powerful points include:

- Easy creation of speaker notes and handouts to accompany a presentation.
- Multiple views that tailor the display to the kind of work you want to do.
- Full control of the color scheme, background, and slide design for great-looking shows.
- Full support of Windows multimedia for electronic shows, including the ability to play sound clips, narration, video clips, and audio CD tracks during a show.
- Easy-to-use animation features that make text and pictures move into slides in fun, eye-catching ways, and also animate the transitions between slides with wipes, dissolves, and other effects.
- Templates and Wizards that preformat various types of slide shows, and may even supply some of the content of a show.
- An easy-to-use facility that prepares and sends your slide show to a popular service bureau via modem.
- Easy text and paragraph formatting with buttons on the Formatting toolbar.
- Automatic, as-you-go spelling and grammar checking, plus checking on-demand.
- Style checking that suggests ways you can change your slides to communicate more effectively.

Outlook 97

Outlook is the only new application in Office 97—sort of. Actually, Microsoft took an old personal scheduling program from Office 95—the little-used Schedule+—and spliced its genes with Windows's built-in e-mail program, the justly unloved Exchange. The offspring of this union between mediocre parents is Outlook, an odd but rather handy program designed to manage all of your computer-based communications—including e-mail and fax—and also organize your life by keeping up with your friends, customers or colleagues (contacts), schedule, and ongoing projects.

Outlook is one program with five faces. In Outlook, you jump from a group of mail folders where you manage messages; to a Contacts folder where you record the names, addresses, and profile information of your contacts; to a Calendar folder where you manage your daily, weekly, and monthly appointments and meetings; to a Tasks folder where you plan projects; and finally to a Journal folder where you review (and optionally add to) a Journal of your activities kept automatically by Outlook.

While managing all of that separate stuff has its own rewards, the real power of Outlook becomes apparent when the five faces start talking to each other. For example, you can use a name in your Contacts folder to quickly address an e-mail message or letter. You can drag a Task to the Calendar to schedule some time to work on that task, or drag names from Contacts to the Calendar to plan a meeting (and also automatically generate an e-mail invitation to each attendee). When the various disparate pieces of information recorded in Outlook begin crossing lines, your reward is effective, efficient management of your time, communication, and projects.

When Does a Job Call for Outlook?

Call on Outlook whenever you need to exchange electronic messages (e-mail or fax); keep track of names, addresses, and phone numbers; plan and track projects; or schedule meetings, appointments, and events.

Key Outlook 97 Features

While discovering and exploring Outlook, be on the lookout for:

- Automatic, customizable Journal tracking of all of your activity in all Office programs and files.
- Support for a variety of messaging services—including Internet Mail, Microsoft Mail, and Microsoft Fax—and the ability to consolidate messaging from multiple services all under the Outlook umbrella.
- Complete messaging capabilities, including receiving messages, composing and sending messages, sending automatic carbon copies, and replying and forwarding.
- Room for keeping detailed information about each contact, including name, multiple mailing addresses, multiple e-mail addresses, multiple phone numbers (including fax and pager numbers), and profile information, such as the contact's birthday, job title, or spouse's name.

- Automatic inclusion of national, secular, and religious holidays in your Calendar.
- An automated meeting planner that can help choose a time for a meeting and generate invitations to all attendees.
- The ability to assign Tasks to others by sending automated task requests.

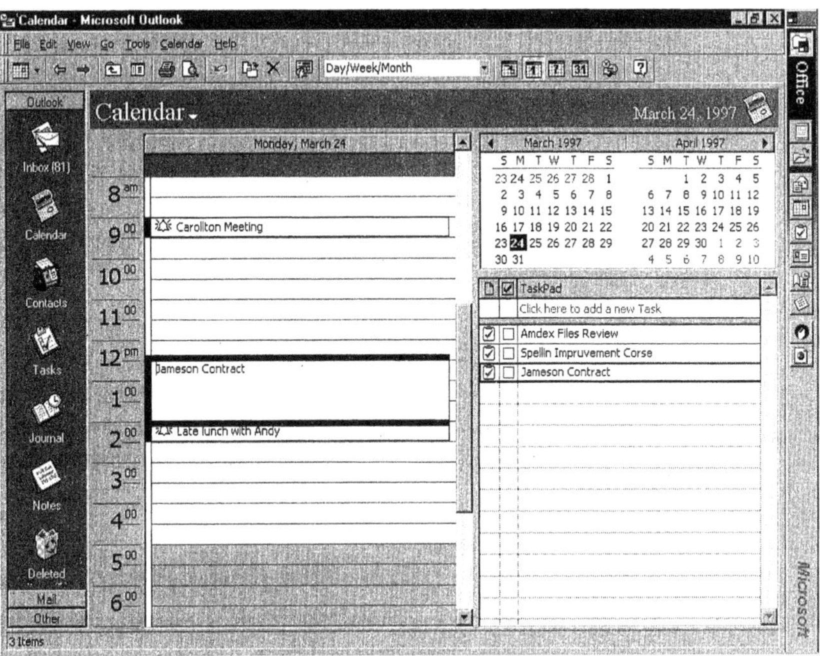

Figure 1-5: Outlook manages your messages, schedule, contacts, journal, and tasks—and the relationships between those items.

Excel 97

As the newest incarnation of the oldest category of PC application software—the spreadsheet—Excel is perhaps the most mature, time-tested application in Office 97. What's amazing about Excel is that all of the history and experience that went into its development have produced a program that's sophisticated when your needs are sophisticated, and simple when your needs are simple.

In Excel, you work in a space called a worksheet, a grid of rows and columns. By entering information into the boxes formed at the intersection of rows and columns—cells—you automatically organize the information you type into neat tables. Excel automatically guesses the type of information you enter in a cell—ordinary text, a number to use in calculations, a date to use in time-based calculations, a dollar amount to use in financial calculations, and so on. While Excel's primary concern is the data in your worksheet—not its appearance—Excel nonetheless provides you with an easy-to-use family of formatting tools for dressing up your tables and text and controlling how they look in print or online.

Once data is recorded in a worksheet, you can use it in powerful, creative ways. You can easily enter formulas that calculate new cell values by performing equations with existing cell data—for example, you can calculate row or column totals, determine statistical variances, or perform financial accounting operations. You can also use your cell data and formula results to quickly generate a wide variety of great-looking charts and maps.

Anytime you change the data in a worksheet, Excel automatically reruns any formulas based on the data, updating the cells that show formula results and also any charts based on calculated values. That enables you to set up a worksheet and its formulas once and then produce quick, accurate results whenever conditions change. It also enables you to analyze and explore your data through "what-if" scenarios. As an experiment, you can change any value used in formulas and instantly see what would happen if that value were to change in real life.

Access is the real database manager in Office 97, but users of the Office Standard Edition don't get Access, and even some users of the Professional Edition may want to do some basic database management—such as sorting or filtering records—but not badly enough to fire up Access. Fortunately, Excel doubles as an entry-level database manager, enabling you to create database tables—lists—in worksheets and then sort, filter, and perform other database operations on the records in the list.

When Does a Job Call for Excel?

Excel is your program of choice when a project demands an easy way to organize information in an orderly table or when some values in the table must be calculated from others—especially when those calculations are financial. Excel is also the place to enter data and produce charts and graphs that you can then import into a Word or PowerPoint document.

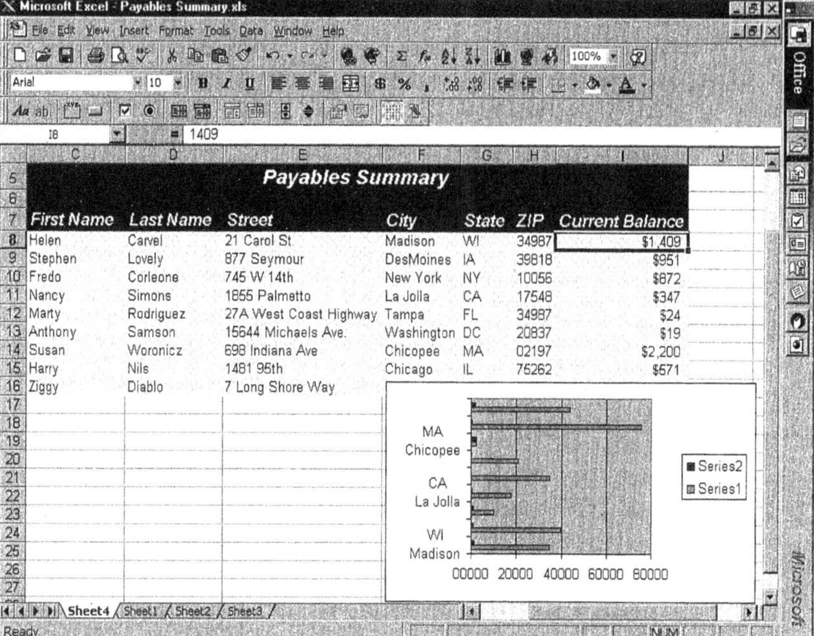

Figure 1-6: With Excel, you can easily organize information in attractively formatted tables and then use that information to produce calculation results, charts, and more.

Key Excel 97 Features

You'll excel by taking advantage of these Excel 97 features:

- Automatic formatting of cell entries, including assignment of number formats.
- Automatic fills, cell entries Excel creates for you by copying the data in a cell or by continuing a series you have begun.
- Quick, attractive formatting of tables through the AutoFormat facility.
- Tools for adding graphical impact to worksheets, including pictures, rules, borders, shading, and color.
- Easy formatting of cell contents with buttons on the Formatting toolbar.
- Functions that enable you to easily perform sophisticated calculations within a formula.

- A Formula Palette that helps you type formulas and functions properly and check the results as you go.
- Easy creation of a wide variety of charts with the Chart Wizard, plus automatic generation of maps based on tables that contain place names.
- Automatic spell-checking.
- Simple, quick database management tools, such as Sort Ascending, Sort Descending, and AutoFilter.
- Special features for formatting worksheets as online or printed forms for collecting data.

Access 97 (Professional Edition Only)

Not long ago, if you wanted to create and manipulate a database on a PC, you did it either in a spreadsheet program (like Excel or Lotus 1-2-3), or in some programmer's playground like dBase. The spreadsheet approach was manageable by nonprogrammers, but limited. The programming approach—while consistently aimed at nonprogrammers—never really caught on beyond the corporate data center.

Access is the latest attempt in a 20-year effort to give everyday computer users the power to easily build and manage a sophisticated database. You get to decide whether that effort has been successful. Certainly, there have been PC databases before Access that were easier to use. (Even Microsoft isn't sure whether Access is for beginners or experts—the program is marketed as a beginner's database, but excluded from the Standard Edition.) But never before Access has a relatively easy-to-use database been so fully capable. Access does stuff on your PC that demanded a mainframe computer only a few years ago.

In practice, Access is not really difficult to master. It requires only a commitment to the job and a willingness to look at data the way Access does. Access sees a database as a table, just as Excel does. Access goes a step further, however, enabling you to create sophisticated databases built from multiple tables containing interrelated data. This relational database model is what makes Access so powerful, and if you take the time to get used to it, you'll be rewarded with a level of control and reporting capability you wouldn't have thought possible.

When Does a Job Call for Access?

Access is your program of choice when you must record, maintain, and analyze large amounts of information, when you need to generate automatic reports based on some of that information, or when you must perform sophisticated data analysis and manipulation operations.

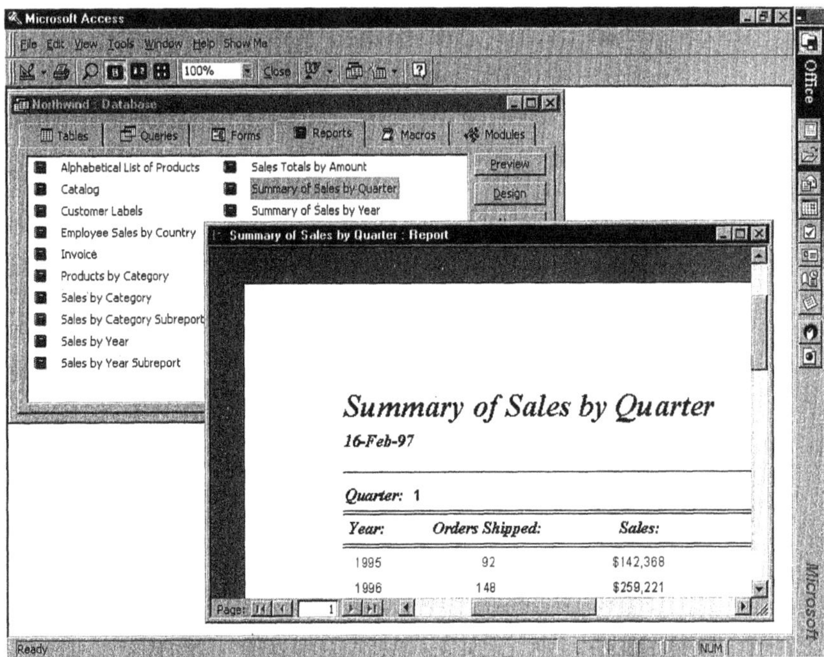

Figure 1-7: Access puts sophisticated data management into the toolbox of everyday Office users.

Key Access 97 Features

To make the most of Access 97, access these important features:

- Powerful, highly customizable sorting and filtering of records.
- Automatic spelling and grammar checking during data entry.
- Easy, quick generation of good-looking reports and tables showing selected data or the results of data manipulations and analyses.
- Quick data summary capabilities such as averages, totals, and statistical variances.

- A Query Wizard to help you phrase queries, powerful commands for sorting and filtering data.
- Relational database capabilities that enable you to update or analyze interrelated data residing in multiple tables.
- Fast generation of printed address labels from a database.
- Customizable forms for entering, editing, and viewing selected data.

Moving On

As you can see, the Office suite is made up of five fat programs that can do an awful lot among them. Except for playing games, you may never need a program that's not part of the Office family.

The feature density of the programs tends to make them look overwhelmingly complex—but don't let that throw you. Each of the programs scales its difficulty level to your ambitions. Achieving easy goals—a quick letter, a simple presentation, a small table—is always pretty easy in Office. Harder projects are, well, harder—but if they weren't, you wouldn't feel so satisfied when you mastered them. And you will.

In Chapter 2, you'll pick up the basics of Office operation—the stuff that works the same in all Office programs. While some of that stuff, such as drag and drop, falls under the heading of general Windows skills, some facilities—like the Office Assistant and the Drawing Tools—are so cool and powerful that they almost qualify as applications in their own right. Move on to Chapter 2, "Getting to Know the Office 97 Environment," and check 'em out.

2 Getting to Know the Office 97 Environment

I grew up in Massachusetts, but never learned to ski. When I lived in Manhattan, I was surprised to discover that nearly every native New Yorker I met had never been to the Statue of Liberty or the top of the Empire State building, and most had never seen a Broadway show. When I lived in Indianapolis, I did so for seven years without once seeing some big auto race they kept telling me about. I've now lived in Central Florida for almost a year without visiting Mickey Mouse. There's no denying it: *length* of experience does not always equal *breadth* of experience, or vice versa.

Even among practiced users of Windows 95 and NT, different folks have different gaps in their Windows skill sets. I know experienced Windows 95 users who had not yet discovered context menus, or many of the ways you can use drag and drop, until I pointed these techniques out to them. Also, not all of us use the same names for the same stuff: what I call "dialogs" you might call "those box things that pop up."

Before you and I can move together into the meat of the book, we need to synchronize our watches and agree on a common vocabulary. In the program sections, you'll be instructed to perform actions by clicking on "toolbar buttons," opening "dialogs," choosing from "drop-down lists," and more. While you may already know from your own experience how to do all of these things, you may not always recognize the words I use to describe them. Also, like most of us, you may have some of those lived-there-but-never-did-it gaps in your Windows background. If you can fill those gaps before moving forward, you'll gain much more from all that follows this chapter.

In addition to getting us all on the same Windows wavelength, this chapter introduces you to various utilities—such as the Office Drawing Tools or the Office Assistant help elf—that play a role not just in one Office program, but in several, or all. Because I have designed the program sections so that you may read them separately, learning about these common elements now saves you from having to review them in the sections on every program where they apply.

Take a quick scan through this easy chapter, and if you discover that you already know about everything it covers, good for you. However, if you see anything new—and I bet you will—be sure to give it a good read. When you begin working with the Office programs in earnest, you'll be glad you did.

Opening & Closing Office Programs

When you learn the Office programs, you'll discover a variety of ways to open and close each program under various circumstances. But just to get you on your way, here's how to get into—and out of—any Office application.

The easiest way to open any Office program is to choose it from the Windows Start menu. From the Taskbar, click Start to open the Start menu. On the Start menu, click Programs. Figure 2-1 shows my Programs menu, but yours will be different, since you and I probably don't have the same programs installed on our PCs.

On the Programs menu, following a short list of program groups, you'll see your programs listed alphabetically. The official name of every Office program begins with "Microsoft," so look around the letter "M" to find your Office programs. To open one of your Office programs, click its name in the Programs menu. When the program opens, its name appears in the title bar—the colored bar at the very top of the program window (see Figure 2-2).

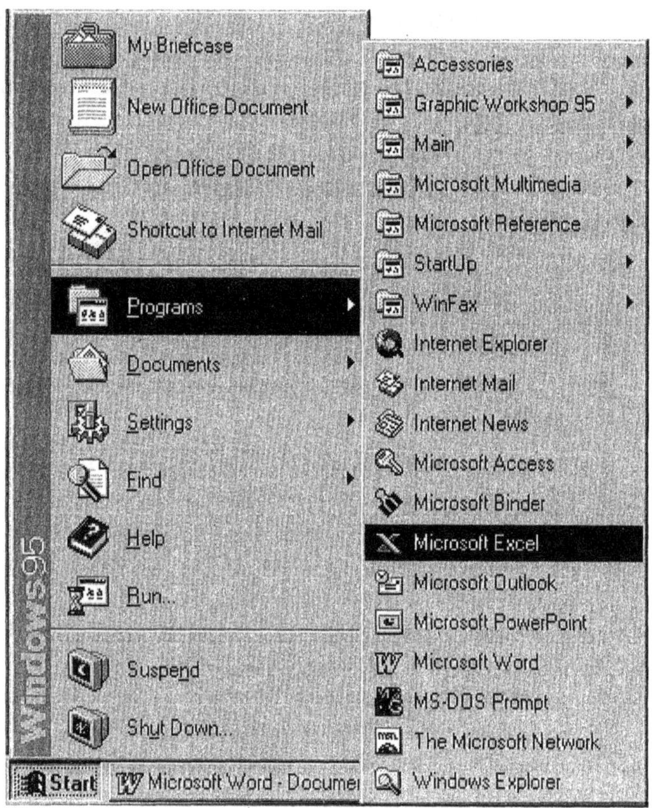

Figure 2-1: Click Start on the Windows Taskbar to open the menus from which you start programs.

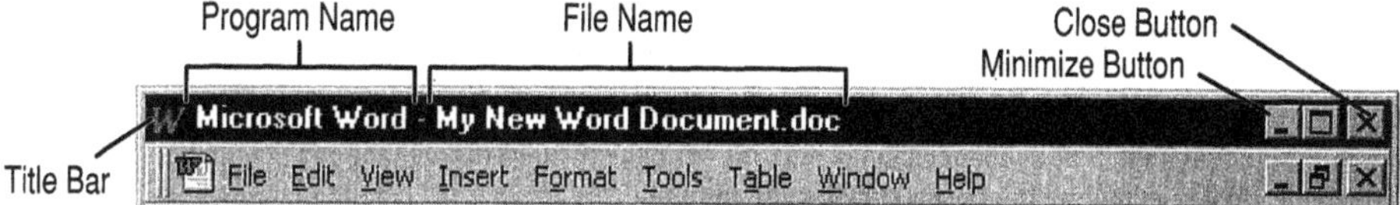

Figure 2-2: Use the title bar—and the buttons that appear at its right end—to identify, minimize, and maximize a program window, and close the program.

Usually, Office programs open *maximized*—the program fills up the whole display—and that's generally the best way to use Office programs. If an Office program opens in a window that doesn't fill your display, you may double-click its title bar to maximize it. To return the window to its previous size, double-click the title bar again.

You have three different ways to close any Office program. All have the same effect:

- Click the *close button*—the X—that appears in the extreme upper-right corner of the program window (see Figure 2-2).
- Press and hold the Alt key, then press F4.
- Choose File | Exit (see "Choosing From a Menu Bar" later in this chapter).

Note that you needn't close one Office program to open another. You can open the Start menu right on top of an open program, and open another. Each open program has its own button on the Taskbar; to switch from one open program to another, click a program's Taskbar button.

However, unless you're comparing files in different programs or moving or copying information from one to another (as you learn to do in Chapter 21, "Collaborating & Integrating With Office 97"), there's rarely a reason to keep multiple programs open, and doing so can slow down the performance of the programs. (In fact, unless you have mucho-plenty memory in your PC, you may be unable to run more than two Office programs simultaneously. See the Introduction or the Appendix to learn about memory requirements.) When you must use multiple programs together, you'll get better performance if you minimize programs you're not using at the moment. To minimize a program, click the minimize button in the program's title bar (see Figure 2-2). When you minimize a program, it disappears from the desktop, but its button remains on the Taskbar so you can redisplay it at any time.

Choosing From a Menu Bar

Just below the title bar—the very top of the window in which a program appears—a row of words appears, beginning with the words File and Edit—the *menu bar*. Clicking on any word on the menu bar drops down a menu of choices, or *items*, as shown in Figure 2-3. Clicking on an item in the menu does one of the following:

- **Performs an action.** The action described by the menu item happens. Pow.
- **Opens a dialog.** A *dialog* opens, on which you choose from among options that control how an action will be carried out. (See "Understanding Dialogs," later in this chapter.)
- **Opens a submenu.** If the item in the menu has an arrow next to it, a *submenu* opens (see Figure 2-3), a new menu to the right, from which you may choose items.

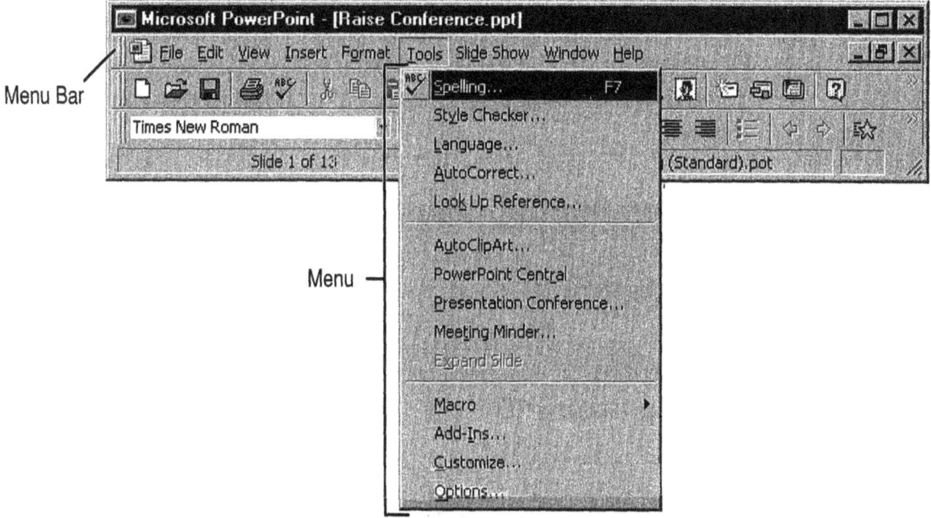

Figure 2-3: Click any item on a program's menu bar to drop down a list of items you can click to do stuff.

In the instructions you'll discover throughout this book, the precise menu items you need to choose to perform an action are shown in order, with vertical bars (|) between each choice. The first item is always one of the main choices along the menu bar. For example, you may see the instruction:

Choose Insert | Picture | Clip Art

You perform the action described by choosing Insert from the menu bar to open the Insert menu, then choosing Picture from the Insert menu to display the Picture submenu, then choosing Clip Art from the Picture submenu.

Using Toolbars

Besides choosing from menus, you perform many actions in Office programs by clicking the buttons—little squares with pictures on them—on *toolbars*, rows of buttons that usually appear right beneath the menu bar (see Figure 2-4). Note that toolbar buttons usually duplicate actions you can also perform by choosing from menus. The toolbar just provides a quicker way to get something done.

In addition to buttons, some toolbars have *drop-down lists* on them. You use a drop-down list to select from a list of options; for example, with the Formatting toolbars available in Word, PowerPoint, Access, and Excel, you can choose the *font* (typeface) of text by selecting from a drop-down list on the toolbar. You learn more about drop-down lists later in this chapter.

Figure 2-4: Toolbar buttons give you quick access to common activities.

Finding the Button You Need

The pictures that appear on all toolbar buttons are designed to help you easily guess what the button does. For example, the Print button in every program's Standard toolbar has a picture of a printer on it; to print whatever you're working on, you click the Print button. On Word's Formatting toolbar, the Bold button—which makes text bold—has a big, bold "B" on it, while the Italic button shows an italic "I" and the Underline button shows an underlined "U." In most cases, when you want to find and use a particular button, you'll quickly identify it on the toolbar by its appearance.

If you ever have trouble finding a particular button on a toolbar, or if you're just curious about what a particular button does, point to a button (but don't click), and allow the pointer to rest on the button for a moment. A *tooltip* appears (see Figure 2-5), telling you the name of the button to which you're pointing. (To see not only the name of the button, but also a detailed description of what a button does, use What's This as described later in this chapter.)

Figure 2-5: To learn the name of any toolbar button, rest the pointer on it for a moment.

Fast Track

You can take a tour of the tooltips on a toolbar to learn what each button does. Point to the leftmost button, and wait a beat until its tooltip appears. Then move the pointer slowly to the right, through each button. As the pointer hits each new button, the tooltip appears.

Showing the Toolbar You Need

Each Office program has many different toolbars you can use, but they don't all appear at once. Instead, only the one or two toolbars containing the most-used buttons appear when you first open the program; each toolbar makes up one full row of buttons beneath the menu bar. If programs were to show all of their toolbars at once, the toolbars would take up the whole application window, and you'd have trouble.

In all Office programs, a toolbar called Standard appears by default; the Standard toolbar contains the buttons you're likely to need most often, such as those for opening a file, creating a file, or printing. You may choose to display other toolbars as you need them. You display any toolbar by choosing View | Toolbars and then clicking the toolbar's name in the menu that appears. You follow the same steps to remove a toolbar you don't want to see anymore. Once you display a particular set of toolbars, that same set appears every time you open the program, until you change toolbars again.

While they rest at the top of your display, the toolbar's names don't appear; but you can learn which toolbars are currently on your display by observing which names on the toolbar menu have checkmarks next to them. Also, note that you can move any toolbar from its spot atop the window—the toolbar area—by working with the double vertical bar that appears at the extreme left end of every toolbar. Double-click that double bar, and the toolbar jumps into the middle of the display as a floating toolbar (see Figure 2-6), which you can drag anywhere you want to put it. (You restore a floating toolbar to the toolbar area by double-clicking the floating toolbar's title area.) Finally, you can change the order in which the toolbars appear in the toolbar area by clicking and holding on a toolbar's double bar and then dragging it where you want it.

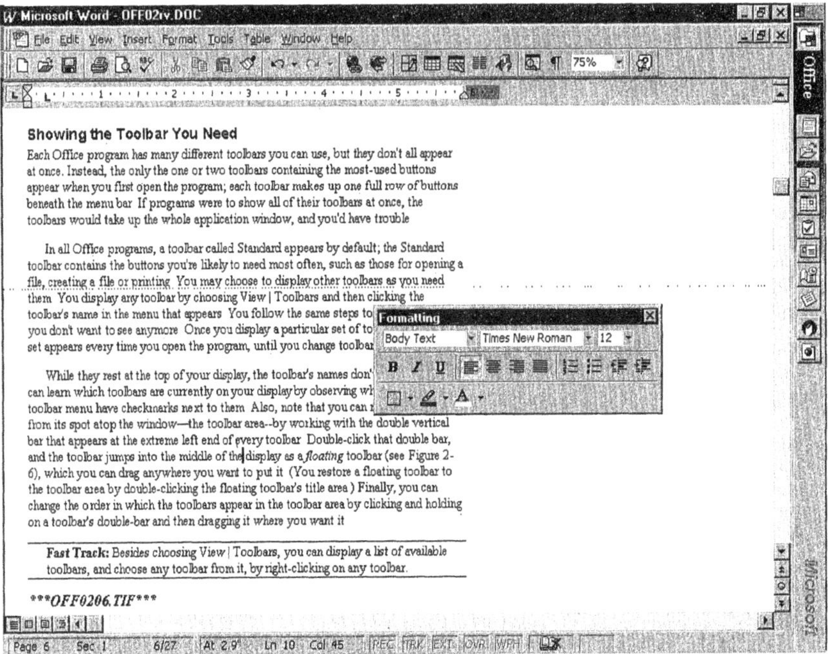

Figure 2-6: To float a toolbar, double-click the double bar that appears at the toolbar's left end.

Fast Track

Besides choosing View | Toolbars, you can display a list of available toolbars, and choose any toolbar from it, by right-clicking on any toolbar.

Scrolling to See More

When whatever you're working on—whether a file, a list of items, or anything else—is so tall or wide that you cannot view it all at once within the window, *scroll bars* appear (see Figure 2-7). When a vertical scroll bar appears along the right side of the window, there is more to see above or below what you're looking at. When a scroll bar appears along the bottom of the window, there is more to see at the sides.

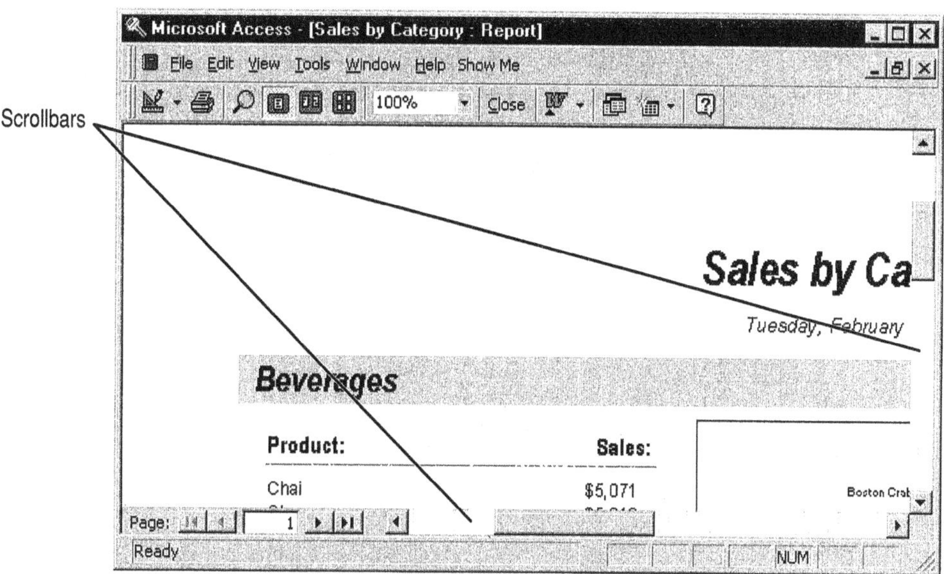

Figure 2-7: Scrollbars enable you to see more than what fits in a window.

It helps to think of the application window as a frame through which you may view something that's larger than the frame. You use the scroll bars to shift the frame up and down or side to side to reveal the hidden parts above, below, or on the sides. Shifting the window this way is called scrolling.

Clicking on any of the arrows that appear at each end of a scroll bar scrolls the window a short way in the direction of the arrow. To scroll a longer way, you may click and hold an arrow, or drag the rectangular box—the slider—that appears between the arrows. Also, any time you see a vertical scroll bar, pressing your PgDn or PgUp keys scrolls the display down or up by one screenful, or use your Up and Down arrow keys to scroll up or down by smaller increments.

Fast Track

In most Office programs, you may make selections on the View menu to magnify or reduce the contents of the window, often reducing or eliminating the need for scrolling.

Dragging & Dropping

Dragging an object means clicking on the object, holding down the mouse button, and moving the mouse. You drag to move any window or dialog from one part of the screen to another, to operate scroll bars, to select text and objects, and much more. Throughout this book, you'll see specific instructions for things you can do by dragging.

When you drag an object to a particular place and then release it, you *drag and drop* it. The main use of drag and drop in Windows is to move files into folders by dragging a file icon to a folder icon, then dropping the file into the folder. But you'll discover some surprising drag-and-drop uses in Office, particularly in Outlook.

Right-Clicking to Use Context Menus

One of the most powerful, least-used tricks in Windows is right-clicking objects to display their *context menus* (see Figure 2-8). A context menu is a list of items specifically related to the object you clicked. For example, if you point to the Windows desktop and click your right mouse button, a context menu pops up, showing items you may click to customize your desktop.

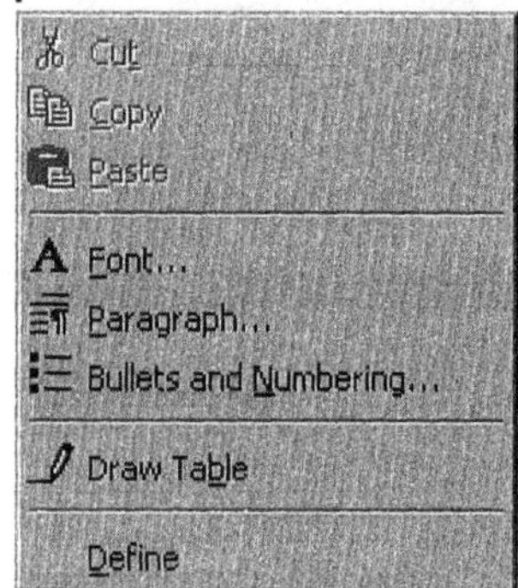

Figure 2-8: Right-click an object to display its context menu.

Throughout this book, I'll alert you to the best opportunities to use context menus. But it's also good to adopt a habit of instinctively right-clicking something you want to work with, to see whether the object's context menu provides you with a useful option. Right-clicking always opens a context menu, or does nothing at all—so you can't make a mistake or hurt anything by right-clicking on it.

Understanding Dialogs

When you choose a menu item or click a toolbar, and a box pops onto your screen, that box is called a *dialog*. On dialogs, you supply information required to complete an action you've started, or choose from among options that affect how the action will be carried out. Each dialog has a name that appears in a title bar at the top of the dialog.

Dialogs come in all shapes and sizes. Most dialogs in Office 97 programs are made up of multiple pages, or tabs. When a dialog has multiple tabs (see Figure 2-9), a sort of onscreen thumb tab—like the tab on a manila file folder—appears at the top of each tab, with the tab's name on it. You click the name to open the tab and use the options that appear there.

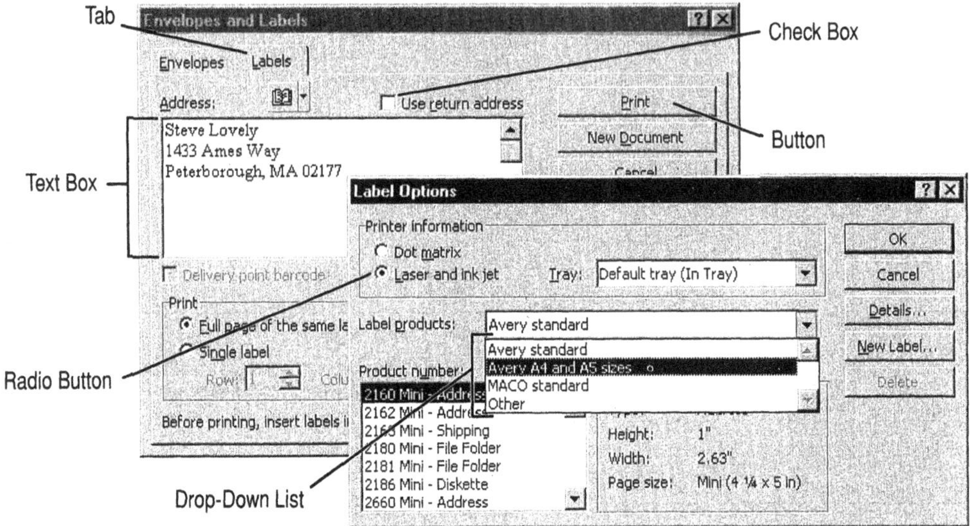

Figure 2-9: On a dialog, you use controls to specify precisely how you want an action carried out.

Using a Dialog

In dialogs and their tabs, you'll supply information and select from among options by using a variety of different controls (see Figure 2-9), including:

- **Text boxes.** A text box is a white rectangle in which you type something. For example, on the dialog you use to save a file, a text box is provided so you can type a file name. To use a text box, you simply click in it and type.
- **Drop-down lists.** A drop-down list looks like a text box, but has an arrow at its right end. If you click on the arrow, a list of options drops down, so you may choose an item in the list by clicking it. You can use many drop-down lists (but not all) two ways: like a text box by typing your entry, or by dropping down the list and choosing from it.
- **Radio buttons.** A radio button is a small circle that indicates whether an option is selected or not. When the circle is white and empty, the option next to it is not selected. When the circle is full and black, the option is selected. Each time you click an option that has a radio button next to it, you select or deselect the option.

- **Check boxes.** A check box is a white square that contains a checkmark when selected, but is empty when not selected. Each time you click an option that has a check box next to it, you insert or remove the checkmark.
- **Buttons.** A button is a small, rectangular box with a name on it. You click the button to perform the action the label describes. Buttons are used for a variety of actions, but most dialogs have at least two buttons: an OK button you click to confirm that you're done choosing options on a dialog, and a Cancel button you click to close the dialog without applying any changes you may have made on it.

Fast Track

A terrific—and often overlooked—accompaniment to working in any dialog is the What's This pointer. Using What's This, you can click on anything in a dialog—a button, an option, a box—and display a description of exactly what that item is all about. To learn about What's This, see "Getting Help" later in this chapter.

Understanding Dialog Defaults

On most dialogs, most or all of the available settings are already made with *defaults*. A default is a setting a program uses or an action it performs automatically, with no input from you, when you do not specify otherwise.

For example, when you open the Print dialog in most Office programs, you may choose from a drop-down list to select a printer to use, and you may use radio buttons and text boxes to choose to print only certain parts of a file. But if you change nothing on the dialog, and just click OK on it, the file is printed using default settings for the printer selection, parts of the file to print, and all other options. Much of the time, these defaults will happen to be the choices you would have made anyway.

Default settings are terrific time-savers, because they match the settings most people are most likely to use. Because of defaults, you'll often find that even in a dialog containing many tabs and settings, you'll want to change only an option or two—or none at all—because most options are already set the way you want them.

Using Office 97 Without a Mouse

Office 97 does not absolutely require a pointing device—a mouse, trackball, or other animal that points and clicks—although using one is strongly recommended. The alternative is *shortcut keys,* keyboard combinations you press to duplicate the actions of "mousy" work like choosing from menus.

Fast Track

Here and there throughout this book, you'll see shortcut key combinations for accomplishing some tasks. When a shortcut key combination is given it appears with a plus sign (+) in it to indicate that you hold down the first key, press the second, then release both. For example, to execute the key combination "Ctrl+P," press and hold Ctrl, press P, and release both keys.

There are a number of special-purpose shortcut keys for performing common tasks; most of them require you to press and hold Ctrl and then press another key. For example, Ctrl+N creates a new file (N for New), Ctrl+S saves a file (S for Save), and Ctrl+P prints a file (P for Print). To help you learn and remember these shortcuts, they appear on menus, right next to the menu items whose actions they duplicate. For example, if you open the File menu in any Office program, you'll see Ctrl+N listed right next to the New item on the menu. (The shortcut key combination is shown on the menu only for your education, not to be used right then; after all, by the time you've opened the menu, you've already done half of the shortcut key's job.)

Although such shortcut keys are valuable, they require memorization and are available only for some activities. A more versatile type of shortcut key combo involves the Alt key and the underlined letters that appear on every menu item and dialog box. This method requires no memorization, and you can use it for almost anything. To select an item or option, you press and hold the Alt key, then press the underlined letter.

For example, on every menu bar, the F in "File" is underlined, so you can press Alt+F to open the File menu. On the File menu, the "P" in the Print item is underlined—so you press P to print. (Once a menu is open, you can choose any item just by pressing its underlined letter; you do not have to press Alt.) In a dialog, each of the options and buttons has an underlined letter. Press Alt plus the underlined letter to select the option or "press" the button.

Besides shortcut keys, other ways to get around without a mouse include:

- **Choosing a dialog tab.** Press Alt+the first letter of the tab name.
- **Scrolling.** Use PgDn, PgUp, and the arrow keys.
- **Moving among text boxes in a dialog.** Press Tab to jump to the next text box, Shift+Tab to jump to the previous one.
- **Choosing from lists.** Use a shortcut key or Tab to move to the list box, then press the Down arrow key to drop down the list.

Shortcut keys can be big time-savers, especially in Word, where you may work faster when you needn't shift your fingers from keyboard to mouse. However, they're really a holdover from the days when mice were optional, and notebook PCs came with inadequate pointing devices. Today, few PCs capable of running Office 97—if any—will lack a good pointer, and Office knows it, having been built with many new ways to use drag and drop and other mouse-dependent techniques.

Can you use Office 97 without a mouse? Sure. But in general, you probably shouldn't.

FYI: Improving Office's Accessibility

While shortcut keys are not the best way to perform most actions in Office programs, people with certain motor disabilities sometimes find key combinations easier to execute than pointing and clicking—especially when shortcut keys are used in tandem with Windows' Accessibility options. All Office 97 programs fully support the Accessibility options, which you enable from the Windows Control Panel.

Open the Start menu and choose Settings|Control Panel to open the Control Panel, then double-click the icon labeled Accessibility Options. On the dialog that opens, you can check check boxes to select features that improve Windows's accessibility to users with motor, sight, or hearing disabilities. For example, a feature called "StickyKeys" enables you to use the shortcut keys (and type capital letters) without holding anything down—that helps folks who use Windows with a mouse stick or who have other motor impairments. For users with hearing disabilities, choices on the dialog's Sound tab make Windows display visual warnings and captions whenever it plays a sound. And on the Mouse tab, a check box enables MouseKeys, which allows you to control the pointer with the keys on your numeric keypad.

In addition to using Accessibility options, users with sight disabilities may choose to adjust various view settings within each program to magnify the display. In particular, raising the Zoom percentage makes text in your files appear larger and sharper. You learn about the view options for each program in the program sections.

Using the Office Shortcut Bar

The Office Shortcut bar is an optional bar of buttons on your Windows desktop that provides quick access to a variety of Office-related activities. When Office 97 is installed, you get the Shortcut bar only if:

- Typical installation is selected, and the PC already had Office 95's Shortcut bar installed on it, or
- Custom installation is selected, and the installer specifically chooses the Shortcut bar from a list of Office Tools while installing.

The Shortcut bar usually lives along the right side of your screen, as Figure 2-10 shows. However, you can drag it to any part of your display. You use the buttons on the Shortcut bar just as you would the buttons on a toolbar; in fact, you can even rest the pointer on a button to display its tooltip.

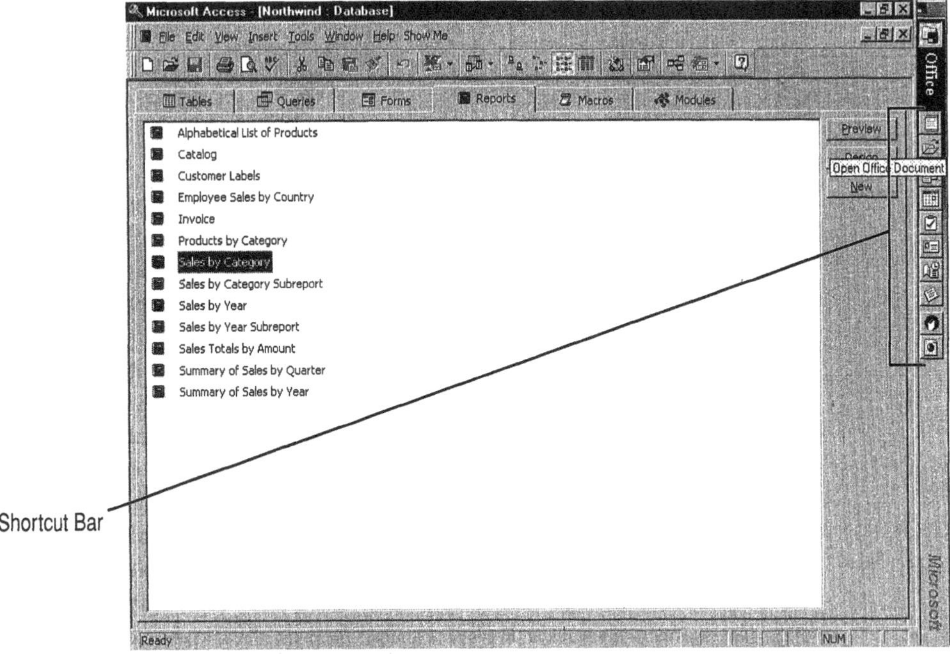

Figure 2-10: The optional Office 97 Shortcut Bar gives you access to some Office activities straight from your Windows desktop.

If you don't see the Shortcut bar on your display, and you decide you'd like to have it, you can add it from your Office CD as described in the Appendix.

Opening Office Programs From the Shortcut Bar

The Shortcut bar is most handy for getting into an Office program through a file, rather than by opening the program. It contains a New Office Document button you can click to open the New Office Document dialog, from which you may select a template to create a new Word, Excel, PowerPoint, or Access file (you learn more about using these templates in the program sections). After you select a template, the Office program that uses the type of template you selected opens, and a new document opens within that program, ready for you to edit. The effect is the same as if you had opened the program first (from the Start menu) and then chosen File | New. The Shortcut bar simply provides you with a different way of going about it.

Also on the Shortcut bar, you may click the Open Office Document button to open any existing file from Word, Excel, PowerPoint, or Access, and open the program at the same time. The button displays the Open Office Document dialog (see Figure 2-11), which lists all of the Office document files in your My Documents folder (on most PCs, that's C:\My Documents). Click the document you want, then click the Open button to open the file and the program used to work with it.

In the program sections, you will discover additional ways to use the Shortcut Bar, if you choose to use it at all.

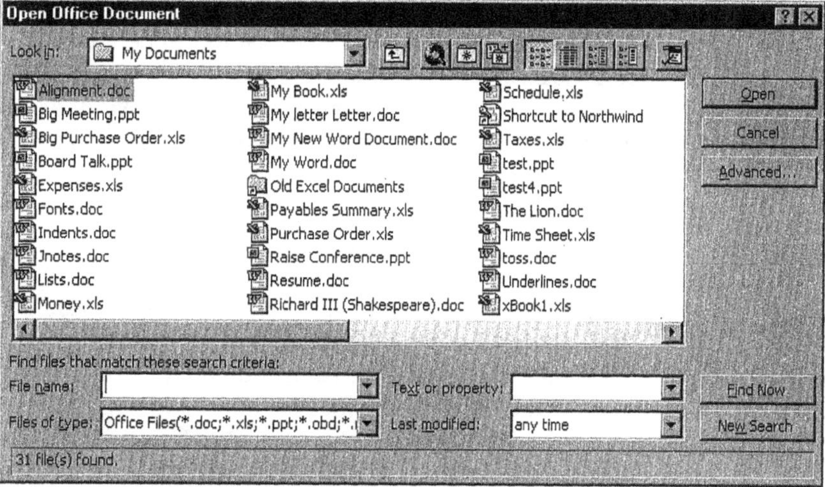

Figure 2-11: Click the Open Office Document button on the Shortcut Bar to open any existing Office 97 file (plus the program used to edit it).

FYI: About "My Documents"

There are other defaults in Office 97 besides what's on the dialogs. Office 97 has a default folder where it prefers to store everything new you create in Office (except, as always, for what you do in Outlook). The folder is called My Documents, and is generally located in the root directory on your hard disk; on most PCs, the folder is C:\My Documents.

When you save a new document, you may optionally choose to store the document in any folder on any disk to which your PC has access—including a shared network disk, if you have privileges there. But if you don't specify a storage location, the file goes in My Documents automatically.

When you use the Open dialog in any program to locate a file to open, the Open dialog always starts out showing the files in My Documents—which makes My Documents the most convenient place to keep them.

You can change any program's default folder from My Documents to another folder by changing the File Locations tab on that program's Options dialog. (See "Customizing Office Applications" later in this chapter.)

Modifying (or Removing) the Shortcut Bar

I have to tell you here and now that lots of people don't like the Shortcut bar, which is why it is only installed under certain circumstances.

First, the Shortcut bar lengthens the time Windows takes to get fully open and ready for work when you switch on your PC. More importantly, Office programs are specially designed to share the screen with the Shortcut bar; when maximized, the programs fit themselves neatly beside the bar so that no part of the program is covered by the Shortcut bar, and vice versa. But the Shortcut bar may cover portions of a non-Office program, blocking your access to the program's scroll bar or other important parts of the window.

If you have the Shortcut bar, and you don't like something about it, locate the tiny button on the bar that's made up of four colored squares (it's at the very top of the bar, if the bar is vertical) and click it. A menu appears with a variety of options for dealing with the Shortcut Bar, among them:

- **Auto-Hide.** The Shortcut bar disappears, and only reappears when you move the pointer to the edge of the screen where you keep the Shortcut bar. This prevents the bar from interfering with non-Office programs.
- **Customize.** Opens a dialog on which you can select from options controlling the behavior of the bar, or customize the bar by adding or removing buttons. Using the dialog, you can even add to the bar buttons that open your favorite programs—even non-Office programs.
- **Exit.** Bids adios to the Shortcut bar. A dialog asks whether you want the Shortcut bar to come back the next time you open Windows, or to go away and stay away. You decide.

Using OfficeArt

OfficeArt is the name collectively applied to Office 97's built-in tools for creating pictures and inserting them in documents you create with Word, PowerPoint, Excel, and Access. (OfficeArt is not available within Outlook. But then, there's really nothing to do in Outlook that would call for art, anyway.)

The OfficeArt tools include:

- **Clip Gallery.** Makes selecting picture, sound, and video files easy. Office 97 includes a library of Popular Clip Art that you can access through the Clip Gallery.
- **Drawing toolbar.** A tool for creating and editing your own drawings.
- **WordArt.** Turns ordinary text into snappy text-based pictures.

The next few pages describe how to use OfficeArt. It's a little early in the game for you to dive right into these tools; this part of the chapter is designed to familiarize you with OfficeArt so you'll have a sense of the possibilities when you begin working in the programs themselves. Feel free at that time to come back here and review.

FYI: Can I Use My Own Pictures, Sound Clips & Video?

Indeed yes. All you need to do is create the file. You can use paint programs, scanners, or digital cameras to produce bitmap pictures, and you can use drawing and charting programs to create vector graphics. You can create movies using video capture boards, or record sounds with the Windows Sound Recorder utility.

In addition, you can use the Microsoft Photo Editor—an optional Office program included on the CD, to control a scanner and also to perform advanced editing and photomanipulation of the scanned image. The final file you create in the Photo Editor can easily be imported by any Office program that supports pictures.

It really doesn't matter how you get the file; that's because Office 97 programs can use—import—virtually all popular picture, sound, and video file formats. After creating the file, you insert it into your documents according to instructions you find in the program sections in this book.

Note that Office programs all share a common library of converters and filters that do the job of preparing files you want to use in Office. While the converters and filters for most common file types are included in the Typical installation, not all of the converters and filters on the Office 97 CD are included. If you follow the instructions in the program sections for importing files into your documents, and the program won't accept the file, the filter for importing that file type has not been installed in Office. See the Appendix to learn how to add converters and filters from the CD.

Picking Multimedia Files From the Clip Gallery

The Clip Gallery (see Figure 2-12) indexes pictures, sound clips, and movie clips by subject, to make selecting any of these objects—collectively known as multimedia files—and inserting the object in an Office document easy. In the programs that support it, you open the Clip Gallery by choosing Insert | Picture | Clip Art.

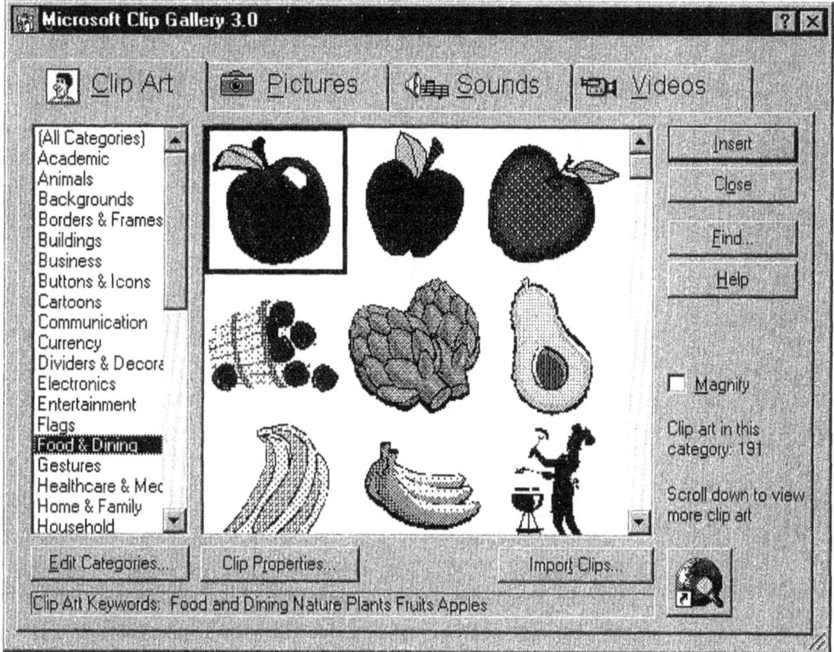

Figure 2-12: The Clip Gallery provides a way to find and insert multimedia files organized by category.

Note that most of the clip art that comes with Office 97 stays on the CD, but can be accessed there by the Clip Gallery. Always insert your Office 97 CD into your CD-ROM drive before opening the Clip Gallery to ensure access to the widest range of files.

The Clip Gallery has four tabs, each of which contains a different type of multimedia file:

- **Clip Art.** Drawing objects, also known as *vector graphics*. These images—generally very graphical in style and appearance—are in the same file format as the pictures you can create with Office's Drawing tool, and you can edit and manipulate them in many different ways in Office documents.
- **Pictures.** *Bitmap* images, such as scanned photos or high-quality artwork. Bitmap images can be more lifelike than drawing objects, but you cannot edit them as many ways in Office programs as drawing objects.

- **Sounds.** Sound clips, represented in an Office document by a speaker icon. Sound clips are used chiefly in PowerPoint presentations, but you may also use them in Word documents designed for presentation online.
- **Videos.** Video clips, represented in an Office document by a frozen image of the first frame of the clip. Like sound clips, video clips are used chiefly in PowerPoint presentations and online Word documents.

To choose a file from the Clip Gallery, you select a tab, then choose an index category from the column on the left side of the tab. The tab shows only the files that match the category you selected. (Choosing the category "All Categories" shows all files in the tab.) You may scroll down to see all files in the tab; in the Clip Art and Pictures tabs, you see small thumbnail versions of each picture to help you choose. In the Sounds and Videos tabs, click any file icon and then click the tab's Play button to evaluate the selected sound or video clip. When the selected file is the one you want, you click Insert to copy it into the document.

To add your own files to the Clip Gallery, open the Clip Gallery tab in which the file you want to add belongs, then click the Import Clips button. A dialog opens, which you use to navigate to and select the file you want to add. After you select the file, another dialog opens, where you choose the Categories in which you want the new file grouped by the Clip Gallery.

Net-Savvy

If you can't find the picture, sound, or video you want in the Clip Gallery, and you don't want to create it yourself, your next best bet is to look in the many multimedia clip libraries on the Web. There you can select from among thousands of multimedia files, download what you want, and either add it to the Clip Gallery or insert the file in a document just as you would insert a file you created.

There are far too many clip sources on the Web to list; instead, here's the address of two Yahoo directories containing links to good file sources:

For pictures, try the links at: http://www.yahoo.com/Computers_and_Internet/Multimedia/Pictures/Clip_Art/.

For sounds and video, try the links at: http://www.yahoo.com/Computers_and_Internet/Multimedia/Archives/.

Before using downloaded clips, be sure to read any copyright notices on the page where you download them from, to be sure you're not violating copyrights. And if you're ever in doubt about whether a clip is copyrighted, don't use it.

Drawing Pictures

From within Word, PowerPoint, and Excel, you can draw your own drawing objects to decorate your documents. These can be as elaborate as you want them to be, or they can be as simple as lines or arrows connecting text or other pictures in the document.

To draw in any of the supporting programs, display the Drawing toolbar (see Figure 2-13) by clicking the Drawing button that appears on each program's Standard toolbar. (Note that the Drawing toolbar, unlike most toolbars, plants itself at the bottom of the display, not the top. But you can move it, or float it, like any other toolbar.) To draw a simple object, click the Line, Arrow, Rectangle, or Oval button. Then click and hold in the document, drag to create the object, and release the mouse button. Besides creating these simple shapes, you can quickly insert more complex shapes by dropping down the AutoShapes list from the Drawing toolbar.

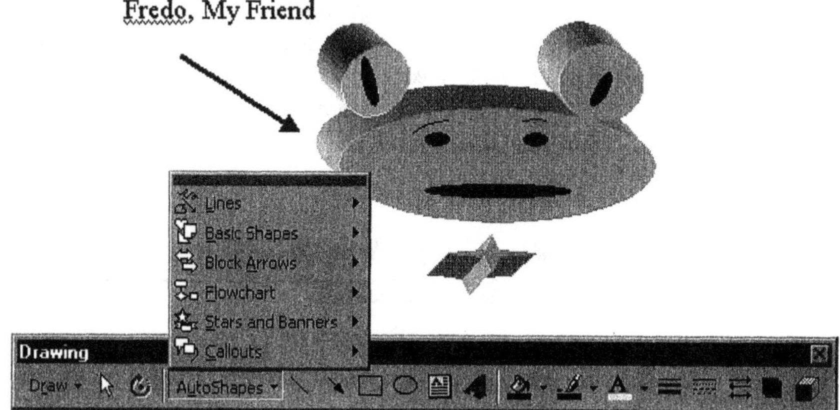

Figure 2-13: Use the tools on the Drawing toolbar to create your own drawing objects.

Once you've inserted the basic shapes in your document, you can manipulate them. You begin by clicking on your drawing object to select it; when you do, its handles appear, little white squares you can click and drag to change the size or shape of the object. (You learn more about handles in the program sections.) Once an object is selected, you can:

- Click and drag the object to change its position.
- Click the Free Rotate button to rotate the object to a different angle.
- Click and drag a handle to edit the size and shape of the object.
- Click the Fill Color button to fill in ovals and rectangles with a selected color.
- Click the Line Color button to choose a color for lines and shape outlines.
- Click the Shadow and 3D buttons to add a three-dimensional look to your shapes.

Fast Track

You create complex drawings by drawing the various lines and shapes that make up the drawing, then grouping them into one.

Begin by drawing and positioning the objects. Next, click the Select Objects button on the Drawing toolbar and click and drag in the document to pull a dashed box around the objects, which selects all of the objects at once. Finally, drop down the Draw list and choose Group. Once you group a drawing, you can move it, change its size, and otherwise treat it as a single object.

If you need to ungroup it later, you can select it and choose Ungroup from the Drawing toolbar.

Turning Words to Art With WordArt

WordArt lets you turn ordinary text into cool, stylized word-based artwork, like the fun and funky text and logos you see in ads. To create WordArt in the programs that support it, choose Insert | Picture | WordArt. The WordArt Gallery opens (see Figure 2-14), where you can choose from among the many available WordArt styles. After you choose a style, another dialog opens in which you type the words you want to use.

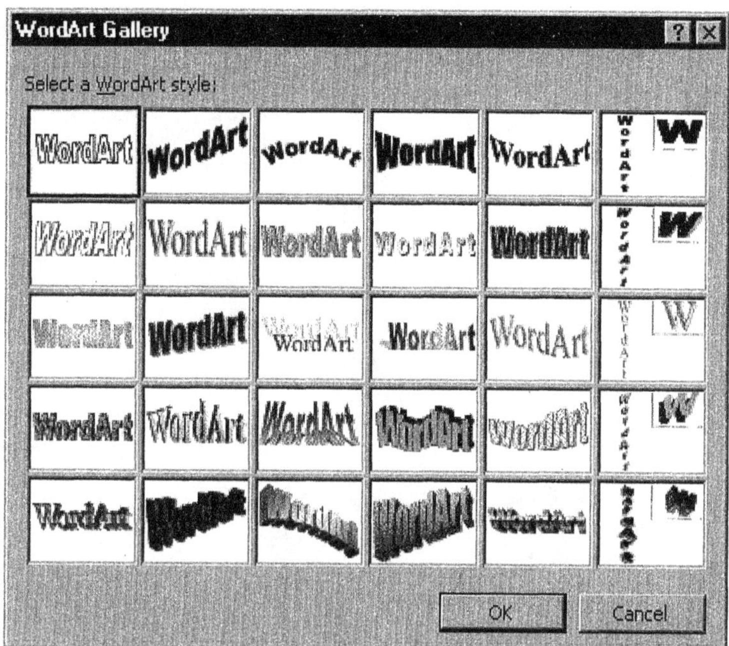

Figure 2-14: Choose a WordArt style to create highly stylized text that you can manipulate as a picture.

When you finish, the new art appears in your file, along with a WordArt toolbar. You can drag the art to position it, or change its size and shape by clicking and dragging its handles, or edit it in other ways by using buttons on the WordArt toolbar.

Customizing Office Applications

Every Office application program has its own Options dialog (see Figure 2-15), and in every Office program you open it the same way: Choose Tools | Options. The Options dialog contains an assortment of tabs on which you can change the appearance and behavior of the program.

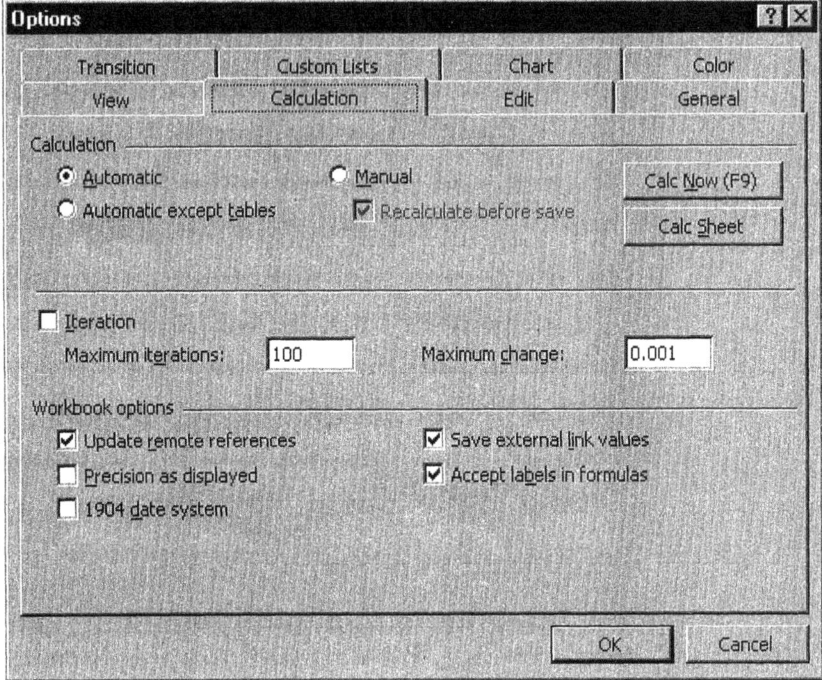

Figure 2-15: Choosing Tools | Options in any Office program opens that program's Options dialog.

In the program sections of this book, you learn how to use some of the more important settings on each program's Options dialog. The Options dialogs simply contain too many options for me to discuss each in detail. The defaults on each program's Options dialog have been carefully selected to configure the program in a way most users will prefer, so while you're learning a program, you're usually better off leaving its Options dialog alone. However, as you gain experience, you may find that you don't like the way some aspects of the program look or behave. When you get to that point, you may find that you can modify the program to your liking by changing settings on the Options dialog.

When you feel ready to change options, be sure to use the What's This arrow (described in "Getting Help") to learn what a setting does before you change it.

Getting Help

The Office 97 programs offer a richer, more versatile set of Help options than most Windows programs. In particular, they add Office Assistant—which you may find either hugely helpful or assertively annoying—to the standard Windows Help facilities, as well as a whole bagful of "Web Help" links that may or may not hook you up to more help online.

The Office Assistant

Perhaps the single most radical new feature of Office 97 is the Office Assistant (see Figure 2-16), an animated cartoon character that pops up to offer help. By default, the Office Assistant pops up immediately when you open any Office program, offering a list of options—in a comic-style word balloon—to help you get started. The character that represents the Office Assistant starts out as a paper clip with eyes, but you can change the character and customize the Office Assistant in other ways, too.

When the Assistant offers you a list of help items in its word balloon, you can click any item to read whatever help text the Office Assistant has to offer, or press the Esc key to close the word balloon and go back to work. When you display the help text the Office Assistant suggests, what you see is generally the same help text you'd see if you navigated to a help topic in the traditional help facility, Contents and Index.

As you work, the Office Assistant stays open in a corner of your screen; you can drag it anywhere on the screen, if it's in your way. Also, if you don't use it for a few minutes, it becomes smaller by about half, making itself less conspicuous.

While open, the Assistant monitors your activities—and blinks its eyes, makes faces, and does various other little animated tricks, just to show off. If the Assistant senses you're having trouble with something, the word balloon opens, offering a list of help items the Assistant guesses may help you accomplish what you're trying to do.

Sometimes, the word balloon doesn't open, but a little yellow light bulb appears within the Office Assistant's window. The light bulb means the Assistant has a tip for you, but it's trying not to impose. To see the tip, click the bulb.

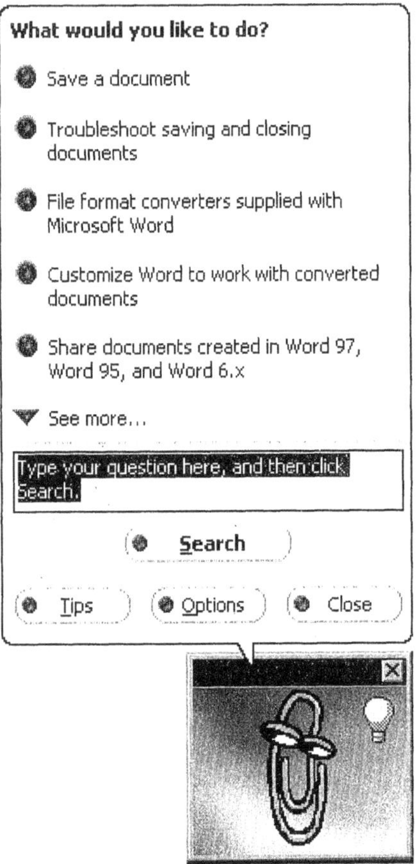

Figure 2-16: The Office Assistant watches over your shoulder and offers help when it thinks you need some.

The Office Assistant isn't limited to making suggestions. You can ask it a question by typing a search term—a word, phrase, or even a whole sentence describing something you want help with—in the text box on the word balloon. (If the word balloon isn't open when you want to ask a question, click the Office Assistant.) For example, in Word, you might type "add a picture" in the word balloon's text box when you want help with adding a picture to a Word document. Then click the Search button in the word balloon, and the Assistant displays a list of help topics it thinks may be related to your problem. Choose one that looks promising or try a different search term.

Hiding the Office Assistant

If you don't want to see the Assistant, you can hide it by clicking the X button in its upper-right corner. You can redisplay it at any time by:

- Pressing F1.
- Choosing Help, and then choosing the top item on the Help menu. (The wording of that item will differ program to program.)
- Clicking the Office Assistant icon anywhere you see it. The icon appears as a button on the far-right end of the Standard toolbar in most Office 97 programs, and also shows up in dialogs here and there.

I should point out that a lot of people don't like the Office Assistant, considering it either too intrusive or too "cutesy." For your own sake, though, I'd advise you to leave it open, at least for the first week or two you use Office. If you find you don't use it, then by all means hide it. But once you get used to it, you may find it handy. And if you don't give it a chance to prove itself to you, you'll never know what you're missing.

Customizing the Office Assistant

On the Office Assistant dialog (see Figure 2-17), you choose the Assistant character and also control the way it behaves. To open the Office Assistant dialog, first insert your Office 97 CD into your CD-ROM drive (it contains the various characters you can select). Then click the Options button that usually appears in the Assistant's word balloon (see Figure 2-16).

Click the Gallery tab to choose a character. On the tab, click Next to move through the nine available characters, which include Albert Einstein, Shakespeare, a cat, and a group of more abstract choices. When you see the character you want, click OK, or move on to the Options tab. Note that changing the character changes only the Assistant's appearance; you still get exactly the same help from it. (Einstein is no smarter than the cat.) On the Options tab, check or clear check boxes to control how and when the Assistant offers help, and when it should leave you alone.

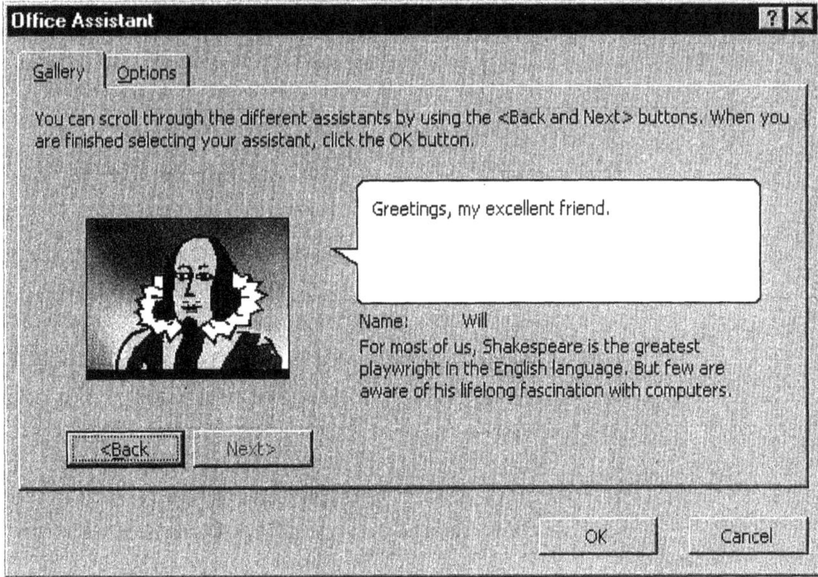

Figure 2-17: Use the Office Assistant dialog to choose a new personality for the Office Assistant.

Fast Track

If you right-click the Office Assistant, a content menu appears, offering items that close the Office Assistant (Hide Assistant), show tips (See tips), open the Options dialog (Options), and more. The context menu also includes an Animate button that you may click to send the Assistant into a brief spasm of rapid animation for no apparent reason.

What's This?

What's This changes the windows pointer to an arrow with a question mark next to it. While the arrow is in that state, you may point to almost anything on the screen—a toolbar button, a menu item, an option in a dialog, a dialog's title bar—to display a brief description of what the object is or how you use it (see Figure 2-18). What's This is a great way to learn more about the various options on a dialog while making choices there, or to learn what different toolbar buttons do.

You can get the What's This pointer in three ways:

- Choose Help | What's This.
- Press Shift+F1.
- Click the question mark button that appears in the upper-right corner of most dialogs (next to the X button).

After you click on something to display its help text, the pointer reverts to the regular Windows pointer, and you may continue working normally in the program or choose What's This again to learn about something else.

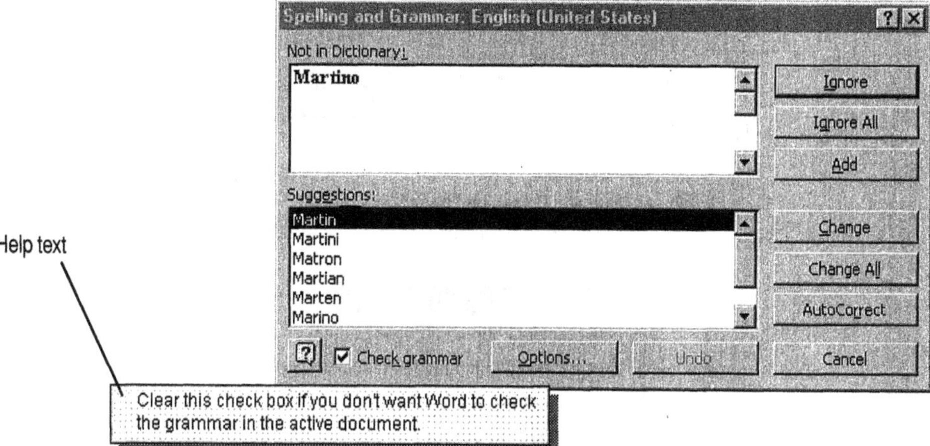

Figure 2-18: When you have the What's This pointer, click on anything to learn more about it.

Contents and Index

The standard Help facility in Office 97 and most other Windows programs, Contents and Index provides the most complete access to a program's Help resources. In all Office 97 programs, you open Contents and Index by choosing Help | Contents and Index.

The Contents and Index dialog (see Figure 2-19) has three tabs:

- **Contents.** A table of contents to the whole help system. Entries that have little book icons next to them represent multiple help topics grouped by subject; click the book to display the individual help topic entries, which have little question mark icons next to them.

- **Index.** An alphabetical index to help topics. Type a word or phrase in the text box at the top of the tab, and the Index scrolls to the help topic in the index.
- **Find.** A search facility for when you come up dry in the Contents and Index tabs. When you click Find, you're provided with instructions for compiling a search database and entering a search term, from which Find produces a list of help topics you may click to display the help.

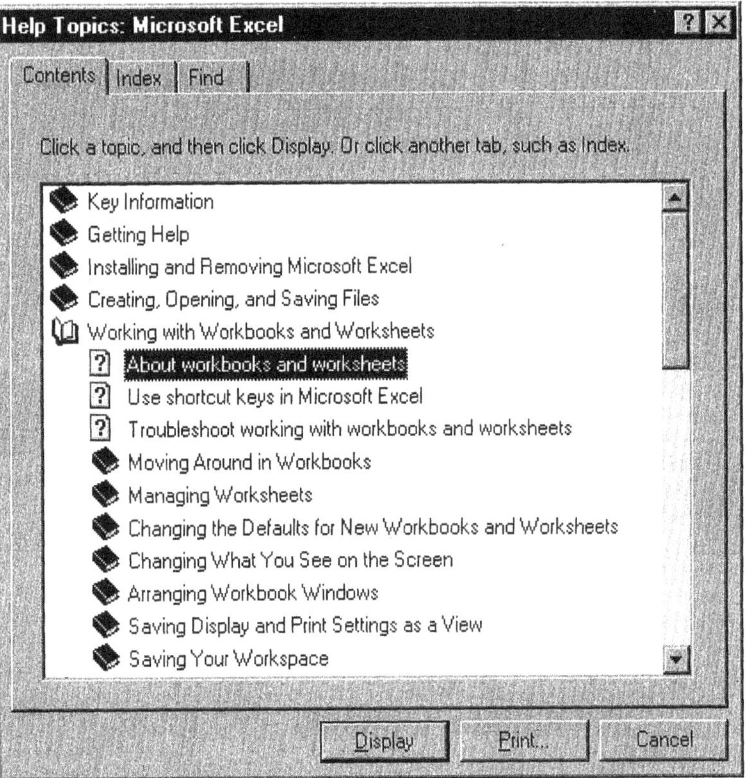

Figure 2-19: The Contents and Index help facility lets you find a help topic by subject, alphabetically, or through a search.

Note that all three tabs lead to the same help topics—they just provide you with three different ways of looking for what you want. When you reach a help topic, it appears like the one in Figure 2-20. At the top of the topic appear three buttons: Help Topics (returns you to the Contents and Index dialog), Back (takes you back to the previous topic you viewed), and Options (displays a list of options for working with the help topic, such as Print Topic).

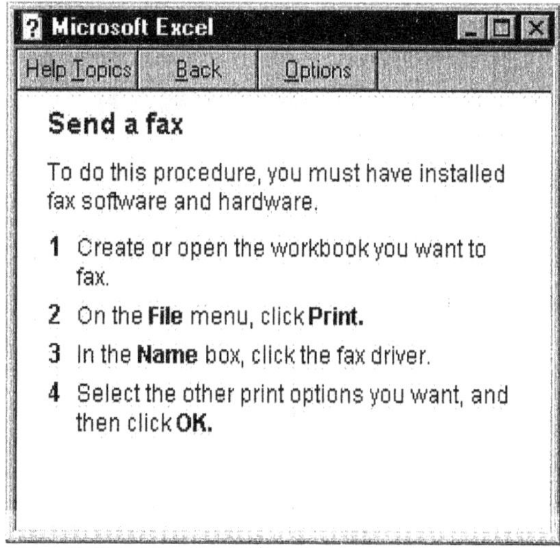

Figure 2-20: Help topics supply the explanations you've requested through the Office Assistant or Contents and Index.

Usually, a help topic simply tells you how to do something, step-by-step. But within a help topic, you may also see a number of objects that can supplement the help:

- **Show me.** Click the Show me button to see an animated walk-through of the task the help topic describes.
- **Underlined words.** Click any word underlined with dashes to see a definition for that word.
- **A gray button with a double-carat (>>).** Click this button to jump to a related help topic.

Web Help

In the Help menu of every Office application, you'll see the item, "Microsoft on the Web." Click that item, and a submenu appears (see Figure 2-21). Each item on this submenu is an Internet shortcut, a link straight to a particular page at Microsoft's Web site.

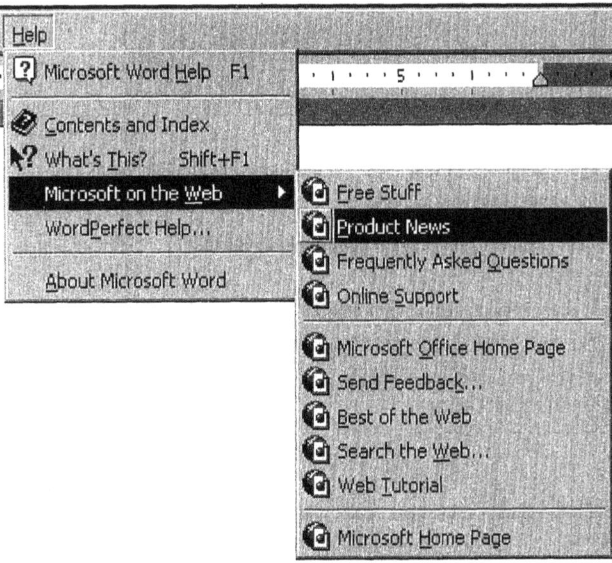

Figure 2-21: If you have the right configuration, the Microsoft on the Web help items take you directly to help resources on Microsoft's Web server.

To use these links, you must have the following:

- **An Internet connection configured in Windows.** A dial-up connection (made through a modem) or through a local network server.
- **Windows's Internet AutoDial feature enabled.** Internet resources initiate the connection procedure. (To enable AutoDial for a typical Windows Internet setup, open the Internet icon in the Control Panel, click the Connection tab, and check the check box for Connect to Internet as needed.)

- **A default Web browser specified.** Opens automatically whenever a Web resource is requested in Windows. Most Windows Web browsers—including Internet Explorer and Netscape Navigator—become the default browser automatically when you install them.

If you have all of this, clicking any of the Microsoft on the Web items opens your Web browser, initiates the Internet connection, and displays the help at Microsoft's Web site. (Depending upon your Internet configuration, you may be prompted to type your Internet password while Windows is connecting to the Internet.)

Web help is a good idea, and by all means you should try it. Depending upon your available memory and other factors, you may find accessing help text this way unreliable, even to the point where it brings your PC to a screeching halt. The combination of Office applications, a Web browser, and network protocols all open and working together is a huge load on most PCs.

Instead of taking your chances with Web help, you may instead want to simply browse the Web directly. Listed below are the principle Web page addresses where you can learn more about Office. I must warn you, however, that at this writing these pages offer surprisingly little actual help. With luck, by the time you read this, these pages will have more to offer:

- General Office information and reference, http://www.microsoft.com/msoffice/.
- Free Office add-ins and accessories, http://www.microsoft.com/OfficeFreeStuff/.
- Office Technical Support, http://www.microsoft.com/msOfficeSupport/.

Net-Savvy

On the Office Shortcut bar, you'll find a button for the Office Getting Results book. If you click this button, it opens your Web browser, then opens a file in your Web browser that contains nothing but a link you can click to connect to the Internet and open Getting Results, a general-purpose, Web-based Office reference book that really doesn't tell you much.

If you don't use the Shortcut Bar, you can go directly to the Getting Results book by pointing your Web browser to http://www.microsoft.com/OfficeReference/GettingResults/.

About the Valupack

The Office Valupack is a library of additional templates, add-ins, sample files, and other useful stuff that is never installed by the Office Setup program. Instead, it sits on your Office CD until you need it. From time to time in the program sections, I'll direct you to files on the Valupack that you may find helpful with the job at hand.

To check out the Valupack yourself, insert your Office 97 CD in your CD-ROM drive, click the My Computer icon on your Windows desktop, and double-click the icon for your CD-ROM drive. A window opens, showing the contents of your Office 97 CD. Double-click the Valupack folder, and explore the folders within it.

Moving On

If you have a feel for all that's in this chapter, you're fully prepared to take on any Office program you like. Don't worry if anything you discovered in this chapter feels fuzzy to you now—it'll come into focus as soon as you have an opportunity to apply it for real. This chapter is just orientation, not graduation.

From here, you may jump straight to any of the Program Sections to learn the specifics of your favorite (or predicted favorite) Office program. Be sure to begin the section with its first chapter, "Getting Started With…," to learn the lay of the land in that program.

If no particular program beckons you, may I suggest that you simply move forward from here straight on to Chapter 3, "Getting Started With Word," for Word may be the only Office program that's used by virtually everyone who has Office.

SECTION II

Word

3 Getting Started With Word

For most people, Word is sort of like a car that can go 140 MPH. You'll never actually drive that fast (I hope), but somehow you enjoy knowing you *could* go that fast.

Word can do so much, and has so many capabilities, that few users apply even a fraction of what Word can do. (Take a look at Word's toolbar—it has more switches and lights than the Space Shuttle.) And that makes perfect sense; you use Word not to give its feature set a workout, but to produce the exact document you want. If that document is a simple one, you'll produce it simply in Word, easily ignoring any extraneous power tools. If the document is elaborate, well, Word has all the gadgets you need to produce the exact document you want, from a book to a brochure to a Web page. You put into Word only as much as you want to get out of it.

In keeping with that principle, this section of the book proceeds from the very simplest of techniques—those that are applied in virtually any document—to more advanced, less-used features in the later chapters. In this first chapter about Word, you get the absolute basics: creating a new Word document, basic typing, saving the document, and finally printing it. And if you're upgrading from an earlier version of Word, here you'll learn how to upgrade your existing Word documents—and documents in many other word processing formats—to Word 97, and vice versa.

You can find all of the toolbar buttons described in this chapter on Word's Standard toolbar, shown in Figure 3-1. If you don't see the Standard toolbar on your screen, point to any spot on any visible toolbar and right-click (or choose View | Toolbars from the menu bar), then click Standard. To display the name of any button on the toolbar, rest the pointer on the button for a moment.

Figure 3-1: Word's Standard toolbar, whose buttons you click in many of the activities in this chapter.

Creating a New Word Document

As you know from Chapter 2, "Getting to Know the Office 97 Environment," if you have chosen to install the Office 97 Shortcut bar, you can create any new Office document (including a Word document) straight from the Shortcut bar. Click the Shortcut bar's New Office Document button to open the New Office Document dialog, then double-click the icon for Blank Document. (Instead of Blank Document, you may select any of the other template files that appear as Word—rather than Excel or PowerPoint—icons. But stick with Blank Document for now—you learn all about templates in Chapter 7, "Working Faster & Easier in Word.") After you double-click the template icon, Word opens, and the new, blank document opens within Word, ready to accept whatever you type.

Of course, you can also create a new document from within Word itself. In fact, you do so automatically each time you open Word from the Windows Start menu. Click Start, then choose Programs | Microsoft Word. Word 97 opens, and a new, blank document opens within it. You may begin working on your document right away. This method of creating a new document is generally more convenient than using the Shortcut bar when using a particular template isn't immediately important.

When Word is open, you can create another blank document at any time simply by clicking the New button on Word's Standard toolbar.

Fast Track

Outside of Word, you can create a new Word document from the Windows New menu. To open the New menu:

1. *Open the folder in which you want the new Word document stored.*
2. *From the folder's menu bar, choose File | New | Microsoft Word Document.*
3. *Then type a name for the document and press Enter. A Word file icon for the new document appears in the folder.*

Alternatively, you can create a new Word document right on your Windows desktop by using the New menu in the desktop's context menu. Right-click any empty area of the desktop, then choose New.

After creating a new document from the New menu, you may open it in Word using any of the methods described later under "Opening Documents."

If you've just created your new, empty document in any way other than using the New menu, your new document does not yet have a real name—it's called Document 1 in the title bar. When you save the document (as described later in this chapter), you also name it. You may save your new document immediately after creating it (even before you type anything), or after you've worked on it for awhile, or anytime you feel like it. Once the document has been saved, its new name appears in the title bar.

Entering Text

The *edit cursor* always appears automatically in the upper-left corner (the *top*) of any newly created document (and also in any pre-existing document that's just been opened). The edit cursor is a simple vertical bar that's a little taller than the letters that surround it; it flashes on and off, so it's easy to see when it rests deep within a forest of words.

The edit cursor is ground zero, the hot spot, the place where anything you do on the keyboard happens within the document. If you press any letter key, the letter appears in the document exactly where the edit cursor was, and the edit cursor moves one place to the right (where the next letter you type appears).

FYI: Cursors & Pointers in Word

Any time you create or open a document, you'll actually see two "cursors"—the edit cursor *and* the regular Windows mouse pointer.

The edit cursor always starts at the top of the document, while the mouse pointer may appear anywhere on your screen. The mouse pointer moves whenever you move your mouse, while the edit cursor moves when you press an arrow key.

When the mouse pointer is within the document window, it looks like a vertical I-beam; elsewhere, it appears just as it usually does in Windows, usually as an arrow. You can use the I-beam pointer to quickly relocate the edit cursor. Point the I-beam pointer to the spot where you want to work, then click. The edit cursor jumps to that spot.

To enter text in a Word document, type away. That's it. As you type, the edit cursor moves to the right and jumps down to the start of the next line automatically when you reach the end of a line. Keep going. Let the genius fly from your fingertips. Go nuts.

You'll learn much more about ways to enter and format text in the upcoming chapters. But here are a few essentials to get you started, in case you're new to typing. (If you've ever typed before—even on a typewriter—most of this stuff is second nature to you already.)

- To type a blank space, press the spacebar.
- To break a paragraph and start a new one, or to insert a blank line, press Enter. (Press Enter only to break a paragraph or insert a blank line, but not to end a line within a paragraph. Unlike a typewriter, a word processor breaks the lines within a paragraph for you.)
- To type an *uppercase*—capital—letter (or the upper character that appears on a key that shows two characters) press and hold the Shift key, then press the letter key.
- To fix a mistake, use your arrow keys or pointer to move the edit cursor to the mistake, then press the Backspace key or Del (Delete) key. Backspace deletes the character to the left of the edit cursor; Del deletes the character to the right of the edit cursor. When the error is gone, type your correction.

Walk-Through: Creating a Document & Entering Text

Follow the steps below to practice creating a Word document and entering text into it.

1. Click Start|Programs|Microsoft Word.

   Word opens with a new, empty document ready for your text. The edit cursor appears at the top of the document.

2. Press Enter twice, to create two blank lines.

   The edit cursor jumps down a line each time you press Enter.

3. Type a paragraph of your choosing, at least two lines long. Don't worry about fixing mistakes; just keep going.

4. At the end of the paragraph, press Enter once, to start a new paragraph.

5. Type a second paragraph of your choosing, at least two lines long.

When finished, leave the document open to save yourself a few steps in the next walk-through. If you want to close Word now, choose File|Exit. Word asks whether you want to save the document. For now, click No when Word asks.

Saving Documents

Unless you're brand-new to computers, you know how important it is to save your work. When you create a new document, it exists only in your PC's memory until it's saved on your hard disk (or a diskette). As you make changes to the document, those changes exist only in memory (not on disk) until you save the document again. If you accidentally switch off your PC—or if a power outage shuts off your PC for you—you may lose a document completely if you've never saved it, or at least lose the changes you've made to a document since the last time you saved it.

While saving is important, forgetting to save is not as dangerous as it once was. Windows and Word 97 work together to protect you from accidentally losing work by failing to save. Suppose you're working on a document and have either never saved it or have made changes since the last time you saved it. If you attempt to close that document, exit Word, or shut down Windows (using the Shut Down dialog), Word immediately displays a prompt asking whether you want to save your work before exiting. Click Yes, and the work is saved. Click No, and it's history. So unless you simply switch off your PC (or your PC is shut down by a power outage) while unsaved work is open in Word, you almost can't make the old mistake of forgetting to save.

But saving isn't only about loss prevention. When you save, you make decisions that affect the way you may work with the document thereafter: the document's name, its storage location, and other important defining characteristics.

The precise steps involved in saving a document are different the first time you save it from every time afterwards. In the next few pages, you discover how to save the first time, and then save subsequent times. You also learn variations on saving, including saving your document under a new name and converting your document to another word processing format.

Saving a Document the First Time

To save the document on which you're working, click the Save button on the Word toolbar (or choose File | Save from the menu bar). The Save As dialog opens, as shown in Figure 3-2. As the top of the figure shows, a folder, My Documents, has been preselected in the Save in box; the folder appearing in Save in is the one where your document will be saved.

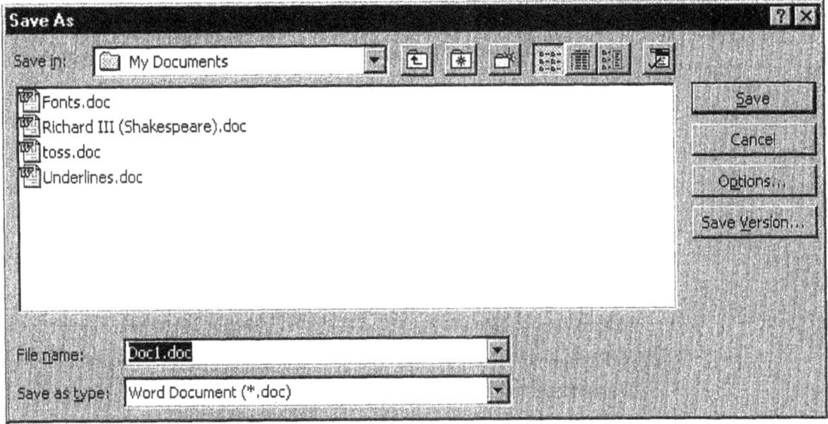

Figure 3-2: The Save As dialog, where saving, copying, and converting documents happens.

FYI: Why "My Documents"?

My Documents is the default folder for Office 97 documents, the folder where Save always stores your documents unless you specifically select a different folder. When you use My Documents as the folder for your work, you don't have to bother choosing a folder when saving. Also, when you want to open the document later, you won't have to do any navigation in the Open dialog to get to it. However, you always have the option to save a document in any folder you wish, or on the Windows desktop, or in a new folder you create right from the Save As dialog.

On the File Location's tab of Word's Options dialog (see Chapter 2, "Getting to Know the Office 97 Environment") you can reconfigure Word 97 to use a different default folder instead of My Documents.

The box beneath Save in lists all Word files in the folder, so you can see with which files your new file will share a folder. Near the bottom of the Save dialog appears the File name box. If you have already typed some text in your document, Word has automatically entered the first few words in the File name box, on the assumption that you may want to use that as a filename. (If you haven't typed anything yet, the stand-in filename is Doc1.doc.) When you first arrive at the Save As dialog, the entry in the File name box is highlighted. While the entry remains highlighted, whatever you type next replaces it.

To name your file and save it in My Documents, type the filename you wish (as you type, the name appears in the File name box), then click the Save button. When phrasing your filename, keep in mind the following:

- Don't type a filename *extension* (the period and three letters at the very end of a complete filename). Word adds .doc automatically; if you type **My Resume** in the File name box, the actual saved name of your document is My Resume.doc. If you attempt to add an extension (for example, by typing the filename **My Resume.Ned**), Word *still* adds .doc (My Resume.Ned.doc).
- You may include spaces in your filename (for example, My Resume or Angry Letter of Resignation), capitalize it any way you want (RESUME or ANGRY letter), and use any combination of letter and number characters (Report1 or 3rd Angry Letter). You may also use punctuation characters, with the following exceptions: / \ < > * . ? " | : ;

(You can memorize this list of characters, or you can adopt my policy—no punctuation of any kind in filenames, ever—and just forget about the whole issue.)

- You can enter long filenames, up to 255 characters (including the filename and the full path to the file; for example, C:\My Documents\Guests.doc is a 26-character filename). But you'll find that short, simple names are more convenient. Not only do shorter names save typing in the Save As dialog, but they also are more likely to fit entirely within dialogs that list your document filenames, and in the filename space allotted beneath the icons. When you can always read the whole filename, you'll locate and organize your documents more easily.

FYI: Extra Rules for Files That Move

If for any reason the document you're saving may be copied later to a computer running Windows 3.1 or MS-DOS, don't use any punctuation or spaces in the filename, and keep the filename to eight characters or less (not including the three-character extension). Windows 3.1 and MS-DOS generally choke on filenames longer than eight characters. If you use a longer filename, you can later create a copy of the file (using Save As, as described later in this chapter) and give the copy a DOS-friendly name.

To save the document in a folder other than My Documents, use the Save As dialog to navigate to the folder you want. You can navigate to other folders in several ways:

- Drop down the Save in list (click on the arrow at the right end of the Save in box), and select from the list. At the top of the list is Desktop, which you may select to save the document on your desktop. You may also select any desktop folder from the list.
- Also in the Save in box list are any disk drives (a:, c:, and so on) to which you have access, including drives on your local network. Click a drive letter to display a list of the folders on that drive. In the list of folders, click a folder to display its contents (folders and Word files). To move back up one level in the folder tree, click the Up One Level button in the Save As dialog's toolbar.

- To create a new, empty folder in which you'll save your document, click the Create New Folder button in the Save As dialog's toolbar. When you click Create New Folder, the new folder is created within the folder that appears in the Save in box.

When the Save in box shows the name of the folder you want, click in the File name box, type a filename, and click the Save button. Be sure to remember how to find the folder—you'll need to navigate to it again when you open the file for another editing session.

Net-Savvy

If the document you're working on will be a Web page, don't click Save. Instead, choose File | Save as HTML, and don't use spaces or punctuation in the file name. To learn more about composing Web pages in Word 97, see Chapter 22, "Office 97 & the Internet."

Saving a Document After the First Time

Once you've named and saved your document for the first time, you needn't fuss with the Save As dialog again. In fact, the Save As dialog appears automatically only the first time you click the Save button (or choose File | Save) for any particular document. Any time you click Save thereafter, Word simply saves the document, with no further input from you—after all, Word already knows the file's name and storage location. While saving the document (which usually takes only a moment or two), Word displays a message in the status line, reporting that it is "Saving..." the document.

FYI: Word Saves You From Yourself

After the first time you save a new document, Word's AutoRecover feature engages. AutoRecover automatically saves a temporary copy of all your open documents every 10 minutes. Should catastrophe strike (lightning kills the power, a kid or coworker yanks your power plug, your PC's warranty expires...), the next time you open Word, the documents that were open at the time of the catastrophe are re-created from the temporary copies made the last time AutoRecover did its thing. You'll never lose more than the last 10 minutes of your labor.

As you work, when AutoRecover does its thing, it doesn't tell you about it, except for a message that appears briefly in the status bar. Unless you happen to notice your hard disk cranking away unexpectedly (which it weirdly does anyway, from time to time, in Windows), you may never notice that AutoRecover is on the job.

To change how often AutoRecover saves the document, or to shut off AutoRecover altogether, change the AutoRecover options on the Save tab of Word's Options dialog (Tools, Options).

Copying a Document in Word

From time to time, you may want to copy a document. For example, you may need to create several different versions of the same document, or several different documents that are very similar to one another. By saving a previously-saved document under a different name (or under the same name, but in a different location), you effectively create a separate copy of that document. Later on, you may then edit each copy independently.

To save an existing document with a new name or location, force the Save As dialog to appear by choosing File | Save As. The Save As dialog opens just as it did when you first saved the document—only now the entry in the Save in box is not necessarily My Documents, but rather the folder where the document was saved previously.

In the Save As dialog, you can:

- Change the entry in the File name box to save a new copy of the document, under a new name, in the same folder as the original.
- Change the folder listed in the Save in box to save a copy of the document in a new location.
- Change both File name and Save in to save a copy under a new name in a different folder.
- Change the file type listed under Save as type to save in a format other than Word 97. See "Converting a Document for Use Beyond Word," later in this chapter.

Make any changes you like in the Save As dialog, then click the Save button to create the copy. (Note that, if you change nothing at all in the Save As dialog and then click the Save button, you accomplish the same thing you would have if you'd just clicked the toolbar's Save button in the first place—you save the original document, using its original name, in its original location. No copy is created. You've wasted time you could have spent learning about bad B movies from the *Cinemania* CD-ROM.)

FYI: What to Watch Out for With Save As

When using Save As, keep two slightly tricky issues in mind:

- After you click Save button in the Save As dialog, the dialog closes and you return to editing in Word. However, the document now open before you is not the original document—it's the copy you just created. (Look at the Word title bar, and you'll see the name of the copy.) Since you just created the copy, Word assumes you want to work on it instead of the original. If you want to work on the original, just open it as you learn to do later in this chapter.
- A copy you create with Save As is a completely independent document. Changes you make to it do not affect the original document, and vice versa. (If you want to link two separate documents so that changes in one affect the other, you'll learn to do so in Chapter 21, "Collaborating & Integrating With Office 97.")

Walk-Through: Creating & Saving a New Document

Follow the steps below to practice saving a new Word document. If the document you created in the preceding walk-through is still open, you can skip Step 1.

1. Create a new document, and type in it anything you want to (your personal manifesto, a list of friends or enemies, a love poem).
2. Click the Save button on the toolbar (or choose File|Save).
   The Save As dialog opens.
3. Make sure the entry in the File name box is highlighted. If it isn't, click it once to highlight it.
4. Type the filename **Walkthrough 3.**

5. Click the Save button in the Save As dialog.
   The file is saved.
6. Add a few words to your document.
7. Click the Save button on the toolbar.
   The document is saved again, without further input from you.
8. Choose File|Save As.
   The Save As dialog opens.
9. Drop down the Save in list, and choose Desktop.
10. Click Save.
    A copy of Walkthrough 3 appears on your Windows desktop.

Converting a Document for Use Beyond Word

Word includes a family of *filters* that can convert a document from Word 97 format into another file format. If all you ever want to do is write in Word, edit in Word, and print from Word, you don't care about filters. But suppose you need to share a document you've created in Word with a friend or colleague who uses WordPerfect, or Microsoft Works, or maybe some word processor you've never even heard of. What then? At such times, you can convert any document from Word 97 format to other file formats for which you have filters.

After conversion, the document may or may not look and behave exactly as it did in Word. If the Word document contained formatting or other features that are not also provided in the other program, those aspects of the file are lost in the conversion. For example, if you convert a document from Word 97 to Word 2.0, the document loses any characteristics based on features included in Word 97 but not in Word 2.0. Ultimately, unless the document you're converting is very simple, its appearance (but not its words) will change in the conversion, and it will probably require some cleanup editing in the other program. But you won't have to retype it or totally reformat it, and that saves a lot of work.

To convert a file, open the Word file you want to convert, then choose File | Save As to open the Save As dialog. At the bottom of the dialog, open the list for Save as type (see Figure 3-3).

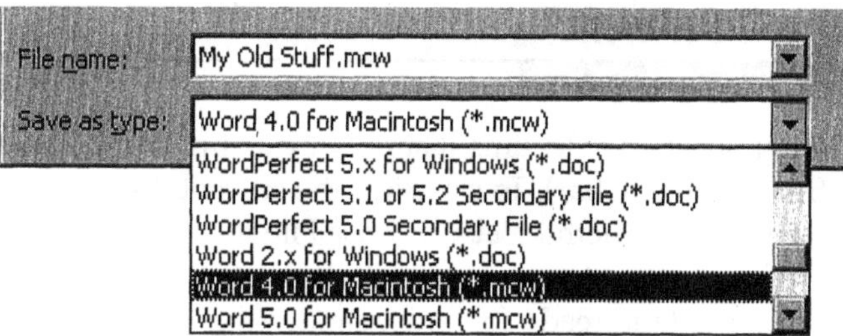

Figure 3-3: The Save as type list.

That list shows all of the filters currently installed on your system. Choose the file format you want, and click Save. Word makes a copy of the document and saves it in the selected format.

FYI: Tips for Fuss-Free Conversions

Before attempting to convert a file, it's a good idea to find out the precise type of file you need to wind up with. For example, if you need a WordPerfect file, in which version of WordPerfect will the file be used?

Note that not all of the filters on the Office 97 CD are installed automatically in the Typical installation. If you don't see a filter you need on the Save as type list, you may be able to add it from the CD (see the Appendix).

If you can't find or add the precise filter you need, consider the following strategies:

- Check whether the program you're trying to convert for can also convert, or *import*, documents from other sources. If so, you may choose to use that program to convert the Word file to its own format.
- Some converters in the Save as type list produce a file format that can be easily imported by a wide variety of programs. Rich Text Format (RTF) preserves much of the formatting in a document but makes the file easy for many other programs to import. The various other "text" converters (for example, Text Only or MS-DOS Text) remove most or all formatting, but preserve all of the text of the document—which makes the document easy to import not only by almost any word processor, but by many other types of programs, as well. The text can be reformatted, if necessary, in the other program.

Closing a Document

You may close a document simply by exiting Word (choose File | Exit from the menu bar). To close just the current document but keep Word open to do something else, choose File | Close.

If you're finished not just with the document, but with everything in Windows (and ready for a nice sandwich), you may shut down Windows while Word (and any documents) are still open. To shut down, choose Shut Down from the Start menu, then press Enter. Windows automatically closes your document, closes Word 97, and closes any other open applications or files, then shuts itself down. When Windows reports that it's OK to do so, you may shut off your PC.

FYI: Don't Touch That Switch!

Never switch off your PC without first using Windows's Shut Down routine. Not only does Shut Down help protect you against accidentally losing unsaved work, but it also performs a number of important, unseen housekeeping chores that Windows must perform to run reliably.

No matter which method you use to close, Word always checks whether any open documents contain changes that have not been saved; if Word finds any unsaved work, it displays the prompt shown in Figure 3-4. To save the document, click Yes; to close without saving, click No. To cancel closing the document and instead return to work on it, click Cancel.

Note that, if you click No, you lose all changes you made to the document since the last time you deliberately saved it, even if AutoRecover has saved the document in the meantime. In other words, if you last clicked Save an hour ago, and you click No when prompted to save before closing, you lose all changes you made in the last hour, even though AutoRecover may have done its thing five minutes ago. AutoRecover rescues you from unexpected shutdowns, not deliberate ones.

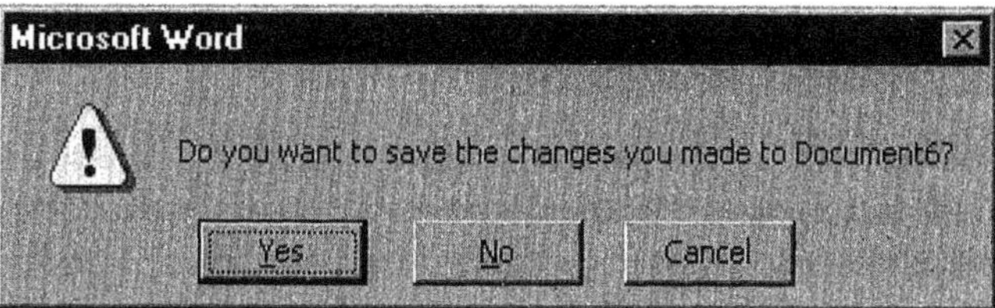

Figure 3-4: Word making sure you don't quit without saving (unless you want to).

Opening Documents

If you're at all like me (and if so, Heaven help you), you don't create most of your documents in one sitting, print them, and be done. You work awhile on a document, then shut down and watch *The Simpsons*. Then you open the document on another day, rework what you've already written, add some more, then go make pizza. The document evolves across a series of writing and editing sessions until either 1) It's perfect, or 2) You run out of time. (Most of the time, it's 2.) When either 1 or 2 happens, the document is said to be "done," whatever that means.

To work on a document through multiple editing sessions, you'll need to locate and open it—and you have a surprising number of ways to do that. Perhaps more important, you can apply some of the available opening methods to the task of importing documents that were originally created in other programs—earlier versions of Word, WordPerfect, Microsoft Works, and others.

Fast Track

Word remembers the names and locations of the last four documents you've edited, and lists them at the bottom of the Word 97 File menu, numbered 1 through 4. Number 1 is the last document you worked on; number 2 is the document you worked on before number 1, and so on. To open any of the last four documents you've worked on, open Word, choose File from the menu bar, then click on the document you want (or press its number).

Also, you'll probably find the last several documents you've worked on listed in your Windows Documents menu. Click the Windows Start button and choose Documents. If you see the document you want to edit listed there, click it. Word opens (if it's not open already) and the selected document opens in Word.

Opening a Word Document

The easiest way to open an existing Word document is not to open Word at all, but to open the document itself. You open any document in Windows—whether it's a Word document, Excel worksheet, saved Web page, or any other file type—by double-clicking its file icon.

Double-clicking a document's file icon works no matter where you find the icon: on your Windows desktop, in any folder, in Windows Explorer, or in a Find dialog. If Word is closed when you open the document this way, Word opens automatically. If Word is already open, Windows switches to Word. Either way, the document you opened appears in Word, ready to edit or print.

FYI: Word 97 Usurps Earlier Versions

If you have an earlier version of Word still installed on your PC, note that all of your Word documents—including those you created with an earlier Word version—now open automatically in Word 97, despite the availability of the older version. See "Opening & Saving Documents From Earlier Word Versions," later in this chapter.

In some circumstances, you may find it easier to open a document from within Word. For example, opening the My Documents folder from outside of Word requires several navigation steps, whether you navigate to the folder through My Computer or through Windows Explorer. Opening My Documents from within Word, however, is a simple matter of clicking a button.

To open an existing document from within Word, click the Open button on the Standard toolbar (or choose File | Open from the menu bar). An Open dialog like the one in Figure 3-5 appears. In the dialog, use the Look in box exactly as you would use the Save in box in the Save As dialog: click your way to any folder, or to the Windows desktop. The window beneath Look in shows all of the Word files (or rather, all files using the extension .DOC) currently stored in the folder selected in the Look in box.

When you have navigated to the folder containing the file you want to open, double-click the file, or single-click it and then click the Open button. Either way, the Open dialog closes, and the selected document opens in Word, ready to edit.

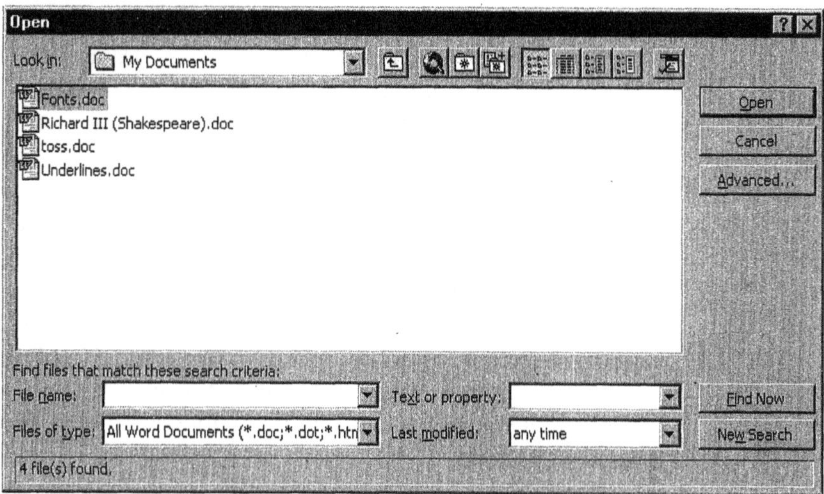

Figure 3-5: The Open dialog, from which you select files to open.

The final way to open a Word document is to click the Open Office Document button on the Office Shortcut bar. Doing so opens the Open Office Document dialog, which works exactly like Word's Open dialog (except that it lists not just the Word documents in the selected Look in folder, but all Office documents—Word files, Excel files, and so on—in the folder). To open a document, use Look in and Up One Level to navigate to the desired folder, then double-click the file.

Fast Track

You may open several documents at once in Word to compare documents or to copy text from one document to another. To open multiple documents, just keep opening documents without bothering to close any that are already open. To switch among your open documents, click Window on the toolbar. You'll learn more about working with multiple documents in Chapter 4, "Working With Text."

Opening & Saving Documents From Earlier Word Versions

If you're upgrading from an earlier version of Word, you probably have some documents that you revise from time to time, or use as boilerplates for new documents you create. If so, you'll be editing these documents in Word 97.

Opening these documents is no problem. Using any of the techniques described earlier under Opening a Word Document, you can open documents from earlier Word versions, including versions 2.0 through 6.0 (for Windows 3.1), version 7.0 (for Windows 95), and Macintosh versions, as well. The file opens just like any other Word document.

When you save the document after editing it in Word 97, you have a choice to make. Word 97 documents are stored in a file format that is incompatible with all earlier versions of Word. When you click Save while working with a document from an earlier version of Word, the dialog shown in Figure 3-6 opens. If you intend to edit the document in Word 97 from now on, click Yes. If you want to preserve the file's original file format so that you can edit it in either Word 97 or in a previous version, click No.

If you click No to preserve the file's original format, note that any changes you've made in Word 97 that require Word 97 will be lost. All text entry always survives just fine—you never lose any of the text of your document when saving in an earlier Word format. But if you've applied some of Word's advanced formatting and automation features—such as engraved or shadow text effects (see Chapter 6, "Adding Pictures, Tables & Borders") or animated text (see Chapter 22, "Office 97 & the Internet")—the effects of your efforts may be lost in the conversion.

Fast Track

If you install Office 97 but also elect to keep an earlier version of Word on your PC (instead of replacing it with Word 97), Office adds to your old Word version a converter for Word 97 documents. From within your old version, you can use the old version's Save As dialog to convert Word 97 documents to the older version. The effect is the same as if you had made the conversion from within Word 97.

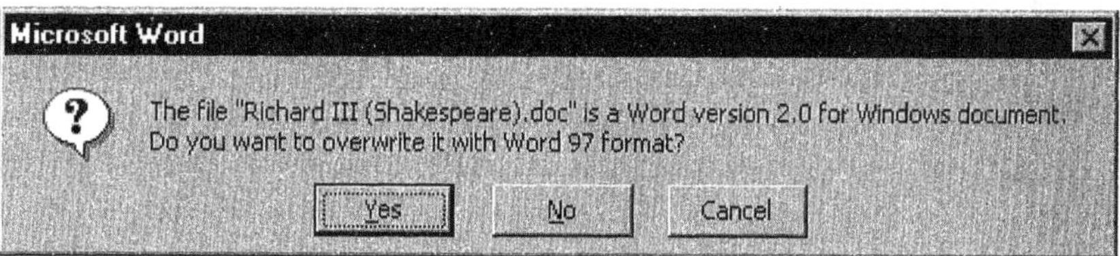

Figure 3-6: Word asks you to choose a format in which to save a document from an earlier Word version.

Opening & Saving Documents From Other Word Processors

The filters installed in Word 97 not only enable you to convert your Word 97 documents to other formats, but also let you open documents from other programs within Word 97 and then save those documents in Word 97 format.

FYI: Special Help for WordPerfect Users

If you're converting from WordPerfect, Word not only converts your documents for you, but also provides a special Help facility just for you and other WordPerfect users.

In Word, choose Help|WordPerfect Help. The Help For WordPerfect Users dialog opens. From a list of WordPerfect Command keys on the dialog, you can select any WordPerfect command and then click Help Text (to read about how the same action is accomplished in Word) or Demo (to ask Word to demonstrate the action).

As a rule, you can't open a non-Word document in Word by double-clicking its file icon. Instead, open Word, then choose File | Open to display the Open dialog (see Figure 3-5, earlier in this chapter). From the Open dialog, you locate and open a non-Word file exactly as you open a Word file—with one catch.

By default, the big box on the Open dialog lists only files with the extension .DOC. Even if you have selected the appropriate folder from the Look in list, the document you want to open won't show up on the list unless its filename extension is .DOC. To make the Open dialog include the type of file you want to open, drop down the Files of type list (see Figure 3-7), and choose the appropriate file type from the list. If you're not certain of the exact filename extension of the file, choose All files from the Files of type list. When the file icon for the document you want to edit appears in the box, double-click it, or click it and click the Open button.

When you attempt to save the file after editing it, you'll see a dialog similar to the one shown earlier in Figure 3-6. On that dialog, you may choose to save the file in Word 97 format or in its original file format.

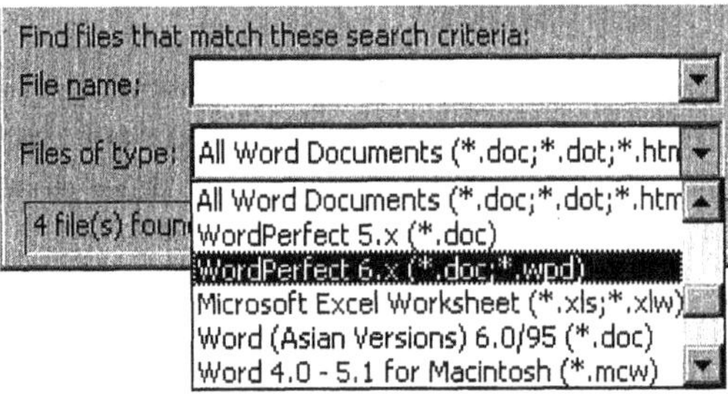

Figure 3-7: The Open dialog's Files of type list, where you choose the type of file you want to open.

Controlling Word's Display

In Chapter 1, "Discovering Office 97," you learned that Word is a WYSIWYG (What You See Is What You Get) word processor, one that shows your document onscreen exactly as it will appear when printed. While that's valuable, it's not always efficient. By making a few simple selections, you can ask Word to sacrifice perfect WYSIWYG to make your editing work easier.

Keep in mind that none of the display-control options that follow have any actual effect on your document or the way it will look when printed. These options simply change the way Word represents that document onscreen, to help you work more efficiently. Since changing your display options can't hurt your document, feel free to experiment with them. Try out different combinations of views, zooms, and so on—it's good practice.

Choosing a View

The *view* describes the extent to which you want Word's display to mimic the final, intended result of your document. You can choose among several different views; each is appropriate for a different kind of editing session. Choose a view by selecting an option from the View menu or by clicking one of the view buttons (see Figure 3-8) at the bottom of the Word window, immediately to the left of the horizontal scroll bar.

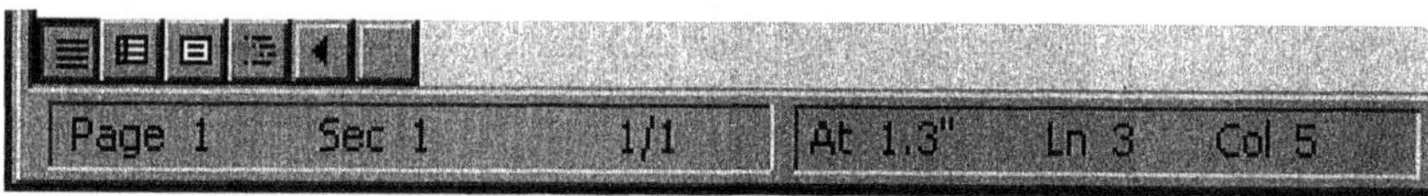

Figure 3-8: Buttons for changing the view, to the left of the scroll bar at the bottom of Word's window.

By default, most of the time you work in Word, you work in Normal view. In Normal view, the text of your pages appears as you intend it to, including all text and paragraph formatting and the correct margins (see Chapter 4, "Working With Text," and Chapter 5, "Designing Pages"). However, if you've added headers or footers to the document, they appear only on the first page, not on every page, as they would in print. Page breaks in Normal view are represented by simple dotted lines between pages. Also, if you've formatted newspaper-style columns (see Chapter 5) in your document, in Normal view each column appears in its proper width, but the columns don't appear side-by-side as they will when printed. Finally, if you've added pictures to your document, you won't see them in Normal view.

The Page Layout view, on the other hand, attempts to represent your document onscreen, as you edit, exactly as it will appear when printed, including headers and footers (in gray), pictures, and actual page breaks that make each page appear to be a piece of paper on your screen (see Figure 3-9).

Because it does not visually break pages or fill space with repeated headers and footers, Normal view is the most convenient view to work in during the text entry and editing phase of document creation. You'll find getting around in your document quicker and easier in Normal view, particularly scrolling from page to page. Depending upon the speed of your hardware, you may also notice that Word performs most quickly when in Normal view. As you near completion of your document (and shift your focus from content to appearance), switch to Page Layout view to fine tune the document's printed appearance.

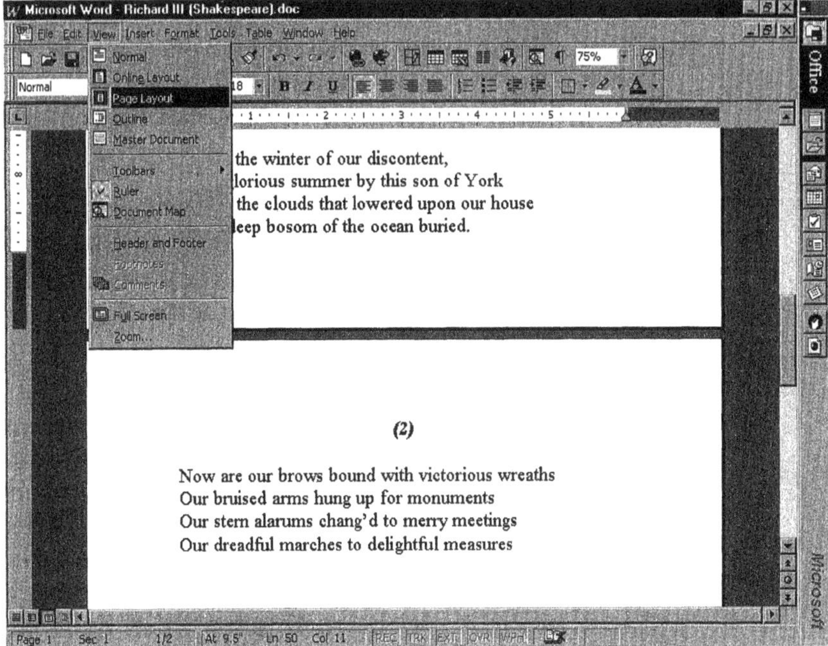

Figure 3-9: Word in Page Layout view, showing page breaks, headers, and footers.

In addition to Normal view and Page Layout view, you have four more view options:

- **Online layout (View | Online Layout).** This view is optimized for sharing the editing of the document across a network (see Chapter 21, "Collaborating & Integrating With Office," and Chapter 22, "Office 97 & the Internet").
- **Outline (View | Outline).** This view organizes your document in outline form, to help you evaluate and fine tune the structure of a long, complex document (see Chapter 22, "Office 97 & the Internet").
- **Master Document (View | Master Document).** This view shows you the *master document* for the multi-file document on which you're working. A master document is a special document used to pull together several separate files into a cohesive single document.

Fast Track

When evaluating your document's appearance, instead of using Page Layout view, you can display the Print Preview. Choose File | Print Preview to display your document in Print Preview.

In the Print Preview, Word shows an entire page—or two pages at a time—so you can accurately predict how the page will appear when printed. However, while you can edit your document in the Print Preview, doing so is a little tricky and cumbersome.

Fine Tuning Word's Display

Three other adjustments to Word's display can help you deal with a variety of tricky circumstances: Zoom, Show/Hide, and Full Screen.

Zoom

Use the Zoom list on the Standard toolbar—or choose View | Zoom—to set the zoom level. Zooms higher than 100% magnify the page, enabling you to see and work closely with very small text and other small page elements. Zooms lower than 100% make the page look farther away; small text may be difficult or impossible to read, but you'll be better able to see and evaluate the overall look of the page. A low zoom combined with Page Layout view enables you to fine-tune your page layout when your document is nearly finished.

On the Zoom dialog (View | Zoom), you can set the view by choosing a percentage, just as you can from the Zoom list on the toolbar. But on the dialog, you can also choose the Zoom by clicking options for:

- **Page Width.** The Zoom percentage is set so that you can see the full page width without scrolling left or right.
- **Whole Page.** The Zoom is set so that you can see the entire page without scrolling left or right or up or down.
- **Many Pages.** The Zoom is set super high so that you can see multiple pages (very *small* pages) all at once.

Show/Hide

Click the Show/Hide button on the Standard toolbar to display all of the *nonprinting characters* in your document (see Figure 3-10). Nonprinting characters are characters you type that are invisible (until you click Show/Hide), but affect the text around them; for example, spaces, tabs (see Chapter 5, "Designing Pages"), and paragraph breaks (what you type when you press Enter).

Show/Hide is useful when you're having formatting troubles that you think may be related to the placement of nonprinting characters. For example, showing the nonprinting characters can reveal whether you've used two spaces or one after a period, or whether you've pressed Tab twice in a place where only one tab character was called for. When you've solved your problem, just click Show/Hide again to hide the nonprinting characters.

Note that, like the other display-control options (views, Zoom, Print Preview), Show/Hide has no effect on the printed appearance of your document. Even if you print the document while Word is displaying the nonprinting characters, the nonprinting characters (eponymously) don't show up on paper.

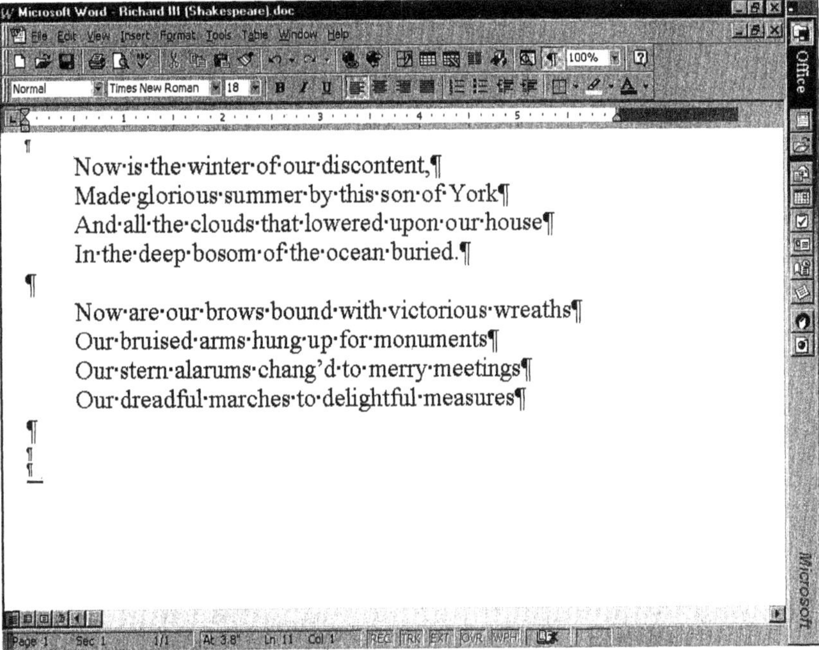

Figure 3-10: Nonprinting characters—paragraph breaks and spaces—appear because I clicked Show/Hide.

Full Screen

Choose View | Full Screen to enter Word's Full Screen mode. Full Screen mode hides almost everything but your document, allowing your document to fill up the whole display. Word's menu bar, status bar, scroll bars, toolbars—even the Windows Taskbar and the Office Shortcut bar—all vanish so that your document can fill up your screen completely. You may find Full Screen mode valuable if you have a small display (as on a notebook PC) or if you find the clutter of Word's tools distracting.

You can edit in Full Screen mode, although you haven't any toolbars with which to work. Instead, use shortcut keys—for example, you can save the document by pressing Ctrl+S or Alt+F+S. Also, you can temporarily restore the menu bar by moving the pointer to the very top of the display or by pressing the Alt key. To get around without scroll bars, use your arrow keys or PgUp and PgDn.

The only thing you see in Full Screen mode besides your document is a small dialog with a single button: Close Full Screen. To exit Full Screen mode and restore all of Word's paraphernalia, click the button, or press Esc or Alt+C.

FYI: Where Am I?

If you're just getting started with your documents, you're probably not thinking too much about how many pages make up your document. But as your skills develop and your documents become more complex, you'll need to know how many pages are in your document, and what page you're on.

When Word's status bar isn't busy telling you something else (like letting you know AutoRecover has engaged), it always reports the precise location of the edit cursor, to let you know where you are. In the leftmost box of the status bar, Word reports (from left to right):

- The page number
- The section number (see Chapter 5, "Designing Pages")
- The number of the current page within the total number of pages. For example, if the status bar reports 26/42, the current page is number 26 out of a total of 42 pages in the document.

Jumping From Page to Page

In Chapter 2, "Getting to Know the Office 97 Environment," you discovered the principal ways you can get around in an Office document: Scroll bars, PgUp, and PgDn. And most of the time you work in Word, you'll use those same methods to move from page to page, while using your mouse or arrow keys to relocate the edit cursor within a page.

When you're working in a long document, however, and you need to get from page 3 to, oh, page 129, you'll get there pretty slowly by scrolling or pressing PgDn. When you need to jump directly to a specific spot anywhere in your document, rely on the Go To tab of the Find & Replace dialog. (Note that you'll learn about the other tabs of this dialog in Chapter 7, "Working Faster & Easier in Word.")

To go straight to the Go To tab (see Figure 3-11), choose Edit | Go To or press Ctrl+G. By default, the choice in the Go to what list is Page, so you can simply type a page number in the Enter page number box, then click the tab's Go To button. The dialog disappears, and your desired page appears in the document window, with the edit cursor positioned at the top of the page.

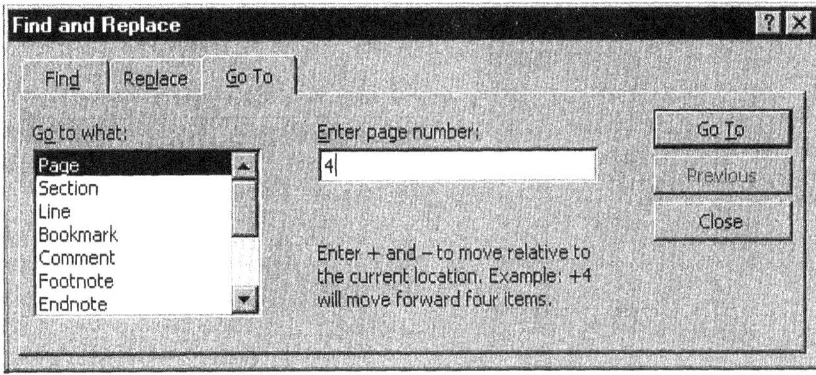

Figure 3-11: The Go To tab of the Find and Replace dialog.

Fast Track

As Figure 3-11 shows, you can also use the Go To dialog to jump to a particular part of your document by choosing Section | Comment or another choice in Go to what. After making your choice, you use the text box to the right to enter whatever identifying information Word requests: Section number, the text of the comment, and so on. (Don't worry if you don't yet know what all the choices in the Go to what list mean; you'll discover most of them in upcoming chapters.)

Perhaps the most useful choice is Bookmark. By choosing Insert | Bookmark, you create an invisible bookmark anywhere in your document to mark a specific spot; for example, you might leave a bookmark where you quit the day's editing session. When you begin the next editing session, you can use the Go To tab to jump directly to the Bookmark and pick up right where you left off.

Printing Your Document

Like so many other things about Word, printing is as easy or as hard as you choose to make it.

Here's easy: To print all pages of the current document on your default Windows printer, make sure the printer is switched on and loaded with paper, then click the Print button on Word's toolbar. That's it. Word and Windows work together to prepare the document for the printer, then transmit it to the printer to be printed. No further input from you is required.

So why do more? Word's Print dialog allows you to control a lot about how your document prints. For example, you may choose to print only selected pages of the document rather than the whole thing. And if your PC is connected to more than one printer (as it might be if you use a local network), you can select the printer to use.

To open the Print dialog (shown in Figure 3-12), choose File | Print. On the Print dialog, you may choose a printer from the Name list, enter a range of pages to print, and more. Most of what you can do on the Print dialog comes into play only when you're working on a long or complex document.

Fast Track

If you have a fax modem installed in your PC and configured for Windows, you can use the Print dialog to fax the document to someone instead of printing it. Most fax boards make Windows think they're a printer. To fax a document instead of printing it, choose the fax board from the Print dialog as if it were a printer.

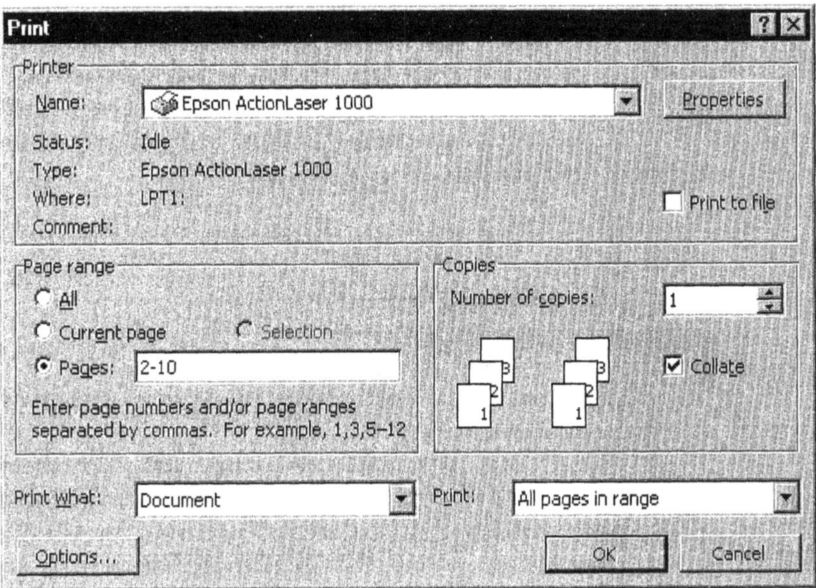

Figure 3-12: The Print dialog.

WYSMNBWYG (What You See May Not Be What You Get)

Theoretically, the printout of your document should be identical in every way to the onscreen version. But when you print, check your printouts very carefully, and prepare to discover some variation between the two, even to the point where pages may not break at the same point they do onscreen. (As a rule, the better your printer, the more accurate its results.)

This isn't really Word's fault, or Windows'; rather, it's the result of your particular printer's inability to accurately print what Windows tells it to. The variations are rarely serious, and you can usually fix their effects by making minor adjustments in your document. Also, the more elaborately you format your document, the greater the likelihood of variation between screen and printer. Throughout this book, you'll be alerted to techniques that are known to baffle some printers. But there's really no way you can predict the outcome; through experience with your printer, you'll learn what it does well, and what it goofs.

Also, keep in mind that different printers produce different results. Among reasonably new laser or inkjet printers, the variation is likely to be slight. But if you print your draft copies on one printer, and then intend to print a final copy on another printer, be sure to check the final copy carefully, and edit the document as necessary to adjust for any surprises.

Walk-Through: Opening & Printing Documents

Follow the steps below to practice opening and printing a Word document.

1. Close (or minimize) Word.
2. Locate the file icon for Walkthrough 3 on your Windows Desktop.
   This is the copy of Walkthrough 3 you created earlier with Save As.
3. Double-click the icon.
   Word opens, and then opens the desktop copy of Walkthrough 3.
4. Choose File|Close.
   Walkthrough 3 closes; Word stays open.
5. Click the Open button on the toolbar (or choose File|Open).
   The Open dialog opens.
6. In the box on the Open dialog, select the icon for Walkthrough 3.
   This is the originally saved version of Walkthrough 3 you saved in My Documents.
7. Click Open.
   Walkthrough 3 opens.
8. Choose File|Close.
   Walkthrough 3 closes; Word stays open.

9. Click the Open button on the toolbar (or choose File|Open).
   The Open dialog opens.
10. Drop down the Look in list, and from the list, choose Desktop.
    The box in the Open dialog shows all of the Word documents on your desktop.
11. Click Walkthrough 3.
    The desktop copy of Walkthrough 3 opens in Word.
12. Add a few words to Walkthrough 3.
13. Click the Print button on the toolbar to print Walkthrough 3.
14. Choose File|Exit.
    Word asks if you want to save Walkthrough 3 before exiting.
15. Click Yes.
    Word saves the desktop copy of Walkthrough 3, then closes.

Moving On

In one short chapter, you've become a fully-functioning Word 97 writer. You can create documents, enter paragraphs, save your work, and print it. In the grand scheme of things, there's not much else to it.

While you discovered here a number of other, powerful techniques—Save As, for example—you probably won't use those techniques often. If you can create a new document, type in it, save it, and print it, you're already on the downslope of the learning curve.

What's left? Well, in this chapter you discovered the absolute basics of entering text into your new document. In Chapter 4, "Working With Text," you'll learn not only how to edit that text, in a powerful variety of ways, but also how to *format* that text, and change its appearance and style. Having discovered how to format text in Chapter 4, you'll move on to formatting the overall look of your pages in Chapter 5, "Designing Pages."

4 Working With Text

I guess there are in this world those extreme right-brain types who want to fiddle with the layout and design of a document before supplying its content. In fact, Word does offer you ways to define how your document will look before you type a word of it—you'll learn how in Chapter 7, "Working Faster & Easier in Word." But for practical reasons, it makes more sense to learn first how to enter and edit the text of your document, then to deal with how your document will look. (If you think I'm being too linear, well…my wife agrees with you. That's what a liberal arts education does to you.)

In this chapter, you build on the skills from Chapter 3, "Getting Started With Word," by getting deeper into text entry and editing. You'll discover such essential editing skills as selecting text and undoing mistakes, plus time-savers like copying text. In the second half of this chapter, you'll begin a transition from left brain to right—from content to style—by learning how to *format* text, change its appearance and personality. That done, you'll be prepared to format the overall look of your pages—full right-brain stuff—in Chapter 5, "Designing Pages." (Man…my wife is right.)

In the first half of this chapter, you'll discover still more stuff you can do with Word's Standard toolbar, which you first met in Chapter 3. In the second half, you'll begin working with Word's Formatting toolbar. Before beginning, it's a good idea to make sure both toolbars are on your screen and ready to go (see Figure 4-1). If you don't see one or both of these toolbars, point to any spot on any toolbar and right-click (or choose View | Toolbars), then click Formatting or Standard. To display the name of any button on either toolbar, rest the pointer on the button for a moment.

Figure 4-1: Word's Standard (above) and Formatting (below) toolbars, which contain buttons for many of the activities in this chapter.

Choosing Text to Work With

Many of the activities in this chapter require *selecting text*, highlighting one or more characters so that the next action you perform affects the entire group of highlighted characters, known as a *text block*.

The simplest and most natural way to select text is to use your mouse. Point to the very beginning of the block you want to select, and click and hold the left mouse button. Drag the mouse to the right (to select only part of a line) or down (to select multiple lines). As you drag, you highlight all text in the pointer's path (see Figure 4-2). When you reach the end of the block you wish to highlight, release the mouse button. The block remains highlighted, ready to accept whatever action you choose to perform on it.

FYI: Make Your Next Move Carefully

Once a block is highlighted, do not press any key or click anything with the mouse except to perform the specific action you want to perform on that block. For example, if you type anything—even a single character—while a block is highlighted, the entire block is instantly deleted and replaced by what you type. That's actually a handy editing feature, as you'll learn later in this chapter. Still, you don't want a careless keystroke to wipe out a block you intended merely to format, not replace.

If you accidentally replace or delete a highlighted block—or do anything else to a selected block that isn't what you intended—you can restore the block to its previous state by clicking the Undo button immediately after deleting—as described in the next section.

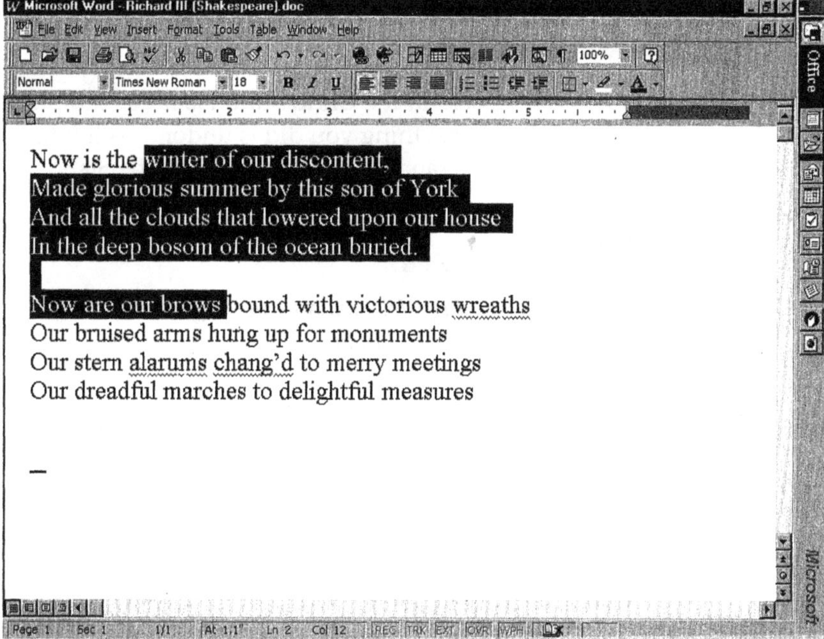

Figure 4-2: Selected text.

If, after you've selected a block, you decide that you do not want to make any changes to that block, you can *deselect* it (remove the highlight) simply by clicking your mouse button once anywhere on the page or by pressing any of the arrow keys.

Besides dragging your mouse, you can select text in a variety of other ways, including:

- Double-click a word to select the word.
- Triple-click a paragraph to select the whole paragraph. (To triple-click, click your primary mouse button three times quickly. Repeating "There's no place like home," is optional.)
- Choose Edit | Select All or Ctrl + A to select the entire document.
- Press and hold the Ctrl key, then click a sentence, to select the sentence.
- Press and hold the Shift key, then press and hold an arrow key, to highlight a selection that begins at the position of the edit cursor and ends wherever you release the arrow key. Shift + Right arrow selects to the right; Shift + Down arrow selects multiple lines down; and so on. (This selection method is convenient if you prefer not to use a mouse.)

Changing Your Mind After Changing Text

The principle behind the Undo button is rather simple: When you click Undo, the very last thing you did is undone, as if it had never happened. You'll find Undo (and its partner Redo) on the Standard toolbar.

Fast Track

If you're using Word sans-mouse*, you can undo by pressing Ctrl + Z or by selecting Edit | Undo.*

If you click Undo immediately after performing some action to a selected block of text, that block immediately returns to its exact state before you performed the action, and also remains selected, to make performing the desired action simple. For example, if you press Del, you delete the selected block. If you then choose Undo, the selected block is restored, and highlighted—ready for the correct action.

Predicting what Undo will do is pretty simple when what you're undoing is a deletion (the deletion is restored) or any action to a selected text block (the text reverts to the way it was before the last action). But Undo is a little trickier when it comes to typing.

When you click Undo after typing something, Undo deletes everything you've typed since the last time you did something besides typing. In other words, if you type three paragraphs in a row without stopping to format something or perform some other nontyping activity, clicking Undo deletes all three paragraphs—it undoes the last uninterrupted typing session. If you type three paragraphs, then go back to fix a mistake, *then* type one more sentence, Undo deletes only that last sentence.

In those really confused moments, you may undo something and then decide that you liked it better before you undid. For those occasions, the Redo button is available. Redo reverses the action of Undo—restoring, essentially, the changes that you thought were mistakes when you clicked Undo. Note that Redo does nothing unless you've already used Undo—without an undo, there can't be a redo.

Fast Track

Sometimes you don't discover a mistake until you've already performed several other actions following your goof. For such times, Word offers the Undo list, which you display by clicking the Down arrow on the Undo button.

The Undo list catalogs the last several actions you performed. If the mistake happens to appear among those actions, select it on the list. Word undoes the error—and *everything you have done since making that mistake. In effect, the Undo list is a time machine that takes your document back to the time just before your last screw-up. (Instead of using the Undo list, you can achieve the same effect by clicking Undo several times in a row. Each click moves back one level in the Undo list.)*

If you value the work you did between making the mistake and discovering the mistake, you might not want to use the Undo list. Instead, simply do whatever is necessary to repair the error. That way, you don't also undo later actions you want to keep.

Walk-Through: Select & Undo

Follow the steps below to practice selecting text, typing to replace a selection, and undoing an error.

1. Open or create any document containing text. (Walkthrough 3—which you created in Chapter 3—will do fine, but you can use any document you don't mind fooling around with.)
2. Point to the very beginning of a paragraph.
3. Click and hold your primary mouse button, drag to the end of the paragraph, and release.
   The paragraph is selected.
4. Click anywhere in the document window.
   The highlight disappears. The paragraph is deselected.
5. Select the paragraph again.
6. Type **This text replaces the selection.**
   The selected paragraph is replaced by your typing.
7. Click Undo.
   The original highlighted paragraph is restored.
8. Click anywhere in the document window.
   The highlight disappears.

Editing Text

As you learned in Chapter 3, "Getting Started With Word," you can easily edit your text as you go along by using the Backspace or Del (Delete) keys:

- Pressing Backspace once deletes one character to the left of the edit cursor.
- Pressing Del once deletes one character to the right of the edit cursor.
- Pressing and holding either key deletes multiple characters until you release the key.

After removing a mistake, you can simply type a correction. But while this technique is effective for fixing typooos (uh, typos), it's not an efficient way to make major changes, such as rearranging paragraphs, making careful insertions within a sentence or paragraph, or making big cuts. In the next few pages, you will discover Word's powerful editing tools.

Fast Track

Every document you create will require some manual editing using the techniques described here. However, Word also includes a family of automated editing tools that can fix your spelling and grammar, apply consistent formatting, and do much more to make editing more accurate and less time-consuming.

You discover automated editing in Chapter 7, "Working Faster & Easier in Word"—but don't jump there yet. Word can do a lot automatically, but not everything. To edit in Word effectively—and to properly apply the automatic tools you discover later—you need to understand the basics of manual editing.

Inserting & Overwriting Text

When you type, you can type in either of two modes:

- **Insert mode.** Your typing pushes the text out of the way, so that no existing text is overwritten.
- **Overtype mode.** Your typing *overtypes*—replaces—any text ahead of it as you go along, just as if you had "typed over" what was there.

Insert is the default mode. That's why you can move the edit cursor to a typo, delete the typo, and type a correction. To switch to Overtype mode, you must locate the OVR indicator in the status bar (see Figure 4-3).

In the right side of the bar, a bank of five three-letter abbreviations appears: REC, MRK, EXT, OVR, WPH. When you're in Insert mode, the OVR indicator is grayed out. To switch from Insert to Overtype mode, double-click the OVR indicator. It changes from gray to black to indicate that you're in Overtype mode. To return to Insert mode (and return the OVR indicator to gray), double-click the OVR indicator again.

Figure 4-3: A black OVR in the status bar, indicating Overtype mode.

Copying, Moving & Cutting Text

Word enables you to delete ("cut"), copy, and move the text contained in any selection very easily, thanks to the Windows clipboard (see the Introduction). Note that Undo can reverse any copy, cut, or move operation you perform.

No matter whether you cut, copy, or move, you always begin by selecting the text with which you want to work. With the text selected, you can:

- **Copy the selection.** Click the Copy button on the Standard toolbar, move the edit cursor to the spot where you want the copy to appear, then click the Paste button on the Standard toolbar. To insert another copy, position the cursor, and click Paste again. You may insert as many copies as you want to, at any time, until the next time you use Copy or Cut.
- **Move the selection.** Click the Cut button on the Standard toolbar (the selection disappears, as if it had been deleted), move the edit cursor to the spot where you want the text moved, then click the Paste button on the Standard toolbar. After moving, you may insert another copy of the moved text by positioning the cursor and clicking Paste. You may insert as many copies as you want to, at any time, until the next time you use Copy or Cut.

- **Cut the selection.** Click the Cut button on the Standard toolbar. The selection disappears. (Note that pressing the Del key has the same effect, and like Cut, Del can be reversed by Undo. However, you may use Del in place of Cut *only* when you intend to delete the selection, not move it. If you plan to move the selection, you must use Cut, not Del.)

FYI: Paste Always Inserts, Never Overtypes (*Except*. . .)

When you use Paste in a move or copy operation, the text is always inserted at the edit cursor position—it doesn't overwrite nearby text, even if you are in Overtype mode.

However, if you select something immediately before pasting, the text you paste replaces the selection.

Fast Track

The actions of the Copy, Paste, and Cut buttons can all be duplicated with menus or keystrokes. You can Copy with Edit | Copy or Ctrl+C; Paste with Edit | Paste or Ctrl+V; or Cut with Edit | Cut or Ctrl+X.

Moving or Copying Text Between Documents

By opening multiple Word documents in the same session, you may copy or move text from one document to another. The steps are exactly the same as the copy and move steps you just learned, except that after clicking Copy (for copying) or Cut (for moving), you must switch to the document into which you want to paste.

For example, suppose you want to copy a paragraph from Final Notice.doc to Pay Up Now.doc. First, select the paragraph in Final Notice, and click Copy. Then switch to Pay Up Now, position the edit cursor at the desired spot in Pay Up Now, and click Paste. Voila!

The only tricky part is deciding how you intend to switch among documents. If you plan to make only a single copy or move between two documents, you may find it simplest to close the first document after clicking Copy or Cut, then open the second for the Paste. However, if you plan to move back and forth several times to make multiple cuts or copies, or if you need to copy or move text among three, four, or more documents, you'll find it more convenient to keep all documents open until you're finished.

Begin by opening the first document. Without closing the first, open the second—it takes over the document window, appearing to have closed the first document. But in fact, the first document remains open. Continue opening documents until you've opened all the files you need.

To switch among your open documents, open the Window menu (see Figure 4-4). All open documents are listed there, in alphabetical order. To switch to any document, choose it from the menu. When you finish with a document, close it—the others remain open until you close them.

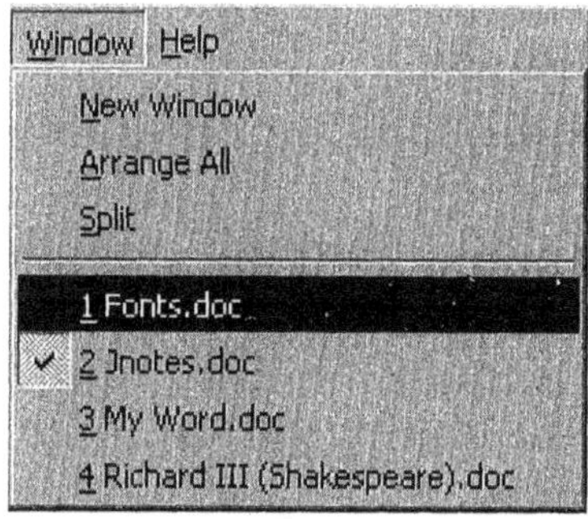

Figure 4-4: The Window menu, from which you may switch among open documents.

Fast Track

If you want to insert the entire contents of a document—formatting and all—into another document, you needn't fiddle with opening multiple documents and making a copy or move. Instead, open the document into which you want the other document's contents inserted, and position the edit cursor at the spot where you want the inserted file's contents to appear.

Choose Insert | File to open the Insert File dialog, which, name aside, is identical to the Open dialog. Using the same techniques available in the Open dialog (see Chapter 3), navigate to the file whose contents you wish to copy, select it, and click OK.

Changing Capitalization

Ideally, you'll type uppercase (capital) letters when you want uppercase letters, and lowercase when you want lowercase. But if later you must make broad, generalized changes to the way you've capitalized stuff, doing so manually can be a pain.

For example, suppose you had used ALL CAPS for all of the headings in your document and then decided to use initial caps (uppercase only on the first letter of each word, as in the headings in this book). You could retype all of your headings. But Word offers a more convenient option: the Change Case dialog (see Figure 4-5).

To use the Change Case dialog, select the text whose case you want to modify, then choose Format | Change Case. Choose the radio button next to the style of capitalization you want. The choices are:

- **Sentence case.** Word capitalizes the first letter of the first word of all sentences in the selection.
- **lowercase.** Word makes all letter characters in the selection lowercase.
- **UPPERCASE.** Word makes all letter characters in the selection uppercase.
- **Title Case.** Word capitalizes the first letter of each word in the selection, as in a title or heading. Note that Title Case does its thing to every word in the selection, including articles (A, The), prepositions (Of, By), and other short words that are often left all lowercase in titles and headings, except when they're the first word.
- **tOGGLE cASE.** Word automatically reverses the case of each letter in the selection. GORILLA becomes gorilla, lake becomes LAKE, Bob becomes bOB, NaCl (sodium chloride) becomes nAcL (nothin').

Observe two important points about Change Case:

- Each of the choices on the Change Case dialog is capitalized in a way that represents its effect.
- Change Case affects letter characters only—numbers and punctuation are unaffected.

Had you already guessed these?

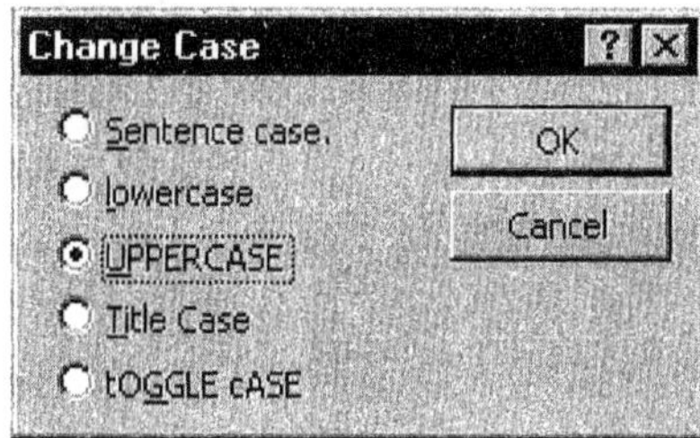

Figure 4-5: The Change Case dialog.

Fast Track

Let's say you just spent three days working on a document for work, and your boss asks to see it. Let's say you provide your boss with the Word file, and he or she then makes a few "minor" changes and returns it. Now unless you have a really good memory or you have the time to compare this new changed document with your original, you won't even know what was changed, right? Wrong! Word provides an excellent tool that allows you to make revisions plainly visible, so that another reader can see exactly what is new—what has been added, deleted, moved, and so on. Read more about this clever feature in "Tracking Changes," a section of Chapter 21.

Counting Words

You know that by printing your document, or checking the status bar, you can learn at any time how many pages you've created. But for many school, office, and professional projects, you need to know the number of words in your document. ("Class, for Monday please write a 500-word essay. Topic: 'Yeast: the Brewer's Friend.'")

To find out how many words your whole document contains, make sure nothing is selected, then choose Tools | Word Count. A dialog like the one in Figure 4-6 appears, reporting not only the number of words, but also pages, characters, and other statistics.

To find out how many words a particular portion of your document contains, select that portion before choosing Tools | Word Count.

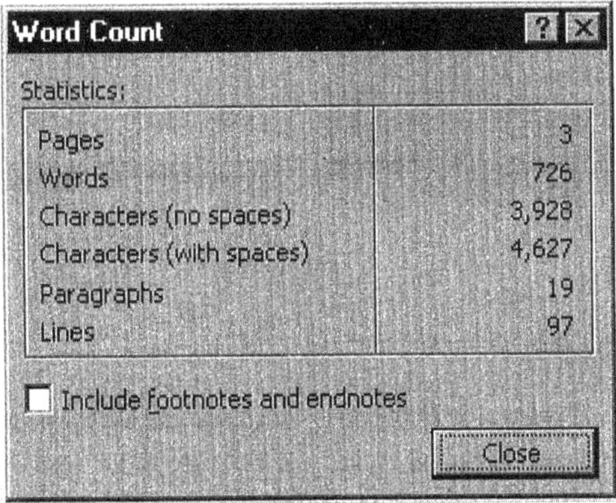

Figure 4-6: The Word Count dialog, showing statistics for the current document or selection.

Walk-Through: Insert, Overtype, Copy, Move

Follow the steps below to practice inserting, overtyping, copying, and moving blocks of text in Word.

1. Open or create any document containing text. (Walkthrough 3—which you created in Chapter 3—will do fine.)
2. Position the edit cursor in the middle of a sentence.
3. Type a few words.

   The Words are inserted within the sentence, without overtyping any existing text.
4. Select the words you just typed.
5. Click the Cut button on the Standard toolbar.

   The selection vanishes.
6. Position the edit cursor at the very end of the document.

7. Click the Paste button on the Standard toolbar.
   The cut selection appears at the bottom of the document. You have moved the selection.
8. Select any paragraph.
9. Click the Copy button on the Standard toolbar.
10. Position the edit cursor at the very top of the document.
11. Click the Paste button on the Standard toolbar.
    A copy of the selected paragraph appears at the top of the document.
12. Click Paste twice more.
    Two more copies appear.
13. Position the edit cursor in the middle of any sentence.
14. Double-click the OVR indicator in the status bar.
    The OVR indicator in the status bar turns from gray to black—you're in Overtype mode.
15. Type a few words.
    Your words replace existing text as you type them.
16. Double-click the OVR indicator in the status bar.
    The OVR indicator in the status bar turns gray—you're in Insert mode.

Formatting Text

A *font,* as you probably already know, is a particular typeface, the general style in which your words appear both onscreen and when printed. Every font has a name, such as Arial, Courier, or Bookman (see Figure 4-7). While the font determines the style of your text, you must also choose a size for the text in that font. In Word, the size is expressed in *points* (one point = 1/72 of an inch) and describes the height of the letters, or rather, the height of the capital letters. In 12-point type, a capital I is 1/6 of an inch high.

In Word, you can choose the font and size for any text in your document. You can even change fonts in the middle of a paragraph, or in the middle of a word. Or you may use a single font throughout a document. Professional-looking documents generally use at least two fonts—one for big type (headings, titles, and so on) and one for the general purpose text, sometimes known as *body text.*

In general, try to use fonts creatively, but sparingly. A document that incorporates four or five different fonts usually appears sloppy and disorganized. Choose two or three fonts that look good together and apply them consistently throughout the document; for example, use font A for all headings, font B for body text, and font C for page numbers.

Net-Savvy

When you're creating a Web page with Word, the level of text formatting you can perform—particularly the use of fonts—is much more restricted than for a document intended for printing. See Chapter 22, "Office 97 & the Internet," to learn why you may want to keep your text formatting very simple in your Web pages.

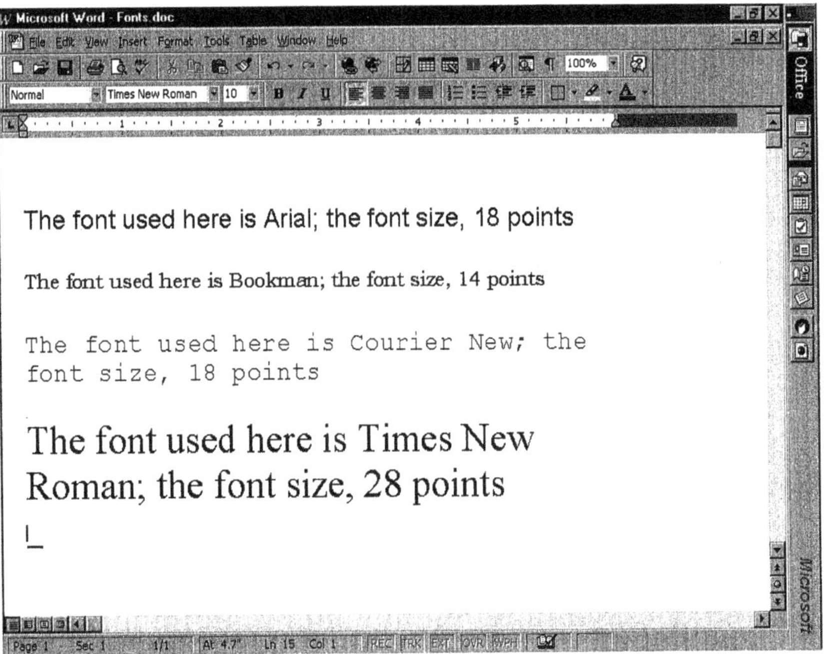

Figure 4-7: A sampling of fonts and sizes.

The fonts available to you in Word are installed not in Word, but in Windows, and are thus available for text formatting in any Windows application that deals with text—including Word, Excel, and PowerPoint. Windows comes with a varied selection of fonts you can use, and a few more are added by Office 97. To see all of the fonts available on your PC, drop down the Font list on the Formatting toolbar, and scroll through the list. As you can see on the list (mine is shown in Figure 4-8; yours may have different fonts in it), most of the default Windows fonts are *TrueType* fonts (in the list, TrueType fonts have a TT before them). TrueType fonts are specially designed for Windows applications to achieve a very close match between what you see on your screen and what you'll get on paper.

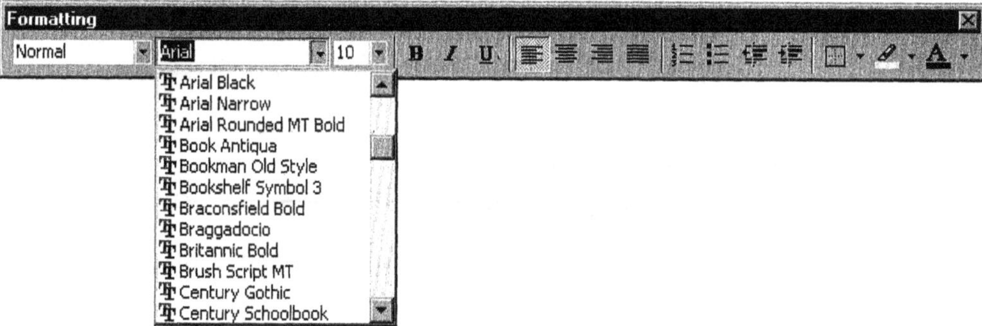

Figure 4-8: The Font list in the Formatting toolbar.

In addition to the TrueType fonts, you may also see a few *printer fonts* (in the Font list, printer fonts have a printer icon next to them). Printer fonts are the fonts already built into your particular make and model of printer. When you install a printer in Windows, Windows adds the printer fonts to your font menu, so you can apply these fonts in your documents, and also see—as you can with TrueType fonts—on your screen exactly how text using that font will appear when the document is printed.

Other than TrueType and printer fonts, there is one more type you may discover in your font list: PostScript fonts. PostScript fonts are fonts which you can print only on a PostScript-compatible printer. If you see PostScript fonts on your Font list, odds are your printer is PostScript-compatible.

Although your PC probably has a good selection of fonts to get you started, note that you can add fonts anytime you want. Font files are available in commercial software packages, in shareware, and from professional font houses. You can learn how to add fonts to your system in the Appendix, "Installing & Configuring Office 97."

Net-Savvy

TrueType, PostScript, and other fonts are widely available for download from the Web. You'll find them at many Web sites, but good starting places include:

Microsoft's Typography page: http://www.microsoft.com/truetype/fontpack/win.htm

Yahoo's Fonts directory at: http://www.yahoo.com/Computers_and_Internet/Desktop_Publishing/Fonts/

Choosing Fonts & Sizes

When you begin typing in a new, blank document, you're already using a font; the name of the font appears in the Font box on the Formatting toolbar, and the size of the type appears to the right, in the Font Size box. This font and size are preselected by the template you happen to be using. (Don't worry about templates for now).

It really doesn't matter what font comes out when you type—you can always change it to any font and size available. To change the font of existing text, select the text you want to change, then drop down the Font list from the toolbar and select a font. To change the type size, leave the text selected (or select it again, if it has been deselected), drop down the Font Size list, and select a point size. Note that the range of available sizes differs from font to font. In general, TrueType and PostScript fonts may be set in a wide range of sizes, while printer fonts may be restricted to just a few sizes.

Keep in mind that Font and Font Size work completely independently. For example, if you select a block that contains text in several different fonts and sizes—for example, the block contains some text in 12-point Arial and some in 10-point Courier—and then choose Bookman from the font list, all of the text in the block changes to Bookman, but the sizes remain unchanged—you wind up with some 12-point Bookman and some 10-point Bookman. Conversely, if you select a multi-font, multi-size block and change only the size, all text in the block changes to the size you selected, but the fonts are unchanged.

FYI: Know Your Font Types

Stylistically, fonts are divided into two basic groups: *monospaced* fonts and *proportional* fonts.

In a monospaced font, such as Courier, every character occupies the exact same amount of space; the letter i is given as much space on the line as m. Monospaced fonts have a typewriterish look to them. Monospaced fonts that may be on your Font list include Courier New and Century Gothic.

In a proportional font, the space *between* the characters remains consistent, while each character takes up only as much space as it needs—i gets a little space, m gets a lot. Proportional fonts are dressier and are used much more often today than monospaced fonts. Most of the fonts on your Font list—including Arial, Bookman, Century Schoolbook, and Times New Roman—are proportional, unless your default printer happens to be incapable of printing proportional fonts. (Any laser or inkjet printer, and most modern dot-matrix printers, can handle proportional fonts. But some older dot-matrix printers, particularly high-speed line printers in many office environments, print only their built-in, monospaced printer fonts.)

Applying Bold, Italic & Underlining

On the Formatting toolbar, to the right of the Font Size button appears a bank of three buttons. These buttons change the look of text, but don't actually change the font. What they do is change the *attributes*, or style, of the text within the selected font. The buttons available are:

- Bold. Makes text **bold.**
- Italic. Makes text *italic.*
- Underline. Underlines text.

Fast Track

Instead of clicking the attribute toolbar buttons, you can use the keyboard to create the same effect: Ctrl+B = ***bold****, Ctrl+I =* italic, *and Ctrl+U = underline.*

These buttons all work the same, doing their bit to selected text. To apply an attribute to text, select the text, then click the desired button. To apply an attribute to text as you type it, click the button, then type, then click the same attribute button again when you're done.

Note that you can combine attributes. Highlight a word, click the Bold button, then click the Italic button, and the text becomes ***bold & italic***. **Bold & underlined**, *italic and underlined*, and ***bold & italic & underlined*** are also possible. However, combining attributes in this way is generally considered overkill. A little emphasis—a single attribute—goes a long way.

To remove an attribute, highlight the text, then click the attribute button again; for example, if the highlighted text is already bold, clicking the Bold button removes the bold.

Fast Track

At the far-right end of the Formatting toolbar appear three more buttons—Outside Border, Highlight, and Font Color. While in effect, these buttons also apply attributes, but their proper use is related more to the application of graphics and color than to text formatting. Along with all of the other graphics- and color-related activities, these buttons are covered in detail in Chapter 6, "Adding Pictures, Tables & Borders."

Walk-Through: Fonts, Sizes & Attributes

Follow the steps below to practice formatting text by applying fonts, font sizes, and attributes.

1. Open or create any document containing text. (Walkthrough 3—which you created in Chapter 3—will do fine.)
2. From the menu bar, choose Edit|Select All.
   The entire document is highlighted.
3. From the Formatting toolbar, drop down the Font list and choose Arial.
   All text in the document is set in Arial.
4. Select any text in the document (but not the whole document).
5. Drop down the Font list and choose Courier New.
   The selection changes from Arial to Courier New.
6. Position the edit cursor at the very top of the document, type a few words (such as a title for your document), and press Enter.
7. Select the new title paragraph you just created.
8. From the Formatting toolbar, make the following selections: Font list = Century Schoolbook; Font Size = 28; Bold button.
   The title at the top of your page is set in 28-point Century Schoolbook, bold.
9. Experiment with fonts, trying out each of the fonts in your list.
   What does each one look like? In what types of documents might you use each font?

Applying Advanced Text-Control Options

Changing fonts, sizes, and attributes from the toolbar is a snap, as you have seen up to this point in the chapter. But you can control the appearance of text to a much finer degree through the Font dialog.

Before opening the Font dialog, select the text you want to format. Then open the Font dialog by choosing Format | Font. The dialog shown in Figure 4-9 opens, with its Font tab preselected.

Observe that the Font tab—like all of the tabs on the Font dialog—includes a Preview pane near the bottom. As you make changes in the tabs, the Preview pane updates automatically to show you the effect you're building. When the Preview pane shows the full effect you're after, click OK.

Fast Track

The Font dialog includes three tabs: Font, Character Spacing, and Animation. The first two tabs are described in this section. The third, Animation, is used only for dressing up documents that will be published online. Online publishing—including animation effects—is discussed in Chapter 22, "Office 97 & the Internet.")

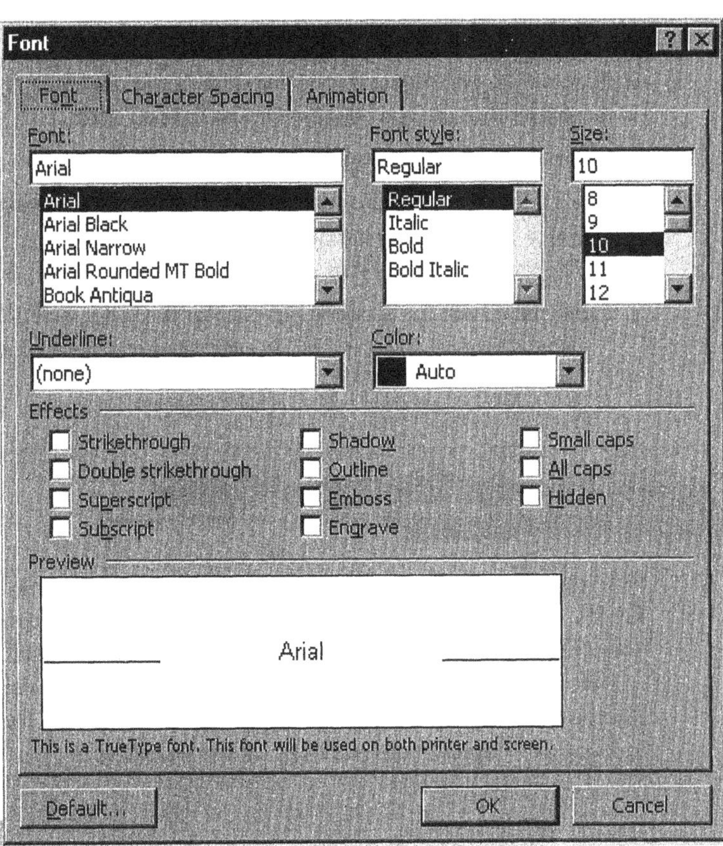

Figure 4-9: The Font dialog.

Using the Font Tab

On the Font tab of the Font dialog, the top row of three items—Font, Font style, and Size—duplicate precisely the font-control activities you have performed with the toolbar. You use Font and Size exactly as you use their toolbar namesakes (the Font and Font Size boxes), while Font Style stands in for the actions of the Bold and Italic buttons (and the combination of those buttons, bold italic). Choosing Regular from the Font Style list removes any bold or italic effects.

Below the top row you'll find ways to do things you cannot do on the toolbar. For example, the Underline button on the toolbar simply applies a solid, unbroken underline under the entire block of selected text (including all words and the spaces between them). By choosing an option from the Underline list on the Font tab, you can achieve a wide variety of underlining effects. Figure 4-10 illustrates the effects of some of the choices on the underline menu. (To test the effect of any item on the list, choose it, and observe the Preview pane.)

Fast Track

The Color list, to the right of the Underline list on the Font dialog, controls the color of text. Using color in your documents requires balancing many considerations, such as where and how the document will be published—online, on a laser printer, on a color printer, and so on. These issues—including the use of the Color list—are covered in Chapter 6, "Adding Pictures, Tables & Borders."

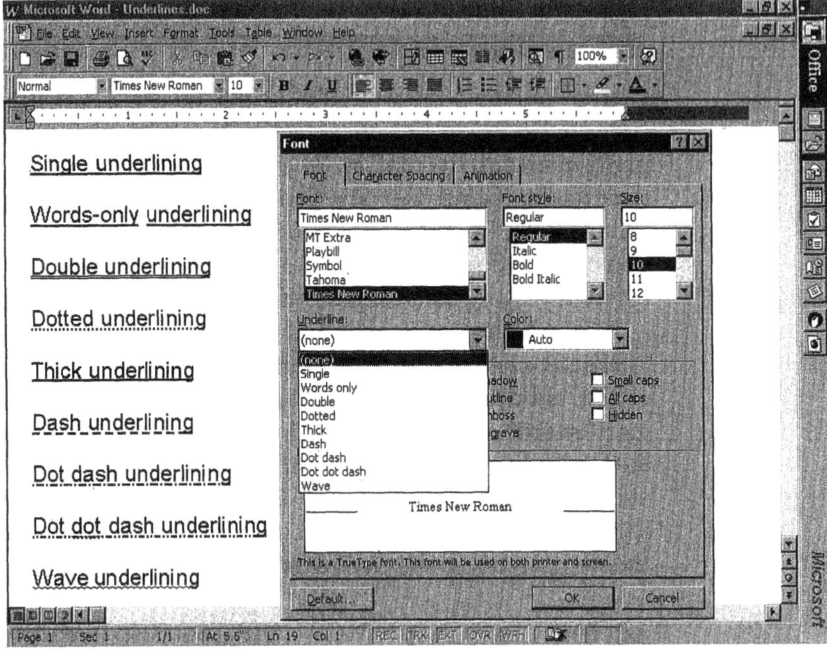

Figure 4-10: Underline options on the Font tab.

The set of Effects check boxes above the Preview pane enables you to apply a wide variety of special text effects, from ~~Strikethrough~~ to ALL CAPS. Many of these may be used in combination. To experiment with the Effects until you achieve the effect you want, click the check boxes and observe the change in the Preview pane.

FYI: Watch Out for Effects Overload

When working with the Effects on the Font tab—particularly those in the center column that includes Shadow, Outline, Emboss, and Engrave effects—keep in mind that such effects are notorious for looking much worse on paper than they do on your screen, even if you use a good laser printer. Similarly, any of the adjustments you can make on the Character Spacing tab (covered next) may be difficult for some printers to produce successfully.

Any time you choose to get fancy with text effects or spacing, be sure to evaluate their printed appearance carefully. You may wind up simplifying your text formatting once you see its effect on paper.

Using the Character Spacing Tab

The Font dialog's Character Spacing tab (shown in Figure 4-11) enables you to make minute adjustments to the spacing of characters in the selected text. As a rule, font designers set the spacing for a font very carefully, to achieve an eye-pleasing effect. Unless you're a type designer yourself, or a professional graphic designer, odds are that you'll diminish the beauty and readability of the type if you fiddle with the character spacing needlessly.

Still, you may choose to change the spacing to achieve a special effect. For example, you may want to s p r e a d o u t s o m e w o r d s in a title or heading to give it a unique appearance (advertisers do that a lot these days with product names and slogans). Or you may choose to squeeze characters closer together to make a particular block of text fit within a restricted space.

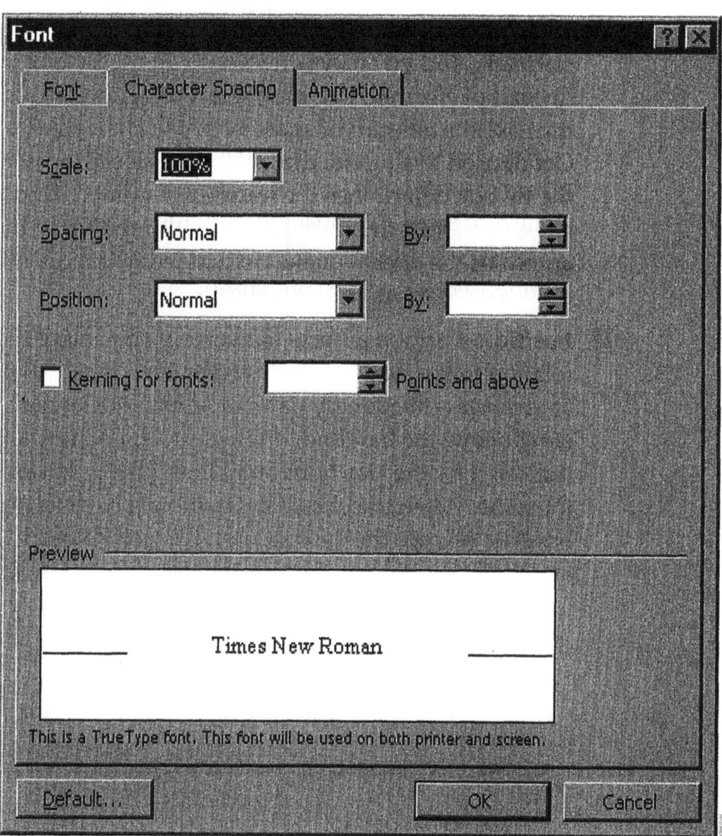

Figure 4-11: The Font dialog's Character Spacing tab.

Fast Track

You can open the Font dialog from a context menu. Select the text you want to format, right-click the selection to open the context menu, and choose Font.

You can adjust the spacing of the selected text in four ways on the Character Spacing tab (note that you can use any of these in combination):

- **Scale.** Scale has no effect on the amount of space *between* the characters; rather, Scale stretches or squeezes the width of the characters themselves. The default choice, 100%, leaves the characters at their normal width, as set by the font's designer. Percentages above 100% make the characters wider, and percentages below 100% narrow the characters.
- **Spacing.** Spacing adjusts the space between the characters. When the default choice, Normal, is in place, the characters are spaced normally, and no entry is necessary in the By box to the right. Instead of Normal, you may select Expanded from the list to increase the amount of space between characters, or choose Condensed to squeeze the characters closer together. Your entry in the By box determines the number of points (72nds of an inch) by which to adjust the spacing. A higher number in the By box always amplifies the effect—makes expanded text more expanded, condensed text more condensed.
- **Position.** Position adjusts the vertical spacing of the selected text in relation to the *baseline*, the invisible line on which the text sits (*descenders*—the dangly parts of letters like lowercase y and j—hang below the baseline). In the Preview pane, the baseline is indicated by the two horizontal lines jutting in from the sides of the pane. When the choice in Position is Normal, all text sits on the baseline (except the descenders). Choose Raised to raise the text above the baseline, or Lowered to lower it below the baseline. The

entry in the By box determines the number of points by which the text is raised or lowered.

- **Kerning.** When font designers design a proportional font, they carefully select the uniform spacing between characters for the best overall effect. Unfortunately, when text is set at larger sizes, some character combinations begin to look like they're too far apart. For example, lowercase f and lowercase i may begin to look too far apart because of the way they're shaped. It's a trick of the eye—the characters are no farther apart or closer together than any others. Still, font designers have found a way to compensate for this phenomenon: kerning pairs. The type designer picks out the particular pairs of letters that begin to look oddly spaced at larger point sizes and builds into the font kerning instructions, spacing guidelines for kerning pairs.

  By checking the check box next to Kerning for fonts, you instruct Word to automatically apply spacing adjustment guidelines to any kerning pairs in the selected text. Because kerning is generally unnecessary and sometimes unattractive at smaller point sizes, you must also select a point size in the box preceding Points and above. For example, if you check the Kerning for fonts check box and select 18 in the Points and above box, kerning will be applied to any text in the selection that is 18 points or larger; any text in the selection below 18 points will not be kerned.

Adding Symbols & Special Characters

In many documents, you may require special characters that appear nowhere on your keyboard. Examples of the more commonly-used special characters appear in Figure 4-12, but in fact, there are hundreds of special characters available. While many such characters are graphical in appearance, they are not graphics; they are text, and as such, you can set them within a line of text and format them in most of the ways you can format any other text.

Word groups these characters into two groups. Each group is represented on a separate tab of the Symbol dialog:

- **Special characters.** Common text characters that do not appear on the keyboard, such as a long (em) dash, copyright symbol, and so on.
- **Symbols.** Unusual characters, such as Greek letters, arrows, and others that are not used often and do not appear on the keyboard, but are part of the character set of some fonts. Symbols also include characters from special "symbol" or "dingbat" fonts, fonts made up completely of icons and symbols rather than letters and number characters. These symbols are used in typing equations or non-English words, or to create fun & funky list bullets and other page dressing.

FYI: Symbols May Not Like Font Changes

The two groups of symbols—Special Characters and Symbols—overlap; some characters may appear in both groups. When that's the case, you're always better off choosing from among the Special Characters than from the Symbols.

Why? Well, the Special Characters are pretty much *font independent*; that is, if you insert a copyright mark in a line of Arial text, you get an Arial copyright mark. If later you change the font of the line to Courier, the copyright mark changes to a Courier copyright mark. Selecting your symbols from the Special Characters list ensures that if you change the font of a text block that contains a symbol, the symbol changes font, too—but it remains the correct symbol.

Conversely, many (but not all) of the choices you may make from the Symbols tab are font-dependent. The inserted symbol will appear, at first, just as you want it to, but if you change fonts later, the symbol may change unexpectedly to an entirely different character.

Whichever tab you choose from, it's smart to recheck any inserted symbols carefully any time you change the font of a block containing symbols.

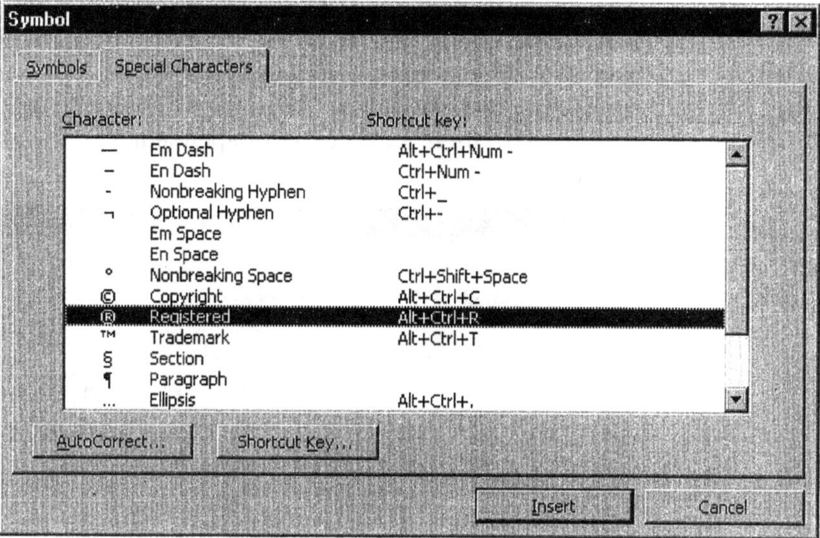

Figure 4-12: The Symbol dialog, where you can get to all those funky characters you can't find on the keyboard.

To insert a symbol or special character, first position the edit cursor in your document at the spot where you want to insert the character. Then open the Symbol dialog (shown in Figure 4-12) by choosing Insert | Symbol.

To insert any of the common special characters, choose the Special Characters tab, select the character you want from the list, and click Insert. The character appears in the document, in the same font and size as the surrounding text.

Inserting a symbol takes a little more effort than a special character. First, click the Symbols tab (see Figure 4-13). Then choose a Font from the list; when you do, the dialog displays all of the available characters for that font, including letters, numbers, punctuation, and any other special characters. To insert a character, click it (it appears enlarged after clicking, so you can get a better look at it), and click Insert.

If on the Symbols tab you choose the top selection in the Font list, (normal text), the dialog displays a list of characters that are available for virtually any of the regular text fonts you may be using in your document. Usually, choices you make from the (normal text) list are, like the choices on the Special Characters tab, font independent, and appear in

your document in the same font as the surrounding text. Below (normal text), the remaining choices on the Symbols tab's Font list are all special symbol or dingbat fonts, populated entirely with symbols and, in the case of dingbat fonts such as Wingdings, funky little pictures. Symbols you choose in these fonts are font-dependent.

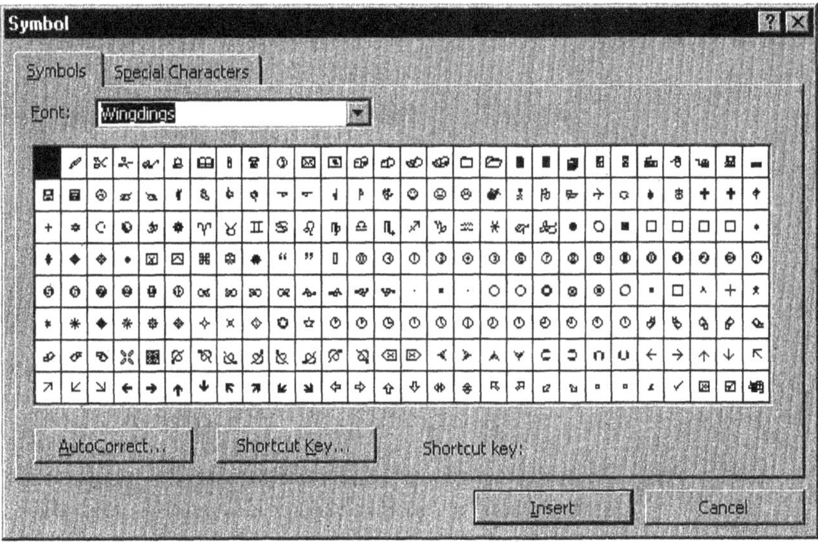

Figure 4-13: Use the Symbol dialog's Symbols tab to insert special characters from symbol fonts, such as Wingdings.

Walk-Through: Symbols

Follow the steps below to practice inserting symbols and special characters in a Word document.

1. Create a new document.
2. Type **New—The 1997 Ford Econolux**.
3. Select what you just typed, and set it in 18-point Arial.
4. Position the edit cursor at the end of the line.
5. Choose Insert|Symbol.

   The Symbol dialog opens.

6. Click the Special Characters tab.
7. Select the trademark symbol from the special characters list, and click Insert.
   Econolux is now trademarked.
8. Select the double dash (--) following New.
9. Choose Insert|Symbol.
10. Click the Special Characters tab.
11. Select the em dash from the special characters list, and click Insert.
    The selection (a double dash) is replaced by an em dash.
12. Position the edit cursor just after the E in Econolux.
13. Press Backspace to delete the E.
14. Choose Insert|Symbol.
15. Open the Symbols tab, and choose (normal text) in the Font list.
16. Find the character É and click Insert.
    É *now begins* Éconolux.
17. Select the word Éconolux, including the copyright symbol.
18. Choose Format|Font.
19. In the Font tab, click the check box next to All caps.
20. Click the Character Spacing tab, and choose a Scale of 150%, and Spacing Expanded By 3 points.
21. Click OK.
    How do you like the results? Too much? Not enough?

Moving On

You're in charge of your words now. You know how to funnel words from your brain into a Word document, to make corrections and revisions, and to edit, manipulate, and polish your writing by selecting text blocks and applying powerful time-savers like copy, move, and undo. You also know how to shape the look and feel of your words to an exacting degree. Gutenberg himself would be astonished at what you can do. Congratulate yourself—you're a font of knowledge, a bold pioneer, a special character, a symbol of excellence. . . . You get my 1/72nd of an inch (my *point*, get it?). Okay, I'll stop.

That's it for words—now the problem is pages. What should your pages look like? What size paper will your document be printed on, how wide are the margins, how many columns does it have? Are paragraphs indented? Are there headers or footers on the pages? Page numbers? You'll learn how to answer all of these questions, and more, all in the course of "Designing Pages" in Chapter 5.

5 Designing Pages

When you speak, it isn't your words alone that communicate your meaning—it's how you say them. Your vocal inflections, pacing, facial expressions, and even your body language work together with your words to get your ideas across. In the same way, the formatting of your text and pages work together with the words to communicate their meaning more effectively. How your words and pages look is as important as what they say.

Open your eyes a little wider, and take in the whole page you're reading right now. Observe the various fonts and sizes, the occasional use of text attributes, the indenting of paragraphs, the width of the margins, the headers, and other aesthetic choices. All of this formatting was carefully selected to make this particular document attractive, easy-to-read, and professional looking. It was designed to help you learn.

What do you want *your* document to look like? Think about who your intended reader is. A friend? A potential customer? Your boss? All three? Do you want it to be a fun, crazy document, or a sober, businesslike one? The formatting choices you make determine your document's personality, and they dramatically affect how your readers perceive your words—and you.

If you've been through Chapter 4, "Working With Text," you already know how to control the look of your text. That leaves three remaining activities that determine your document's appearance:

- **Page layout.** Choosing the geometry and organization of the page: paper size and orientation, margins, headers and footers (text automatically repeated at the top or bottom of each page), columns.
- **Paragraph formatting.** Choosing the look and behavior of paragraphs within the page layout: alignment, indenting, automatic list formatting, tab settings.
- **Graphical formatting.** Adding pictures, tables, borders, color.

The graphics I'll save for Chapter 6, "Adding Pictures, Tables & Borders." Here, under the catchall of page design, you'll discover both layout and paragraph formatting (a.k.a. "the chicken and the egg"), because of the way these two phases of page design are inextricably linked. You can best judge your indents, tabs, and other paragraph stuff only within the space allotted to those paragraphs by the page layout, so laying out pages first makes sense. On the other hand, performing both text and paragraph formatting before laying out pages allows you to play around with the page layout and accurately assess the overall impact of any changes to margins, header space, and so on. So it's a crapshoot.

Now, if I'm anything, I'm flexible. Live and let live, I always say. Don't snap like an oak, I say—bend like bamboo. So I hope you'll interpret my approach to this conflict—namely, "tell 'em how to do page layout and paragraph formatting without saying which comes first" —as evidence of open-mindedness and a desire to empower you (rather than as ambivalence and cowardice, which is, of course, the frank truth).

In this chapter, you'll learn how to complete the formatting of your document, paragraphs, and pages together. Which you do first is your business. Once you've tried a little of both activities, I'm sure you'll discover an approach that feels natural to you. Trust your instincts. The Force will be with you.

Net-Savvy

Laying out an online document or a Web page is an entirely different sack of worms from laying out a printed document, with an entirely different set of rules and limitations. While the material in this chapter is essential to controlling the look of a printed document, little in this chapter has any relevance to online documents. You'll learn about the layout of online "pages" in Chapter 22, "Office 97 & the Internet."

Understanding & Creating Sections

For short, simple documents, you may want to lay out pages one way and have that layout apply to every page in the document. But more often than not, you'll want to use different layouts for different parts of the document. For example, you may want the *header* or *footer*—repeated text that appears at the top or bottom, respectively, of every page—to change with each major part of the document. Or you may want to create a title page, or introductory pages for each part of the document, with an entirely different look from the rest of the document—different margins, headers, and footers.

To accomplish this, you could break the document up into multiple files, then give each file its own layout. But this is an inconvenient way to vary the layout in shorter documents. A better way is to break a single document file into multiple *sections*. To each section, you can apply unique page formatting—margins, headers and footers, page orientation—without affecting the rest of the document.

To start a new section within your document, you must insert a *section break*. First, position the edit cursor in your document immediately preceding the material that belongs in the new section. Choose Insert | Break from the menu bar to open the Break dialog shown in Figure 5-1. From the Break dialog choose one of the four options listed under Section breaks:

- **Next page.** A *page break* is inserted at the edit cursor position, and the new section begins with the very top of that new page.
- **Continuous.** The new section begins at the edit cursor position, with no page break.
- **Even page.** The new section begins on an even-numbered (left-hand) page. One or two page breaks are inserted automatically to force the new section to the top of an even-numbered page, creating a blank odd-numbered page, if necessary.
- **Odd page.** The new section begins on an odd-numbered (right-hand) page. One or two page breaks are inserted automatically to force the new section to the top of an odd-numbered page, creating a blank even-numbered page, if necessary.

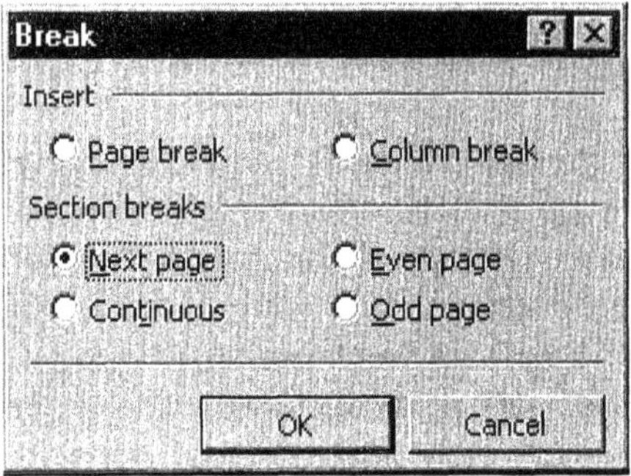

Figure 5-1: The Break dialog, where you make section breaks, page breaks, and column breaks.

Fast Track

If you choose Continuous, the layout settings from the preceding section—including the top, left, and right margin settings, and the header—will still apply to the page on which the new section begins. On that page, only elements following the section break, such as the footer and bottom margin—are affected by any layout changes you make.

The most common application of Continuous is to change the number or layout of columns within a page. For example, the top half of a page may have two columns, then the bottom half (following the section break) may have only one. See "Working With Columns" later in this chapter.

Whichever starting point you choose, the new section begins at that point and continues to the next section break, or to the end of the document, if you create no more sections.

Once a section is created, you apply layout settings to it by locating the edit cursor anywhere within the section and then changing the Page Setup dialog as described in the next several pages.

FYI: Entering Measurements

In many of the activities in this chapter, you'll need to enter measurements in text boxes. For example, you'll need to supply measurements for the width of the margins.

On most text boxes that collect measurements, you'll see an Up arrow and a Down arrow on the right side of the box; you can click the arrows to increase or decrease the measurement. Still, you may need to type a measurement in such a box, so it's important to learn how right now.

Type all measurements in inches, using decimal fractions when necessary (.5" = 1/2 inch; .75" = 3/4 inches; 1.25" = 1 1/4 inches, and so on). Don't bother including the quote mark (") to indicate inches; Word fills in the quote mark for you.

Setting Up the Page

By "setting up the page," I mean defining the geometry of your page by determining such things as the width of the margins, the size of the paper your document will be printed on, and more. The phrase "setting up the page" is meant to help you remember the name of the dialog on which you do all this stuff—the Page Setup dialog.

You might expect to open the Page Setup dialog from the Format menu, but you'd be *wrong*—it's on the File menu. (Who knew?) Choose File | Page Setup to open the dialog (see Figure 5-2). Then modify any entries you wish in the four tabs of the Page Setup dialog, according to the instructions you'll find on the next several pages. Note that defaults are supplied for all Page Setup entries—you needn't change everything, just change what you want to.

Fast Track

In Normal or Page Layout view, you can also open the Page Setup dialog by double-clicking on a margin area of the ruler that appears below the toolbars. A margin area appears at each end of the ruler, colored gray.

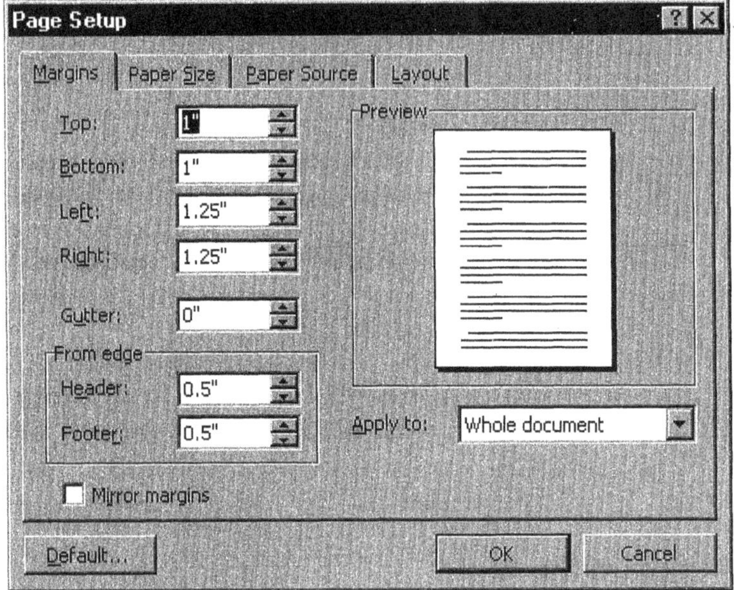

Figure 5-2: The Margins tab.

Every tab on the Page Setup dialog has a Preview pane. Any time you make a change, the Preview pane immediately displays how that change affects your pages.

Also on every tab, the Apply to list appears. From this list, you'll choose to which portion of the document the changes you're making now apply. The choices are:

- **Whole document.** Changes you make now to the Page Setup dialog affect the whole document.
- **This section.** Changes you make now to the Page Setup dialog affect only the section that now contains the edit cursor. (This option is available only if you have split up your document into sections.)
- **This point forward.** Changes you make now to the Page Setup dialog affect the page containing the edit cursor and all pages that follow it. Pages preceding the one containing the edit cursor are unaffected.

Fast Track

On every tab of the Page Setup dialog, you'll also see the Default button. Clicking the Default button changes the template *of the current document to match the Page Setup settings you've chosen. The new setup is then applied not only to the current document but also to all new documents you create from then on using the same template as the current document.*

Using a template, the Page Setup dialog, and the Default button, you can quickly change the layout of a whole family of related documents. See Chapter 7.

Margins

On the Margins tab (see Figure 5-2), you set the margins of the page, including not only the left and right margins you may think of first, but also top and bottom margins, plus special margin adjustments to dress things up.

In the Top, Bottom, Left, and Right boxes on the tab, enter margin widths in inches.

FYI: Top & Bottom Margins Include Headers & Footers

When figuring top and bottom margins, consider the margin to be the space between the edge of the paper and the space allotted for the regular text of your document—*not* the space between the edge of the paper and any header or footer you may create.

The header or footer can appear within the space allotted to the margins, while all of the other text in your document is forced out of that space. For example, if you have a 1" top margin, the top line of text in your document will begin 1" below the top edge of the paper, but the header may sit just 1/2" from the edge.

While headers and footers don't obey top and bottom margins, they do obey left and right margins.

In the From edge box, you choose the position of your Header and Footer (both of which you learn how to create and format later in this chapter). If you don't intend to use headers or footers in your document, you can ignore the From edge box.

If you intend to create headers or footers, use the From edge box to choose the distance from the edge of the paper (top edge for Header, bottom edge for Footer) to the header or footer itself. Note that these settings are entirely independent of the top and bottom margin settings.

FYI: Don't Upset Your Printer

When choosing margins and From edge settings, keep in mind the mechanical limits of your printer. For example, most laser printers cannot print within .25" of any edge of the page (they grab the paper in that quarter inch). When using such a printer, all of your margin settings (and your From edge settings, if you use headers or footers) must be .25" or greater.

If you choose margins that exceed your printer's capabilities, Word automatically warns you with a special dialog. On that dialog, you can click Fix to automatically set all margins to the minimum required by your printer. Or, if the printer's limitations don't matter to you—if, for example, you will print the document on a printer other than the one currently defined as your default Windows printer—choose Ignore on the dialog to instruct Word to accept whatever margins you choose.

The remaining options on the Margins tab—Gutter and Mirror margins—make special adjustments that are required only for documents that will be bound in some way and printed on both sides of each page. The adjustments are necessary for two reasons:

- The edge of the page that goes to the binding—the *inside* edge, or *gutter*—tends to lose a quarter-inch or so of readable space, because of the binding. (Unless you're one of those evil people who open books so wide that the binding breaks—and if so, I think you and I use the same public library.)
- What makes a bound document look attractive isn't consistent left and right margins, but consistent inside and outside margins. As in this book, the outside edge is the right side of a right-hand page, and the left side of a left-hand page. So unless you enter identical measurements for the Left and Right margins, the inside margin will change page to page, as will the outside.

The Gutter box solves the first problem. By entering a measurement in the Gutter box, you instruct Word to automatically add that measure to the margin on the gutter side of the page. For example, if you choose 1" margins for both Left and Right, then enter **.25"** in Gutter, Word automatically adds an extra .25" to the inside margin (the right margin of all left-hand pages and the left margin of all right-hand pages) to add a little breathing space for the binding.

Mirror margins solves the second problem. If you check the check box in Mirror Margins, Word changes the Margin tab. Where once you could enter measurements for "Left" and "Right" margins, you'll see instead boxes for defining "Inside" and "Outside" margins. The Inside margin setting is applied to whichever margin faces the binding (in addition to any measurement in Gutter), and the Outside entry is applied to the edge opposite the binding. This makes all outside margins the same, and all inside margins the same, page to page. (Note that Mirror margins is irrelevant if the measurement in Inside is the same as that in Outside, or if Left matches Right.)

Fast Track

In Page Layout view or in Print Preview mode, you can use the rulers to adjust margins. The horizontal ruler appears just below the toolbars, and the vertical ruler appears to the left of the page. (If you don't see the rulers, choose View | Ruler.)

The gray areas on the ends of the rulers indicate the current margins. Point carefully to the spot where the gray margin meets the white part of the ruler. The pointer becomes a double-pointed arrow, and a tooltip appears, reporting which margin—Left, Right, Top, Bottom—you're about to adjust. Click and drag to change the margin, then release.

Paper Size

"Paper size" describes the dimensions of a page of your document in its finished form. These dimensions are figured into the formatting of your documents within the margins. For example, if you tell Word that the paper is 7" wide, and you've set 1" margins left and right, Word formats your text within a 5" column (7" minus the margins). You tell Word about the paper size on the Paper Size tab (see Figure 5-3).

It's important to understand that the "Paper Size" dimensions do not have to match the actual size of the paper on which you will print the document. For example, you may print your document on regular letter-size paper (8.5" x 11") but intend to trim it, after printing, to 5" x 7". Or you may print on letter-size paper for draft copies, intending to later print the final copy on smaller paper, perhaps on a different printer. By defining your intended page on the Paper Size tab, you instruct Word to properly format the document for its intended page size, regardless of the actual paper used to print it.

To choose a paper size, select any of the standard paper sizes (Letter, Legal, A4, etc.) from the Paper size list. If none of the paper sizes matches what you want, enter the precise Width and Height of the paper in the boxes provided.

Also on the Paper Size tab, you'll select an *orientation* by clicking one of the radio buttons provided. If the pages of your document will be taller than they are wide (like this book), choose Portrait orientation. If pages are wider than tall (like a bank check or a computer screen) choose Landscape.

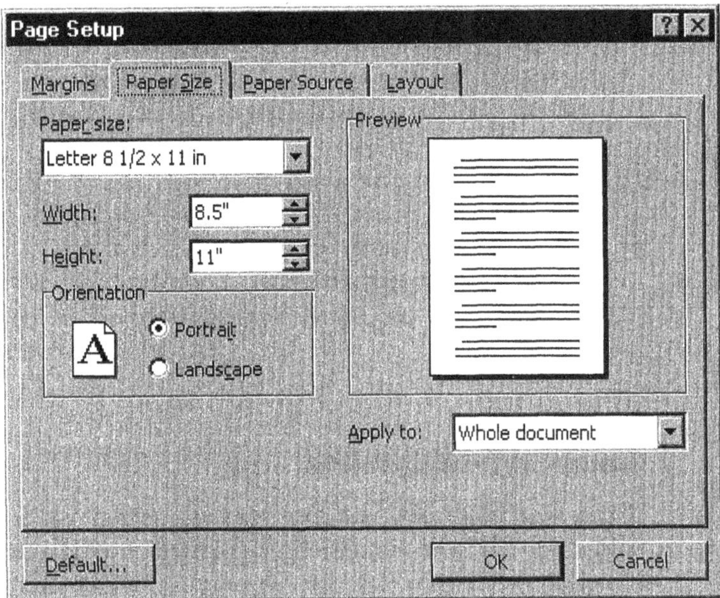

Figure 5-3: The Paper Size tab.

Paper Source

Some printers have multiple *paper sources*, trays or stacks from which they can draw paper for printing. For example, your PC might be connected to a network laser printer that has two paper trays, one containing letter-size paper (8.5" x 11") and one containing legal-size paper (8.5" x 14") or maybe envelopes. On the Paper Source tab, choose which tray to use to print the document at hand.

FYI: Paper Source Peculiarities

If your printer does not have multiple paper sources, you can ignore the Paper Source tab. Isn't that nice?

Don't trust the Paper Source tab to know whether your printer has multiple trays. It will probably list several paper source choices regardless of what your printer can do.

Finally, regardless of the Paper Source settings, you may be able to change the Paper Source at any time through the Print dialog.

The Paper Source tab includes two lists from which to choose: First page and Other pages. By choosing two different paper sources from these lists, you can print the first page of a document (or section) from one source, and the rest from another. This enables you to print, for example, the first page of a document on a fancy or colored paper stock while printing subsequent pages on regular paper stock. It also enables you to print envelopes along with letters when printing an automated mailing. See Chapter 7, "Working Faster & Easier in Word."

Layout

The Layout tab is a lie—almost everything on the other tabs of the Page Setup dialog pertains to page layout, too, so just who does this Layout tab think it is, anyway? In fact, the Layout tab would more properly be labeled the Miscellaneous tab, but "Miscellaneous" doesn't fit easily in the space provided. On the Layout tab, you define a few final, optional aspects of your page layout.

The Section start list lets you start a new section, to which the current page setup will be applied. Selecting from the Section start list has the same effect as using Insert | Break to start a new section (see "Understanding & Creating Sections"), and includes the same options.

By default, a header or footer you enter is repeated throughout a document (or section) identically on every page (see "Adding Headers & Footers" later in this chapter). You can change this behavior in two ways using the entries in the Headers and Footers box:

- **The Different odd and even check box.** By checking the Different odd and even check box, you instruct Word to permit you to enter two headers or two footers—one header or footer for right-hand pages, a different one for left-hand pages (as in this book). Using different odd/even headers in this way is common in long documents; for example, you may wish to put the document title in the header on left-hand pages, and a chapter or section title on right-hand pages.
- **The Different first page check box.** By checking the different first page check box, you instruct Word to permit you to enter a header or footer on the very first page of the section or document that's different from the header or footer in following pages.

Fast Track

You may use the check boxes in the Headers and Footers box to eliminate headers or footers from selected pages. For example, to omit the header from the first page, check Different first page and then don't bother to type a first-page header. To omit footers from left-hand pages, check Different odd and even, then don't type a header for the even-numbered pages. See Adding Headers and Footers later in this chapter.

Finally, Vertical alignment allows you to specify how Word should spread the lines of text vertically within the page. In general, the Vertical alignment has no effect on any page that is full—top to bottom—of text, including paragraph breaks. But on pages that aren't full, Word can align the text within the page three ways:

- **Top.** The text starts at the top of the page, and stops wherever it stops, leaving some empty space at the bottom. This is the default choice, and also the best choice except when you're going for an unusual effect.

- **Center.** The text is centered vertically within the page, leaving equal amounts of empty space above the text and below it. Center provides an easy way to perfectly center a title within a title page.
- **Justified.** Extra space is automatically inserted between lines to spread out the text so that it always completely fills the page, top to bottom. Justified causes the line spacing to vary page to page, and creates truly weird results when a page runs more than a few lines short of a real full page.

FYI: Printing Line Numbers in Your Document

If you need line numbers printed in your document (as is required in some types of contracts and other legal documents), click the Line Numbers button in the Layout tab. A small dialog opens in which you can define where (how far from the text) and how (numbered consecutively throughout the document, restarting at every page, etc.) you want line numbers to appear. (If you want to number only a portion of the document, select that portion before opening the Page Setup dialog and choosing your line numbering.)

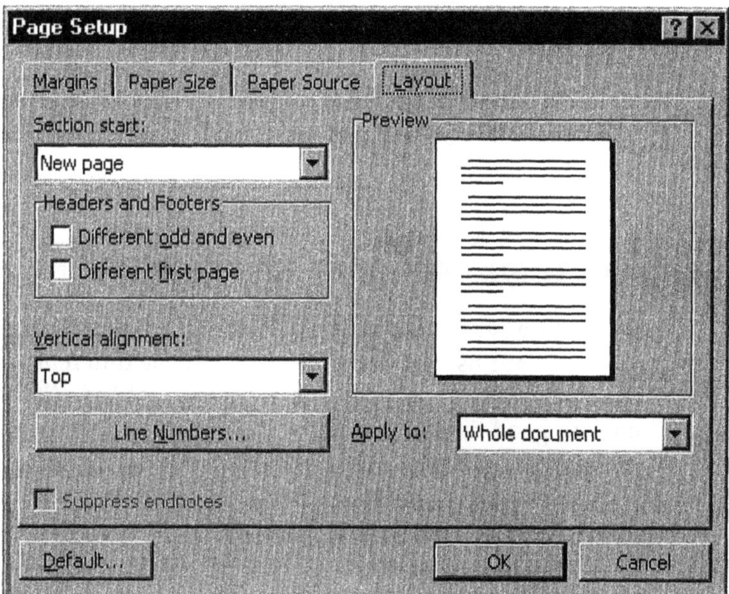

Figure 5-4: Use the Layout tab to control a few miscellaneous aspects of the page layout.

Walk-Through: Page Layout

Follow the steps below to practice setting up pages.

1. Open or create any multi-page document you're comfortable experimenting with. (If necessary, use Save As to make a copy you can play around with while not affecting the original.)
2. Print the document.
3. Choose File|Page Setup.
   The Page Setup dialog opens.
4. On the Margins tab, double the width of all four margins.
5. Click OK.
6. Print the document again, and compare it to the earlier printout, paying special attention to differences in the width of the text and in the places where pages break.
7. Choose File|Page Setup.
8. Open the Layout tab.
9. In Section start, choose Continuous.
10. In Vertical alignment, choose Center.
11. Click OK.
12. Print the document again, and compare it to the earlier printout, paying special attention to the space above and below the text of each page.

Adding Headers & Footers

In the Page Setup dialog, you decided where to put your headers and footers (Margins tab), and whether to enable different headers and footers for odd and even pages or for the first page (Layout tab). So now's a good time to make 'em.

To review, a *header* is any text you want to appear regularly at the very top of every page (or every other page, if you've used the odd/even option in the Layout tab), and a *footer* is text you want to appear at the very bottom of the page (or every other page). You should choose all of your header and footer options in the Page Setup dialog before adding the headers and footers themselves.

If your settings in the Page Setup dialog enable multiple headers and footers within the document, you must supply each different header and footer separately (see "Working With Multiple Headers & Footers"). If your page setup does not permit multiple headers or footers, you can enter your header and footer on any page in the document, and Word will automatically repeat it on every page.

To add a header or footer, choose View | Header and Footer. As Figure 5-5 shows, three things happen:

- The view switches to Page Layout view (if you were not already in Page Layout view).
- The Header and Footer dialog opens.
- Above the dialog, a dashed box labeled Header appears—the *header space*. The edit cursor appears within the header space.

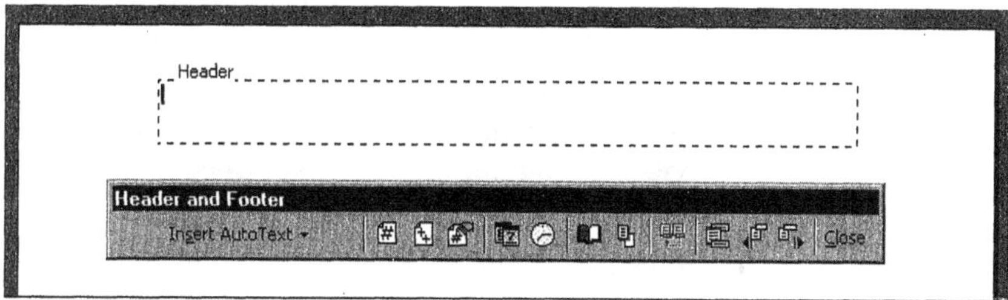

Figure 5-5: Header and Footer dialog.

Fast Track

When you're already in Page Layout view, your headers and footers appear in gray on each page of the document. You can open the Header and Footer dialog and edit the header or footer by double-clicking the gray header or footer on any page.

To add a header, type your header and apply any formatting you wish, including text formatting—font, font size, attributes, and so on—and paragraph formatting (see "Formatting Paragraphs" later in this chapter).

To add a footer, click the Switch Between Header and Footer button on the Header and Footer dialog. A dashed box labeled Footer opens (the *footer space*). Type your footer and format it any way you wish.

Working With Multiple Headers & Footers

By now you know that your headers and footers can change within a document. You can define a different header and footer for each section in your document, and within a section or document, you can use different headers or footers for odd and even pages or a different header or footer on the first page from those used in the rest of the section or document.

That's a confusing tangle of possibilities, so here's a simple way to deal with it. You need remember only one basic rule to use multiple headers and footers: Identify all pages or sections that are permitted to have a unique header or footer, and supply one there. For example:

- If your document has multiple sections, add a header and footer on any page within each section; Word automatically repeats that header or footer throughout the section.
- If the page setup permits different odd and even headers and footers (Layout tab), add a header and footer on any odd page, and add a header and footer on any even page—Word automatically repeats the headers and footers on their respective odd/even pages throughout the section or document to which the page setup applies.
- If the page setup uses the different first page option (Layout tab), go to the first page of the section or document to which the setup applies and enter a header and/or footer there, then go to any other page to supply the header and footer for the rest.

Of course, any place you may use a header or footer, you may also choose not to supply a header or footer and leave the header space or footer space blank. For example, if you don't want the first page of a section to have a header, use the Different first page option, then don't add a header on the first page. To print footers on odd pages but no footers on even pages, use the Different odd/even option, add a footer on any odd page (it will repeat on all odd pages), but add no footer to any even page.

Finally, you may have places where you're permitted to have a different header or footer, but nevertheless want to continue the header or footer from the previous page or section. If so, go to the section or page where you're required to supply a new header or footer, open the Header and Footer dialog (and jump to the footer space, if adding a footer) then click the Same as Previous button on the Header and Footer dialog. The header or footer from the preceding page or section is copied to the new page or section.

Fast Track

If a required new header or footer will be only slightly different from the preceding one, you can save yourself some typing and formatting. Go to the page or section where you must enter the new header or footer, use the Same as Previous button to copy over the previous header or footer, then just edit the copy to create the new, unique header or footer.

Adding Page Numbers & Other Stuff to Headers & Footers

You can add page numbering, the current date, and other useful information in the header or footer easily through the buttons on the Header and Footer dialog. These buttons don't insert just text, but also insert *field codes* (see Chapter 7), special coding that allows Word to update changeable information in your document automatically. For example, page numbering will automatically change as necessary if you add pages to or delete pages from your document; Word will also update dates automatically as the days go by.

The easiest way to use this feature is to click the Insert AutoText button on the Header and Footer dialog. A list of choices drops down; each choice is a predefined header or footer. For example, if you open the Header space and then choose Author, Page #, Date option from the Insert AutoText list, you get a one-line header in which your name appears on the far left, the page number is centered, and the current date appears on the far right.

Fast Track

Some of the information AutoText uses is pulled from the document's Properties sheet, which you can open by choosing File | Properties. Some items on the Properties sheet are filled in for you (for example, on the Summary tab, Word names you the Author if Word is registered in your name), but you can add to and edit the information in the Properties sheet, as you'll learn in Chapter 21, "Collaborating & Integrating With Office 97."

After adding a header or footer from the Insert AutoText list, you can change the text formatting—fonts, font sizes, attributes—to whatever you want. However, it's best to restrict your changes to formatting—

don't try to edit the text of the header itself. If you do, you may scramble the coding so that it no longer works properly, and you'll have to create your header all over again. If you don't like any of the AutoText choices as written, you're better off creating your own header or footer.

Instead of using AutoText, you may use the other buttons in the Header and Footer dialog to insert field codes into your own text. For example, type the word Page and a space, then click the Insert Page Number button on the Header and Footer dialog. A field code for the page numbering is inserted following Page. Word automatically replaces that code with the correct page number.

Fast Track

If all you want in a header or footer is page numbering, you needn't fiddle with the Header and Footer dialog. Just choose Insert | Page Numbers to open the Page Numbers dialog. In that dialog, you can choose where to show the numbers (header or footer) and where along the header or footer space to display them (left, right, center, and so on).

Working With Columns

Despite assertions to the contrary, all documents have *columns*. The document you're reading right now isn't column-free—it's a one-column document. The text is organized in one fat column, running from margin to margin.

But when folks talk about columns, they're usually describing newspaper-style columns, sometimes called *snaking* columns, that divide your text into two or more vertical strips. The columns automatically snake, or wrap, so that when your text reaches the bottom of a column, it continues at the top of the next column, to the right. Columns are a great way to give your document a snazzy, periodical look that is most appropriate for newsletters, magazines, or brochures—and less so for instructional documents or lengthy documents, such as books. Not surprisingly, column-formatted documents work best when pictures are incorporated into the layout. See Chapter 6.

FYI: With Columns, the View Makes a Big Difference

When you use two or more columns, all columns appear in Page Layout view just as they would appear when printed. In Normal view, however, you see only a single column, not multiple columns (the spots where columns break are indicated with dashed lines labeled Column Break). The single column you see in Normal is the proper width—you can see how each column will look, you just can't see columns side-by-side.

In general, you'll find heavy editing easier in the one-column Normal view. Switch to Page Layout when the text is almost final, and the layout takes precedence.

To define columns, choose Format | Columns to open the Columns dialog (see Figure 5-6). The simplest and most effective way to define columns is to double-click any of the five Presets, all of which have been carefully predesigned to produce attractive results:

- **One.** A single column (like this book) from margin to margin. (If you don't like the way your document looks in multiple columns, you can use the One preset to switch it back.)
- **Two.** Two columns of equal width, .5″ apart.
- **Three.** Three columns of equal width, .5″ apart.
- **Left.** Two columns—a narrow column on the left and a right column twice as wide—.5″ apart. This preset (and the Right preset, as well) provides two columns but visually divides the page by thirds—2/3 on one side, 1/3 on the other.
- **Right.** Two columns—a narrow column on the right and a left column twice as wide—.5″ apart.

Fast Track

You can change the number of columns in the middle of a page by inserting a Continuous section break and then changing the column settings following the break. For example, you may create a newsletter-style layout with two columns on the top half of the page and one below.

If you want more than three columns, or if you want to fine tune the width and spacing of columns, enter a Number of columns, then enter the Width and spacing for each column in inches (or check the Equal column width check box to automatically make all columns equally wide).

Finally, to dress up a document with two or more columns, check the Line between check box. A vertical line appears in the exact center of the space between any two adjacent columns.

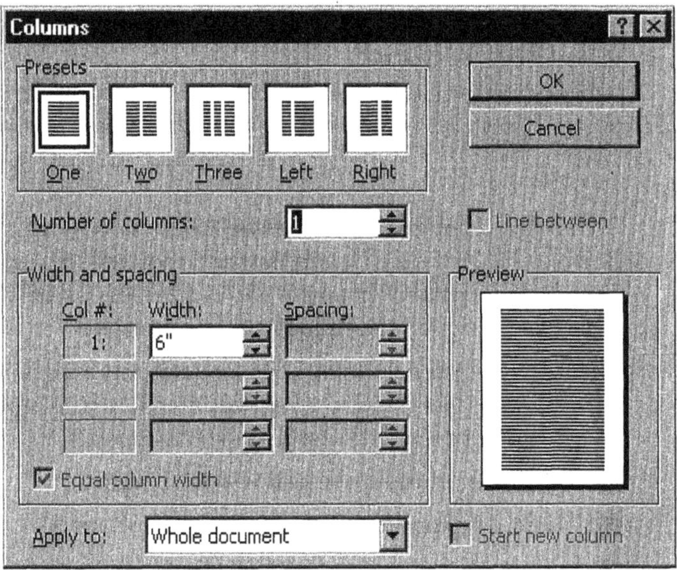

Figure 5-6: The Columns dialog.

Fast Track

To create from one to four equal-width columns in a hurry, click the Columns button on the Standard toolbar. A four-column picture drops down from the button. To choose two columns, point to the second column (from the left) in the picture, then click. To choose three or four columns, click the picture's third or fourth column. To revert a multi-column document or section to a single column, click the picture's leftmost column.

Breaking Pages & Columns

Throughout your document, Word breaks pages and columns automatically whenever the text reaches the bottom margin. These automatic breaks are called *soft breaks*, because they move within the text automatically whenever necessary. If you add half a page of text to a document, Word automatically changes soft breaks to accommodate it.

As your document nears completion, you'll want to nail down the page and column breaks, making sure each major part—section, chapter, and so on—begins on a new page, and making sure that columns break where you want them to. To do that, you insert *hard breaks*—page breaks and column breaks that always break the page or column at the same spot in the text, regardless of subsequent changes. Also, Word can automatically dress up your document by making some smart decisions about where to apply its automatic page breaks. For example, you can instruct Word never to automatically break the page in the middle of a paragraph.

You'll learn to add hard breaks and also to control Word's soft breaks in the next few pages.

Inserting & Removing Hard Breaks

To break a page or column, position the edit cursor where you want the break to happen, then choose Insert | Break from the menu bar. The Break dialog opens (shown earlier in Figure 5-1), from which you can choose to insert either a Page break or a Column break. In Normal view, hard breaks appear as dashed lines labeled "Page Break" or "Column Break." In Page Layout view, the breaks appear as they will print.

To delete a hard page or column break, select the break (starting before the break, ending after the break) and press the Del key (or click the Cut button on the standard toolbar). Instead of first selecting the break, you may position the edit cursor immediately after the break, then press Backspace.

Controlling Line & Page Breaks

Line and Page Breaks is a tab on the Paragraph dialog. While you'll learn about using the rest of that dialog later in this chapter, the Line and Page Breaks tab is important here because it sets the rules for how and when

Word inserts its automatic soft breaks. You can modify the rules, and by doing so enable Word to place its soft breaks intelligently, so that more of the breaks in your document can be Word's automatic soft breaks instead of the hard breaks you insert manually.

Why are soft breaks preferable, other than the fact that you needn't insert them yourself? Experience teaches us that a document is never finished when we think it is. We'll polish it up, put the hard breaks right where we want them, and then suddenly discover that there are changes to make.

The more hard breaks your document contains, the more likely it is to fall apart when edited. Perfectly positioned page and column breaks are suddenly all wrong after the edits, and you must carefully delete and reposition them all, one by one. Certainly, if a major section of your document must always begin on a new page, a hard break is one way of ensuring that it does so (though not the only way, as you'll see). But other breaks you may insert, for aesthetic reasons, to manage breaking points almost always end up wrong as soon as you make even minor changes. To the extent that you rely on Word to properly format your document with soft breaks, the document will reformat itself after any edits. You may need to make only minor cleanup changes to the breaks, or even none at all.

To use the Line and Page Breaks tab, select the portion of the document to which you want the rules you choose to apply. Choose Format | Paragraph, then click the Line and Page Breaks tab. The whole tab (see Figure 5-7) is check boxes. Check a box to enable a particular policy. The choices are:

- **Widow/Orphan control.** When you permit Word to break pages in the middle of a paragraph, two unattractive things can happen: The paragraph breaks right before its very last line, so that the last line appears all by itself on the top of the next page (a *widow*), or it breaks right after its very first line, so that the first line appears all by itself at the bottom of the page (an *orphan*). A check in this check box forces Word to break the page immediately before the paragraph to prevent an orphan, or to move the break a few lines up in a paragraph to prevent a widow.
- **Keep lines together.** A check here prevents Word from inserting a soft break in the middle of a paragraph. If the bottom of the page is reached mid-paragraph, Word breaks the page immediately before the paragraph.

- **Keep with next.** Instructs Word to never insert a break between the selection and the paragraph that follows it. Use this check box to ensure that particular paragraphs always share a page.
- **Page break before.** Ensures that the page always breaks immediately before the selection. For elements that you want always to begin on a new page, this is a good alternative to a hard page break. If a full page precedes the selection, Word doesn't add an extra break. If the preceding page is not full, Word puts in a soft break.
- **Suppress line numbers.** If you've instructed Word to print line numbers (as described earlier in this chapter), this check box prevents the numbering for the selection.
- **Don't hyphenate.** By default, at the end of a line Word breaks and hyphenates words according to accepted conventions about when to break a word and where in the word the break can occur. If you'd prefer that Word not hyphenate, but rather always break a line between two words, check this box.

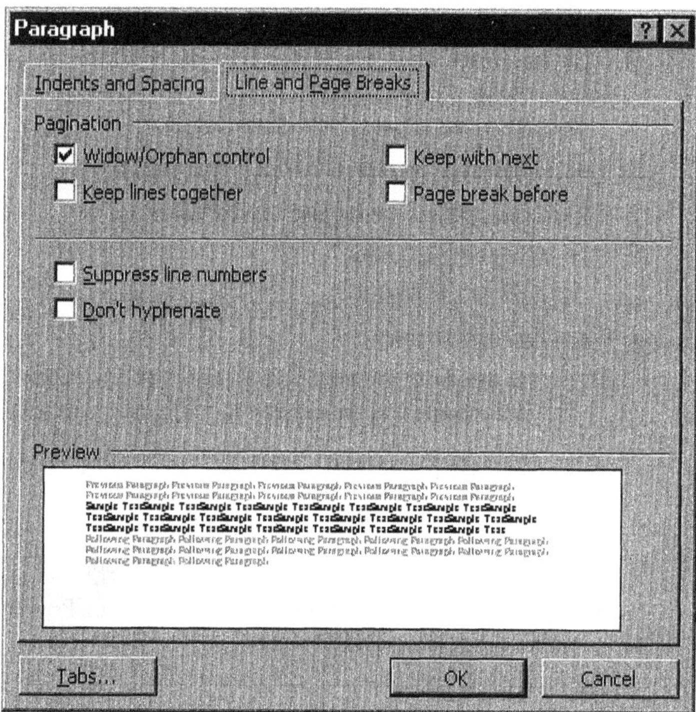

Figure 5-7: The Paragraph dialog's Line and Page Breaks tab.

Walk-Through: Headers, Footers & Columns

Follow the steps below to practice working with headers, footers, and columns.

1. Open or create any multi-page document you're comfortable experimenting with. (If necessary, use Save As to make a copy you can play around with while not affecting the original.)
2. Position the edit cursor somewhere near the middle of the document.
3. Choose Insert|Break.
   The Break dialog opens.
4. Under Section breaks, choose Next page, then click OK.
   On the page following the edit cursor position, a new section begins.
5. Without moving the edit cursor, choose View|Header and Footer.
   The Header and Footer dialog opens, and the edit cursor appears in the header space.
6. Choose any header you wish from the Insert AutoText list.
   The AutoText header appears in the header space.
7. Click the Switch Between Header and Footer button on the Header and Footer dialog.
   The edit cursor appears in the footer space.
8. Type and format any text you wish in the footer.
9. Click Close on the Header and Footer dialog.
10. Choose Format|Columns.
    The Columns dialog opens.
11. Click the Three preset.
12. Make sure the entry in Apply to is This section, then click OK.
    The section containing the edit cursor is reformatted to three columns.
13. Observe the Section number reported in the status bar, and scroll forward until the Section number changes.
    The edit cursor is in the section you created in Step 3.
14. Add a new header and footer for the new section.
15. Print the document (or review it in Page Layout or Print Preview).
    How is the document different now?

Formatting Paragraphs

First off, it's important to be clear on what a "paragraph" is—to Word, anyway. A paragraph is any block of text not interrupted by a paragraph break. A paragraph can be a single character, a word, a sentence, a group of lines, or pages and pages of text—as long as no paragraph breaks interrupt the flow of the text, it's a single paragraph, even if it runs across multiple pages or columns. Any place you've pressed Enter (which inserts a paragraph break), one paragraph ends, and another begins—even if the return appears after a single character.

That understood, the next several pages describe ways you can control the look and feel of the paragraphs in your document.

Fast Track

To apply paragraph formatting, you need not select the whole paragraph. You need only locate the edit cursor anywhere within the paragraph, then choose your paragraph formatting from the toolbar or menu bar. The formatting is automatically applied to the whole paragraph, even though you didn't select anything. You cannot apply paragraph formatting to only part of a paragraph.

To apply paragraph formatting to multiple paragraphs, hold down and drag your mouse to highlight anywhere within the first paragraph to anywhere in the last one. All parts of all paragraphs that have any part of them selected will take on the formatting you choose—including the unselected portions of the first and last paragraph.

Aligning Paragraphs

Alignment describes the way the lines of a paragraph are organized on the page. There are four alignment buttons on the Formatting toolbar; each applies one of the four types of alignment. The four types are described below, and illustrated in Figure 5-8:

- **Left (the default).** All lines of the paragraph align evenly on the left side (*flush left*), while the right ends of the lines are permitted to break at their natural break points to create an uneven, or *ragged*, right side. In a left-aligned paragraph, the first line is often indented by a tab, and so does not line up exactly with the lines that follow. But the paragraph is still said to be left-aligned.

- **Center.** Each line of the paragraph is centered; both sides of the paragraph run ragged. Except for special effects—such as poems or ad copy—center alignment is rarely used for multi-line paragraphs, and is generally used for centering titles, headings, or other text elements less than one line long.
- **Right.** All lines of the paragraph align evenly on the right side, and the left side runs ragged. Right alignment fights the reader's eyes—which are trained to always jump back to a consistent left side to start each new line—and is thus used sparingly for effect, not as a standard paragraph format.
- **Justified.** The spacing between words in the paragraph is automatically adjusted so that each line spreads completely across the page. Both left and right sides are flush; no side is ragged. Justified alignment can create a dressy look, but with certain fonts or narrow columns, some lines may appear unnaturally spaced out or squeezed together.

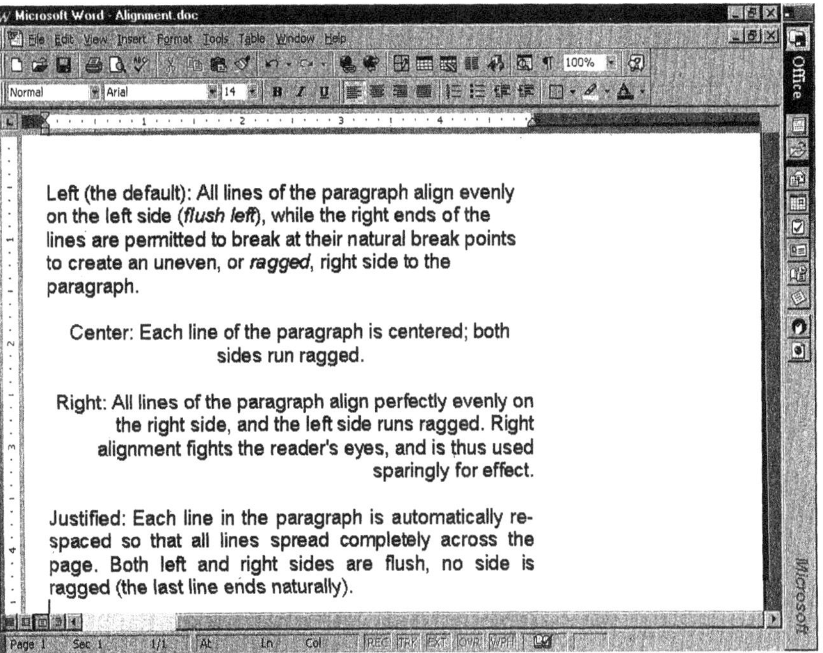

Figure 5-8: Ways you can align paragraphs.

To change the alignment, locate the edit cursor anywhere within the paragraph, then click the appropriate button—Align Left, Center, Align Right, or Justified—on the Formatting toolbar.

Fast Track

Instead of clicking toolbar buttons, you may change a paragraph's alignment by positioning the edit cursor within the paragraph, then pressing Ctrl+L (for left), Ctrl+R (for right), Ctrl+J (for justified), or Ctrl+E (for center). Yes, I know—one might expect center to be Ctrl+C, but that key combo is already taken by Copy. See Chapter 4.

Indenting Paragraphs

When you *indent* a paragraph, you push it away from the margin on one side. Most of the time folks indent, they *left indent*—push the paragraph in from the left margin, as shown in Figure 5-9. While the left side of the paragraph is pushed in, the right margin prevents the right end of the paragraph from moving to compensate; indenting makes the paragraph narrower, and usually longer.

To make a quick and easy *left indent*, position the edit cursor anywhere within the paragraph you want to indent, then click the Increase Indent button on the Formatting toolbar. The paragraph is indented to the first *tab stop* (see "Working With Tabs" later in this chapter). Click Increase Indent again to indent the paragraph further, to the next tab stop. To shift the indent back one tab stop, click Decrease Indent.

Fast Track

To control left indents even more precisely, and to create special types of indents, such as right indents and hanging indents, choose Format | Paragraph to open the Paragraph dialog. The Indents & Spacing tab on the Paragraph dialog includes controls for precise indenting, plus fine control of other aspects of paragraph formatting, such as line spacing.

Alternatively, the horizontal ruler includes triangular slides that control indents. To learn how to use them, consult Word's Help index under indentation, with ruler.

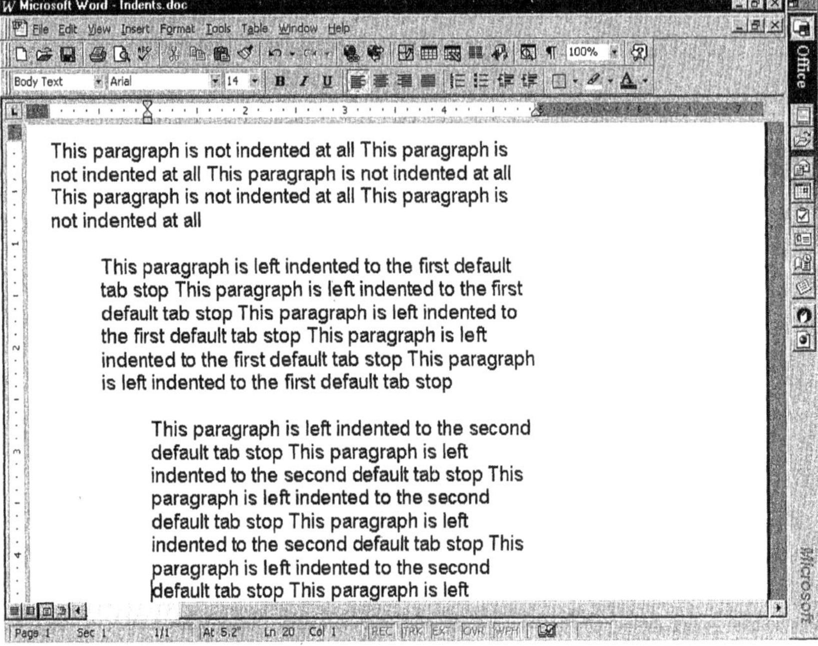

Figure 5-9: Before and after indenting.

Formatting Lists

If you really wanted to, there's no reason you couldn't simply type your lists and then dress them up with indenting. But Word's list formatting tools do the job much more conveniently, and better, for two reasons:

- Word automatically creates two types of lists: Bulleted and Numbered. In a bulleted list, an attractive bullet symbol flags each list item. For numbered lists, Word automatically adds the number to the beginning of each list item, automatically numbering the items consecutively. More important, Word automatically renumbers the list for you if you later add or remove any items.
- Word automatically formats lists with *hanging indents*. In a hanging indent, the whole paragraph is indented, except for the first line, which isn't indented. The first line "hangs" back from the rest of the paragraph (see Figure 5-10). This touch allows the bullets or numbers to line up nicely in their own column on the left while the text of each list item appears indented.

Each item in a list is a separate paragraph—whether the item is a single word or a dozen lines of text. That's important to keep in mind, because when you create lists, you're always applying list formatting to multiple paragraphs. Generally, it's easiest to type your whole list first, without worrying about formatting it as such. Just type out each list item, pressing Enter once between each item so that each is its own paragraph. (Don't bother typing the numbers or trying to insert the bullets—Word takes care of that.) When you're finished typing the list, select all of its paragraphs (select from anywhere within the first list item to anywhere within the last), then choose your desired list formatting as described next.

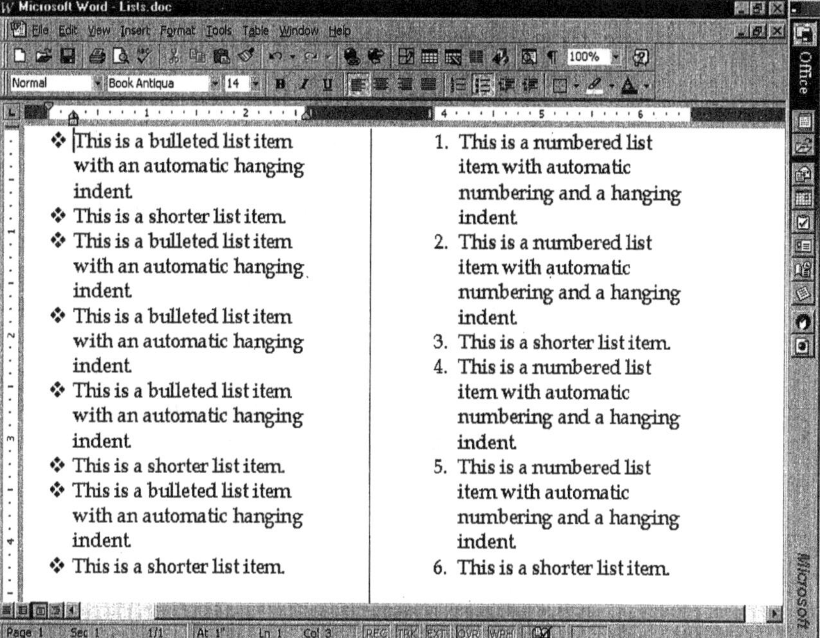

Figure 5-10: Types of lists.

Quick & Easy List-Building

Once your list items are all typed and the list has been selected, format the list by choosing a button on the Formatting toolbar:

- To create a bulleted list, click the Bullets button.
- To create a numbered list, click Numbering.

That's it. Once your list is created, you can change it in a number of ways:

- Click Increase Indent or Decrease Indent to adjust the hanging indent.
- Add list items. Position the cursor between two list items, and press Enter. A new bullet or number is added automatically, and you can type the item. (If the list is numbered, the list is automatically renumbered to accommodate your additions.)
- Customize the bullet style, numbering scheme, or other aspects of the list using the techniques described next, in Advanced List Formatting.

To undo list formatting (revert list items to normal paragraphs), select the items and click the toolbar button (Bullets or Numbering) you used previously to create the list.

Fast Track

If you make extensive changes to the text of a list after formatting it, eventually the formatting may get a little scrambled, with some items formatted like regular paragraphs or with the numbering messed up. This happens when your edits break the list in such a way that Word thinks it's not one list, but several separate lists.

To straighten out the list, just select the whole list again, and apply the desired list formatting. Word re-interprets the selection as a single list and applies the formatting consistently.

Advanced List Formatting

To more precisely control the appearance of your lists, select the list (before or after applying any list formatting with the toolbar) and choose Format | Bullets and Numbering. The Bullets and Numbering dialog opens (see Figure 5-11).

The Bullets and Numbering dialog has three tabs. Any changes you make on these tabs—or on a few other dialogs you can reach through buttons on these tabs—reformats the selected list or makes the selection

into a list. By experimenting with the selections on these tabs, you'll discover many ways to dress up your lists. Here's a tour through the most important:

- **Bulleted tab.** Click any of the boxes shown to choose a new bullet style. If you don't care for any of the choices, or if you want to fine tune the indent of the list, click Customize to open the Customize Bulleted List dialog. That dialog features a few more bullet choices to select, and a Bullet button which opens a dialog from which you may choose any symbol to use as a bullet (see Chapter 4, "Working with Text," to learn more about working with symbols).
- **Numbered tab.** Just like the Bulleted tab, the Numbered tab offers a selection of different numbering styles, plus a Customize button that opens a Customize Numbered List dialog. On that dialog, you choose among different numbering styles, and fine tune the indents (Number Position and Text Position). Also on the Customize Numbered list, you can select a Start At number or letter, to choose to begin at a later spot than the default (1, A, i, or a).

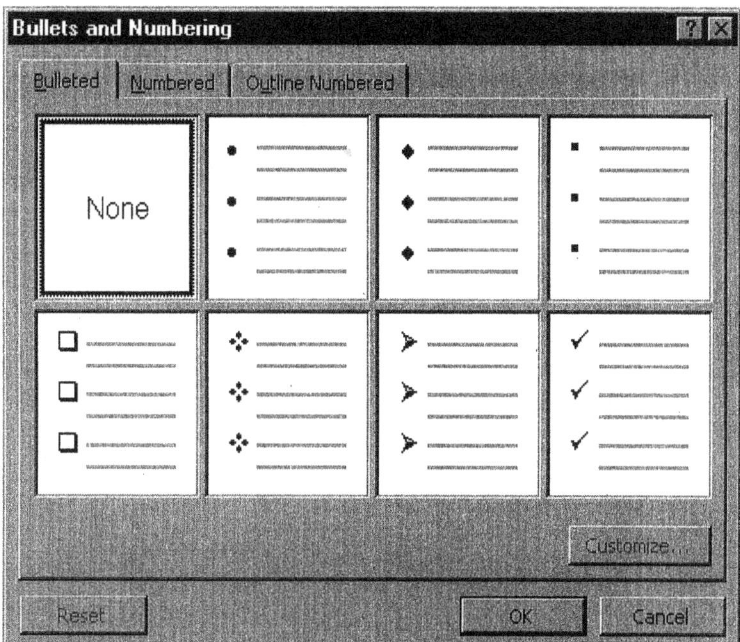

Figure 5-11: The Bullets and Numbering dialog.

Fast Track

In rare circumstances, you may choose to restart the numbering somewhere in the middle of a list. For example, you may want the list to be numbered from 1 to 10, then to start over again at 1 on the 11th item.

Position the edit cursor anywhere within the list item at which numbering should start over. Then choose Format | Bullets and Numbering, click the Numbered tab, and click the radio button next to Restart numbering. If you change your mind later, you can restore the old numbering scheme by clicking the button next to Continue previous list.

- **Outline Numbered tab.** This tab creates a type of list you can't create from the toolbar. An outline numbered list has multiple levels, as an outline does (see Figure 5-12). Word can automatically number such lists, applying a different number style to each level and restarting the numbering where appropriate. When typing such a list, choose the level of each item by pressing Tab before the item until it is indented to the desired level.

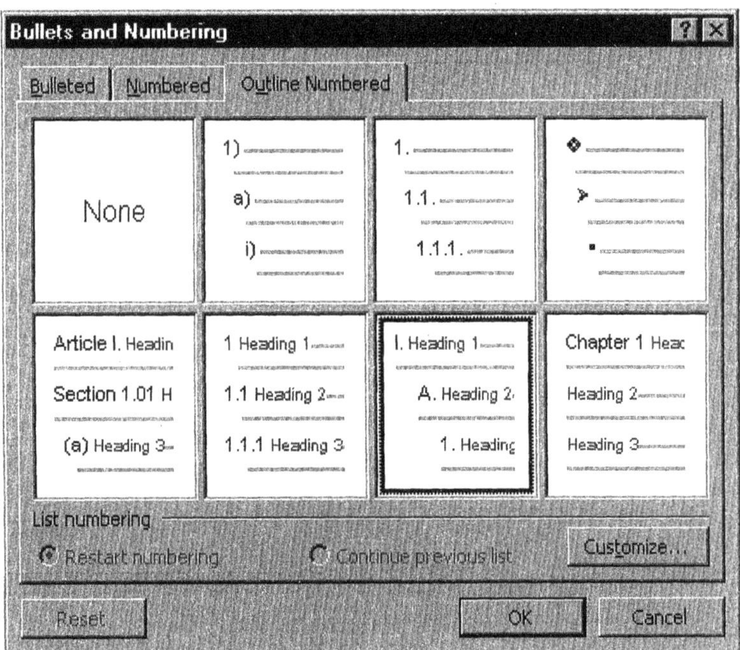

Figure 5-12: Choosing a format for an Outline Numbered list.

Working With Tabs

Tabs play many parts in Word. They can indent the first line of a paragraph, line up items in a list, or automatically align a column of numbers. Like indenting, tabs can push text away from the margins. But unlike an indent, a tab affects only one line of text. A tab at the beginning of a paragraph indents just the first line, not the whole paragraph.

Every time you press the Tab key while working in your document, you insert a tab character into your text. Like a space or paragraph break, a tab is a *nonprinting character*. A tab pushes the character next to it in a particular direction.

Fast Track

Ordinarily, you don't see the actual tab character in your document; you just see its effect. But sometimes you may want to see exactly where your tabs (and other nonprinting characters) are actually placed in your document. To display all nonprinting characters in the document, click the Show/Hide button on the Standard toolbar.

Setting Tab Stops

A tab character aligns the text it precedes to a preset point, called a *tab stop*. Typically, there are multiple tab stops spread out along the width of the document. Starting at the left margin, pressing the Tab key once moves the text to the first tab stop (from the left), pressing Tab twice moves the text to the next tab stop, and so on.

Tab stops come in four different types. The most commonly used, a left tab stop, does exactly what you expect from tabs: The tab pushes the text away from the left margin, aligning the character following the tab with the tab stop. The three other types are:

- **Right tab stop.** Pressing tab when the next tab stop is a right tab pushes the text away from the right margin, aligning the character following the tab with the tab stop.
- **Center tab stop.** Pressing tab when the next tab stop is a center tab centers the text following the tab character around the tab stop.

- **Decimal tab stop.** Pressing tab when the next tab stop is a decimal tab stop pushes a number following the tab until its decimal point (or its presumed decimal point, if it doesn't contain one) aligns with the tab stop. Decimal tabs are used to align a column of numbers properly.

In a document that has no specific tab stops set, Word assumes *default tab stops*—all left tab stops—at every .5" from margin to margin. Each time you press Tab, the text to the right of the edit cursor is pushed half an inch to the left. Press tab three times, and you push the line to the right by 1.5 inches. Note that the default tab stops are also used by the Increase Indent and Decrease Indent buttons on the Formatting toolbar to determine how far to indent a paragraph.

By setting your own tab stops, you can replace the default tab stops with tab stops of your choosing, and set any type of tab stop, as well. The best way to choose tab stops is with the Tabs dialog. Begin by selecting the paragraph(s) to which you want the tab settings to apply. Then choose Format | Tabs to open the dialog (see Figure 5-13).

On the Tabs dialog, you can enter a measurement in Default tab stops to determine the amount of space between each of the default, left tab stops. Alternatively, you can define and set specific tab stops, one by one. First, in Tab stop position, enter the distance from the left margin (regardless of the tab type you're creating); for example, enter **2.5** to create a tab stop 2.5" from the left margin. In Alignment, choose the type of tab stop, then click the Set button. The position of the new tab appears in the box beneath Tab stop position. You may then set another tab stop by choosing a new position and alignment, or click OK to close the dialog.

To remove a tab stop, highlight its position in the list beneath Tab stop position and click the Clear button.

FYI: Leader Characters

The Tabs dialog lets you optionally select *Leader characters*. Leader characters fill any empty space on the line created by the tab with a dotted line, dashed line, or solid line. (The default choice, None, inserts no leader character.)

The most common use of leader characters is to run dotted lines in a table of contents—an effect you can achieve by aligning page numbers to a right tab stop and using a dotted leader character.

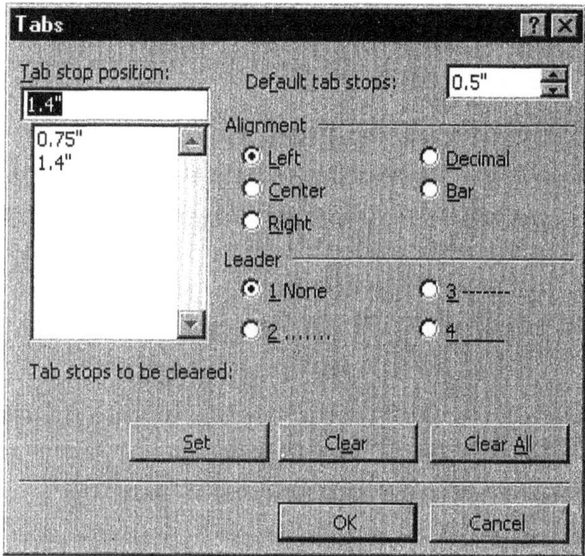

Figure 5-13: The Tabs dialog.

Instead of using the Tabs dialog, you can set tab stops on the horizontal ruler. Begin by selecting the paragraph(s) to which you want the tab stops to apply. Point to the spot along the ruler where you want to put a left tab stop, and click. A left tab stop marker appears on the ruler. You may click back in the document and continue editing, or click another spot on the ruler to add another left tab stop.

To add a right, center, or decimal tab stop, you need to change the tab stop type in the square at the extreme left end of the ruler. By default, the left tab stop symbol appears in the square. Each time you click the square, the type changes:

Left tab

Center tab

Right tab

Decimal tab

To insert a tab stop, click the square until your desired tab stop type appears there, then point to the spot on the ruler where you want to insert the tab stop, and click. The tab stop marker deposited on the ruler matches the type you selected.

Walk-Through: Paragraph Formatting

Follow the steps below to practice applying paragraph formatting.

1. Open or create any multi-page document you're comfortable experimenting with. (If necessary, use Save As to make a copy you can play around with while not affecting the original.)
2. Locate (or create) any group of three paragraphs in a row.
3. Position the edit cursor within the first paragraph.
4. Click the Center alignment button on the Formatting toolbar.
   The paragraph is centered on the page.
5. Position the edit cursor within the second paragraph.
6. Click the Increase Indent button on the Formatting toolbar once.
   The paragraph is indented to the first tab stop.
7. Click the Decrease Indent button on the Formatting toolbar once.
   The paragraph is not indented.
8. Select from anywhere in the first paragraph to anywhere in the third.
9. Click the Justified alignment button on the Formatting toolbar.
   All three paragraphs are justified.
10. Click the Bullets button on the Formatting toolbar.
    The three paragraphs become a bulleted list.
11. Click the Bullets button on the Formatting toolbar.
    The list formatting is removed.
12. Choose Format|Tabs.
    The Tabs dialog opens.
13. Click Clear All.
    All tab stops for the selected paragraph are removed.
14. Enter **.75** in Tab stop position.
15. Click Set, then OK.
16. At the very beginning of each of the three paragraphs, press Tab.
    Each paragraph has an indented (tabbed) first line.

Moving On

There's so much to page design—a zillion little settings and options and controls. Fortunately, it's usually just the big stuff that really counts—margins, headers and footers, columns. The rest is largely fine tuning, and you may be able to ignore most of it unless 1) You're working on a document that requires great precision, or 2) You're obsessive-compulsive. In either case, even complex page design isn't so tough if you approach it by making the broad strokes first, then selectively fiddling with any other settings that appear to require your attention.

It's fitting, though, that you understand all of the ways you can dress up your document with nothing but page design and text formatting. For you see, in Chapter 6 you'll discover the cool stuff—pictures, tables, borders, and color. While all of the cool stuff has a dramatic impact on the look of your document, a lot of folks get so wrapped up in that stuff that they shortchange the page design. They wind up with documents whose graphical pizzazz is undercut by bland, careless text and page formatting.

You, on the other hand, know how to create a snappy page with nothing but a few fonts, some carefully composed headers, and a loving heart. So when you get into graphics, you'll apply them as an enrichment of a good design, not as a cover-up for a poor one.

6

Adding Pictures, Tables & Borders

The basic mechanics of adding pictures, tables, and borders to your Word documents are amazingly simple—so simple, in fact, that if you're even a moderately experienced user of Windows applications you could probably figure it out yourself over lunch.

The problem with all this graphical stuff is that getting it into your document is only half the battle. The real challenge in adding graphics is sorting among, and applying, the unbelievably varied array of options for how those graphics can look. For example, inserting a clip art file in your document is a snap—a few clicks and it's done. *Then* all you have to do is decide whether text should flow around, over, or under the picture; whether the picture should move with the text it's next to or stay in the same spot on the page no matter what happens to the text; whether it needs a border or shading, and what type of border or shading; whether it's the proper size and orientation.... You get the general idea.

You'll find all this simpler if you think of graphics as mere content, just as the text you type is content. Whether the object at hand is text or graphics, the job always takes two steps: 1) Put the raw content into the document, and 2) Format the content by applying any of a wide range of options to it.

In this chapter, you'll discover all of the ways you can add graphical impact to your Word documents. While the most obvious example is adding pictures, related techniques such as defining borders and creating text boxes are equally important to making your document appealing.

And while a table may at first seem like text, when you think about it, a table is a graphical way of treating text—so you'll learn about table-making here, plus a few, final surprise visual tricks Word 97 puts into your bag.

In the course of doing all this, you'll encounter two toolbars (see Figure 6-1)—Picture and Tables and Borders—you haven't seen before. Unlike the Standard and Formatting toolbars, these graphics-related toolbars open automatically whenever you do something that may require their help, and close when you're finished—so you needn't choose to display them all the time. However, if you want to display them (even if only to check 'em out), choose View | Toolbars and then choose the name of the toolbar you want to display.

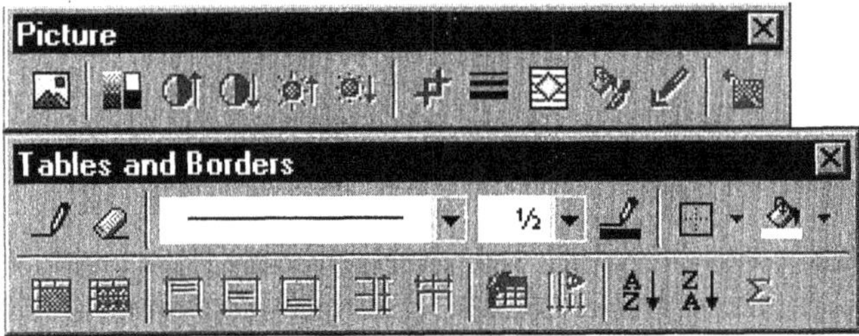

Figure 6-1: The Picture and the Tables and Borders toolbars.

FYI: *Get* Pictures in Chapter 2, *Use* Them Here...

The Office environment provides a variety of powerful graphical tools, including OfficeArt (the Clip Gallery and Drawing Tools), WordArt, and an optional Photo Editor for advanced editing. These tools are considered part of the Office environment because you use them the same way whether in Word, Excel, PowerPoint, or Access.

In Chapter 2, "Getting to Know the Office 97 Environment," you not only learn about using these tools, but also about the many other ways you can acquire and create picture files. To learn how to incorporate those pictures into a document, consult the application chapter:

- Word: This chapter
- PowerPoint: Chapter 9, "Designing Presentations"
- Excel: Chapter 15, "Formatting Workbooks"

Adding Pictures to Documents

Before adding a picture to your document, you must:

- Decide roughly where in the layout of the document the picture belongs.
- Know where the picture file is stored on disk.

FYI: Understanding Color

To a varying degree, almost everything you do in this chapter allows you to add color to your document. For example, you may add a color picture, or you may lay a transparent, colored highlight over selected text.

While Word exerts no limitations over how you may work with color, when working with color you must keep in mind how your document will be published. If the document is intended for online publishing, either in native Word format or as a HyperText Markup Language (HTML) file (Web page format), you can pretty much do anything you want to color-wise—although you must consider a few compatibility issues you'll learn about in Chapter 22, "Office 97 & the Internet."

When your document is intended for printing, however, you must consider how well—if at all—your intended printer handles color. While a good printer will reproduce the same colors you see (green onscreen will be green in print), subtleties of color—the precise hue and saturation—will almost always differ.

Inserting a Picture

To insert a picture, begin by positioning the edit cursor roughly where you want the picture positioned in your document. (Don't worry about creating an empty space for it or positioning it exactly—that stuff comes later.) Choose Insert | Picture. A submenu like the one in Figure 6-2 appears.

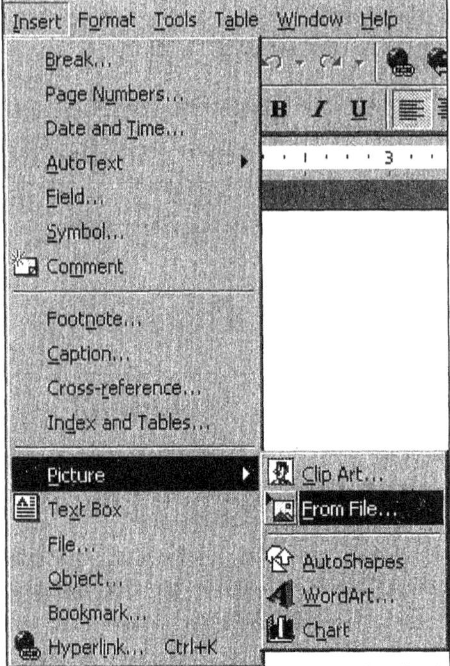

Figure 6-2: The Picture submenu.

Fast Track

To insert a picture into a header or footer, position the edit cursor in the header space or footer space as explained in Chapter 5, "Designing Pages." Then choose Insert | Picture. This is a great way to dress up a document by displaying a company logo or other picture at the top or bottom of every page.

To select the picture for formatting (see "Formatting a Picture" later in this chapter), first open the header or footer space containing the picture, then click the picture.

From the Picture submenu, choose Clip Art to insert a picture from the Clip Gallery (as described in Chapter 2), or choose From File to insert any type of picture file you have on disk.

If you choose From File, the Insert Picture dialog opens (see Figure 6-3). By default, the dialog opens in the Office 97 Clip Art folder. You're free to choose any of the Clip Art pictures from the Insert Picture dialog, although if it's Office Clip Art you want, you'll find using the Clip Gallery more convenient than using the Insert Picture dialog.

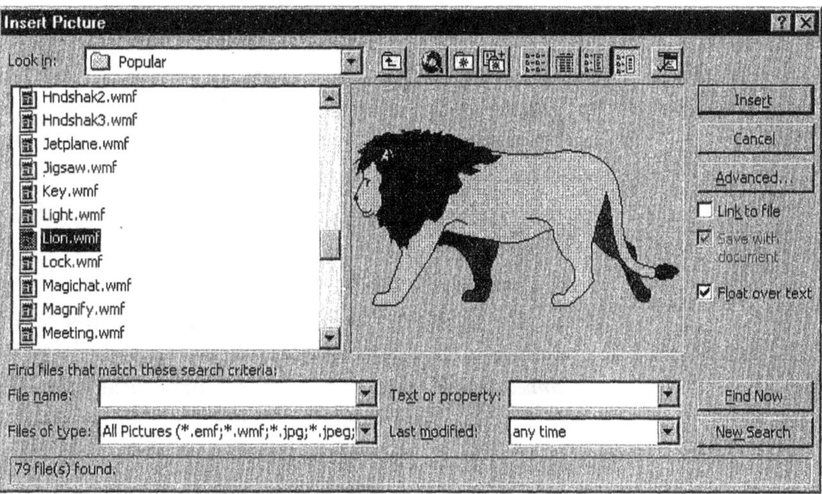

Figure 6-3: The Insert Picture dialog.

Net-Savvy

When you publish a document on the Web in the standard file format (HTML), all pictures in the document should be in either of two standard file types supported by Web browsers: GIF (Graphics Interchange Format, supported by all graphical browsers) or JPEG (Joint Photographic Experts Group, supported by fewer browsers than GIF, but by all market leaders such as Netscape Navigator and Internet Explorer).

When you save a Word file in HTML format, Word automatically converts all picture files—including OfficeArt—to GIF format, except for JPEG images, which are left in their native format. That frees you to use any pictures you wish—OfficeArt, scanned photos, and so on—in a Word document that will wind up on the Web.

To navigate to the folder that contains the picture file, begin by dropping down the Look in list to choose a folder, disk, or the desktop. When the icon for the picture appears in the box, click it to select it. The picture appears in the Insert Picture dialog's Preview pane, so you can verify that the file you've selected contains the picture you really want. If the file is of a type that you must convert before it can be inserted, the Preview pane displays a message that the preview is unavailable. Also, note that the Preview pane may not show the picture at its full size.

Clicking Insert plugs the picture into the document and closes the Insert Picture dialog. Before you click Insert, however, you may want to choose from among the three optional check boxes that appear along the right-hand side of the Insert Picture dialog:

- **Link to file.** When this check box is checked, the picture file doesn't actually become part of the Word document file. Instead, the picture is kept separate but is linked to the Word file so that the picture appears to be part of the document when you display or print it. Linking has certain advantages and disadvantages over *embedding* (making the picture part of the Word file), as you'll learn in Chapter 21, "Collaborating & Integrating With Office 97."
- **Save with document.** When this check box is checked—it's available only when Link to file is checked—Word automatically copies the picture file to the same folder as the document (if the picture file was not in that folder to begin with). This option helps you keep a Word file and its linked pictures together.
- **Float over text.** When this check box is checked (which is the default), the picture "floats" on the page so that you can position it anywhere, without regard to text or other elements on the page. Floating enables you to precisely position the picture on the page and to control how text wraps around it. If you remove the checkmark, the picture is inserted as an *inline* picture, one that's essentially part of the flow of the text and cannot be positioned except by paragraph formatting options such as left, center, or right alignment. You'll learn more about floating later in this chapter.

When you click the Insert button to insert the picture, three things happen:

- The picture appears in your document roughly at the edit cursor position.
- The Picture toolbar appears.

- The view switches to Page Layout view (if you were not already in Page Layout view). Note that you will not see the pictures in your document when in Normal view.

You may now adjust the picture's formatting or its position within your document. See "Formatting a Picture" and "Positioning a Picture," coming up next.

FYI: Which Comes First: Picture Format or Picture Position?

After you insert a picture, it doesn't really matter whether you format the picture's appearance and then adjust its position on the page, or position first, then format. However, some formatting changes—especially changing the size and shape of a picture or cropping it—inadvertently change the picture's position, too. So you'll usually save yourself some jumping back and forth between formatting and positioning if you format first, then position.

Fast Track

When working with larger pictures, you may find formatting and positioning the picture most convenient if you reduce the Zoom percentage by choosing from the Zoom list on the Standard toolbar.

Formatting a Picture

Immediately after you insert a picture, it is automatically *selected* for editing. Unlike selected text, a selected picture isn't highlighted; instead, the perimeter of the image is marked by tiny squares called *handles* (see Figure 6-4), and the Picture toolbar appears. (If you see handles but don't see the Picture toolbar, choose View | Toolbars | Picture.)

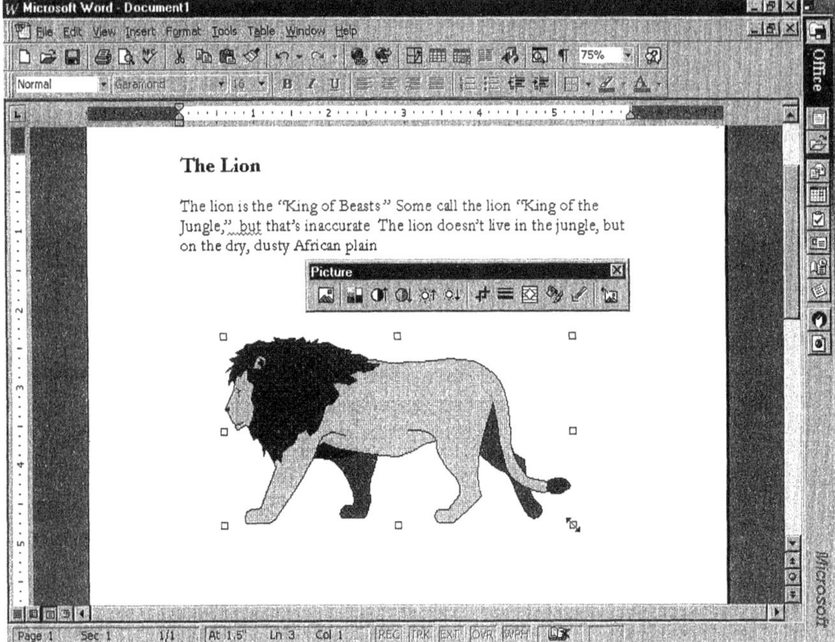

Figure 6-4: Selected picture showing handles and the Picture toolbar.

The handles enable you to use your mouse to change the size and shape of the picture or to *crop* it (trim the sides to remove parts you don't want). The Picture toolbar enables you to fine tune a picture's contrast level, brightness, and other characteristics, much as you might adjust your TV's picture. In the next few pages, you'll learn how to use handles and the Picture toolbar to change an inserted picture's appearance.

Although a picture is preselected immediately after you insert it, you can later select and format the picture at any time while editing the document that contains it. Begin in Page Layout view (pictures do not appear in Normal view). Point to the picture (when the pointer is over a picture, it changes to a four-pointed arrow) and single-click; the handles and Picture toolbar appear.

When you finish formatting a picture, deselect it by pressing Esc or by clicking anywhere in the document except on the picture. The handles and Picture toolbar disappear, and you may return to working with the text and page design of your document.

Fast Track

You can apply most of the formatting and positioning techniques you'll discover in the next several pages to any type of picture, whether an OfficeArt file (Clip Art or Drawing object) or a bitmapped file. However, when working with OfficeArt you have additional options, including ways to group separate drawing objects together so that you can format and position them as if they were a single picture. See Chapter 2, "Getting to Know the Office 97 Environment."

Sizing a Picture

To change the size of a picture (*scale* it), point to a handle that appears at a corner. When on a corner handle, the pointer changes to a two-pointed arrow that points directly toward—and away from—the center of the image. Click and hold the mouse button and drag to resize the picture—drag away from the picture's center to enlarge it, or drag toward the center to reduce the picture. When the size is what you want, release the mouse button.

You can change the overall geometric shape of a picture in the same way that you scale it—by grabbing and dragging a handle. However, while dragging a corner handle scales a picture, dragging any of the other handles changes the picture's shape. For example, dragging the top or bottom handle away from the center of the picture stretches the height of the picture without affecting its width; dragging the top or bottom handle toward the center shortens the picture.

Note that when you change a picture's shape, you distort the original proportions of the image; for example, if you drag up the top handle on a picture of a person, the person will appear unnaturally thin (like the actors on *Friends*). Playing with the shapes of pictures this way is best left to abstract (rather than natural) subjects, unless you're going for an unusual or unnatural effect.

FYI: Undoing Picture Formatting

You can undo any type of picture formatting in any of three ways:

- Use Undo to reverse formatting you've done within your last few edits in Word. (To learn more about Undo, see Chapter 4, "Working With Text.")
- Click the Reset Picture button on the Picture toolbar to remove all formatting and restore the picture to its original appearance when first inserted.
- Apply new formatting that's the opposite of the old; for example, if you've shrunk a picture, enlarge it.

Cropping a Picture

Cropping a picture means cutting off a slice of the image on one or more sides to remove an unwanted portion. For example, if a scanned photograph shows both Michael and Fredo, but you want to show only Fredo in your document, you can crop out Michael.

To crop, click the Crop button on the Picture toolbar. The pointer changes to a crop pointer, which looks just like the icon on the Crop button. Point to a handle, click, drag toward the center of the picture to crop, then release. What you crop depends on which handle you click:

- To crop just one side (top, bottom, left, or right) of the picture, point to a handle on that side and drag inward.
- To crop the top or bottom while also cropping a left or right side, point to a corner handle. When you drag toward the center, the sides that meet at the selected corner are cropped together. By dragging at different angles, you can crop more or less of each side involved. Try it!
- To crop opposite sides of the picture, or three or four sides, just do multiple crops.

To remove cropping (restore a cropped portion of an image), just crop again, but drag away from the center of the image rather than toward it. You may also use Undo to undo cropping.

Controlling Brightness, Contrast & Color

Four buttons on the Picture toolbar—More Contrast, Less Contrast, More Brightness, Less Brightness—allow you to fine tune the contrast and brightness levels of a picture. As a rule, there's no point fiddling with these controls until you see the picture printed, so you can see whether the printed contrast and brightness are appropriate. If not, adjust the picture with the buttons.

Each time you click one of the buttons, the picture changes by a small increment. By clicking a button several times, you can make a noticeable change. For example, clicking More Brightness once makes the picture a tiny bit brighter. Clicking More Brightness five or six times makes it a lot brighter. The tiny increments give you subtle control over contrast and brightness.

FYI: Formatting Can Scramble Pictures

Different picture file formats respond differently to various kinds of picture formatting. While OfficeArt files retain their image quality no matter how you format them, many bitmapped pictures may develop severe *artifacts*—unattractive flaws—when scaled, and especially when shaped. Cropping, brightness/contrast adjustments, and other formatting techniques are less likely to create artifacts but may still create unattractive results in some circumstances.

Unfortunately, I can't offer a reliable way to predict which types of bitmap files respond poorly to what formatting—a wide range of factors determines the effect of formatting on a picture, including not just its file type, but also the number of colors or levels of gray it incorporates, the presence or absence of certain textures or line patterns, the amount of scaling or other formatting applied (and in what combination), and others.

Try to acquire picture files that require as little formatting in Word as possible—ones that are the proper size and shape to begin with. When you create a picture yourself with a paint program or scanner, perform any necessary scaling or other manipulation within the paint or scan program before inserting the file in Word. And whenever possible, favor OfficeArt pictures—whether Clip Art or Drawing objects you create—over bitmaps, so you can format all you like without worrying about artifacts.

Positioning a Picture

When you insert a picture, you place it in the general vicinity where you want it to appear. However, careful page design usually dictates that you'll have to adjust a picture's position, especially after formatting. Also, after inserting and formatting a picture, you need to select among a group of options that determine how you want the text around that picture to flow in relation to the picture.

You can choose to lock a picture into a spot on the page so it stays in that spot no matter what happens to the text around it, or you can anchor the picture to a paragraph so that it always stays with its paragraph, wherever that paragraph may move in response to changes in the document.

To position a picture anywhere you want and to control how text wraps to it, you must *float* the picture. If, when inserting a picture, you uncheck the Float over text check box in the Insert Picture dialog, the picture is *inline*; that is, it is part of the text.

An inline picture moves with the text, and responds to paragraph formatting; for example, if you apply center alignment to a selection containing an inline picture, the picture will be centered on the page.

You can apply any of the picture formatting tools described earlier—scaling, shaping, cropping, brightness, and contrast—to an inline picture, but you cannot apply any of the following positioning techniques, such as text wrapping.

To change a picture from inline to floating, right-click the picture and choose Format Object to open the Format Object dialog (which is identical to the Format Picture dialog described later in this chapter), choose the Position tab, and check the check box next to Float over text.

To position a picture in your document, point to the picture, click and hold the mouse button, then drag to the desired spot and release. Once the picture has been positioned, select options from the Position tab of the Format Picture dialog to control how the picture responds to changes in the document. To open the Format Picture dialog, select the picture (if it is not already selected), then click the Format Picture button on the Picture toolbar. (Alternatively, you can right-click the picture and choose Format Picture from the context menu, or select the picture and choose Format | Picture from the menu bar.)

After the Format Picture dialog opens, choose the Position tab (see Figure 6-5). On the Position tab, the entries in the boxes for Horizontal and Vertical (and their respective From boxes) have been preselected for

you by Word, based on where you dragged the picture to. These boxes are used to locate the picture at a precise spot within the page by recording the distance between the picture and a horizontal page element (such as a paragraph) and between the picture and a vertical element (such as a column). In general, you needn't fiddle with these boxes, though you may use them to fine tune the distance between the picture and the adjacent margin, paragraph, or column.

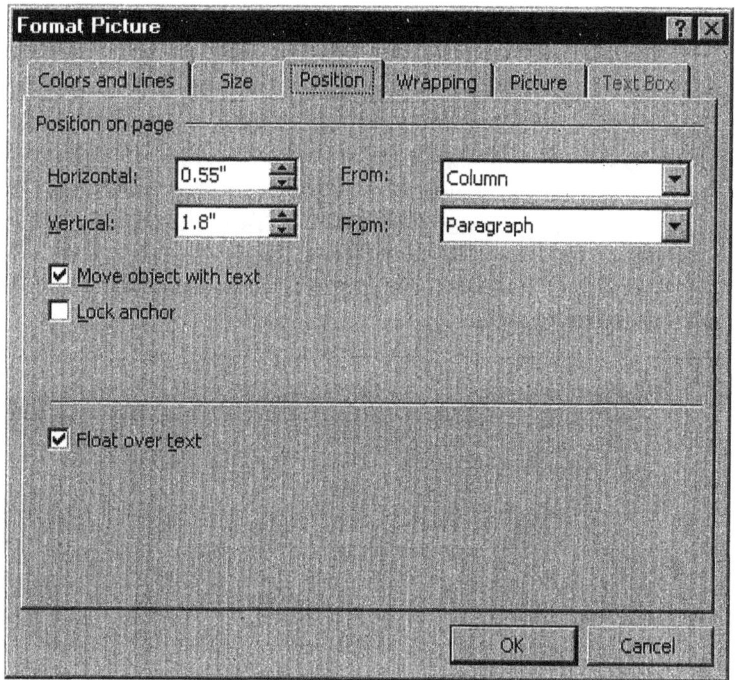

Figure 6-5: The Position tab.

The meat of the Position tab is in two of the check boxes: Move object with text and Lock anchor. When neither of these is checked, the picture remains in the same position on the page regardless of what happens to the text around it. For example, if you position a picture at the bottom of the page and then add text to the page, the new text doesn't "push" the picture onto the text page; some of the text that was above the picture jumps to the next page instead, so the picture can stay where it is.

If you check Move object with text, the picture's position is tied not to the page, but to the adjacent paragraph. The picture always maintains its position relative to the paragraph and column, but moves up and down on the page—and from page to page—as the text moves. If you check Lock anchor, the picture not only moves with the text, but also stays on the same page as the text it is anchored to no matter where that text moves.

Choosing How Text Wraps

The final step in integrating a floating picture into your page is determining how text wraps around it. You can accomplish this most easily by selecting the picture and then clicking the Text Wrapping button on the Picture toolbar. A list of wrapping options—each one a button that graphically illustrates a way text can wrap in relation to the picture—drops down, so you can select your desired wrapping style.

For more options and finer control of wrapping, visit the Wrapping tab of the Format Picture dialog. Right-click the picture and choose Format Picture from the context menu, then choose the Wrapping tab (see Figure 6-6).

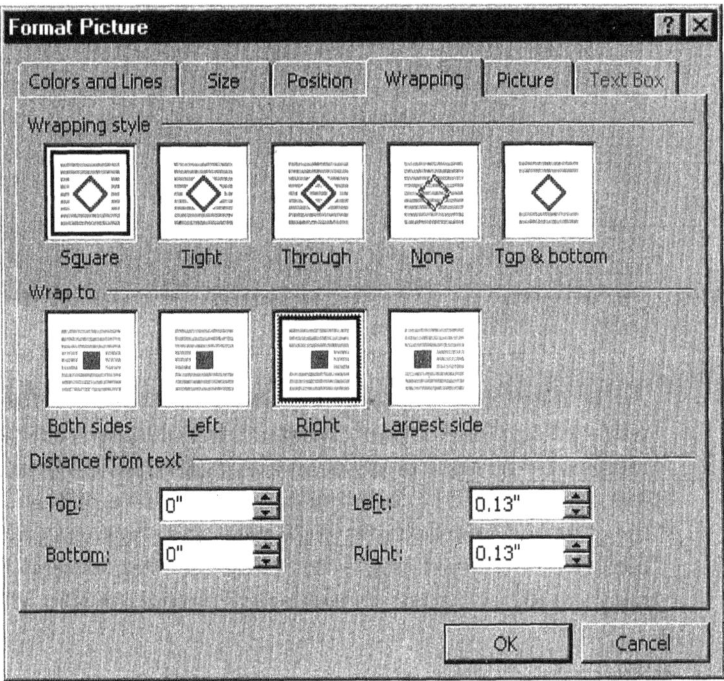

Figure 6-6: The Wrapping tab.

On the wrapping tab, choose a Wrapping Style from the top row of buttons. Note that two of the buttons—Through and None—don't wrap text around the picture, but run text through the picture:

- **Through.** OfficeArt objects may have "empty" areas within them. (Bitmapped pictures do not have empty areas; when the picture is a bitmap, Through has the same effect as the Tight wrapping style.) For example, if a picture has been created by the grouping of two objects, space between the two objects may be considered empty. The Through option wraps text around the picture (just like Tight), but also runs the text within any empty areas.
- **None.** The text doesn't wrap at all—it runs straight through the picture. Whether the text runs on top of the picture or is covered by it depends on whether the picture is configured to be in front of text or behind text. See "Overlapping Pictures, Text & Boxes," later in this chapter.

If you select any of the first three Wrapping styles—Square, Tight, or Through—you may also choose a Wrap to option from the second row of buttons. The default Wrap to option—Both sides—allows text to wrap on both sides of the picture (provided there's room between the picture and the margins). The Left and Right Wrap to options each prevent wrapping on one side, while the Largest side option allows text to wrap only on the side of the picture where there's the most room.

Finally, the Distance from text boxes at the bottom of the wrapping tab enable you to increase or decrease the white space between the picture and the text on any side. If you think there's too much white space, or too little, between the picture and the text around it, decrease or increase the measurements in Distance from text until you get the effect you want.

Changing the Wrap Shape

When using the wrapping options that wrap text tightly around the edges of a picture, the results may not always be what you expect. Sometimes apparently irregularly shaped pictures include an invisible rectangular background, to which the text will wrap instead of wrapping to the parts of the picture you see. Other times, the wrapping around irregular shapes looks uneven—the text appears too close to the image at some spots, too far at others.

You can fix either of these problems by editing the picture's *wrap points*, invisible points that form an outline around the picture. When Word wraps text, it wraps not to the picture, but to the invisible wrap points, which loosely follow the contours of the picture. By adjusting the wrap points, you reshape the outline, and thus change the way text wraps around the picture.

To edit wrap points, select the picture, click the Text Wrapping button on the Picture toolbar, and then choose Edit Wrap Points from the list. A dashed outline appears around the picture, dotted by black squares at any corners. Grab and drag any part of the line, or any black square, to change the shape of the outline. When finished, deselect the picture.

Walk-Through: Insert, Format, Position Picture

Follow the steps below to practice inserting, positioning, and formatting a picture.

1. Open a document containing text.
2. Choose Insert|Picture|From File.
   The Insert Picture dialog opens.
3. In the box of folders, double-click Popular.
   The box lists picture files in the Popular folder.
4. Scroll down the list and select the file Flower.wmf.
   A rose appears in the Preview pane.
5. Click Insert.
   The Insert Picture dialog disappears, and the rose appears in your document.
6. If the Zoom level is higher than 50%, drop down the Zoom list on the Formatting toolbar and choose 50%.
   The Zoom level drops to 50%, to make seeing and working with the picture easier.
7. If the picture is not already selected, point to it and click to select it.
   The handles and the Picture toolbar appear.
8. Point to the handle at the lower right corner of the picture.
   The pointer becomes a two-pointed arrow.
9. Click and drag the pointer about halfway toward the center of the image, then release.
10. Point to the picture so that the pointer becomes a four-pointed arrow.
11. Click and drag the picture over any paragraph, then release it.

12. Right-click the picture and choose Format Picture from the context menu.
    The Format Picture dialog opens.
13. Choose the Wrapping tab.
14. On the Wrapping tab, choose Wrapping style Tight, then click OK.
    The text wraps tightly on all sides of the picture.

Creating Text Boxes

A *text box* is exactly what it sounds like: a box containing text. The beauty of a text box is that, while it contains text, it can be treated much like a picture. You can scale a text box, change its shape, or apply borders and shading to it. Most important, you can drag a text box to any spot on your page and control how text wraps around it, just like a picture. Also like a picture, a text box can float—so it can sit on top of text, a picture, or another text box, or lie behind them (see "Overlapping Pictures, Text & Boxes" later in this chapter).

To create a text box, choose Insert | Text Box. The pointer becomes a crosshair, and the Text Box toolbar opens (see Figure 6-7). To create a small, square text box (you can change its size and shape later), click where you want the text box to go. To create a text box of a particular size and shape, point the crosshair to the spot where you want to position the upper left corner of the text box. Click and hold, then drag downward and to the right. When the shape and size are what you want, release the mouse button.

Figure 6-7: A text box floating on top of a picture.

Once your text box is created, you can work with it in many ways, including:

- **Select the text box.** Click the text box. Handles appear, along with a hashed border around the entire box, to indicate that the box is selected.
- **Enter and format text.** Click inside the box so that the edit cursor appears there, then type or edit as you wish. You can apply any text formatting or paragraph formatting you wish to the text within the box.
- **Format the text box.** Select the text box and drag its handles exactly as you would to scale or shape a picture.
- **Entering tables and pictures.** Click inside the box so that the edit cursor appears there, then insert a picture or table as you normally would. Note that sizing the text box has no effect on the size, shape, or format of a table or picture inside the text box.
- **Position the text box.** Select the text box, then point to the hashed border (the pointer becomes a four-pointed arrow). Click and drag to move the box, then release.
- **Choose text wrapping and other options.** Select the text box, then point to the hashed border (the pointer becomes a four-pointed arrow). Right-click the border and choose Format Text Box from the context menu. Use the dialog that appears—Format Text Box—exactly as you would use the Format Picture dialog to format a picture.

Fast Track

You can change the text direction *of the text in a text box, turning normal text (running left to right, like other text in the document) sideways so that it runs top-down or bottom-up. Select the text box, then click the Text Direction button on the Text Box toolbar until you get the text direction you want.*

Overlapping Pictures, Text & Boxes

Floating pictures, text boxes, and text can overlap one another in Word documents. If you don't want these objects to overlap one another, be careful not to overlap elements when positioning them, and don't use the

None text wrapping style when choosing wrapping options for pictures and text boxes.

However, if you want to create overlapping effects—such as text running on top of a picture or a text box overlapping a corner of a picture to create a graphical caption (refer back to Figure 6-7), you'll need to control the order of overlapping elements—what's on top of the stack, what's beneath it, what's in between.

Begin by positioning your floating pictures and text boxes and choosing wrapping options without regard to order. Then find any improperly ordered overlaps, and choose the order of each element by right-clicking the element and choosing Order from the context menu. A list of choices appears as shown in Figure 6-8.

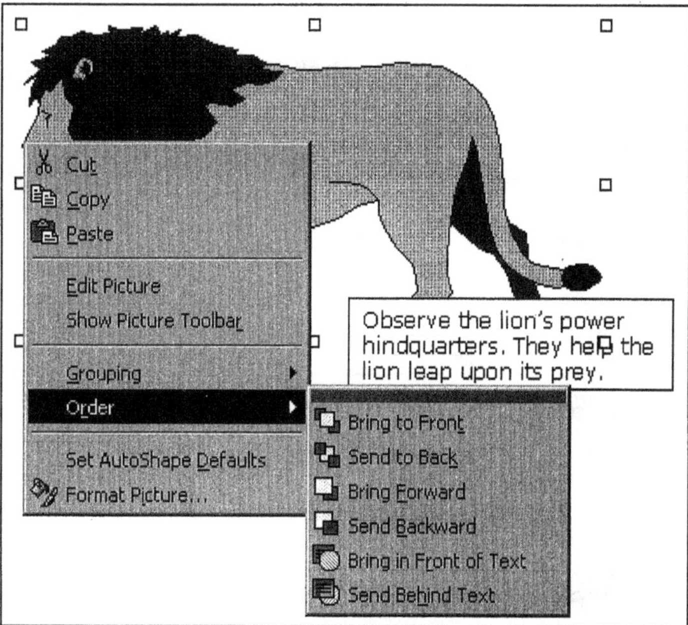

Figure 6-8: The Order submenu.

To put the selected object on top of any it overlaps, choose Bring to Front. To put the object under any it overlaps, choose Send to Back. When more than two objects are involved, use Bring Forward and Send Backward to change the selected object's place in the stack one level at a time.

To make an object cover text (when the wrapping style for the object is None), choose Bring in Front of Text. To allow text to run over the object, choose Send Behind Text.

Making Tables

As with so many things in Word, making tables is a two-part job. First comes format—defining the rows and columns of the table—then comes content, creating and formatting the contents in each box or *cell* within the table.

There are two basic types of tables: simple and complex (see Figure 6-9). A simple table is just what you expect: a grid of rows and columns wherein each column has the same number of rows. A complex table is one in which some columns have more rows than others, or vice versa. Most tables are simple, so that's the type you learn to create first in this section. Following simple tables, you'll learn how to enter table content, then how to create complex tables with Word's Draw Table facility.

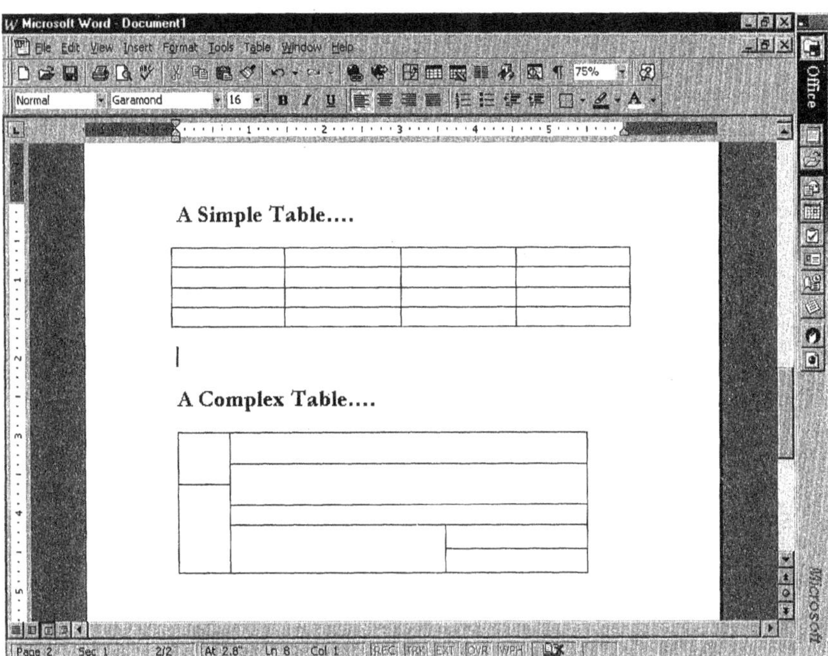

Figure 6-9: Examples of simple and complex table types.

When creating tables, keep in mind that the initial table you create need not match exactly the table you'll end up with—in fact, it probably won't. When you create a table, you create a rough repository for the table's contents, just a place to put stuff. As the table evolves, you can adjust its column widths and row heights, customize its borders, add shading, and much more.

Fast Track

Three different Office 97 applications can create tables: Word, Excel, and Access. Since you can import an Excel or Access table into Word, you may choose to create a table for a Word document in any of the three applications.

Which application should you use for tables? That depends a lot on which program you're comfortable with. Even when Access is the ideal tool for a given table, you may want to use Word anyway if Access isn't your bag. However, all things being equal, here are the rules of thumb:

Use...	***If the table requires...***
Word	*Fancy text formatting (lists, hanging indents, fine control of spacing, etc.).*
Excel	*Fancy calculations, data analysis, or charts generated from table data.*
Access	*Table contents automatically generated by searching and sorting a database.*

Also, when you need a table in a PowerPoint presentation, you'll find importing it into the presentation easiest if you create the table in Word.

To learn about importing an Excel table (or an Access report) into a Word document, or a Word table into PowerPoint, see Chapter 21, "Collaborating & Integrating With Office 97."

Creating a Simple Table

To create a simple table, position the edit cursor where you want the table to appear, then, on the Standard toolbar, click the Insert Table button. A grid of boxes opens (see Figure 6-10); move the pointer down to highlight the number of columns in the table, then across to choose the number of rows. Click to insert the table.

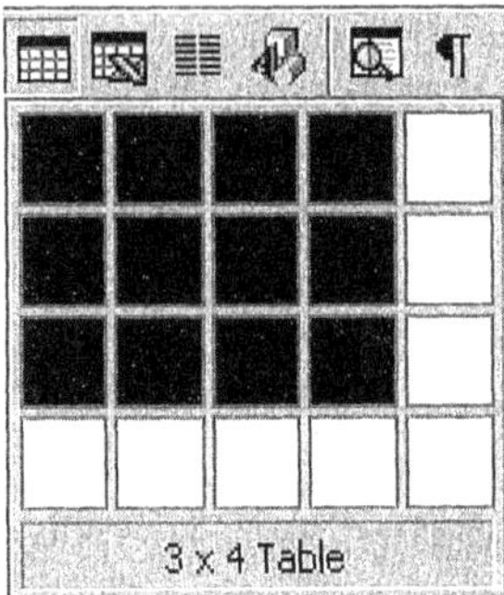

Figure 6-10: A simple table grid created by the Insert Table button.

The largest table you can create with the Insert Table button is four rows by five columns. To create a larger simple table, choose Table | Insert Table. The Insert Table dialog opens (see Figure 6-11). Choose the Number of columns and the Number of rows. Then choose an option in Column width. The default option, Auto, creates a table that runs the full width of the page (margin to margin) made up of equally wide columns. Alternatively, you can select a measurement for the columns in Column width. (Remember that you can always fine tune column widths later.)

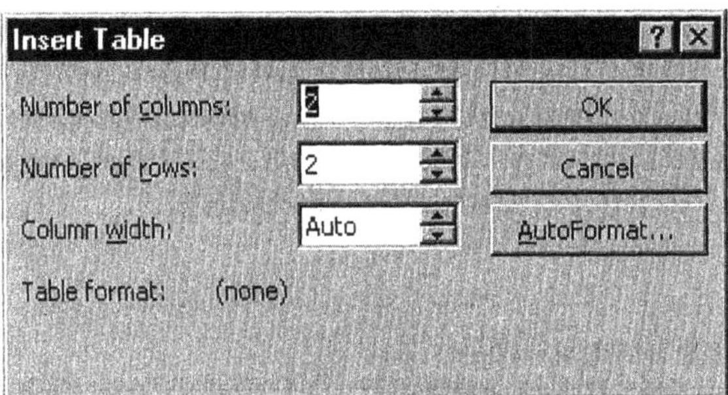

Figure 6-11: The Insert Table dialog.

Creating & Formatting a Table's Contents

Once your table is set up, point to a cell and click to supply that cell's contents. You can type in a cell to enter text, or click in the cell and choose Insert | Picture to put a picture in the cell. To move to another cell, click in the cell you want to go to, or press Tab to jump from the current cell to the next one (to the right). If the content you provide requires it, the height of the row automatically increases to accommodate it.

You may format the text in a cell exactly as you would format text anywhere else in the document. See Chapter 4, "Working With Text." You may select text and apply character formatting, including fonts, font sizes, attributes, and symbols. You may also apply paragraph formatting—but it works a little differently than it does outside of a table cell. For paragraph-formatting purposes, a cell acts like a whole page. For example, if you position the edit cursor within a paragraph in a cell, then click the Center alignment button on the Formatting toolbar, the paragraph is centered within the cell (not within the page as a whole). The other alignment, indenting, and list buttons all do their regular thing, too, but relative to the cell, not the page.

Fast Track

In addition to applying regular text formatting techniques to text in cells, you may also apply a few formatting options available from the Tables and Borders toolbar.

Begin by selecting the cells you want to format (see "Selecting Tables & Cells," next). Then click a button on the Tables and Borders toolbar:

- *The Align Top, Center Vertically, and Align Bottom buttons let you format the contents of the selected cells to vertically align at the top, center, or bottom of the cell. (You can control the horizontal alignment in the cell with the regular Left, Center, and Right alignment buttons on the Formatting toolbar.)*
- *The Change Text Direction button tilts text in the selected cells so that it runs top to bottom or bottom to top, rather than left to right. You might use this option, for example, to create row headings whose text runs bottom to top.*
- *The Sort Ascending and Sort Descending buttons rearrange the selected cells so that their contents appear in alphabetical/numerical order (ascending) or reverse-alphabetical/numerical order (descending).*

Selecting Tables & Cells

By selecting a group of table cells, you can conveniently perform a variety of actions that affect all cells in the selection. The most natural way to select table cells is to click in a cell and drag across other cells until all desired cells are selected. Other ways to select table cells include:

- To select a single cell—Click the left edge of the cell.
- To select a row or column—Place the edit cursor within the desired row or column, and choose Table | Select Row or Table | Select Column.
- To select a whole table—Place the edit cursor within the table and choose Table | Select Table.

Once you've selected the cells to work on, you can:

- Apply text formatting, to format the text in all selected cells the same way.
- Choose Table | Merge Cells (to change two or more cells into one) or Table | Split Cells (to split each cell into two). You can use this technique to turn a simple table into a complex one, or vice versa.
- Apply borders or shading to only the selected cells. For example, you can highlight column headings in a table by selecting the cells containing the headings and applying a heavier border or shading to them than to the rest of the table.
- Select a row or column of cells, and choose Table | Delete Cells to remove a portion of the table and all of its contents.

Finally, if you select the whole table, you can use copy and paste (to copy the table) or cut and paste (to move the table). See Chapter 4, "Working With Text."

FYI: Delete Cuts Content, Not Cells

When you select cells and press the Del key, only the cell contents are deleted—the empty cells remain. To delete the cells themselves, or rows or columns from a table, select the cells and choose Table|Delete.

Drawing a Complex Table

Using Word's Draw Table facility, you can "draw" a simple or complex table. Click the Tables and Borders button on the Standard toolbar (or choose Table | Draw Table). The Tables and Borders toolbar opens (see Figure 6-12) and the pointer becomes a pencil. The pencil draws the grid lines of the table when you click and drag.

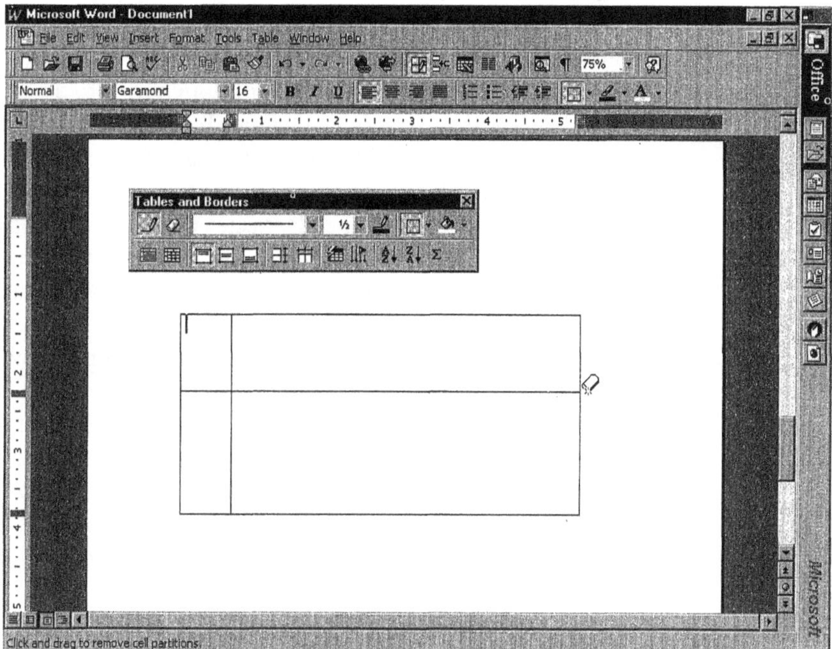

Figure 6-12: Drawing a complex table.

To create a column, point to where you want the top of the column to appear, and drag downward; as you drag, a dashed line appears to indicate the line you're drawing. When you've reached the end of your desired column, release the mouse button. To create a row, point to where you want the left end of the row to appear, then drag to the right. Split rows or columns into smaller rows or columns by clicking on their grid lines and then dragging new grid lines within them. To erase a row or column, click the Eraser button on the Tables and Borders toolbar, click a line in the offending table element, drag to highlight the portion to erase, then release.

When finished drawing your table, press Esc to restore the regular pointer. Then enter the table's contents or adjust its format as desired.

Adjusting Column Width & Row Height

As you develop your table and add its contents, you'll inevitably want to adjust the column widths. The row heights change automatically to accommodate your cell entries, but you may decide to adjust row heights, as well.

The most natural way to adjust column widths and row heights is to drag the grid lines of the table. If you point very carefully to a vertical grid line in a table, you'll see the pointer change to a vertical double bar with a horizontal arrow on each side. To change the column's width, click and drag to the right or left. You can adjust row height in the same way by dragging the horizontal grid lines up or down. To change the height or width of selected cells, rather than whole rows or columns, first select the cells, then click and drag the grid lines within the selection. Note that the width or height of the selected cells will no longer match up with the rest of the row or column.

Word can automatically resize a selected group of rows or columns to make them all of equal width or height. To create equal-width columns, select the columns and choose Table | Distribute Columns Evenly. To create equal-height rows, select the rows and choose Table | Distribute Rows Evenly. (Instead of using the Table menu, you may select the rows or columns and use the Distribute Columns Evenly or Distribute Rows Evenly buttons on the Tables and Borders toolbar.)

Working With Borders, Shading & Color

A *border* is a rectangular box that can appear around almost anything in a Word document: a picture, a text box, a table, a paragraph, selected text within a paragraph, or even a whole page. Within a border—which may be visible or invisible—you can add *shading*, a color or pattern (or both) that lends extra emphasis or visual variety to your document.

You control the look of borders and shading by selecting from among the following characteristics:

- Line color—The color of the border lines.
- Line style—A straight line, squiggly line, zigzag, dashed line, and so on.
- Line weight—The thickness of the line (expressed in points, just like font size).
- Sides/Grid lines—On which sides of the selected object (or on which grid lines in a table) the border appears.
- Fill color—The color of the shading.
- Pattern—A line pattern or dot pattern that adds texture to the shading (may be used in combination with fill color).

Now, to make borders and shading as confusing as possible, Word offers four different ways to apply them. While having options is terrific, the benefit of having four ways to do borders and shading is undercut by three problems:

- No type of object (text, pictures, tables, etc.) works with all four methods.
- Only one method, the Borders and Shading dialog, gives you complete control over all characteristics of the borders and shading.
- Terminology is used inconsistently method to method; for example, fill color is called "Fill color" in one method, "Highlight color" in another, and "Shading color" in another.

Fortunately, there's one part of this job that's reliable: You always begin by selecting the object to which you want to apply borders and shading. Once the object is selected, you can apply the borders and shading method that meets your needs.

On the next several pages, I describe each of the four ways you can apply borders and shading—including to which objects you can apply each method, and which characteristics you can control.

FYI: Tables Carry Extra Border Options

Border lines can appear on any or all of the four sides of a picture, text box, paragraph, page, or selected text. However, a table isn't a single box—it's many boxes, since each cell is a box unto itself.

You can select a whole table and apply borders and shading to it. When you do, you can use the Outside Border button on the Tables and Borders toolbar, or the Preview pane of the Borders and Shading dialog, to selectively apply or remove the border line from any grid line on the table. (When a table grid line has no border line applied to it, it appears gray on your display and will not appear at all in print.)

Alternatively, you can select only part of a table and apply borders and shading to that part that are different from the borders and shading used in the rest of the table. For example, you might apply shading to a single row to make it stand out, while not shading other rows.

Formatting Toolbar

This option quickly applies simple borders or colored highlights to selected paragraphs, text, text boxes, and tables (but not pictures).

- Click the arrow on the Outside Border button of the Formatting toolbar. A box of options appears, from which you can choose the sides to which you want to apply borders. This option provides no control over line weight, style, or color.
- Click the arrow on the Highlight button of the Formatting toolbar. A box of options appears, from which you can choose the color of the shading. This option provides only a fraction of the shading options available with other methods.

Colors & Lines Tab

This option applies a border on all sides, or shading, to a selected picture or text box. On the tab, shading is called *fill color*; a fill color shades a text box in the selected color, or shades empty areas of a picture.

To open the tab shown in Figure 6-13, right-click a picture and choose Format Picture from the context menu (or right-click a text box and choose Format Text Box). Then click the Colors and Lines tab.

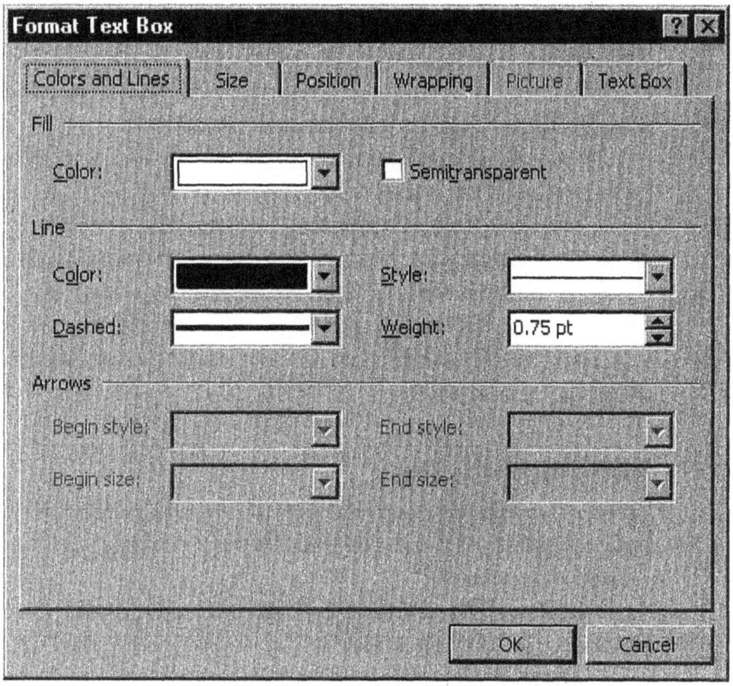

Figure 6-13: The Colors and Lines tab.

Choose a Color (in the Fill area of the tab) to apply a fill color to the selection, or choose the top item in the color list—an empty box—to apply no shading. (Check the Semitransparent check box to allow items behind the picture or text box to be seen through a fill color.) In the Line section of the tab, choose among options for the border's color, style, and weight.

Fast Track

To create a cool solid line—a horizontal rule*—under a header or over a footer (or to apply shading to a header or footer), apply borders and shading to the text of the header or footer.*

For example, to create a rule under the header, open the header space (choose View | Header and Footer), select the header text, then apply a border using the Formatting toolbar or the Borders and Shading dialog (covered later in this chapter).

Tables & Borders Toolbar

This option applies any of several types of borders or fill colors to a table. Select all or part of the table, and open the Tables and Borders toolbar (choose View | Toolbars | Tables and Borders).

Choose the sides and grid lines to which you want to apply a border by clicking the Outside Border button (which works just like the Outside Border button on the Formatting toolbar) and choosing from the list. Note that you can achieve better control of which grid lines get borders by using the Borders and Shading dialog instead of the toolbar.

Customize the line by selecting from the toolbar's lists for Line Weight, Line Style, and Border Color. Choose any desired fill color from the Shading Color button.

Borders & Shading Dialog

This option applies the widest available range of border and shading options and is available for selected text, paragraphs, text boxes, and tables (not pictures).

Begin by selecting the object, then choose Format | Borders and Shading. The Borders and Shading dialog opens, as shown in Figure 6-14. On the Borders tab, choose the overall look of the border under Setting, then fine tune the look of the lines by choosing from the Style | Color and Width (weight) lists. To selectively add or remove the border from any side of the object, click a side of the image in the Preview pane.

Fast Track

You can put a border around a selected page, all pages in a section, or all pages in a document. First, locate the edit cursor anywhere in the page, section, or document on which you want to put a border. Then choose Format | Borders and Shading and click the Page Border tab.

Choose from among the options on the Page Border tab, which are identical to those on the Borders tab. When finished, choose an item from the tab's Apply to list to apply the page border to the whole document, the current section, just the first page of the current section, or all pages in the current section except for the current page.

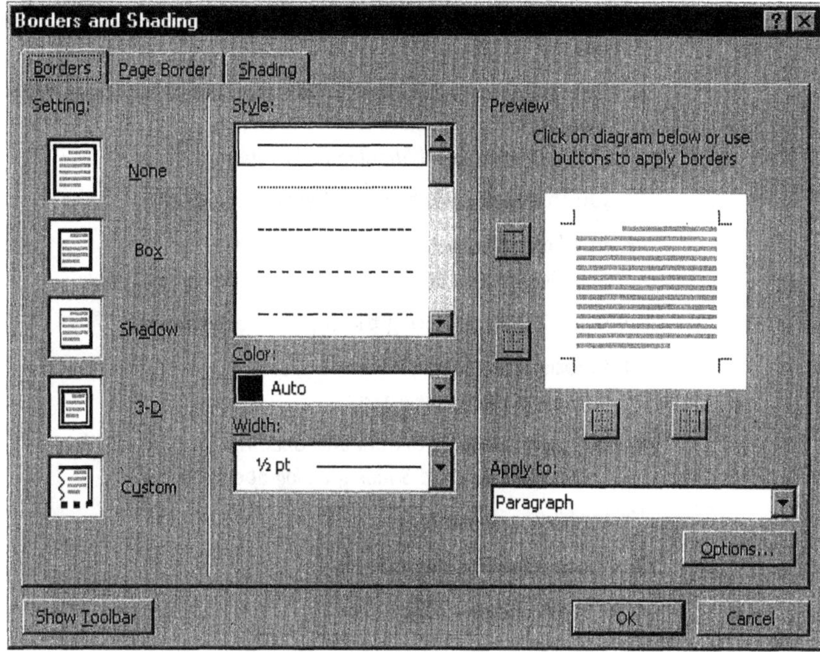

Figure 6-14: The Borders tab.

To shade the selection with a fill color or pattern, click the Shading tab and select from among the fill color and pattern options provided.

Walk-Through: Tables & Borders

Follow the steps below to practice working with tables and borders.

1. Open or create any document.
2. Position the edit cursor in the document, and click the Insert Table button on the Standard toolbar.
   The grid of table columns and rows drops down.
3. Move the pointer down and to the right to highlight three rows by four columns (3 X 4).
4. Click.
   A simple 3 x 4 table appears in the document.

5. Click in any cell(s) you wish and practice entering and formatting text in cells.
6. Click in any cell (but don't select the cell), and choose Format|Borders and Shading.
   The Borders and Shading dialog opens.
7. On the Borders tab under Setting, choose All.
8. In Width, choose 3 pt, then click OK.
   A three-point border appears on all lines of the table.
9. Click in any cell along the top row of the table.
10. Choose Table|Select Row.
    The top row is selected.
11. Choose Format|Borders and Shading.
    The Borders and Shading dialog opens.
12. In Width, choose 6 pt.
13. Choose the Shading tab.
14. In Style, choose 20%.
15. Click OK.
    The top row of the table has a border twice as thick as the rest of the table and is shaded with a 20% gray pattern.

Moving On

The applications included with Office 97 cover a lot of different activities, but curiously, serious computer graphics creation isn't one of them. There's no shortage of such Windows programs outside of Office 97, including such animals as Corel Draw! and Adobe Illustrator, if you need more advanced graphics tools than those accessible through Word.

In practice, creating pictures is one discipline, and integrating them into documents is another—that's why many companies have both graphic artists and desktop publishing pros on-staff. Still, Word gives you a level of control over the formatting and positioning of pictures that until very recently was the exclusive province of desktop publishing software and beyond the toolset of an ordinary Word processor. And yes,

through Office's Clip Gallery, Drawing toolset, and Microsoft Photo Editor, you can provide your own pictures, to a limited extent. Nevertheless that stuff is really extracurricular, as far as Word is concerned. Word doesn't care where the picture comes from or how it was created; Word's job is to fit the picture within the page, and it does that well.

Again, you'll find working with pictures in Word easier if you mentally separate the job into two parts: getting the picture into the document (a quick trip to the Insert Picture dialog or Clip Gallery), then fiddling with its formatting and positioning (beginning with the buttons on the Picture toolbar), when necessary, to create precisely the effect you want. Tables, similarly, are a two-part job: mapping out the rows and columns, then entering the contents of each cell.

Now that you know how to add graphical flair, you know how to do just about everything that you can do to a Word document. So why does another chapter about Word remain? Well, I must confess that for many of the activities you've already learned how to perform—and a few you haven't—Word offers a faster, easier, or more powerful way to get the job done. Don't get mad—I had a really good reason for dragging you through the hard way first. I'll explain everything right at the start of Chapter 7, "Working Faster & Easier in Word."

7

Working Faster & Easier in Word

"It's the last chapter about Word," you may say, "and *now* you're telling me how to do stuff faster and easier than I did it in earlier chapters? Is this some kind of cruel joke?"

No joke. I had a really, *really* good reason. See, you're probably either of two types of readers: a complete newcomer to Word, or an upgrader from a previous version. If you're an upgrader, you probably haven't read all of the preceding chapters; you've just skimmed the stuff that's new, and worked your way here quickly, so your patience hasn't been taxed—and besides, as a user of an earlier Word version, you already knew that a number of time-savers were available to you.

But if you're new to Word, then it's important that you know the mechanics of a document before you turn those tasks over to an automated helper. For example, a *template*—which you learn how to use in this chapter—can automatically apply page formatting like margins and paper size, so you don't have to bother. But unless you already know something about page formatting and how it's applied, how can you determine if a template's settings are right for you? More importantly, if you decide you want to use the template but also modify some of the formatting it applies (as most users of templates inevitably do), you have to know how.

By first showing you the nuts and bolts of document creation and formatting, I've given you the tools to control every aspect of your documents, to produce exactly the look you want or need. Now you'll discover a number of shortcuts that can make creating, formatting, editing, or producing some types of documents quicker and easier. But make no mistake—nothing you learn in this chapter is a replacement for knowing the techniques you picked up in Chapters 3 through 6, just as the availability of a spell-checker (which you also learn about here) doesn't mean you can ignore spelling as you type.

No shortcut is perfect. Knowing the nuts and bolts enables you to enjoy the shortcuts when they apply, but not to be dependent on them. I want you to control Word—not the other way around.

FYI: More Ways to Use What You Learn . . .

The first two sections in this chapter cover two types of files that help you create and format new documents more quickly and easily: Wizards and templates.

Many of the Wizard files and template files included with Office 97 are copied to your PC in the Typical installation—but some aren't. If you want to see or install other templates that are included with Office, run Office setup (see the Appendix) and choose Add/Remove. From the list that appears, select Microsoft Word and click Change Option, then select Wizards and Templates and click Change Option.

Finally, a few more Wizards and templates are included in the Valupack folder on the Office 97 CD. Choose Valupack, then Word, then Templates to open a folder of additional Wizards and templates. Copy any you like to your Templates folder as described later in this chapter.

Wizarding Up a New Document

Word includes a family of *Wizards* for quickly producing any of several common types of documents, including letters, faxes, resumes, mailing labels, and many more. You already know about Wizards—they're the little routines used throughout Windows to take you step-by-step through tricky tasks like installing programs (including Office 97).

Like any Windows Wizard, you use a Word Wizard simply by starting it up and then doing whatever the Wizard tells you to do. To begin, click File | New to open the New dialog. (Don't click the New button on the

toolbar; it creates a new document without opening the New dialog.) In the tabs of the New dialog, you'll see two kinds of files which are distinguished by their filename extensions:

- .wiz—Word document Wizards
- .dot—*templates* (see "Working With Templates," later in this chapter)

Browse among the tabs to locate a Wizard whose name suggests that it might fit what you want to produce. For example, if you intend to write your resume, open the Other Documents tab and choose Resume Wizard.wiz. When you find a likely candidate, click it once to select it. The Preview pane in the New dialog shows you a sample of the kind of document the selected Wizard produces (see Figure 7-1). When you've selected the Wizard you want, click OK to start the Wizard.

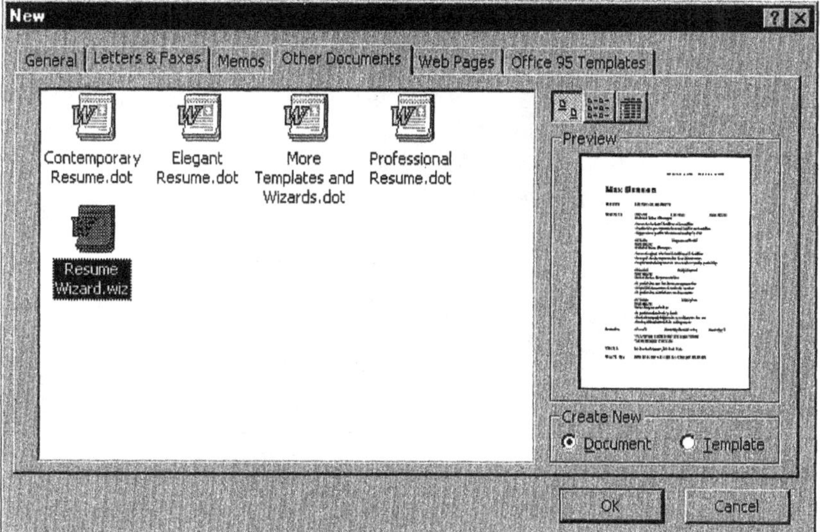

Figure 7-1: You can select a Wizard file (and see a Preview of it) in the New dialog.

A Wizard dialog opens, as shown in Figure 7-2, offering instructions for using the Wizard. Click through the Wizard's dialogs as instructed, choosing among options or supplying text when the Wizard tells you to. To advance to each new dialog, click the Next button; to go back to an earlier dialog to make a change, click Back. Like the Resume Wizard shown in Figure 7-2, many Wizards offer a sort of index along the left side of the dialog. The index helps give you a sense of what the Wizard will require of you; it also enables you to jump directly to any dialog in the Wizard simply by clicking on any entry in the index.

When you've supplied the Wizard with all of the entries it requires, click the Finish button (or click Finish at the bottom of the Index). The Wizard generates the document, opens the document in Word, and the Wizard closes. You may edit or expand the Wizard-produced document however you like, save it, or print it.

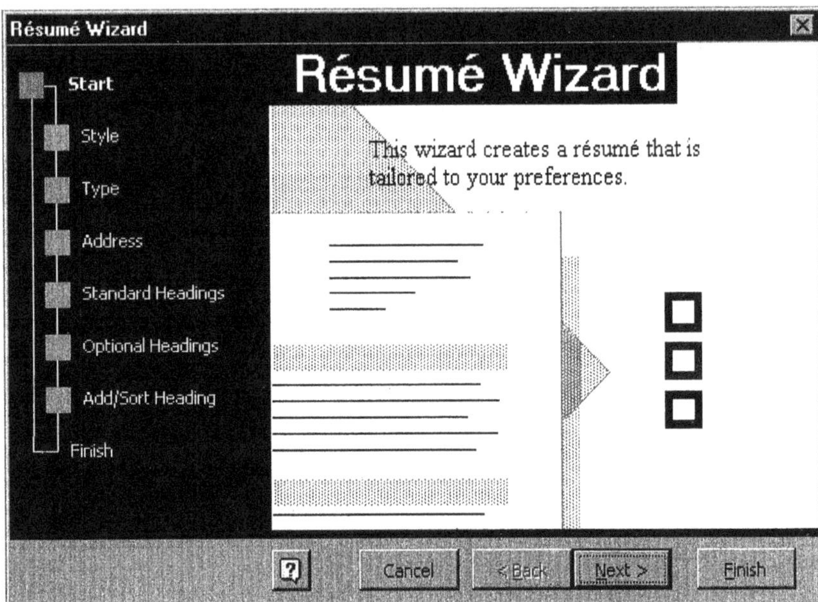

Figure 7-2: A Word document Wizard leads you step-by-step through creating the document.

FYI: Letter Wizard

On the assumption that letters are the most oft-composed documents for most Word users, Microsoft has included in Word 97 a special Letter Wizard that doesn't behave like other Wizards.

First, you start the Letter Wizard by choosing Tools|Letter Wizard. (There are several letter-making Wizards among the Wizards in the Templates file, but they're not the same as the Letter Wizard.) And if you use Word with the Office Assistant, whenever you do something in a new document that suggests you may be composing a letter—for example, typing an address or starting a line "Dear Fredo," Office Assistant asks whether you want help with writing a letter. If you say you do, the Assistant opens the Letter Wizard.

The other way the Letter Wizard differs from other Wizards is that it isn't really a Wizard—it's just a four-tab dialog. On the dialog, you choose options defining the style and layout of the letter, and also enter such standard letter elements as the recipient address, salutation, and closing. A Preview pane in the Letter Wizard shows you the letter you're creating as you go.

Working With Templates

A *template* is a prefab document, a head start on a document you'll create.

The template contains settings for page layout, paragraph formatting, character formatting, headers and footers, and more so that you don't need to define all of these elements yourself. In fact, a template may even contain some of the text of the document, or pictures. When you use a template, all you have to do is supply whatever the template doesn't supply—usually just the text—and you're finished. Instead of both writing and formatting your document, you plug your writing into a preformatted shell.

Using a template has two benefits. The first and most obvious is that a template saves you time when you create a new document. But another, less obvious benefit comes into play when you create a group of documents that share common formatting or portions of text in common. By basing all of the documents on the same template, you ensure that they're formatted consistently, and have common elements—including any common text they may share—defined in advance.

Net-Savvy

You can download new Wizards and templates from the Microsoft Word Free Stuff page. If you have a default Web browser configured in Windows, open Word and choose Help | Microsoft on the Web | Free Stuff. Or point your browser to http://www.microsoft.com/OfficeFreeStuff/Word/.

When downloading new templates or Wizards, be sure to save them in your Templates folder (or move them there after downloading). For most Office users, the Template folder is C:\Program Files\Microsoft Office\Templates. If your PC is on a local network, the Templates folder may be called User Templates or Workgroup Templates.

Using an Existing Template

The easiest way to use a template is to select it when creating a new document. You can choose a template either from Word's New dialog (File | New) or from the New Office Document dialog (see Chapter 2, "Getting to Know the Office 97 Environment").

The filename extension of a Word template is .dot. In the New dialog (see Figure 7-1, earlier in this chapter), click among the tabs, and locate a template whose tab and filename suggest a close match for the type of document you want to create. Single-click the file icon to select the template; the Preview pane in the New dialog shows you a sample of the kind of document the selected template produces.

When you've found the template you want to use, check the lower right corner of the screen to make sure that Document (not Template) is selected under Create New, then click OK. A new document, based on the template, opens in Word. Add to and edit the document any way you want to, and save it or print it as needed.

Note that some templates include built-in instructions, prompting you to "Click here and type . . ." something or other. For example, at the top of the document that appears when you open Elegant Letter.dot (in the Letters & Faxes tab), you'll see the line "CLICK HERE AND TYPE COMPANY NAME." When you click that text, the whole line is automatically selected, and whatever you type next replaces the instruction and is formatted as a letterhead.

Finally, some templates have sample text built into them, to help you visualize the document. For example, if you create a new document based on the template Elegant Resume.dot (in the Other Documents tab), you'll see that you have a resume for somebody named RICH ANDREWS. Unless you're him, you'll need to replace the contents of his resume with yours.

FYI: Templates Aren't Married to Their Docs (Part I)

When working on a document that you created with a template, you can change anything you want to change in the document—including the stuff the template contained. For example, if the template contained margin settings, you may nevertheless change the margins in the document; if the template contains text, you may edit, reformat, or even delete that text in the document.

Changes you make to the document have no effect on the original template or to other documents based on the same template. You can edit the document all you like, and the template remains the same. Also, if you move or copy the document, you needn't move or copy the template along with it. The document is fully independent of the template.

Obviously, the more you change stuff that was part of the template, the less useful the template has been to you. Still, it's important to remember that the template really just helps you start a document. Once the document is open, you can do anything you want with it—it's just a document like any other.

Creating or Editing a Template

To create a template, all you need to do is create a document that contains all of the stuff you want to include in the template. A template can include:

- Text
- Pictures
- Page layout (settings on the Page Setup dialog; see Chapter 5, "Designing Pages")
- Styles for paragraph and character formatting (see "Working With Styles" later in this chapter)

Begin by creating your document, just as you would any other document. As you work, you may save the document, just as you would any other. You can even begin with an existing document and edit it to create the document that will become the template.

When the document contains all of the elements you want featured in the template, open the Save As dialog by choosing File | Save As. In the File name box, give your new template a name that describes the type of document it creates. In the Save file as type list near the bottom of the dialog, choose Document Template (*.dot); the entry in Save in automatically changes to the Templates folder. Choose (or create) a folder within Templates in which you want to store the template, and click the Save button. The template is now available from the New dialog for creating a new document. (You can save a template anywhere—it needn't live in the Templates folder. However, the Templates folder is as good a place as any, and if you use it, you'll locate the template more quickly when you need it.)

Instead of creating a new template from scratch or from an existing document, you can edit a template—whether one included with Office or one you created yourself previously. To edit a template, open it as you would an existing document—choose File | Open, navigate to the Templates folder, and choose a template. (The Templates folder is usually C:\Program Files\Microsoft Office\Templates. If your PC is on a local network, the Templates folder may be called User Templates or Workgroup Templates.) Make any changes you want, then save the template.

By default, the template is saved as a template (.dot) file. If you wish, you may use the Save As dialog to change the filename (to create a new, edited copy of an existing template), but be careful not to change the entry in Save as type—it must be Document Template (*.dot).

FYI: Templates Aren't Married to Their Docs (Part II—the Sequel)

Just as changing a document does not affect the template on which it's based, changing the template does not affect any documents previously created with that template. Changes you make to a template affect only the documents you create with it *after* you've changed it.

There's one little exception to this rule: If you make changes to the *styles* the template contains, you can optionally instruct Word to update the styles in documents based on the template. See "Working With Styles" later in this chapter.

Fast Track

When you create a new document but don't choose a template, Word automatically uses a template called Normal.dot. The new, blank document based on Normal.dot appears whenever you open Word from the Start menu, click the New button on the Standard toolbar, or choose Blank Document from the Open dialog.

By editing the Normal.dot template, you can change the formatting of this default document. For example, if you'd like to be able to click the New button and instantly begin work on a document that has 1-inch margins all around and uses Arial as its default font, simply edit the Normal.dot template to match these settings.

You'll find Normal.dot in your Templates folder. While you can edit the Normal.dot template any way you wish, don't move it from the folder where you find it. When you create a new, blank document, Word looks for the Normal.dot template in your Templates folder. If Word can't find it there, Word automatically creates a new Normal.dot using its default settings.

Working With Styles

A *style* is a collection of formatting characteristics—including both character formatting (fonts, font sizes, attributes) and paragraph formatting (alignment, indentation, line spacing, list formatting)—that define how you want a block of text treated.

By creating and using styles in Word, you can conveniently format whole blocks of text without the bother of separately applying each formatting characteristic. Styles not only save formatting time, but also help you make the formatting consistent within a document—all headings use a heading style, the body text is always formatted with the body text style, and so on.

More important, by using styles you enable yourself to make sweeping formatting changes to entire documents easily, because changing the formatting applied by a given style can automatically change every text block in the document formatted that way. For example, if you've formatted all of your chapter headings with a style called Heading 1, and then decide you'd like to change the font used for those headings, you can simply change Heading 1 so that it applies a different font.

There are two basic types of styles: paragraph and character. A paragraph-type style can apply both paragraph formatting and character formatting, and always affects an entire paragraph, even if only a portion of the paragraph is selected when you apply the style. A character-type style includes only character formatting, and may be applied to all or part of a paragraph.

Fast Track

The styles saved with the Normal.dot template are automatically available for use in any document, even if the document is based on another template instead of Normal.dot. You can make a new style you create accessible from within any Word document by adding that style to Normal.dot.

Applying a Style

All of the styles available in the current document are available from the Style list on the Formatting toolbar (see Figure 7-3). The styles available in any document include:

- All styles that are part of the template on which the document is based.
- All styles in the Normal.dot template.
- Any new styles Word has created for you as you've developed the document.
- Any new styles you have created for the document (if any).

To apply a style, select the text to which you want the style applied and then choose the style from the Style list. Observe that each item on the Style list is formatted to approximate the look that the style applies. Also, to the right of any paragraph-type style in the list, a paragraph symbol appears (¶); to the right of a character-type style, an underlined letter "a" appears (a).

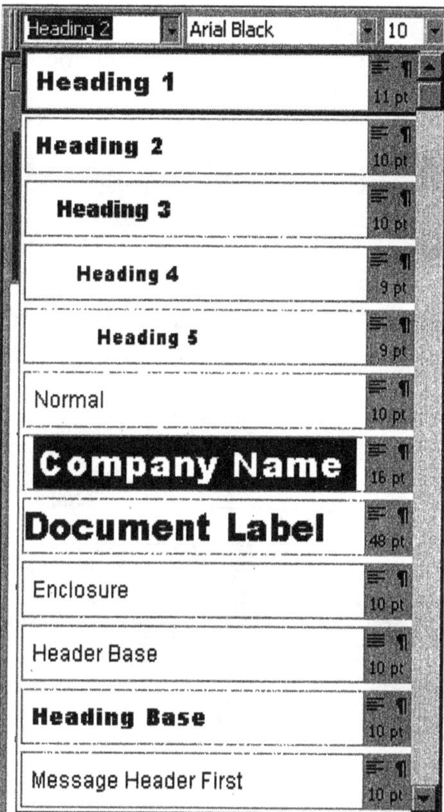

Figure 7-3: Apply a style by choosing from the Styles list on the Formatting toolbar.

If the style is a paragraph-type style, and you want to apply it to a single paragraph, just position the edit cursor anywhere within the paragraph and choose the style. If the desired style is a character-type style, or if you want to apply a paragraph-type style to more than one paragraph, select the text to which the style should be applied, and choose the style.

To preview the look of a style before applying it, select the text you want to format, then choose Format | Style. The Style dialog opens as Figure 7-4 shows, with previews of the paragraph and character formatting the style applies. Beneath the preview, a somewhat cryptic Description of the style appears; if you look at it carefully, you'll see that it includes a font name, font size, and other information. In the Styles list, choose the style you want to preview. When you find the style you want to use, click the Apply button.

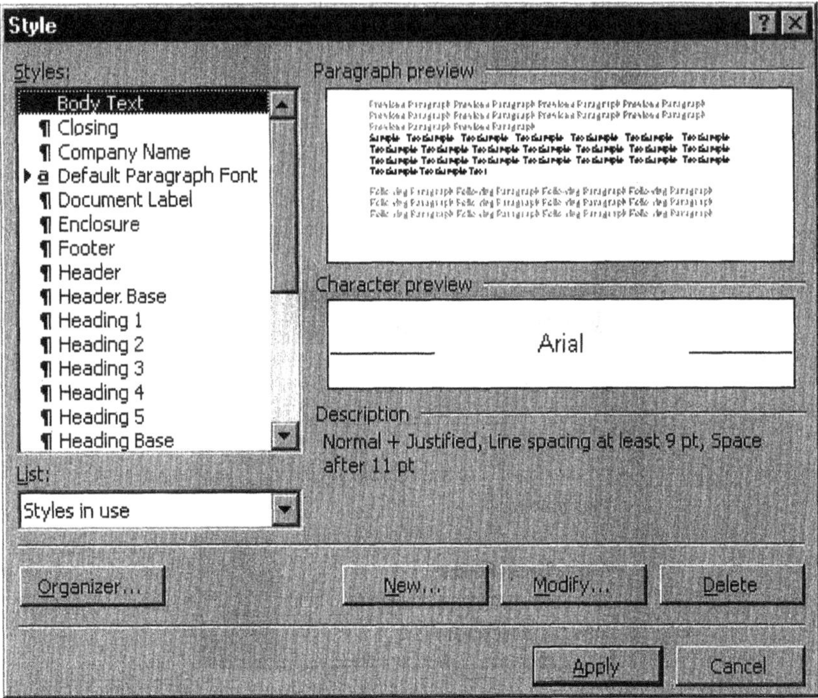

Figure 7-4: In the Style dialog, you may select and preview a style, or click buttons to Modify or Delete styles and create New ones.

Fast Track

If you make manual formatting changes to a selection, and then decide you preferred the way the selection was formatting previously, you can always revert it to its old appearance with Undo. But you may find it easier to simply re-apply the selection's original style.

Choose the style from the Style list, and a dialog appears, asking whether you want to update the style to match the selection's formatting (see Changing a Style, later in this chapter), or reapply the style's original formatting to the selection. Click the radio button next to Reapply, then click OK.

Creating or Changing a Style

As you format text blocks in Word, Word automatically creates new styles. For example, if you center a line of text at the top of a document, and format it in a large font size, Word will guess that the line is a title, and will create a new style called Title based on the formatting you applied. The styles Word comes up with may be useful to you, or they may not be.

You can deliberately create new styles and add them to the current document or template. If you add a new style to a document, it's available only in that document. If you add it to a template, it's available in any document based on that template. If you add a style to the Normal.dot template, it's available in all documents, regardless of the template on which they're based.

Making a Paragraph Style the Easy Way

The easiest way to create a new paragraph-type style is to format a paragraph in the way you want the style to format paragraphs, then create the style from that formatting.

First, select your preformatted paragraph. Click in the Style box on the Formatting toolbar, but instead of selecting a style from the list, type a name for the new style and press Enter. The new style name is added (alphabetically) to the Style list, and the paragraph you used to create the style now has that style officially applied to it. You may apply your new style anywhere in the document.

If you save the document as a template, any new paragraph styles you've created using this method become part of the template, and may be applied in other documents based on the template. If you save the document as a Word document, the new styles you've created are available only within the document.

Defining a New Character or Paragraph Style

To create a character-type style (with no paragraph formatting), choose Format | Style to open the Style dialog, then click the New button on the Style dialog to open the New Style dialog (see Figure 7-5). On the New Style dialog, you can create not only a character-type style, but also create a paragraph-type style and apply to it optional controls that are unavailable with the easy method described earlier.

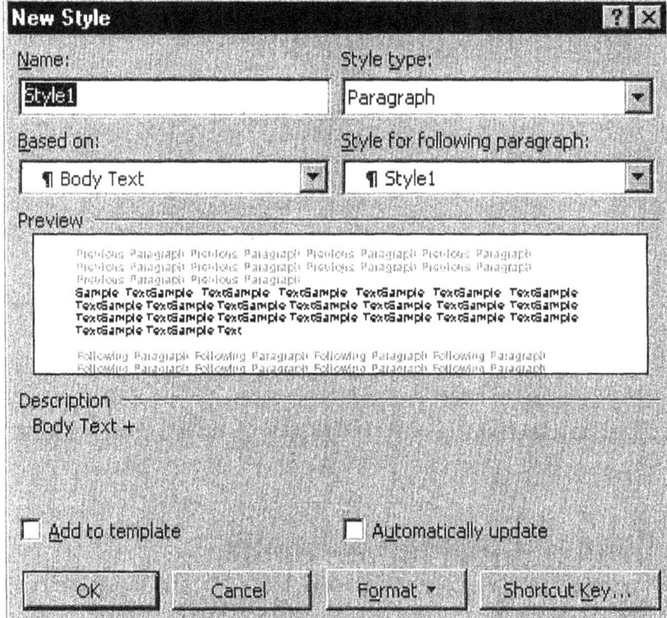

Figure 7-5: Define a new style by choosing options on the New Style dialog.

On the New Style dialog, begin by giving the style a Name, and choose a Style type (Paragraph or Character). In the Based on list, you can select an existing style that's a close match for the one you want to create, to save yourself some work defining the style. For example, if the only difference between an existing style called "Heading" and the one you want to create is the font size, choose Heading in Based on. If no existing style is close to your desired style, choose the top entry in the Based on list, which is (no style) for paragraph-type styles or (underlying properties) for character-type styles.

In Style for following paragraph (which is available only when you've selected Paragraph as the Style type), you may choose an existing style to be automatically applied to any paragraph that follows a paragraph using the style you're creating. For example, when you create a style for headings, you may specify that you want to always use a body text style for the paragraph following a heading. While using this option applies the style automatically to the following paragraph, you can, if you want, apply a different style or formatting to that paragraph within the document.

Finally you're ready to select the formatting for the new style. Click the Format button near the bottom of the New Style dialog to drop down a list of formatting options—Font, Paragraph, and so on. Selecting any one of these brings up the regular dialog used for that type of formatting; for example, choosing Font brings up the Font dialog so you can choose the font, font size, and character spacing. Using any of the available dialogs, apply whatever formatting you want to. Each time you complete a formatting dialog, you return automatically to the New Style dialog, where the Preview shows you how the style looks with the changes you've made so far.

Fast Track

Near the bottom of the New Style dialog appear two check boxes you can use to control two optional aspects for applying the style.

- *If you check the check box for Add to template, the new style is added not only to the current document, but also to the template on which the document is based.*
- *If you check the check box for Automatically update, Word changes the style definition automatically if you change the formatting of text to which the style has been applied. This option enables you to change style definitions on the fly from within a document, but it also creates a potential for accidentally changing whole style definitions when you merely wanted to change the formatting of a paragraph.*

When you finish formatting and the Preview pane shows what you want to see, click OK on the New Style dialog. The new style is added to the Style list on the Formatting toolbar.

Changing a Style

To change a style, choose Format | Style to open the Style dialog, then click the Modify button to open the Modify Style dialog. The Modify Style dialog is identical to the New Style dialog (see Defining a New Character or Paragraph Style); just change whatever you want to on the dialog, and use the Format button to edit the formatting. When finished, click OK on the Modify Style dialog.

After you change a style, you can make the changes effective in existing documents. This allows you to change the formatting in one or more documents, automatically, simply by making changes to styles applied in those documents. Begin by changing the style, and be sure to check the Add to template check box on the Modify Style dialog.

After opening any document based on the template, if you want the styles changes applied in the document, choose Tools | Templates and Add-Ins. On the Templates and Add-Ins dialog that opens, check the check box for Automatically update document styles. The style modifications become effective in the current document, and any new styles you've added to the template become available in the current document.

Fast Track

To change styles on the fly, select a block of text to which the style has been applied, then change its formatting to match what you want the style to do. Then choose the style from the Style list, and a dialog appears, asking whether you want to update the style to match the selection's formatting or reapply the style's original formatting to the selection. Click the radio button next to Update, then click OK. The style definition is changed, and all text in the document formatted with that style changes to match the new formatting.

Walk-Through: Templates & Styles

Follow the steps below to practice working with templates and styles.

1. Choose File|New.

   The New dialog opens.

2. In the New dialog, click the Other Documents tab.
3. Click the template Elegant Resume.dot.

   A preview of the Elegant resume appears.

4. Click OK.
5. Select the name (RICH ANDREWS, whoever that is) at the top.
6. Type your name (note that you needn't press Shift; the name is capitalized automatically by the style).
7. Under OBJECTIVE, click the instruction that appears.

8. Type a brief description of your life goals.
9. Position the edit cursor anywhere within your name at the top of the resume.
10. Drop down the Style list, and choose Document Label.
    The name is reformatted in the Document Label style. (You may have to fix its capitalization now.)
11. Save the resume, for practice. Don't actually submit it anywhere unless you happen coincidentally to have been a salesperson for Arbor Shoe.

AutoCorrecting & Formatting Text

When you think of using a word processor to automatically check your work, you probably think first of spell-checking. Word indeed will spell-check the heck out of your documents, and check your grammar for good measure—as you'll learn soon in "Checking Spelling and Grammar."

But first you'll discover a group of handy tools called AutoCorrect features, for lack of a better word. Unlike spell-checking—which you fire up as needed—most of the auto-correcting features are on duty all of the time, checking and correcting your typos, cleaning up certain types of text formatting, and even finishing words and phrases for you when you type just the first few letters. That's more "AutoHelpingYouOut" than "AutoCorrecting," but that's names for ya.

Using Word's AutoCorrect Features

All of the AutoCorrect features depend upon Word's ability to know—and, in a few cases, guess—how you want certain types of errors and other text handled. Thus the most important step in using AutoCorrect is choosing among the many options on the AutoCorrect dialog to tell Word what you want done and what you want left alone.

To begin, open the AutoCorrect dialog by choosing Tools | AutoCorrect. Consult the next several pages to learn how to complete each of the four tabs of the AutoCorrect dialog.

As you learn about AutoCorrect, keep in mind that choosing precisely the options you want to apply takes some experience, some trial and error. If you were to check every check box on the AutoCorrect dialog—instructing Word to fix every mistake it thinks it sees—you might find that Word keeps trying to fix things that you want left alone, stuff that looks to Word like an error, but isn't to you (you're entitled to your editorial opinion). Through experience, you'll learn how to tune the AutoCorrect dialog to match the way you work.

AutoCorrect

On the AutoCorrect tab (see Figure 7-6), choose the errors you want Word to fix automatically. Note that Word makes AutoCorrect changes instantly and automatically, and does not prompt you or otherwise inform you when making a change. For example, if the top check box in the AutoCorrect tab, Correct TWo INitial CApitals, is checked, when you type "GOdzilla," Word automatically changes the word to "Godzilla" the moment you finish typing it.

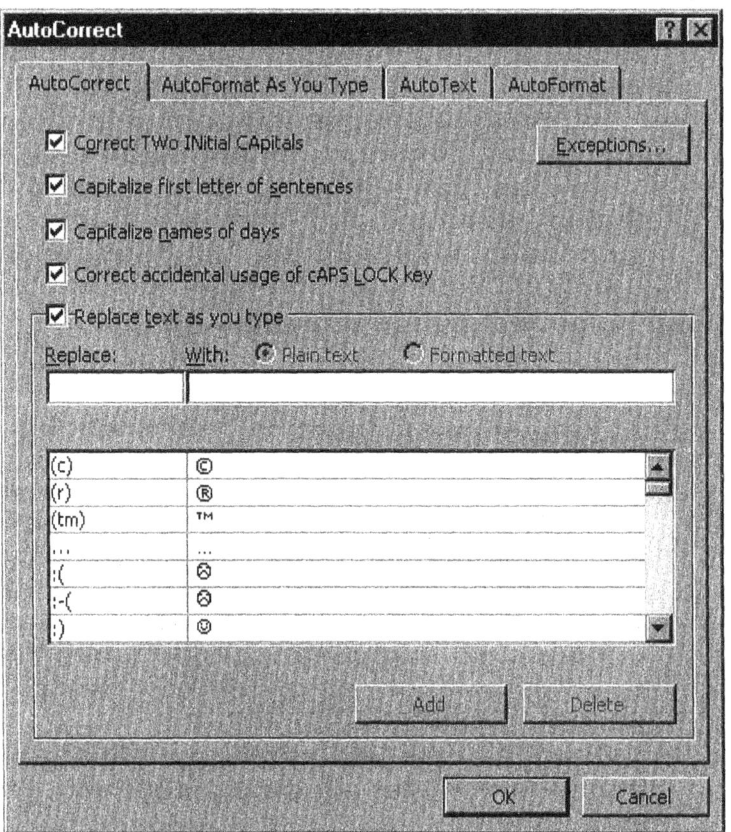

Figure 7-6: The AutoCorrect tab—where you control how Word makes automatic fixes—is the first of four tabs in the AutoCorrect dialog.

Fast Track

While you'll learn in the next few pages how to customize and operate Word's AutoCorrect features, the four tabs of the AutoCorrect dialog contain so many correction/formatting options that not all can be described in detail here. If you want to know specifically what an option on a tab does, just choose Help | What's This?, then point to the desired option and click. An explanation of the option's effect appears.

In the top four check boxes of the AutoCorrect tab, check the check box for any of the four common capitalization errors listed if you want Word to correct it automatically. Note that Word is pretty smart about how it applies these capitalization repairs. For example:

- The fix for two initial capitals comes into effect only when the word has three or more letters, and only when you capitalized the first two letters, but not all letters. Thus mistakes like "DOg" get fixed, but Word doesn't prevent you from typing "PC" or "VCR."
- The fix for accidental use of the Caps Lock key is applied only when the first letter of a word is lowercase, and the rest is uppercase (since that's what happens if Caps Lock is on and you try to capitalize the first letter only of a word). For example, Word assumes that "kING kONG" is a mistake, and repairs the phrase to "King Kong." But if you type "KING KONG," Word assumes you're just using all-caps for emphasis, and leaves it alone.

Fast Track

If your AutoCorrect settings are preventing you from applying some special capitalization you require—for example, if you really want to use two initial caps on a word, as you might with some unusual company names—you have two options. First, of course, you can open the AutoCorrect dialog and uncheck the check boxes that are thwarting you. Alternatively, you can select the characters you want to control capitalization for, choose Format | Change Case, and choose a case for the selected characters. Change Case settings override AutoCorrect.

When the fifth check box on the AutoCorrect tab, Replace text as you type, is checked, all of the items in the list below the check box go into effect. In each case, Word automatically replaces text you type—specified in the left column of the list—with different text or a special character.

If you scroll through the long list, you'll see that the predefined entries insert a number of commonly used special characters when you type their standard typewriter-based equivalents. Type (c), and a real copyright symbol is inserted in its place. Beneath the special characters in the list are entries for dozens of the most common typing errors; there's a list entry to change "adn" to "and," "mesage" to "message," and so on. (Note that AutoCorrect doesn't actually check your spelling—it simply makes the replacements in the list. To learn how to check spelling as you type, see "Checking Spelling & Grammar" later in this chapter.) Fixes for a few especially common grammatical errors appear in the list, as well.

Net-Savvy

By default, Word's AutoCorrect feature turns most smileys*—the little faces made of characters and used to express emotions on the Internet—into neat little graphical faces that show the same emotion.*

You can edit or delete any entry in the list you don't want, and more importantly, you can add your own new entries. Odds are that the mistakes you make often are already there (My big one, typing "comapny" for "company," is there), but if you want to change the list:

- To add a new entry, click in the Replace box and type the error, then click in the With box and type its correct replacement. Click the Add button to add the new entry to the list.
- To delete an existing entry, select it from the list, and click the Delete button.
- To edit an existing entry, select it from the list, edit it in the Replace and With boxes as desired, then click the Replace button (which appears in place of the Add button when you edit an existing entry).

Fast Track

If there's a long or difficult word you type often, you can add an entry to the AutoCorrect list to make Word automatically type the word for you.

For example, suppose you work for McGillicuddy, Inc., and must type that long and tricky name often in your documents. In the Replace box, enter a short nonsense word—a word you know you'll never type for any other purpose, such as "mgc." Then enter "McGillicuddy, Inc." in the With box and click Add. Whenever you type the word "mgc" in a document, Word automatically replaces it with the full company name.

You can achieve a similar result with AutoComplete (see "AutoText (& AutoComplete)," later in this section). But AutoCorrect is more convenient for this purpose than AutoComplete because with AutoCorrect, Word makes the change automatically, while Word prompts you to accept or reject an AutoComplete entry.

AutoFormat

AutoFormat works a lot like AutoCorrect, except that it applies certain types of paragraph formatting and special character formatting instead of correcting. You actually have two different AutoFormat facilities in Word:

- **AutoFormat As You Type.** As soon as you type anything AutoFormat is programmed to format, Word applies the formatting, just as AutoCorrect automatically applies its changes.
- **AutoFormat On Demand.** Word AutoFormats nothing while you're typing. Instead, when you want Word to autoformat, you choose Format | AutoFormat to open the AutoFormat dialog and instruct Word to work through the document, applying the formatting as it goes. Also unlike AutoFormat As You Type, the on-demand flavor optionally enables you to approve or reject each change.

Each AutoFormat flavor has its own tab in the AutoCorrect dialog (the AutoFormat As You Type tab appears in Figure 7-7; the AutoFormat tab is similar). You do the same thing in both dialogs: check the check boxes for formatting you want applied. You needn't work as if you had to use one or the other; you may want some types of changes applied as you go along, and others applied selectively on demand.

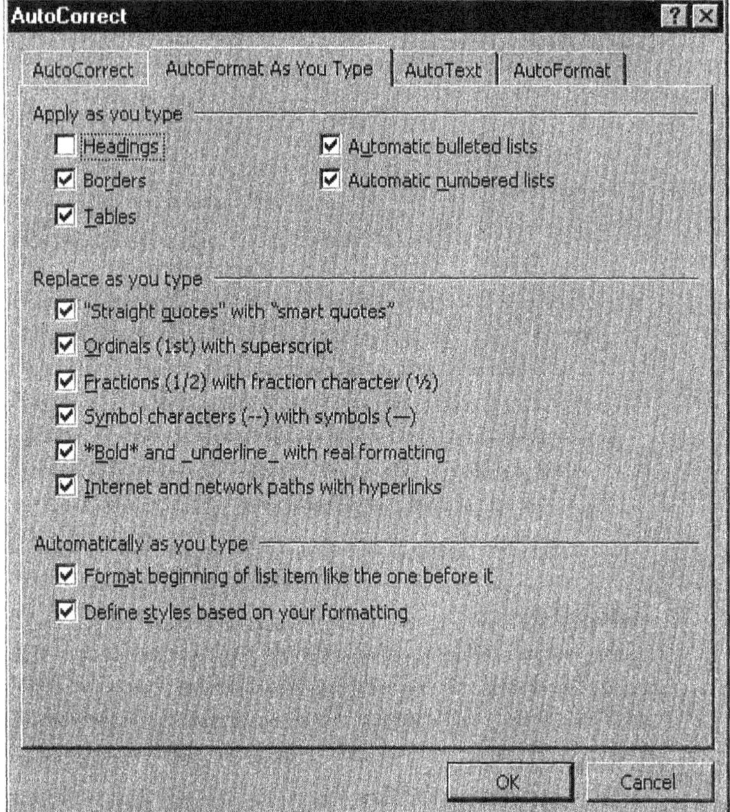

Figure 7-7: Choose formatting options from the AutoCorrect dialog's AutoFormat As You Type tab.

How Word decides what to format depends on a system of intelligent guesses. For example, if at the beginning of a line you type a dash or asterisk, then a space or tab, then some text, Word guesses that you're starting a bulleted list, and formats the line accordingly (if the Automatic bulleted lists check mark is checked). If a number and a space or tab starts the line, Word guesses you're typing a numbered list, and applies numbered list formatting.

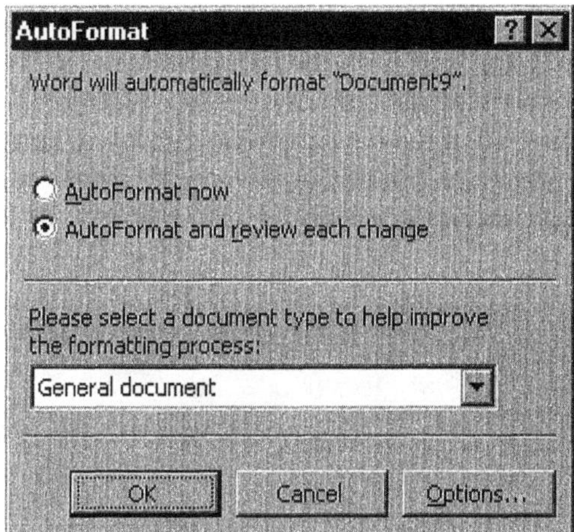

Figure 7-8: You use the AutoFormat dialog to initiate "on-demand" automatic formatting.

After you've chosen your check boxes, the selections on the AutoFormat As You Type dialog are applied automatically as you work. To apply the formatting selected on the AutoFormat tab, choose Format | AutoFormat to open the AutoFormat dialog (see Figure 7-8). On the dialog:

- To AutoFormat the entire document with no further input from you, choose AutoFormat now and click OK.
- To AutoFormat the entire document and then review changes, select AutoFormat, review each change, and then click OK. Word autoformats the entire document, then opens a dialog you may use to review each change, accept or reject changes, and edit the styles Word has applied.

AutoText (& AutoComplete)

"AutoText" is Word's way of describing words and phrases that are used often in documents. You are so likely to use such phrases as "To Whom It May Concern," "Best Wishes," or even your own name in your documents that Word maintains a list of such items and offers you two ways to insert them in your documents without actually typing them.

A long list of AutoText entries is predefined in Word; you can review the list by scrolling through it on the AutoText tab (see Figure 7-9). When you select any item in the list, you can preview its effect by watching the tab's Preview pane. To add a new entry of your own, simply type it in the box under Enter AutoText entries here, and click the Add button. To delete an AutoText entry, select it in the list and click the Delete button.

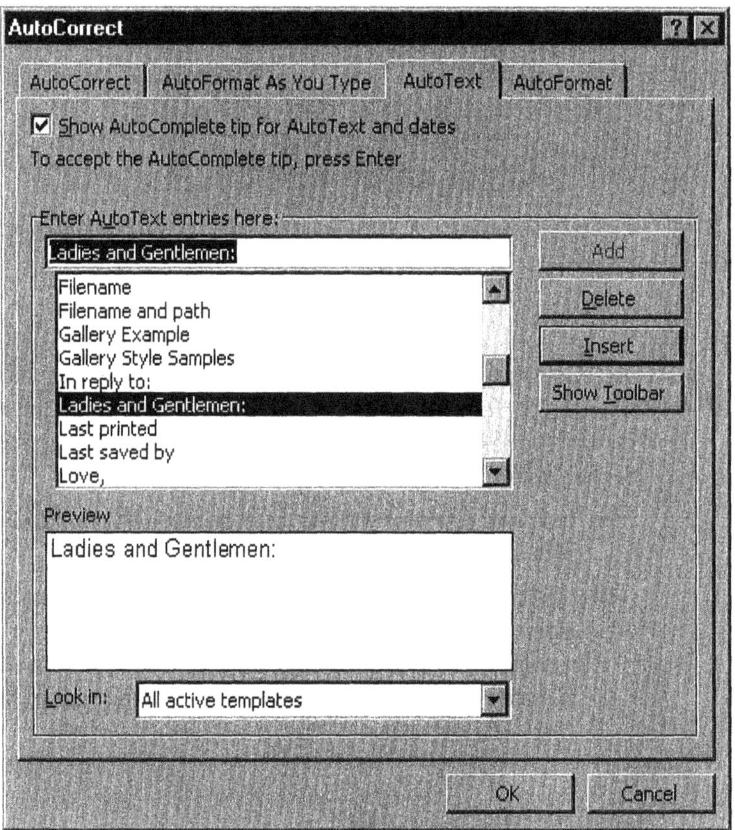

Figure 7-9: Use the AutoCorrect dialog's AutoText tab to create and modify shortcuts to many different types of text entries.

In your document, you can insert items from the AutoText list in either of two ways:

- **AutoText toolbar.** Click the Show Toolbar button on the AutoText tab (or choose View | Toolbars | AutoText) to show the AutoText toolbar (see Figure 7-10). Any time you need an AutoText entry, position the cursor in your document where you want the insertion made, then click All Entries on the AutoText toolbar. A list of categories drops down; choose a category, then choose an entry from the list that appears.

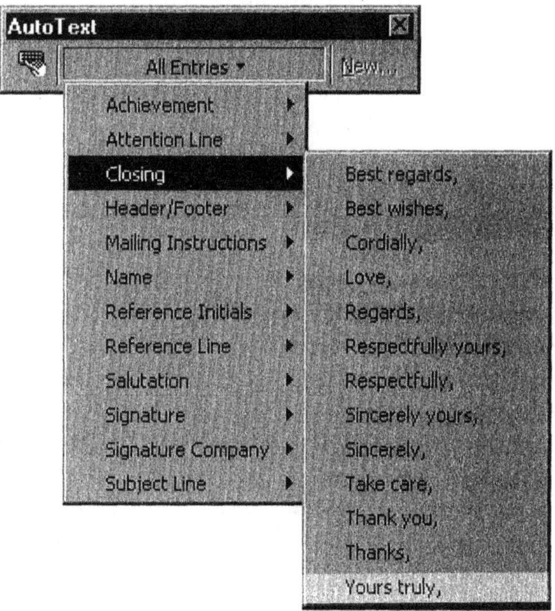

Figure 7-10: You may insert any of your AutoText entries by choosing from the AutoText toolbar.

- **AutoComplete.** Check the check box at the top of the AutoText dialog to enable AutoComplete. When AutoComplete is enabled, any time you type the first several characters of an AutoText entry, AutoComplete guesses what you're trying to type and displays a tip box (see Figure 7-11). To accept AutoComplete's suggestion, press Enter; to reject it, just keep typing.

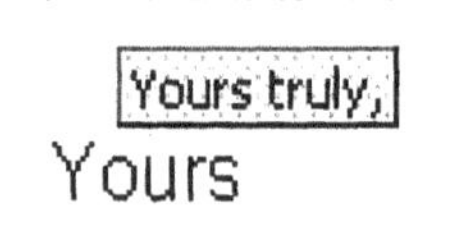

Figure 7-11: Press Enter to accept changes suggested in an AutoComplete tip.

Note that the number of characters you must type before AutoComplete kicks in varies. In some cases, you need type only the first four characters. In other cases, you must type enough of the word or phrase for AutoComplete to distinguish what you're typing from among several possibilities in the list. For example, you must type "Best w" before AutoComplete suggests "Best wishes." Until you type the "w," AutoComplete must wait to see whether you're aiming for "Best wishes" or "Best regards."

Checking Spelling & Grammar

Spell checking is a great benefit and also a trap. The trap is that sometimes you may pay too little attention to spelling when writing or reviewing your document because you know you'll spell-check it later. As you know if that trap has ever caught you, spell-checkers are terrific at locating obviously misspelled words, but incapable of discovering when you've used the wrong word—"to" for "two," "your" for "you're," "lose" for "loose," and so on.

That's why Word's grammar-checking—which works just like its spell-checker—is so important. For casual correspondence, you may not care whether you've ended a sentence with a preposition, or split an infinitive. But the grammar checker is also quite adept at using the structure and context of a sentence to determine when you've used the wrong word. Grammar checking is great when you're unsure of your grammar, but just as important as an adjunct to spell-checking.

Word's spell-checking and grammar-checking can both do their thing on the fly as you type, or on demand. You'll learn both methods in the next few pages.

Fixing Spelling & Grammar as You Go

To instruct Word to check your spelling and grammar automatically as you type, choose Tools | Options to open the Options dialog, then choose the Spelling & Grammar tab (see Figure 7-12). There you'll find check boxes for Check spelling as you type and Check grammar as you type, along with a variety of other options.

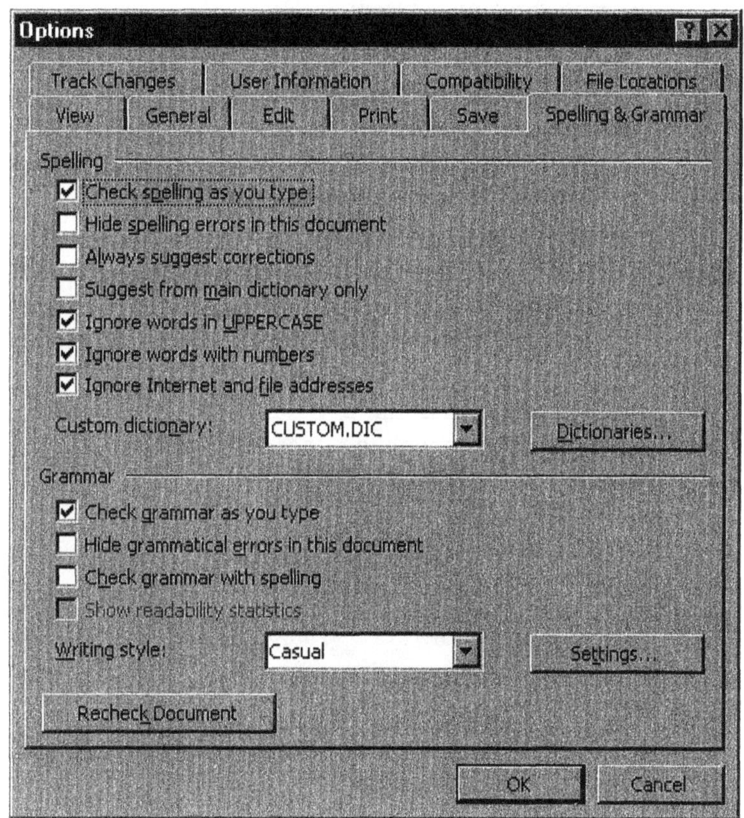

Figure 7-12: Control how and what Word checks by making choices on the Spelling & Grammar tab of Word's Options dialog.

If you've checked these check boxes, as you type Word automatically runs a red zigzag underline beneath words and phrases whose spelling and/or grammar are suspect. If you don't want the word or phrase corrected, just ignore the underline; it doesn't show up in print. To solicit Word's help with fixing the spelling or grammar of a zigzag-underlined item, right-click it. A context menu (see Figure 7-13) opens, suggesting alternatives (in bold, if any suggestions are available) to the item. From the context menu, you can:

- Replace the zigzag-underlined item with a suggested alternative by clicking on an alternative.
- Instruct Word to stop interpreting the underlined item as an error by choosing Ignore All. Word will no longer zigzag underline the word anywhere it appears in the document.
- Apply other options from the Spelling and Grammar dialog (see the next section, "Spell & Grammar Checking On Demand") by clicking Spelling or Grammar (one of the two options appears on the context menu, depending upon the nature of the error).

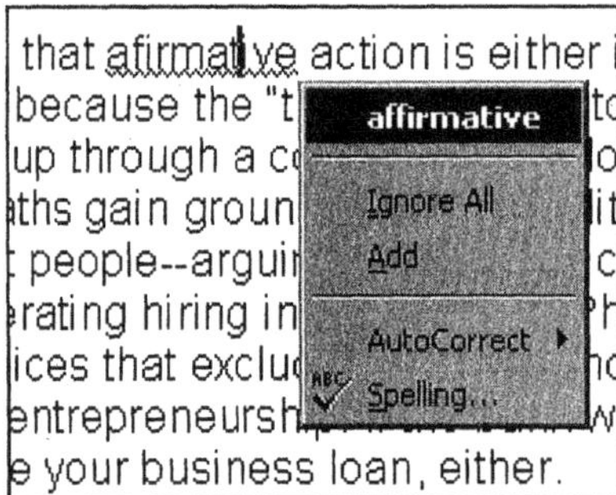

Figure 7-13: To fix spelling and grammar on-the-fly, right-click items Word underlines with a zigzag.

FYI: Tell Word Which Grammar Matters

Different writers, and different types of documents, require different levels of grammatical precision. For example, in a letter to a client or customer, you may care whether you've properly hyphenated compound words; in a letter to your Uncle Sal, you may not (besides, Uncle Sal wouldn't know the difference).

To help Word decide how strictly to watch the grammar in your writing, open the Spelling & Grammar tab of the Options dialog, then click the Settings button to open the Grammar Settings dialog. At the top of the dialog, you'll find a list on which you can select a Writing style to tell Word what general sorts of grammar rules to apply. Beneath the Writing style is a complete list of the grammar and style errors Word can identify. By checking the check box for an item in the list, you tell Word to spot such errors; by leaving a check box blank, you tell Word not to be picky about the error.

At the bottom of the Grammar Settings dialog appear three lists for controlling how Word treats three common punctuation policies. By picking from each list, you may instruct Word to enforce a rigid policy for each (for example, to require that final series comma, a.k.a. the Harvard comma), or to ignore these issues so you can apply your own judgment.

Spell & Grammar Checking On Demand

To spell-check (and, optionally, grammar-check) a document, click the Spelling and Grammar button on the Standard toolbar or choose Tools | Spelling and Grammar. The Spelling and Grammar dialog opens (see Figure 7-14), showing the first detected mistake following the edit cursor position. (You needn't go to the top of a document before starting the spell-check; if you begin in the middle of a document, the spell-check begins there, checks through the end of the document, then jumps to the top of the document and continues checking until it's come full-circle.)

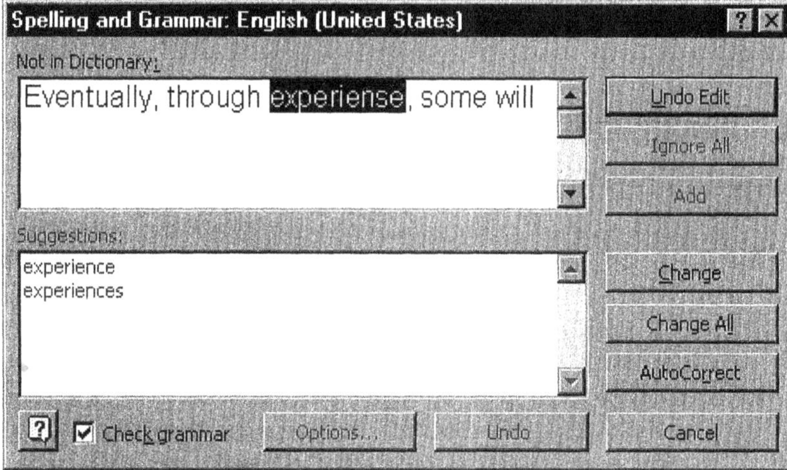

Figure 7-14: Use the Spelling and Grammar dialog to choose how (or whether) Word fixes errors it finds.

If you want Word to check both grammar and spelling, make sure that the check box at the bottom of the dialog, Check grammar, is checked. If you usually want to check grammar and spelling together, click Options on the Spelling and Grammar dialog and make sure Check grammar with spelling is checked in the dialog that appears. If you do that, the Check grammar check box on the Spelling and Grammar dialog is checked by default, but you can uncheck it any time you don't want grammar checked along with spelling.

Two boxes appear in the dialog. The top box shows the error Word has found; the box's label changes to describe the type of error found—Capitalization, Not in Dictionary, and so on. The bottom box shows corrections Word suggests, if Word can come up with any. For each error located, you can do any of the following:

- Select one of the suggestions and click the Change button to replace the error with the suggestion (or Change All to replace all instances of the error in the document with the replacement), then move ahead to the next error. (If no suggestions appear, the error is such that Word can't guess what the correction might be.)
- Click the Ignore All button to ignore this particular error throughout the document. Note that Ignore All doesn't affect variations of the same word. If "Saab" is picked out as a mistake and you choose Ignore All, Word no longer considers "Saab" an error in this document, but continues to hit on "Saabs" or "Saab's" as errors.

- Click the Ignore button to ignore this particular instance of the error but to still identify the same word as an error if it comes up elsewhere in the document.
- Click on the error in the top box and edit it to correct it, then click the Change button to replace the error with your correction (or Change All to replace all instances of the error in the document with your correction) then move ahead to the next error.

Fast Track

After choosing a suggestion or typing/editing a change, but before clicking Change, you can click the AutoCorrect button on the Spelling and Grammar dialog to add the error and its correction to the AutoCorrect list. Word can then fix that mistake automatically any time you commit it in the future. See "Using Word's AutoCorrect Features" earlier in this chapter.

- Click the Add button to add the error to the dictionary so that it will no longer be identified as an error in this or any other documents using the same dictionary. Add is a good choice when the word is just a name you may type often, but one Word doesn't recognize.

After you've spell-checked a document, Word remembers the words and phrases it thought were errors but you told it to Ignore. The next time you run the spell-checker, Word will ignore those errors automatically.

Finding & Using Synonyms

Word includes a built-in thesaurus to help you write more effectively. Using the thesaurus, you can find synonyms or antonyms to many words to vary the vocabulary in your document or to apply a more interesting (or more descriptive) word than the first word you thought of. Judicious application of a thesaurus can make your writing more colorful (bright, vivid, brilliant, resplendent, cool . . .).

To find a synonym or antonym, position the edit cursor anywhere within the word for which you want a synonym or antonym. Choose Tools | Language | Thesaurus to open the Thesaurus dialog (see Figure 7-15). In the dialog, use the list on the left to choose from among the various Meanings of the selected word. In the list on the right, a list of synonyms to that meaning appears. (To see a list of antonyms on the right, choose Antonyms from the Meanings list.) Choose a synonym or antonym from the Replace with . . . list, and click the Replace button to replace the selected word with the synonym or antonym.

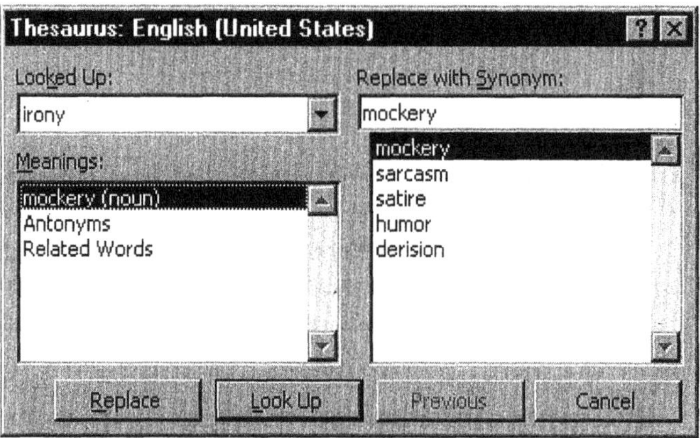

Figure 7-15: Use Word's Thesaurus to pick a word that's better . . . improved . . . superior . . . more suitable . . . .

Finding & Replacing Text & Formatting

Word's find and replace capabilities enable you not only to locate specific text anywhere within your document and replace it with different text of your choosing, but also to locate and replace formatting—for example, you could replace any underlining in your document with italics, or make all instances of a selected word **bold.** Perhaps most important, you can find and replace instances of a style, so you can replace one style with another everywhere it's applied in the document.

Fast Track

Three items on Word's Edit menu—Find, Replace, and Go To—all open the same dialog, Find and Replace, although each opens to a different tab. Choosing Edit | Replace is the quickest option for the task at hand, since that goes straight to the Replace tab. But in practice, you can use any of the three ways to open the dialog, then just choose the tab you want.

To use find and replace, begin by opening the Find and Replace dialog (choose Edit | Replace). When you first open the tab shown in Figure 7-16, only the top two text boxes show, and the tab features a button labeled More. You can perform very simple text replacement operations with the basic tab, or click More to reveal advanced options. (If you reveal options with the More button, clicking the Less button hides them again.)

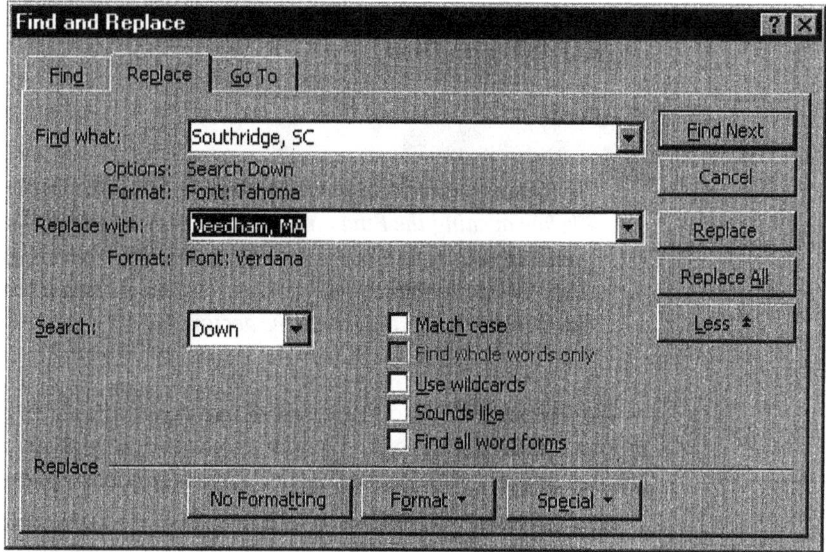

Figure 7-16: Click the More button to reveal all of the Replace tab's options.

The Find and Replace dialog has three tabs: Find, Replace, and Go To. The Find tab is used simply for finding stuff without changing it; you use Find exactly as you use the Find portions of the Replace tab, which you're about to learn. (To learn about the Go To tab, see Chapter 3, "Getting Started With Word.")

To find and replace text only, click in Find what and type the exact text you want replaced. Then click in Replace with and type the replacement. Click Find Next; Word locates the first instance it can find of the Find what text, and stops there.

To then handle the replacement, you may:

- Click Replace to replace the text and automatically jump to the next instance Word can find.

- Click the Replace All button to instruct Word to replace every instance of the text found in the document without prompting you again.
- Click Find Next to leave the current instance of the Find what text unchanged and move on to the next.

Note that when you replace text this way, the changes do not affect formatting in any way—the replacement is formatted exactly as the original was. Capitalization is ignored when finding the word—if you type "John" in Find what?, Word finds John, john, and JOHN. When replacing, Word attempts to capitalize the replacement text as the original was capitalized.

Fast Track

To find and replace only within a portion of a document, select the portion before opening the Find and Replace dialog. Word will first perform the find and replace within the selection only. When finished with the selection, Word displays a dialog asking whether you want to continue finding and replacing for the rest of the document.

To perform more sophisticated searching and replacing, click the More button on the Replace tab. The tab expands to reveal advanced search/ replace options you enable by checking their check boxes. For example:

- Check the check box for Match case to force Word to find only words that match the text *and* the precise capitalization of the entry in Find what. If the entry in Find what is John, Word finds John but not john or JOHN. Also, when this option is checked, the replacement is inserted exactly as you typed it, with no changes to its capitalization. Using Match case, you can easily repair a capitalization error throughout the document.
- Check the check box for Find whole words only to prevent Word from finding the Find what text when it is part of another word. For example, if Find what is "John," Word finds "John" but not "Johnny" or "John's."

Fast Track

Check the Find all word forms box to instruct Word to find not only the word in Find what, but also other forms of the same word, and to replace with the appropriate form of the word in Replace with. For example, if you replace run with walk and have the Find all word forms check box checked, Word replaces run with walk, ran with walked, running with walking, and so on.

For this to work, of course, the Find what and Replace with entries must both be the same part of speech. While this is a powerful option, it's a tricky one. Use it sparingly, and proof carefully after using it. Using the grammar checker will help you locate any errors you may inadvertently create by using this option.

The Format and Special buttons at the bottom of the dialog let you find and replace formatting and special characters. You can find and replace formatting or special characters wherever they occur, or you can use formatting or special characters to modify a text-replacement operation. For example:

- To replace underlining with *italic*, click in the Find what box, click the Format button, choose Font, and choose the underline formatting in the Font dialog. Then click in the Replace with box and follow the same steps to put italic in the Replace with box. (Observe that text appears beneath each box to describe formatting you're finding or replacing.)
- To replace the phrase Misty Jones in Arial font with Mr. James in Courier, type Misty Jones in Find what and then click Format | Font to choose Arial. In Replace with, type Mr. James and click Format to choose Courier font for the Replace with box. Word will find Misty Jones when that text is set in Arial, but ignore it when it's in another font. When you choose to replace, the replacement will be Mr. James in Courier font.

Walk Through: Replace

Follow the steps below to practice replacing text.

1. Create a new document based on the Elegant Resume.dot (in the Other Documents tab of the Templates).
2. Choose Edit|Replace.
   The Find and Replace dialog opens, with the Replace tab showing.
3. In Find what, type **Southridge, SC**.
4. In Replace with, type **Needham, MA**.
5. Click Replace All.
   All instances of Southridge, SC are replaced. Can you find examples of Southridge that weren't replaced, because they didn't include "SC"?
6. Clear all text from Find what, and leave the edit cursor there.
7. Choose Format|Font to open the Font dialog.
8. Choose Italic in Font style, and click OK to close the Font dialog.
9. Repeat the gist of steps 6, 7, and 8 to clear the Replace with box and put bold italic formatting there.
10. Click Replace All.
    All italic text in the document becomes bold italic.
11. Click in the Find what box, and click the No Formatting button to clear the formatting instructions from Find what.
12. In Replace with, type **Needham**.
13. Click in the Replace with box, and click the No Formatting button to clear the formatting instructions.
14. Choose Format|Highlight to add a highlighting instruction to Replace with.
15. Click Replace All.
    Needham is highlighted throughout the document.

Repeating & Copying Formatting

Creating and applying styles really is the best way to apply the same formatting to various text blocks spread throughout your document. But in case the need arises, you should be aware that Word offers two ways to quickly copy formatting.

The first way, Repeat, works sort of like Undo in reverse. When you press the Repeat key (F4, or Ctrl+y) Word repeats the last action you performed. Repeat may be most useful when you need to format separate paragraphs the same way throughout a document. Format the first paragraph as desired, then move the edit cursor to the next paragraph requiring the same formatting and press Repeat. You can use Repeat to repeat a single formatting operation—applying a style, a font, a font size, and so on.

The second method, Format Painter, copies all of the formatting from one block to another. It's less convenient than Repeat, but while Repeat can repeat only a single formatting instruction at a time, Format painter copies all of the formatting instructions—style, font, font size, attributes, and paragraph formatting—from one block to another. To use Format Painter, select the text whose format you want to copy, then click the Format Painter button on the Standard toolbar; the pointer becomes a paintbrush. Point to the text you want formatted, and click (to format the whole paragraph) or click and drag (to format a selection within the paragraph, or multiple paragraphs).

Assembling & Printing Mailings

When mailing is your object, Word provides two great ways to help you.

First, when all you want to do is print a few envelopes or format some mailing labels, Word provides the Envelopes and Labels dialog (Tools | Envelopes and Labels). The dialog has two tabs: Click the Envelopes tab (see Figure 7-17) to choose an envelope size and type the address, or click the Labels tab to choose a label size and style and supply the address. The Envelopes and Labels dialog saves you the trouble of defining the page layout for envelopes and labels, which can be a tricky proposition.

Fast Track

On each tab in the Envelopes and Labels dialog, an Address Book button appears. Click the button to quickly copy names and addresses from your Outlook Address Book.

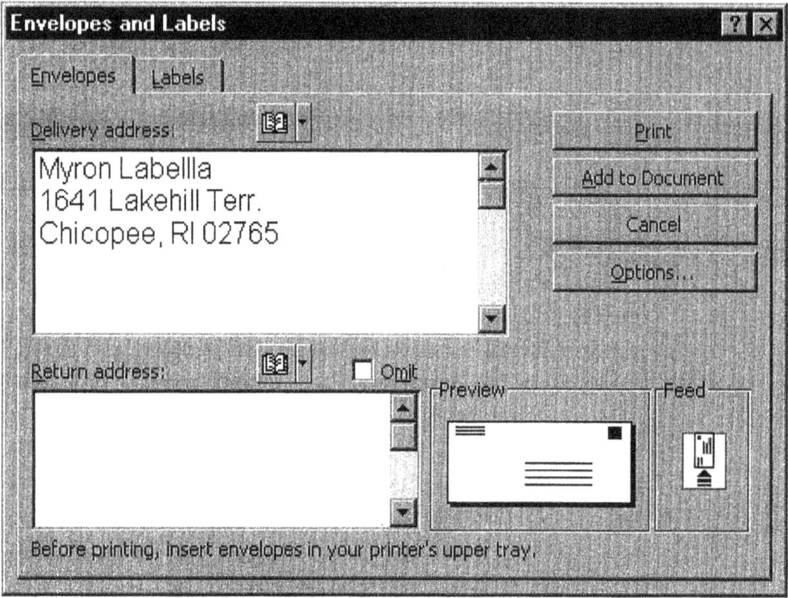

Figure 7-17: The Envelopes and Labels dialog makes quick work of creating and formatting addressed materials.

For more complex mailing projects, Word offers *mail merge* facilities. Mail merge, as you may already know, is a word processor's way of automatically combining a document—a form letter or other document intended for multiple recipients—with a file of names and addresses to crank out a separate document for each addressee, ready to mail. Mail merge is a four-step job. You must:

1. Create the form letter or other document.
2. Choose the *data source*, the file of addresses or other information you want plugged into the document.
3. Compose the document, inserting *fields* where mail merge will plug in information from the data source.
4. Instruct Word to run its mail merge routine to produce the final documents by plugging each entry from the data source into a separate copy of the document.

Word 97 provides a Mail Merge Helper—which is sort of like a Wizard, only not quite as helpful as a Wizard—to take you through these steps. To use the Helper, choose Tools | Mail Merge. The Mail Merge Helper opens, as shown in Figure 7-18. You can call on the helper at any point while working on a mail merge document—even when you started without its help. (In fact, after many of the actions you perform on the Mail Merge Helper dialog, the dialog disappears. If you need more help from it, just reopen it.)

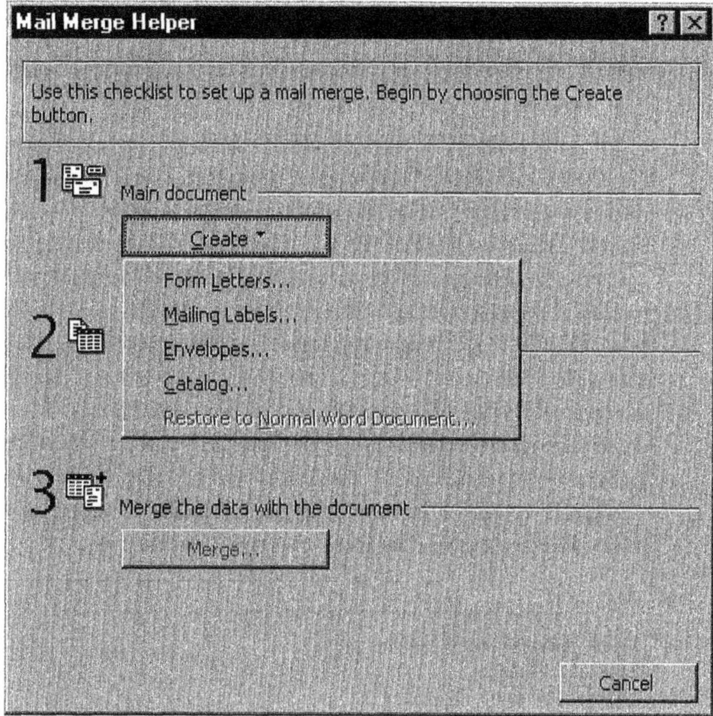

Figure 7-18: The Mail Merge Helper takes you through the steps of merging a mailing list with a document.

To create your mail merge document, click the Create button. A list of different types of mail merge documents—Form Letter, Labels, and so on—drops down. Choose the type that best matches what you want to create.

For the data source, Word can use a variety of different types of data files. Perhaps most importantly, Outlook's Address Book is available as a data source for Word's mail merge, so that you can automatically address Word form letters, envelopes, or labels to the folks in your Outlook Address book.

Click the Get Data button in the Mail Merge help to display a list of options for the data source. Then choose:

- Create Data Source to display a dialog you use to type your data now.
- Open Data Source to open an existing Word data file (one you created previously with Create Data Source).
- Use Address Book to use an Outlook Address Book as the data source.

After choosing the data source, you're ready to compose and edit the form letter. Click the Edit button in the Create Document section of the Mail Merge Helper. The document appears, along with the Mail Merge toolbar. Enter the text of the form letter and format it as you wish.

In the document where you want the Mail Merge data plugged in, position the edit cursor where you want the data to go, then click the Insert Merge Field button on the Mail Merge toolbar. A list of fields—for example, First name, Last Name, and so on—drops down. The list includes all types of information included in the data source you selected. Choose the field from the list. The name of the field appears in the document, surrounded by double carats (<< >>), as shown in Figure 7-19.

When the form letter is complete, click the Merge button on the Mail Merge Helper or choose Tools | Merge Documents.

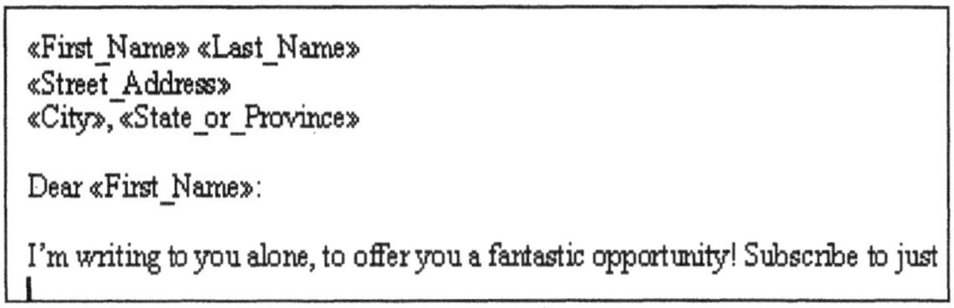

«First_Name» «Last_Name»
«Street_Address»
«City», «State_or_Province»

Dear «First_Name»:

I'm writing to you alone, to offer you a fantastic opportunity! Subscribe to just

Figure 7-19: Mail merge data fields appear surrounded by double carats (<< >>).

Moving On

Whither now? That's a question I can't answer, since I don't know which Office 97 applications you plan to use (nobody uses 'em all—I don't care what Microsoft says).

If you have a hankering to do some Internet authoring, you may want to jump ahead to Chapter 22, "Office 97 & the Internet," to learn how you can use Word to compose Web pages, send e-mail, and link Word documents to online text and data.

Or you can jump ahead to another Office application—beginning, of course, with the first chapter in the section covering that application.

Of course, failing other plans, you can always stay with the program, and move straight ahead to Chapter 8, "Getting Started With PowerPoint," the first of three chapters about the presentation-maker PowerPoint. In fact, there's some logic to doing so, since PowerPoint is the most Word-like of the other Office 97 applications. In fact, if you've already grappled with most of this Word section, you'll find PowerPoint refreshingly simple. Take a peek.

SECTION III

PowerPoint

8

Getting Started With PowerPoint

There's no business like show business. And make no mistake, PowerPoint is a show-biz program—Office 97's own Flo Ziegfeld.

Think about it: If all you wanted was some boring old transparencies to help your audience get a nice afternoon nap, you could easily write 'em up in Word, and save yourself the learning curve and hard drive space a presentation program demands. But making an effective presentation means sparking audience neurons with audio-visual stimuli, and it also means making the presenter (who I assume is you, but needn't be) look polished and professional, a class act. PowerPoint helps you create and perform such shows.

Learning to use PowerPoint is a lot like learning to cook. There are so many possible projects, if you set out to understand it all at once, you'll quickly turn in your spatula. However, creating any one specific show—or recipe—is a pretty straightforward activity, a step-by-stepper. You'll find the whole topic easier to deal with if you first gain an overview of PowerPoint's capabilities and starting points, then deal with the details of show-making. That's what this chapter offers.

In this quickie chapter, you'll pick up an understanding of what you can create with PowerPoint and of how you may present each type of show PowerPoint produces. You'll also learn the ropes of getting PowerPoint going and getting around within it. Armed with these basics, you'll be well prepared to move on to Chapter 9, "Designing Presentations," where you'll learn how to produce your show. In Chapter 10, "Livening Up Your Presentations," you'll learn how to enhance your show with advanced features.

Before beginning, note that you learn to perform several activities in this chapter from PowerPoint's Standard toolbar (see Figure 8-1). PowerPoint comes preconfigured to display the Standard toolbar, but if you don't see its buttons on your display, open PowerPoint and choose View | Toolbars | Standard.

Figure 8-1: Use PowerPoint's Standard toolbar to perform many of the activities in this chapter.

Creating a New Show

Which comes first in a PowerPoint show—the words or the slides on which the words appear? Well, in practice, they evolve in tandem.

- You typically begin by jotting down some, but not all, of the words.
- Then you format those words in their slides.
- Next, you expand and edit the text in the slides.
- Thereupon you tweak the look of the slides some more or add new ones.

Unless you're a frighteningly well-structured human being, creating a PowerPoint show usually requires a lot of hopping back and forth between dealing with text—or rather, content—and dealing with appearance.

When you open PowerPoint from the Windows Start menu (choose Programs | Microsoft PowerPoint), a special sort of startup dialog opens automatically, as shown in Figure 8-2. On the dialog, you may select any of the three radio buttons under Create a new presentation to start a new show; the details of all three approaches are covered in Chapter 9, "Designing Presentations." By selecting the bottom radio button, Open an existing presentation, you bring up the Open dialog so you can open an existing presentation file. (You learn how to use the Open dialog in "Opening Existing Presentations," in the next chapter.)

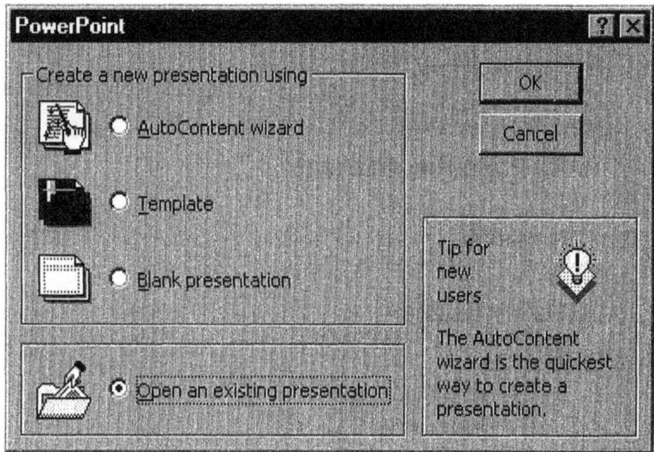

Figure 8-2: Get productive quickly by choosing a starting point from PowerPoint's handy all-purpose startup dialog.

Although the startup dialog in Figure 8-2 may help you get started on the day's PowerPoint session, there's nothing on it that you can't also do from PowerPoint's regular menus. On the dialog, you may click Cancel, or press Esc, to close the dialog and begin working in PowerPoint any way you wish.

But while you needn't know all the words to get started, you do need to address the overall look and structure of your presentation before trying to nail down the details of content and formatting. PowerPoint has two ways of helping you accomplish this:

- AutoContent Wizard
- Templates

Whichever way you get started, you wind up with what I call a *proto-presentation*, a collection of fully formatted slides populated mainly with suggestions for content where your words must go (see Figure 8-3). You complete your presentation by replacing the suggestions with your own text and by changing the slide design or adding, moving, or removing slides however your fancies dictate.

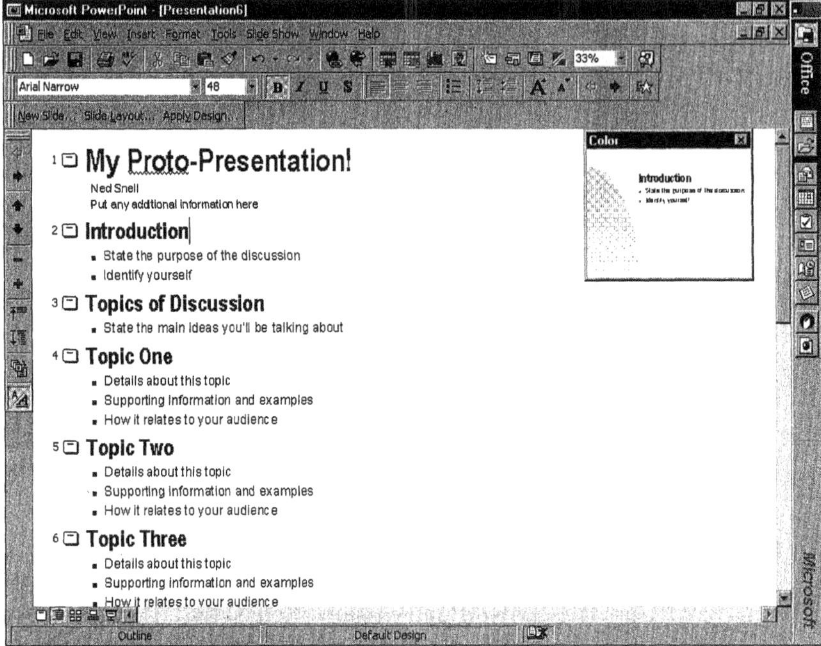

Figure 8-3: When you use the AutoContent Wizard or a template, you get a proto-presentation *with sample text you will replace with your own content.*

In the next few pages, you learn how to create your proto-presentation with the AutoContent Wizard or with a template. Following this section, you learn how to turn your proto-presentation into your own show, beginning with Editing Text.

Jump-Starting With AutoContent Wizard

When you open PowerPoint, you can jump straight into the AutoContent Wizard by choosing it from the opening dialog. If you've already cleared the opening dialog, but want to use the AutoContent Wizard, choose File | New to open the New Presentation dialog. In the dialog, click the Presentations tab, then double-click the file icon for AutoContent Wizard.pwz.

However you open it, the AutoContent Wizard starts you off with the dialog shown in Figure 8-4. Beginning with this dialog, you'll click your way through just five dialogs to tell the Wizard a little about the presentation you're trying to create. To advance to each new dialog, click the Next button. To go back at any time to dialogs you've already visited, click Back. Or, instead of using Next and Back, you can jump directly to any dialog in the Wizard by clicking an item in the index that always appears along the left side of the dialog.

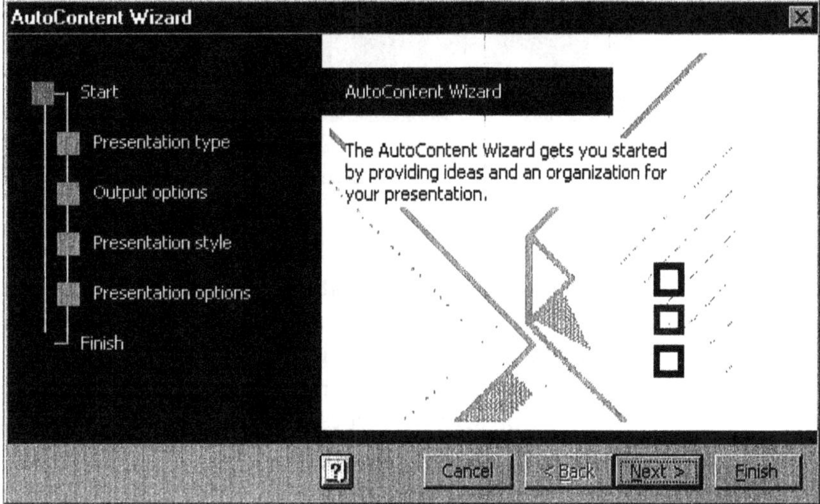

Figure 8-4: The AutoContent Wizard helps you start a new presentation.

When finished filling in the dialogs (described next), move to the Finish dialog, then click the Finish button there. The proto-presentation opens in PowerPoint, ready for you to begin editing the text.

Presentation Type

In the Presentation Type dialog, you choose a presentation on which yours will be modeled. I've chosen the Sales/Marketing type of presentation, as Figure 8-5 shows. The presentation you choose need not be exactly what you want to create—you'll edit the results later. But the more closely your choices on this dialog match what you want to produce, the less work you'll have to do later.

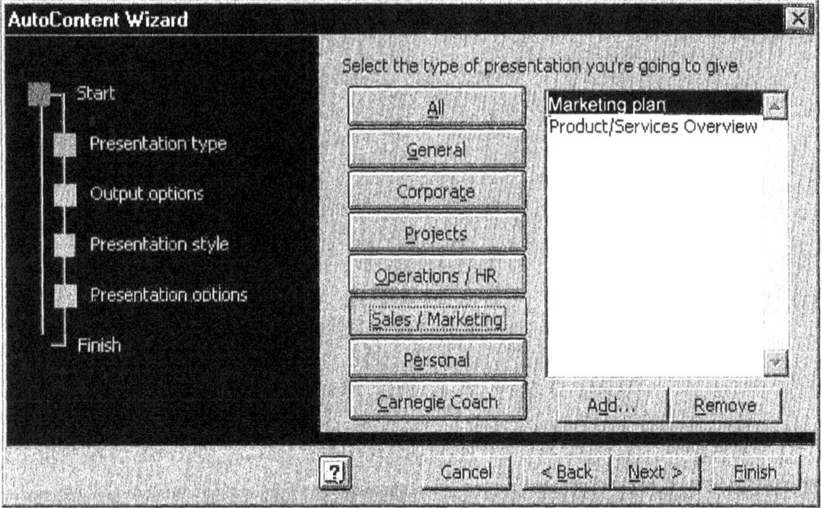

Figure 8-5: In the AutoContent Wizard, you select a Presentation Type.

Begin by clicking the button that most closely matches the general type of presentation you plan to create. After you click a button, the list in the dialog offers a collection of different presentations of that type. By selecting Sales/Marketing, the Marketing Plan and Product/Services Overview presentation types appear. (The All button lists all of the presentations available from the other buttons combined. The Carnegie Coach button lists presentations based on Dale Carnegie sales training techniques.) Choose your best match from the list, then click Next to move ahead.

Output Options

In the Output Options dialog, click one of the radio buttons to choose how the presentation will be shown. The Wizard chooses some of the formatting options and other elements based on the choice you make here. More importantly, the Wizard uses your choice on this screen to determine which options to offer on the next dialogs.

Presentation Style

The Presentation Style dialog (which is not available, or necessary, if you choose Internet | Kiosk from the Output Options dialog) lets you choose from among the various methods you may use to present a show of the type you selected in Output Options.

Presentation Options

The options you see on the Presentation Options (see Figure 8-6) dialog vary, depending on the choices you made in the Output Options and Presentation Style dialogs. Typically, this dialog offers you an opportunity to create some of the text of the presentation. For example, this dialog may include text boxes for your presentation title, your name, and other information. The Wizard may use this information for creating your title slide, or for creating slide headers or footers that include the title and/or your name. Although filling in the Presentation Options dialog may make your proto-presentation more finished at the start, consider this dialog optional—it really doesn't offer anything you can't add yourself later.

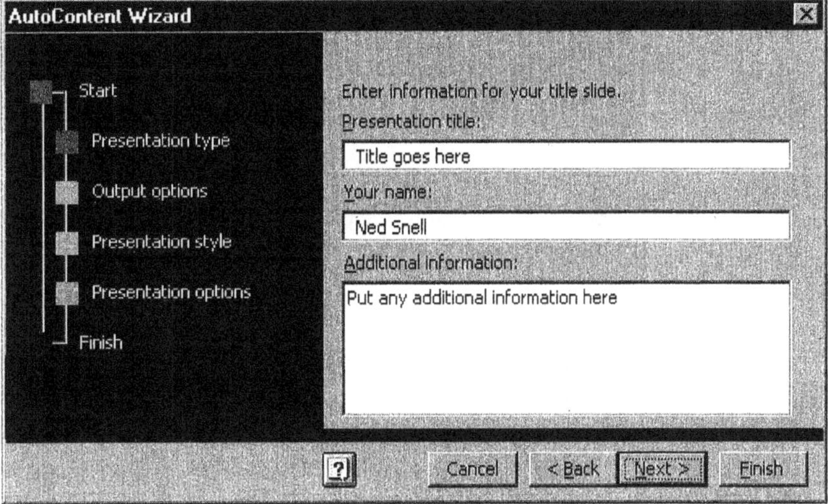

Figure 8-6: The AutoContent Wizard's Presentation options let you define your new show more specifically.

Using Templates

In case you hadn't already guessed, all the AutoContent Wizard really does is help you choose a template, add a little text to it, and select from among a few options. If you're confident in your ability to choose a template for yourself, you may want to forego the Wizard and simply create your proto-presentation by choosing a template.

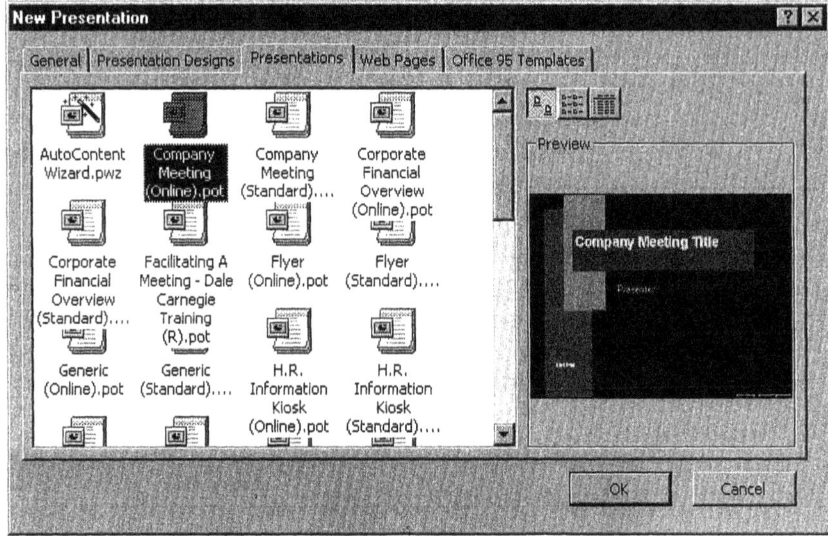

Figure 8-7: Choose File | New to see the templates you can use to create a new show.

Begin by choosing File | New. The New Presentation dialog opens, as shown in Figure 8-7. The template files—which have the filename extension .pot—are grouped into tabs:

- **General.** Typically the General tab provides only one template, Blank Presentation.pot, a very basic, no-frills design for no-frills shows.
- **Presentation Designs.** The templates in this tab are designs only—they offer no sample text or content suggestions. You may want to use one of the Presentation Designs templates when you want a template's help with slide design, but not with content.
- **Presentations.** Each template in this tab includes both slide design and suggested content. The Presentations templates not only provide you with a prebuilt design, but also give you a head start on the structure and content of your show. These are your best bet when you want a template's help with the look of your slides and with their content. Note that the Presentations templates are the same ones offered by the AutoContent Wizard. (The Wizard itself, AutoContent Wizard.pwz, also appears in the Presentations tab.)

Fast Track

The names of some of the templates in the Presentations tab include the word "Online" in parentheses. (Don't think these templates are for making Web pages—the Web page templates are in the Web pages tab.)

For each "Online" template there is another template in the Presentations tab that has the same name, except that "Online" is replaced by "Standard." The online template includes features that can be used only if the show will be presented electronically—for example, the template may feature on-slide buttons so the viewer can control the show interactively. The standard version omits such techno-frills so that you have the option of presenting it electronically or in print, slides, or transparencies.

- **Web Pages.** This tab includes templates you use only when you'll publish the show on the World Wide Web or on an intranet based on the Web. See Chapter 22, "Office 97 and the Internet," to learn more about these templates.
- **Office 95 Templates.** If you had PowerPoint 95 installed on your PC before you installed Office 97, your old PowerPoint 95 templates are all available from this tab. All are fully compatible with PowerPoint 97.

FYI: Taking Text From Elsewhere

If you already have an outline of your presentation typed up in Word—or if you prefer to compose your text in Word—you can easily convert that outline into slide text.

Begin by formatting your Word document. To get the best results, pick out each slide title in your Word outline and apply the style Heading 1 to it. As you work, keep in mind that slides look best when you limit the contents of each to a few lines.

When finished with your Word outline, save it, then switch to PowerPoint. Choose File|Open to display the Open dialog. In the Files of type list, choose All outlines. Navigate to the Word file containing the outline, and double-click it. The Word outline opens in PowerPoint as a new presentation, in Outline view. Each line that used the Heading 1 style is the title of a new slide.

In Chapter 21, "Collaborating & Integrating With Office 97," you'll discover other ways to move information from Word—and other Office 97 programs—into PowerPoint.

To choose a template, find one whose name suggests that it may be a close fit to what you want to produce. Remember that you won't find a perfect fit—you're going to do some editing, no matter which template you choose. But the closer your choice, the less work you'll have to do later. Click the icon for a template to see a preview of its appearance in the Preview pane.

When you've selected the template you want, click OK. What happens next depends on which tab you chose from:

- If you chose from the Presentations tab, the first slide of the proto-presentation opens in Slide view. You may begin replacing the template's content suggestions with your own content, as described in "Editing Text" later in this chapter.
- If you chose from the Presentation Designs tab, or chose Blank Presentation from the General tab, the Slide Layout dialog opens so you can select a layout for the first slide in the presentation. Choose one that includes all of the types of objects—text, pictures, and so on—you intend to include on the first slide. After you make your choice, the proto-presentation opens, containing one simple slide in the layout you selected. You may build your presentation from there by adding slides, text, a background, and so on.

FYI: Slides Are Populated With *Placeholders*

Each object that can appear in a PowerPoint slide appears in its own *placeholder*, an invisible box. Different kinds of objects have different placeholders with different properties—there are text placeholders, picture placeholders, chart placeholders, and so on.

Placeholders enable you to easily rearrange and compose the various objects in a slide, as you'll learn in Chapter 9, "Designing Presentations." If you've read Chapter 6, "Adding Pictures, Tables & Borders," you'll soon notice that text placeholders in PowerPoint work just like Word's text boxes and that other placeholders behave like picture outlines.

In addition to the text placeholders that hold the sample text, some of the Presentations templates include other types of placeholders. For example, the first slide of the template Product Overview includes a picture placeholder for a photo of your product. When a template you choose includes such placeholders, you may fill them with what they're designed to hold, or delete them.

Saving Presentations

Of course, as you work on your presentation, you need to save it from time to time. If you attempt to exit PowerPoint or close Windows without first saving your work, PowerPoint displays a dialog asking if you want to save the file; click Yes on the dialog to open the Save As dialog (see Figure 8-8). Despite this safeguard, it's smart to save often while developing a show. You can save as soon as you create a show and any time you feel like it thereafter.

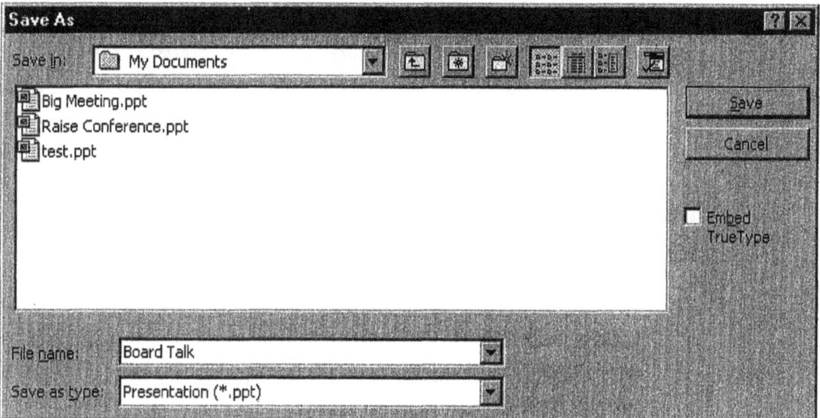

Figure 8-8: Use the Save As dialog to choose a file name and storage location for your show.

To save, click the Save button on the Standard toolbar or choose File | Save. The first time you save, the Save As dialog opens so you can give your show a name and select a folder in which to store it. After that first Save, clicking Save or choosing File | Save simply saves your file without opening a dialog.

On the Save As dialog, the Save in box at the top shows the folder in which the file will be saved; by default, that folder is your Office 97 My Documents folder, but you can drop down the Save in list to choose a different folder. The box beneath Save in shows the .ppt files that are already stored in the Save in folder.

When Save in shows the folder you want to use, click in the filename box and type a name for your presentation. Don't type the filename extension; the Save As dialog adds .ppt to the end of your filename automatically. The filename can include multiple words (Trade Show) and can be up to 255 characters long. However, the full path to the file—C:\Program Files . . . and so on—is included in the 255-character limit. As a rule, you'll find working with your files easier if you keep your filenames under 20 characters, not counting the path. Also, while some punctuation characters are permitted in filenames, some are not—so to keep your life simple, just don't use punctuation in filenames.

After supplying a filename, click Save to save the file. The Save As dialog closes, and you may return to work on the presentation.

Fast Track

To save a file in .pps format, choose PowerPoint Show (.pps) from the Save as type list.*

Choosing a View

Perhaps the most important part of dealing productively with a presentation is choosing the right *view* to work in for a given task. Throughout this PowerPoint section of the book, I'll always tell you which view works best for the task at hand.

You switch easily among the views in either of two ways. First, all views are available from the View menu on PowerPoint's menu bar. Also, a row of tiny View buttons appears in the lower-left corner of the PowerPoint window (see Figure 8-9). As with toolbar buttons, these view buttons feature tooltips—rest the pointer on a button for a moment to display a label telling you which view that button opens.

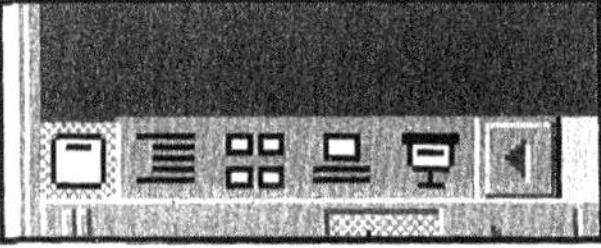

Figure 8-9: The View buttons let you switch quickly among PowerPoint's views.

In addition to the views described here, there's another, special-purpose "view" that's not included among the View buttons or in the same section of the View menu with the others: Black and White view. See "Printing Transparencies" in the next chapter to learn about Black and White view.

Slide View

Slide view is just what it sounds like. You see one slide, big and lovely, in the PowerPoint window (see Figure 8-10). The number of the slide you're viewing appears in the left end of the PowerPoint status bar at the bottom of the window.

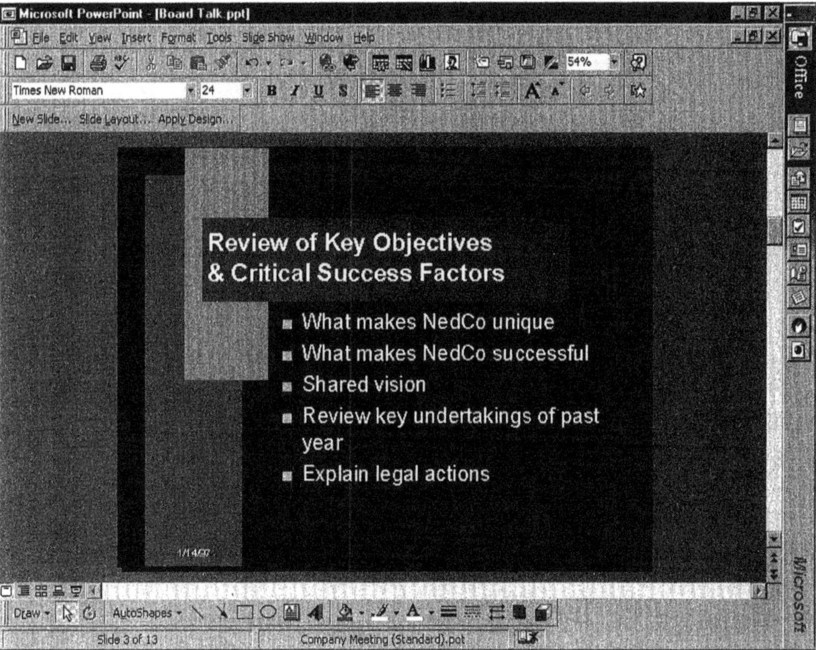

Figure 8-10: In Slide view, you work with one slide at a time.

Slide view gives you the best look at individual slides and is best suited to fine tuning the text and design of individual slides as the show nears completion. When in slide view, you can edit the text of the slide you see, edit the design and layout of that slide, and even apply some types of slide formatting—such as a new background or color scheme—to the presentation as a whole. You may also run the spelling and style checkers for the whole presentation while in Slide view.

To move from slide to slide while in Slide view, press PgDn (to advance forward in the presentation), PgUp (to move toward the beginning of the show), or scroll up or down in the show with the vertical scroll bar.

To see and work with minute details of a slide, you can increase the Zoom percentage to "zoom in" closer to the slide, magnifying its details (see Figure 8-11). Choose View | Zoom to open the Zoom dialog and choose a percentage, or drop down the Zoom box in the Standard toolbar. (The Standard toolbar appears in PowerPoint by default, but if you don't see it, choose View | Toolbars | Standard.)

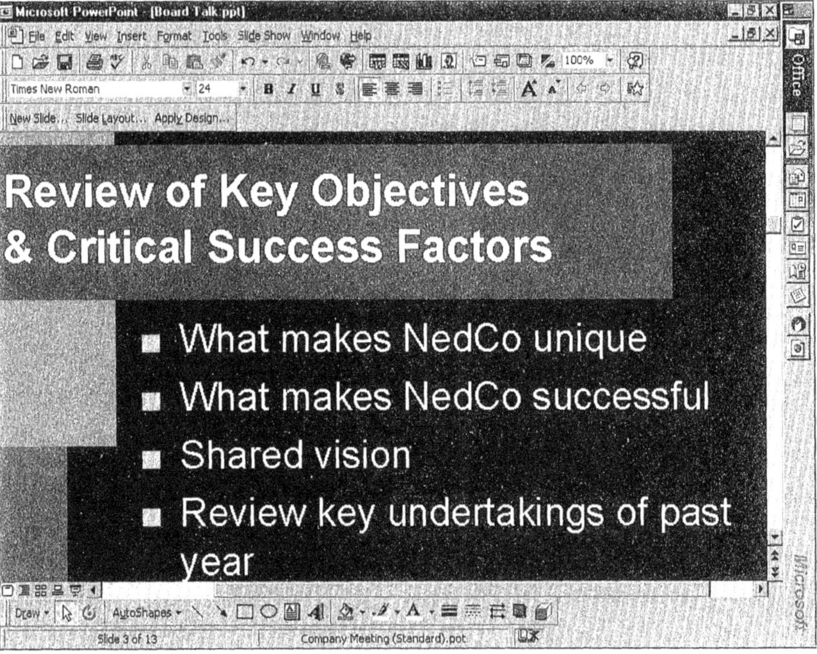

Figure 8-11: Raise the Zoom percentage to magnify the slide for detailed work.

Outline View

In Outline view, you can focus on writing and editing the text of your presentation. Outline view shows the entire presentation as a text outline (see Figure 8-12). This not only makes navigating among slides while editing text easier but also lets you evaluate the general organization and flow of your show without the distraction of the slide designs. To the left of each slide title appears the slide's number.

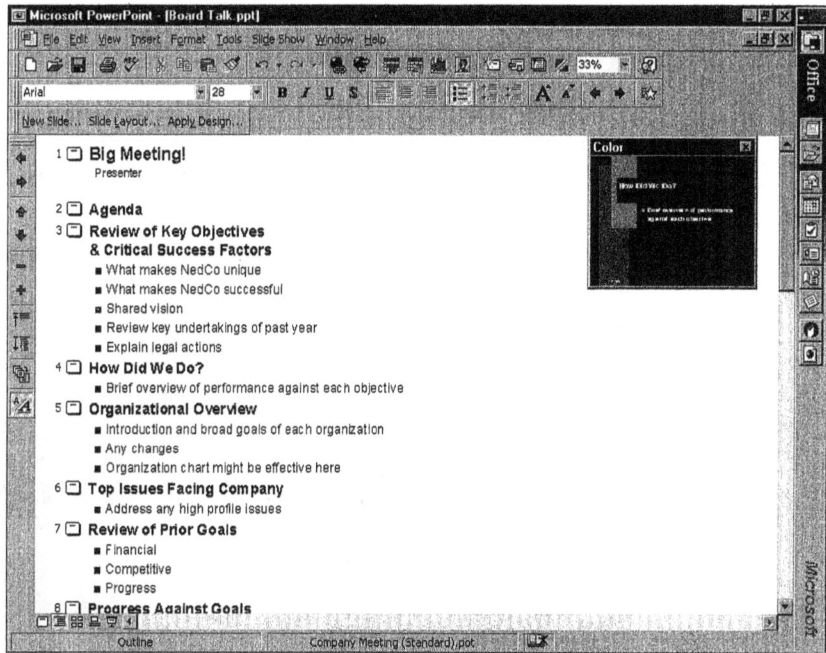

Figure 8-12: Enter, review, and organize the text of your whole show in Outline view.

Of course, Outline view doesn't completely ignore the aesthetics of your slides. First, the text in the outline appears fully formatted, exactly as it will appear on the slides, including the selected fonts, sizes, and more (everything but color). Also, the *slide miniature* appears, as Figure 8-12 shows. The slide miniature shows you a thumbnail version of the slide in which you're working in the outline.

To see the miniature for a particular slide, click the slide icon that appears right next to the slide number, or just click anywhere in the slide's text to locate the cursor there. The slide miniature shows you the slide's appearance. (If you don't want to see the slide miniature, just click its Close button, the X in the slide miniature's upper-right corner.)

Fast Track

While working in Outline view, you may instantly display any slide in Slide view by pointing to the slide's icon (between the slide number and title) and double-clicking.

Slide Sorter

Slide Sorter view (see Figure 8-13) is best applied to evaluating the structure and flow of your show and changing that structure by adding, deleting, or moving slides. The number of each slide appears beneath it.

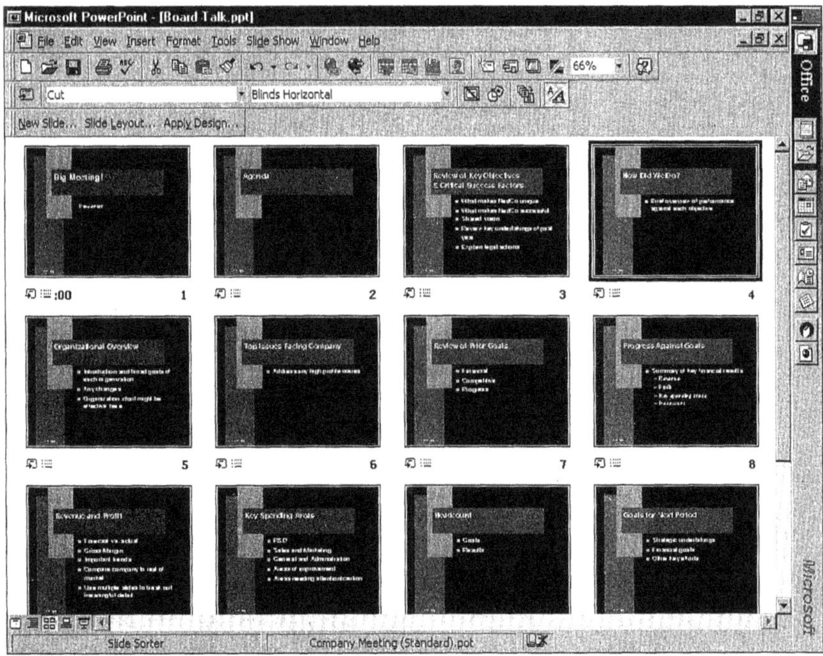

Figure 8-13: Work with the order of slides in Slide Sorter view.

You can't edit or format text or make manual slide layout changes in Slide Sorter view, although you can perform most slide formatting tasks, such as changing the background or color scheme of slides. To open any slide you see in Slide view, point to it and double-click.

The number of slides you see at one time depends upon the Zoom percentage. By default, the Zoom is set at 66%, and 12 slides appear on one full-screen window. If you increase the Zoom percentage (through the Zoom list on the Standard toolbar or by choosing View | Zoom), fewer slides appear per screen, but those that do appear are larger and easier to read. If you reduce the Zoom, more slides appear at once, but each slide is smaller.

If the Zoom you choose to work in can't show all of your slides in one screen, use the vertical scroll bar to scroll the window to see more slides.

Slide Show

The look of Slide Show view depends on whether you've configured the show as a full-screen (presenter-run or kiosk) show or as a windowed, viewer-run show. A full-screen show takes over the entire display (see Figure 8-14), hiding PowerPoint and even the Office shortcut bar. A windowed view displays the show in a window, with the Web toolbar available to help the viewer navigate.

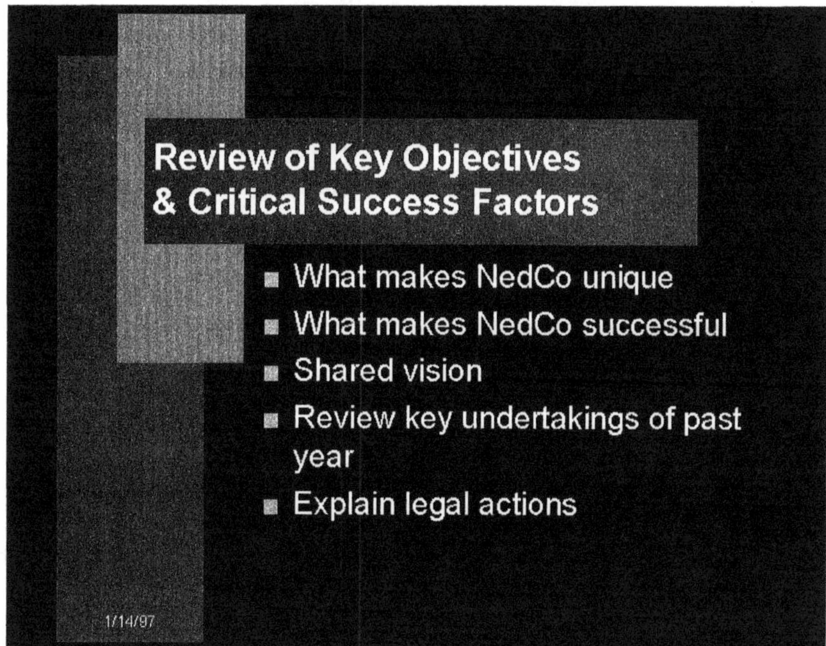

Figure 8-14: Review, rehearse, or present your show in Slide Show view.

In Slide Show view, you can step through the slides just as you would when giving the presentation (or as a viewer does in a kiosk or windowed show). This view plays two important roles, enabling you to:

- Present a show electronically.
- Evaluate and practice a show that will later be output to transparencies or slides. Slide Show view helps you ensure that your show is finished and ready to go before you prepare slides or transparencies.

You can start Slide Show view from the View menu or View buttons, like any other view. However, when you're in Slide view, or when you have selected a particular slide in Outline or Slide Sorter view, the two options work slightly differently. View | Slide Show always starts the slide show from the very first slide. The Slide Show button starts with the current slide (in Slide view) or with the selected slide (in Outline or Slide Sorter view).

When in Slide Show view, you can:

- Advance to the next slide in the show by pressing PgDn, the Down arrow key, or the Right arrow key.
- Back up to the previous slide in the show by pressing PgUp, the Up arrow key, or the Left arrow key.
- Point and click to activate any onscreen buttons or links you've created in an electronic presentation.
- Press Esc to close Slide Show view and return to the previous view.

Modifying Wizards & Templates

Substantial text editing requires *selecting* the text on which you want to work. As you probably know, you can select text in almost any Windows program—PowerPoint included—by pointing to the beginning of the selection, clicking and holding the mouse button, dragging to the end of the selection, and releasing the button. However, I recommend a different selection strategy when doing the big replacement job of changing a proto-presentation into your own show.

You can work with your text on the slides themselves (in Slide view) or in Outline view. I recommend doing most of your heavy-duty text entry and editing in Outline view, in part because text entry and editing is easier in Outline view, and also because working in Outline view helps you better manage the structure and flow of your show. Outline view also forces you to focus on the real content of your show without the distraction of the visuals. Once your text is pretty well done, you can then work with it in Slide view to fine tune its appearance.

Editing Text

To edit in Outline view, simply select and edit at will. You can work with the outline very much as you would in any word processor. To add a new item to a list, position the edit cursor at the very end of a list item line, and press Enter. To delete any line, select it and press Del.

The same selecting and editing techniques apply in Slide view—with one difference. Before you can edit text, you must click it to open the text placeholder that contains the text. Often, the text in a slide will actually appear in multiple placeholders—for example, one for the title and another for the bullets.

When you click on any text in Slide view, a hashed outline appears around the text, showing the borders of the placeholder (see Figure 8-15). The edit cursor appears within the text at roughly the spot where you pointed. Within the selected placeholder, you may select and replace text exactly as you would in Outline view. You can double-click to the right of a line to select it so you can type a replacement or delete the line. You can point and click—or use your arrow keys—to move the edit cursor within a line and make edits.

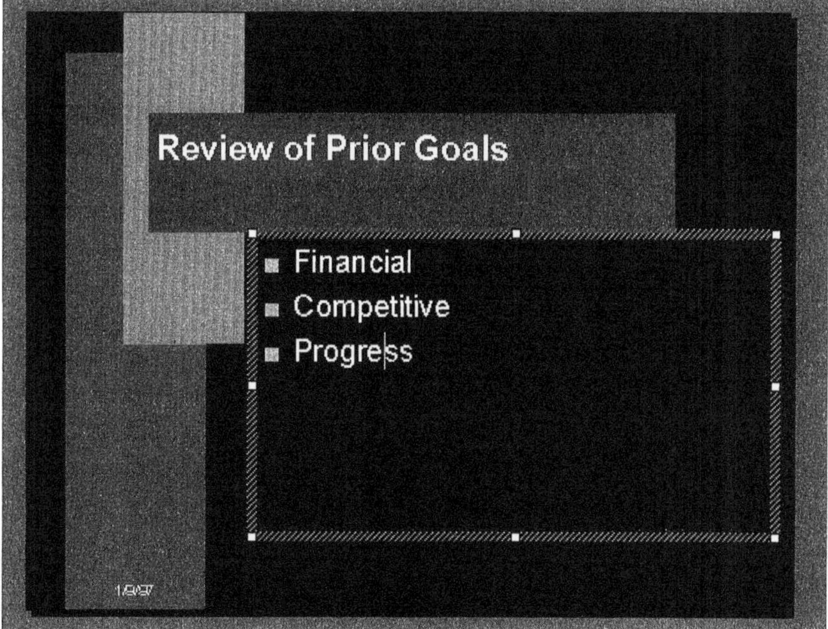

Figure 8-15: Slide text is contained in text placeholders.

When done editing the text in a placeholder, click on another text placeholder to edit its text, or simply deselect the placeholder by clicking in the empty part of the screen to the left or right of the slide.

Walk-Through: Starting a Show, Editing Text

1. Choose File|New.
   The New Presentation dialog opens.
2. Click the Presentations tab.
3. Click Marketing Plan (Standard).pot.
   A preview appears in the Preview pane.
4. Click OK.
   The first slide of the proto-presentation appears.
5. Switch to Outline view (click the Outline View button in PowerPoint's lower-left corner or choose View|Outline).
6. Point just to the right of the title, [Product Name], and double-click to select the title.
7. Type a name for your product.
8. Point to the right of the first bullet (Market Past, Present) and double-click to select it.
9. Type any new text to replace the first bullet line.
10. Click at the end of the first bullet line to position the edit cursor there, and press Enter.
    A new bullet line begins.
11. Type some bulleted text.
12. Double-click the slide icon for Slide 4 to see Slide 4 in Slide view.
13. Point to the very end of the last bullet line, and click.
    The text placeholder appears, and the edit cursor appears at the end of the line.
14. Press Enter to start a new bullet line.
15. Type some text.

Changing Text & Attributes

There's a science to the presentation and organization of text in presentations. And as pedestrian as it may seem, the pattern followed in most of the slides produced by PowerPoint's templates works—a bold, big slide title stating a main point, followed by bulleted items supporting or expanding upon that point. I alert you to this not to inhibit you, but to let you know that you're likely to get a pretty effective presentation if you stick pretty close to what the template gives you. Fiddle too much with the text formatting, and you may improve the slide—then again, you may detract from it, and in doing so, make your own show less effective than it might be.

That said, PowerPoint gives you complete control over the appearance of the text in your slides. You can choose the *font* (typeface) of text and its size, make text bold or italic, and more. You can turn lines of text into a bulleted list (or vice versa), and align text to the left side, right side, or center of the text box that contains the text. All of the controls required for this formatting are featured on the Formatting toolbar, shown in Figure 8-16. If you don't see the Formatting toolbar, choose View | Toolbars | Formatting.

Figure 8-16: Change the look of your show easily with the buttons on the Formatting toolbar.

Fast Track

In Character Formatting, next, you learn how to change the way your text looks in all of the available ways but one: color. The color of text is determined by the color scheme. See "Changing Color Schemes" in the next chapter.

You can apply character formatting—font, size, or *attributes* (bold, italic, underline, shadow)—to any group of characters you wish, from a single character, to a word, to a whole slide or group of slides.

Begin by selecting the text you want to format. Use the same selection techniques you use to edit text, in Outline or Slide view. In addition, you have a few extra ways to select when applying character formatting:

- When no text is selected, any character formatting you apply affects the whole word in which the edit cursor appears.
- To select a whole slide so that any character formatting affects all text in the slide, single-click the slide's icon in Outline view.

After making your selection, apply your desired formatting from the Formatting toolbar. To change the font and font size, drop down the Font list and select from among the fonts installed on your PC, and drop down the Font Size list to select a size for your text. (To learn more about Windows fonts, see Chapter 4, "Working With Text.")

To change the attributes of selected text, click the Bold, Underline, Italic, or Shadow button. Note that you can click any combination of these buttons to combine their effects—bold italic, italic shadowed, and so on. To remove attributes, click the button again; for example, to revert bold text to regular text, select the text and click the Bold button.

Fast Track

To quickly increase or decrease the size of selected text without fiddling with the Font Size list, click the Increase Font Size or Decrease Font Size button on the Formatting toolbar.

Paragraph Alignment & Spacing

In PowerPoint, all of the text before a paragraph break is called a *paragraph*, even though most paragraphs in slide shows are only one line long, or less. The slide title is a paragraph, and each item in a list is also a paragraph, even if the item contains only a single word.

Unlike character formatting, paragraph formatting—alignment and spacing—always affects entire paragraphs. If you select nothing before applying the formatting, the paragraph containing the edit cursor gets the formatting. If you make a selection within a paragraph, the formatting still affects the whole paragraph. If you start a selection in one paragraph and run it through several others, the formatting affects all paragraphs that have any part of them selected.

The alignment buttons on the Formatting toolbar—Left, Center, and Right—align a selected paragraph or paragraphs within their placeholder. For example, click Center to center the selected paragraph within the placeholder. Pay special attention to the fact that alignment is relative to the placeholder, not the slide as a whole. If you want to center text on the slide, you need to use the Center button to center it in the placeholder and also position the placeholder so that it is centered on the slide (see "Rearranging Placeholders" in the next chapter).

To increase or decrease the space between paragraphs, select the paragraphs whose spacing you want to modify, and click Increase Paragraph Spacing or Decrease Paragraph Spacing on the Formatting toolbar.

Bulleted Lists

PowerPoint understands that most presentations are made up mainly of slide titles followed by bulleted lists. That's why most templates and slide layouts format your show that way, and that's also why PowerPoint helps you format lists easily.

To turn any paragraph into a bulleted list item, position the edit cursor in it and click the Bullets button on the Formatting toolbar. To change a group of paragraphs into a bulleted list, run a selection from anywhere in the first paragraph to anywhere in the last, then click Bullets. (To change a bulleted item back into an ordinary paragraph, select it and click the Bullets button.)

PowerPoint supports *nested lists*, lists that contain other lists, which may contain other lists, and so on (see Figure 8-17), as in a table of contents or structured outline. As in an outline, each new hierarchical level in the list is distinguished by being indented further to the right and by a unique bullet character.

Once you've formatted a paragraph as a bullet list item, you can easily change its level by positioning the edit cursor in it and clicking Promote or Demote on the Formatting toolbar. Each time you click Demote, the item is indented farther to the right and automatically takes on the bullet character of the level it occupies. Promote has the opposite effect, moving an item or items higher up in the list structure. You can run a selection through multiple bulleted items and then Promote or Demote them together.

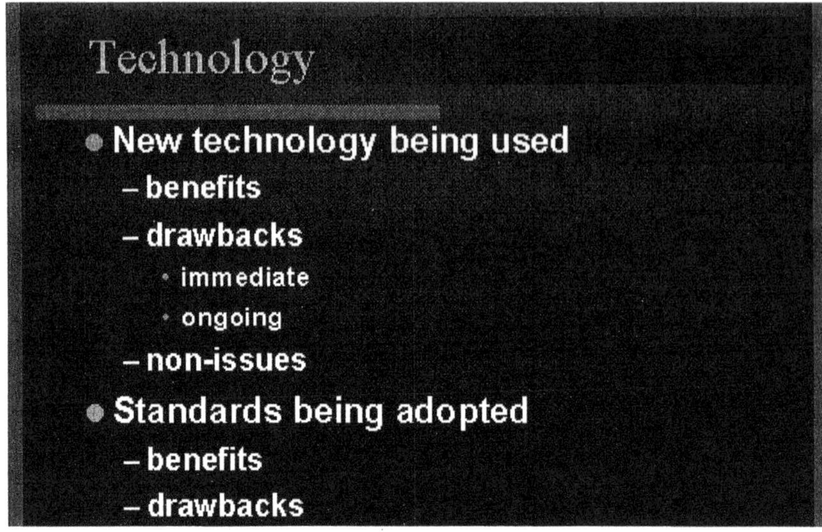

Figure 8-17: When your lists contain lists, you've got nested lists.

Although PowerPoint does a great job of automatically assigning unique bullet styles to all levels in lists, note that you can apply a different bullet character, color, and size to selected list items. Select the items, then choose Format | Bullet to open the Bullet dialog (see Figure 8-18).

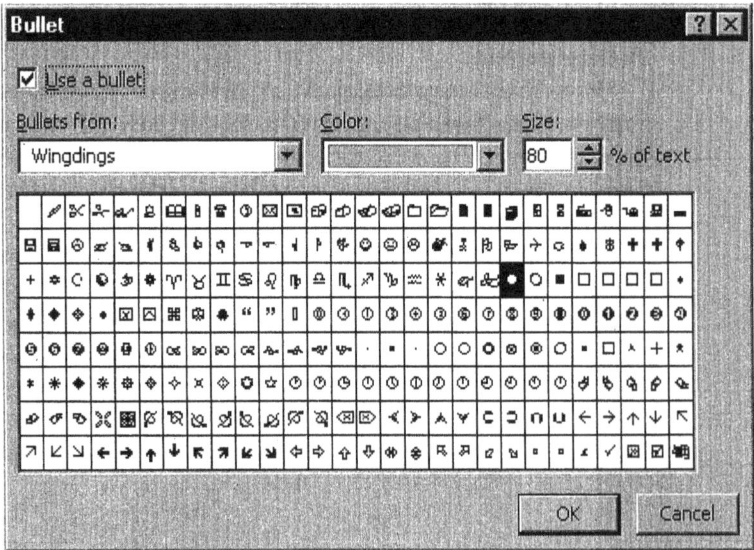

Figure 8-18: Choose a bullet style and other options from the Bullet dialog.

In the Bullet dialog, click the bullet character you want to use. By default, the choice in Bullets from is Normal Text, which applies the same basic bullet regardless of the font in which the bullet text is set. But if none of the bullet characters shown appeals to you, choose a font from the Bullets from list to see more bullet character choices. (A default Windows font in the list, Wingdings, has some great bullet choices.) You may also choose a special color or size for the bullets from the lists provided.

Fast Track

To create a nicely formatted list that doesn't have bullets, select all paragraphs that make up the list (and click Bullets if the list has not already been made a bulleted list), then open the Bullet dialog and clear the check box for Use a bullet.

Checking Spelling & Style

If you've given—or seen—many presentations, you know how humiliating misspelled slide text can be. I once saw a sales presentation in which the product name was misspelled on every slide. (It was one of those old computer product names like "PCcalcX2.5," so nobody knew the difference. But still...)

PowerPoint not only checks your spelling, but also two aspects of your presentation's style:

- **Visual clarity.** The style checker alerts you to slides where the text may be too small, or where there may be too much text on one slide.
- **Case and end punctuation.** The checker alerts you to inconsistent capitalization—for example, a slide title that's not capitalized the same way as others—and inconsistent end punctuation—for example, three items in a list end with a period while a fourth doesn't.

To check spelling and style, choose Tools | Style Checker. (Note that you can check spelling from any view.) A dialog opens like the one in Figure 8-19. Check the check boxes for what you want checked on this pass, and click OK.

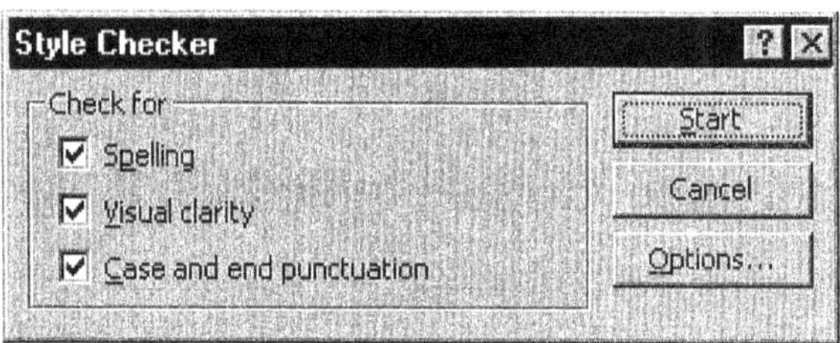

Figure 8-19: PowerPoint checks spelling like Word, but also checks your presentation style.

Fast Track

To check spelling without checking style, click the Spelling button on the Standard toolbar, or choose Tools | Spelling.

PowerPoint checks spelling first. When it locates a word that may be misspelled, a dialog opens like the one in Figure 8-20. Read the word in the top text box carefully. If it's correct (as it may be if it's a name), click Ignore (to ignore just the current instance of the word) or Ignore All (to ignore the word throughout the presentation).

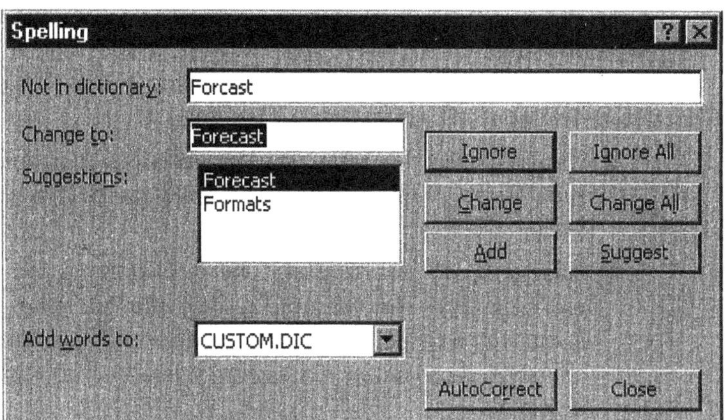

Figure 8-20: Use the Spell Checker to fix spelling.

If the word is incorrect, review the Suggestions box to see whether Word has suggested a correct replacement. If so, click the correct suggestion. If not, edit the word in the Change to box to correct it. After clicking a suggestion or editing Change to, click Change.

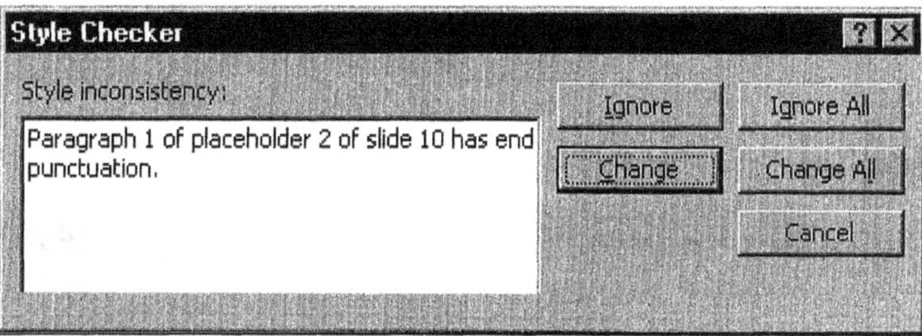

Figure 8-21: Use Style Checker to evaluate and improve your presentation style.

After PowerPoint completes the spell-check, the Style Checker opens (see Figure 8-21). In the Style inconsistency box, the Style Checker describes each language usage problem it encounters:

- Click Change to enable the checker to automatically fix the error, or Change All to change the error anywhere it appears in the presentation.
- Click Ignore to ignore just the current instance of the style problem, or Ignore All to ignore the same problem throughout the presentation.

Adding, Moving & Removing Slides

Changing the order of slides, and adding or deleting slides, is easiest to do when in Slide Sorter view. Note that when you make any of the changes described below, the slides in your presentation are renumbered automatically, as necessary.

As you begin to apply what you learn in this section—particularly deleting a slide—keep in mind that you can use Undo to undo any slide addition, removal, or relocation (click the Undo button on the Standard toolbar or choose Edit | Undo).

Begin by switching to Slide Sorter view (click the Slide Sorter view button in PowerPoint's lower left corner or choose View | Slide Sorter). Next . . .

- **To add a slide:** Click between slides where you want to insert a new slide. (You may click to the left of the first slide, or to the right of the last, to add a slide at the beginning or end.) A vertical bar appears where you clicked. Click the New Slide button on the

Standard toolbar (or choose Insert | New Slide). The New Slide dialog opens (see Figure 8-22), showing the available slide layouts. Click a layout to select it, then click OK.

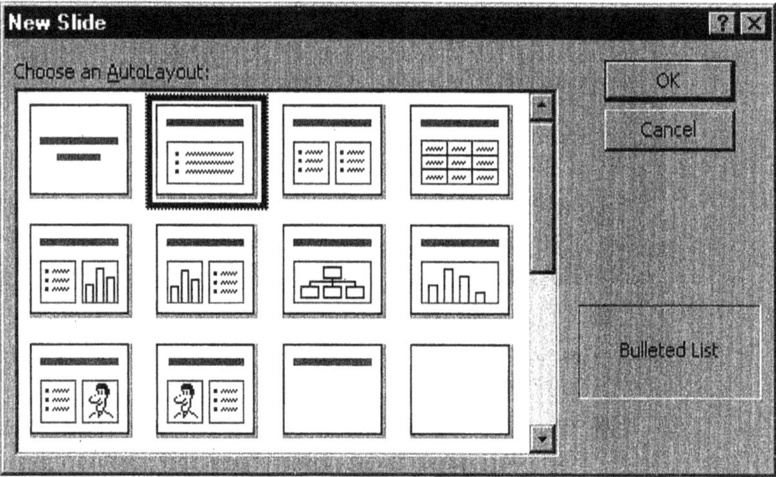

Figure 8-22: Choose an AutoLayout when adding a new slide.

Fast Track

If you want to add a slide that will contain text or formatting that's very similar to an existing slide, select the slide you want to duplicate, then choose Insert | Duplicate Slide. An exact copy of the selected slide appears immediately following it in the presentation. You may edit the duplicate any way you wish or move it elsewhere in the show.

- **To delete a slide:** Click the slide to select it (a black border appears around the slide to show that it is selected). Press the Del key.
- **To move a slide:** Point to the slide. Click and hold, then drag the slide over the slide whose spot you want the moved slide to take. When you release the button, the slide is moved.

Walk-Through: Formatting Text, Adding/Moving/Removing Slides

1. Create a new presentation based on the template Project Overview (Standard).pot (in the Presentations tab).
2. Switch to Outline view.
3. Highlight the title of the first slide (Project Overview).
4. On the Formatting toolbar, click the Increase Font Size button twice.
   The size of the title text increases by 10 points.
5. In the second slide, beneath the bullet list item "Ultimate goal of project," add two new items:
   - Short-term
   - Long-term
6. Start a selection anywhere in Short-term, and run it to anywhere in Long-term.
7. On the Formatting toolbar, click Demote to indent the new bullet items and change their bullet.
8. With the new bullets still highlighted, chose Format|Bullet to open the Bullet dialog.
9. Pick a fun and funky bullet, and click OK.
10. Switch to Slide Sorter view.
11. Click Slide 6 to select it, and press Del.
    Slide 6 disappears, and the following slides are renumbered.
12. Click and hold on Slide 4, drag it over Slide 7, and release.
    Slide 4 becomes Slide 7, and other slides are renumbered as necessary.
13. Click in between Slides 2 and 3.
14. On the Standard toolbar, click New Slide.
    A new Slide 3 appears, and other slides are renumbered as necessary.

Moving On

Got a feel for PowerPoint? Feeling creative? OK, then . . . move ahead to Chapter 9, where you'll learn how to create presentations quickly and beautifully. Nearly all of what you learn in Chapter 9 is medium-independent—that is, you apply the same techniques whether the presentation you're making is destined for transparencies, slides, or electronic presentation.

In Chapter 10, "Livening Up Your Presentations," you'll supplement your authoring skills by learning how to add to your show all of the electronic gadgetry PowerPoint supports, including animation, movies, sound, and much more. You'll also learn the ins and outs of configuring and presenting an electronic extravaganza.

9 Designing Presentations

The last time I had to produce a PowerPoint presentation, I had been invited to speak at a conference in Bermuda. Of course I was very excited to be going to Bermuda, and I knew about the conference months in advance. So I really can't explain why I didn't start working on my presentation until the day before my departure. (I wanted it to seem fresh?)

I'm not trying to wriggle off the hook, but I know that my behavior was more the rule than the exception. Most people who must author their own presentations do so not as part of their daily responsibilities, but in addition to them—in crisis preparation for the "Big Sales Meeting," or customer confab, or what have you. And while we all start out hoping to create a state-of-the-art slide show, in the end we're often grateful to have a dozen colorful text slides with only one typo each.

This chapter has been designed in recognition of that reality. It is designed to help you create a good-looking presentation as quickly as possible, by first covering the basics. You can move through just the first few sections of this chapter to produce an attractive show fast. After that, call the airport—if your flight has been delayed, you can proceed ever deeper into this chapter, discovering how to fine tune your show and customize it precisely to your tastes, needs, or whims.

Opening Existing Presentations

Like all Office 97 applications, PowerPoint remembers the filenames of the last four files you've opened and lists them at the bottom of the File menu. To quickly open any of the last four presentations you've worked on, choose File, then click the presentation's filename on the File menu.

If the file you want isn't on the File menu, you can open it from PowerPoint's Open dialog (Figure 9-1), which you can display in any of three ways:

- On PowerPoint's startup dialog, choose the radio button next to Open an existing presentation and click OK.
- Click the Open button on PowerPoint's Standard toolbar.
- Choose File | Open.

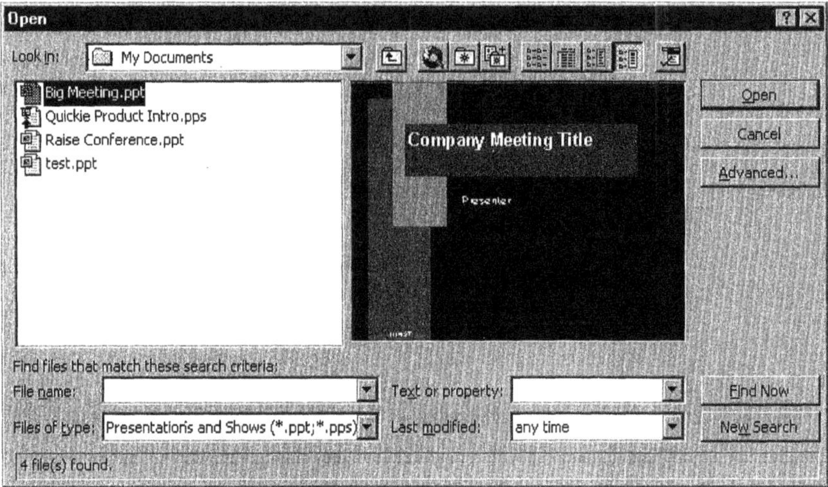

Figure 9-1: Use the Open dialog to navigate to and open an existing presentation.

In the Open dialog, the Look in box names the current folder, and the large box beneath Look in lists all of the presentation (.ppt or .pps) files in the current folder. Drop down the Look in box and use it to navigate to the folder containing the file you want to open. When the file you want appears in the list, click it once to select it; an image of the selected file's first slide appears in the box on the right side of the dialog. When you're sure you've found the file you want, click Open.

Fast Track

When you open a .pps file by opening its file icon in Windows, the show opens automatically in Slide Show view. However, when you open a .pps file from the Open dialog, it opens for editing in Slide view, exactly as a .ppt file does.

Fast Track

Using the Open dialog, you may convert presentations created with Harvard Graphics or Lotus Freelance to PowerPoint format. First, you must install the presentation converters from the Office 97 CD, as explained in the Appendix. (The converters are not included in the Typical installation.) In the Office 97 install program, you'll find the converters listed in the options for Microsoft PowerPoint.

After installing the converters, return to PowerPoint. In the Open dialog, drop down the Files of type list and choose the type of presentation (Harvard Graphics or Lotus Freelance) you want to open. Use the Open dialog's Look in list to navigate to the folder containing the file, then select the file and click Open. PowerPoint converts the file to PowerPoint format and opens it, ready for your edits and enhancements.

Besides opening PowerPoint from the Start menu, you can open it by opening a file of a type registered to PowerPoint in Windows's File Types registry. From any file list in Windows 95—the desktop, a folder, Windows Explorer, or Find results—you open a file by double-clicking its file icon.

While opening any PowerPoint file opens PowerPoint, things happen a little differently depending upon which of the basic PowerPoint file types you open. Table 9-1 describes the PowerPoint files and explains what happens when you open each. (Examine the icons carefully. All are similar, but each is slightly different.)

File icon and extension	Description	What happens when you open it
.ppt	A PowerPoint presentation.	PowerPoint opens in Slide view (see "Choosing a View," in Chapter 8), so you may work on your presentation.
.pps	A presentation configured to open in Slide Show view.	PowerPoint opens in Slide Show view. Other than opening in Slide Show view, a .pps file is just like a .ppt file. You can watch the show, or choose another view to edit the presentation.
.pot	A PowerPoint *template*, used to get a head-start on creating a presentation.	PowerPoint opens, and a new presentation is created based on the template file.
.pwz	A PowerPoint Wizard, which leads you step-by-step through a PowerPoint activity. (The only PowerPoint Wizard included with Office 97, AutoContent Wizard.pwz, helps you start a new presentation by selecting a template for you.)	PowerPoint opens, and the Wizard opens to prompt you through the task.

Table 9-1: PowerPoint files and their actions when opened.

Fast Track

To quickly find and open any of PowerPoint's template (.pot) or Wizard (.pwz) files, click the New Office Document button on the Office 97 Shortcut bar. The tabs Presentations and Presentation Designs include only PowerPoint files. The General tab and Web Pages tab group a few PowerPoint templates with other file types, but you can identify the PowerPoint files by their file icons (see Table 9-1).

Rearranging Slide Elements

Text formatting and *slide formatting*—choosing the colors, background, layout, and other aesthetics of the slide—go hand in hand. Often after changing the text formatting, you'll want to fiddle with the slide formatting, and vice versa. Each changes your perception of the other.

For example, if you make text larger, the larger text may suddenly seem too close to another object onscreen, and you'll want to reposition the placeholders to restore the compositional balance of the slide. Or changing the background fill of a slide may make text harder to read, so you'll want to change the font, enlarge the text, or apply attributes to it to help it stand out against the new background.

Fast Track

To radically change the look of an existing presentation, you can apply a new design template to it. Applying a different design template does not affect the content of your presentation, but it may change much of the text formatting, and also many of the slide formatting options that follow.

Note that if you feel you need the radical overhaul of a new design, the template you chose was probably a bad fit for what you wanted to create. If you've not put much effort yet into the content of your presentation, you may be better off starting over and choosing a different template from the Presentations tab.

To apply a new design to an existing show, click the Apply Design button on the Standard toolbar, or choose Format | Apply Design. A dialog opens, showing a list from which you may choose (and preview) any of PowerPoint's Presentation Designs templates. Alternatively, you can use the dialog's Look in list to navigate to one of your own presentations and copy its design to the current show.

The arrangement of placeholders on a slide is called the slide's *layout*. PowerPoint has 24 predefined AutoLayout options, each containing a different layout.

When you create a presentation with the AutoContent Wizard or from a template on the Presentations tab, an AutoLayout is assigned to each slide for you. When you use a Presentation Designs template or Blank Presentation, the AutoLayout dialog opens so you can choose an AutoLayout for the first slide. When you add slides, you're always prompted to choose an AutoLayout.

You can change the layout of a slide in either of two ways: pick a new AutoLayout, or manually rearrange the placeholders. Both techniques are described next.

Changing the Slide Layout (AutoLayout)

To change the slide layout, select the slide whose layout you want to change, then click the Slide Layout button on the Standard toolbar (or choose Format | Slide Layout). The Slide Layout dialog opens.

In the thumbnail pictures of the available layouts, the horizontal gray bars represent placeholders for title text, while the other boxes feature tiny graphics to help you understand the types of placeholders they contain—a cartoon face for a picture placeholder, a film clapper for a movie clip, and so on. Click on any layout option to see a description in the box on the right side of the dialog. When you've clicked the layout you want, click Apply.

If the selected slide contains placeholders that are not included in the AutoLayout you select, don't worry—all of your objects remain on the slide. For example, if the slide has a picture placeholder, and the AutoLayout has no picture but does have a chart placeholder, your slide will wind up with both a picture and a chart. However, since the AutoLayout had no built-in spot for the extra placeholder, you'll need to manually rearrange the placeholders (as described next) to make everything fit.

Rearranging Placeholders

To reposition, resize, and reshape any placeholder, begin by clicking it to select it and reveal its border (see Figure 9-2). Along the placeholder border, you'll notice little squares—called *handles*—on all sides and corners.

- To reposition the placeholder, point to any part of the border *except* a handle. The pointer becomes a four-pointed arrow. Click and hold the mouse button, drag the outline to the new position, and release to drop it there.

- To change the size of the placeholder without changing its shape, point to a corner handle. The cursor becomes a two-pointed arrow. Click and hold, then drag toward the placeholder's center to shrink it or away from its center to enlarge it.
- To change the placeholder's width (without affecting its height), point to a handle on either side (but not on a corner). The cursor becomes a two-pointed arrow. Click and hold, then drag toward the placeholder's center to narrow it or away from its center to widen it.
- To change the placeholder's height (without affecting its width), point to a handle on the top or bottom (not on a corner). The cursor becomes a two-pointed arrow. Click and hold, then drag toward the placeholder's center to shorten it or away from its center to make it taller.

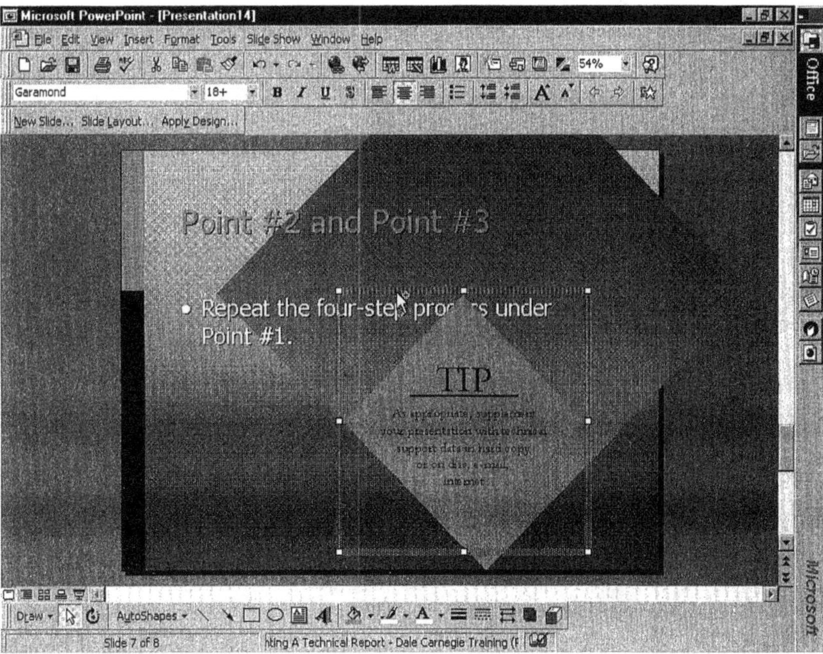

Figure 9-2: Use drag and drop to rearrange placeholders.

Dealing With Overlapping Objects

When objects overlap—as they often may, accidentally, when you change the AutoLayout of an existing slide—you can always adjust size and position to make everything fit without overlapping.

Of course, you may sometimes *want* placeholders to overlap. For example, to place a small caption on top of a picture (as you learn to do in Chapter 10, "Livening Up Your Presentations"), you must lay a text placeholder atop a picture. You may also create fun designs by overlapping multiple picture placeholders.

The trick with overlapping objects is choosing the *order* of each—whether an object is *in front* (covering all others), *in back* (behind all others), or somewhere between front and back when three or more objects overlap. To choose the order of a placeholder that overlaps others, point to it and right-click. The placeholder is selected, and a context menu opens (see Figure 9-3). From the context menu, choose Order, then the place in the order which you want the selected object to hold.

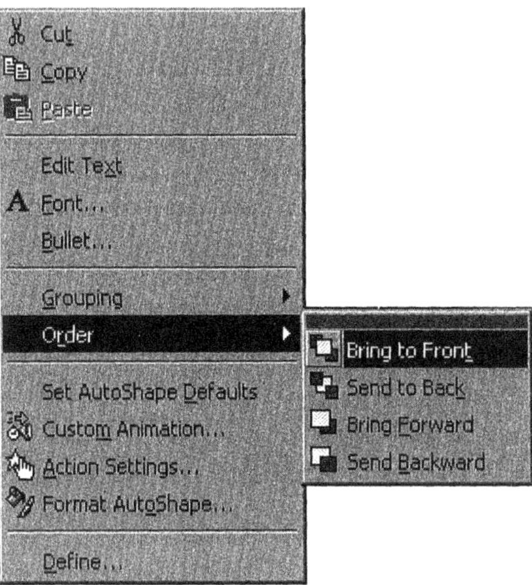

Figure 9-3: Right-click objects and choose Order from the context menu to choose the order of overlapping objects.

Changing Slide Colors

The *color scheme* is the combination of different colors used in slides. The scheme assigns a different color to each element in the slide—one color for the background, another for the text, and so on. Each template includes one or more predefined color schemes, designed so that the colors complement and contrast one another and suit the type of show the template is designed to support.

Changing Color Schemes

You can change the color scheme for selected slides or for an entire presentation. Begin by selecting the slides whose colors you want to change (if you plan to change the scheme for the whole show, it doesn't matter which slides are selected). Choose Format | Slide Color Scheme to open the Color Scheme dialog shown in Figure 9-4.

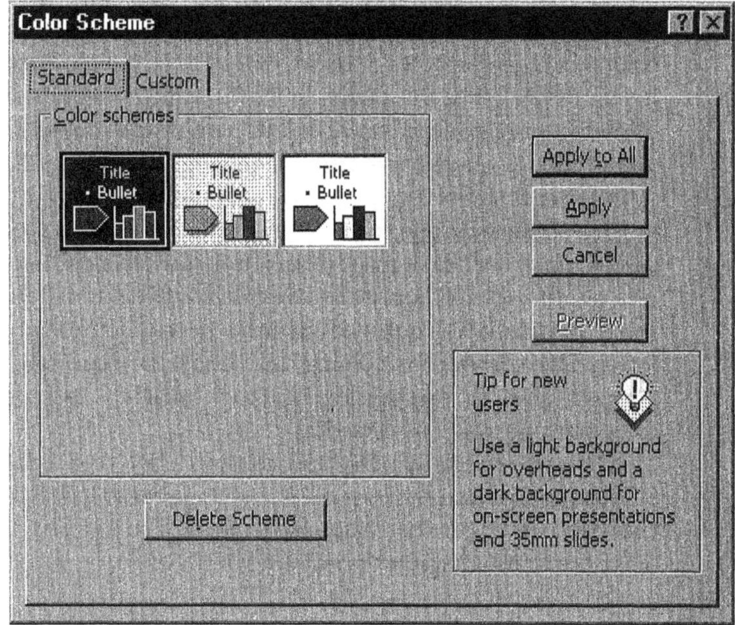

Figure 9-4: Use the Color Scheme dialog to pick the color of each element in a slide.

To use one of the schemes included with the template, select one of the schemes shown in the Standard tab, and click Apply to apply the scheme only to selected slides, or Apply to All to apply the scheme to the whole presentation.

Fast Track

The little thumbnail examples of the Standard color schemes may not provide you with a full sense of how the scheme will appear in your slides. To get a better idea, click the Preview button on the Color Scheme dialog. The current slide takes on the selected color scheme—just temporarily. (You may have to drag the dialog out of the way to see the slide.) Note that the Preview is just that—no change is actually made to your slides unless you click Apply or Apply to All.

To create a new scheme, click a scheme in the Standard tab that's closest to the scheme you want to create, then click the Custom tab (see Figure 9-5). The color squares next to each slide element in the list of Scheme colors show the color from the scheme you chose in the Standard tab. For any element whose color you want to change, click the element's color box, then click the Change Color button. A dialog opens like the one in Figure 9-6. While this dialog looks the same no matter which slide element you selected, observe that its name varies depending on what you're choosing a color for—Shadows color, Background color, and so on.

In the dialog, the big bug-eye hexagon shows the full range of colors you may choose, while the gaggle of little hexagons beneath the big one offer various shades of gray, from white (the leftmost hexagon) to black (the rightmost). To choose any color or gray, point to it and click. The tiny hexagon you click is outlined in white. In the square that appears in the lower-right corner of the dialog, the bottom of the square shows the Current color (the one you're changing), while the top shows the New color (the one you've selected).

When you're happy with your choice, click OK to return to the Color Scheme dialog. You may proceed to change the color of another element, click Preview to see the custom scheme applied to a slide, or click Apply or Apply to All to apply the scheme.

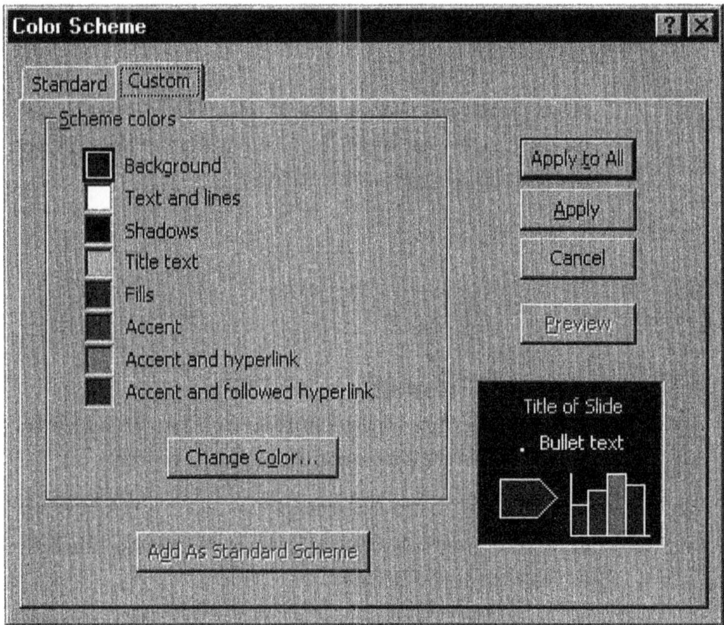

Figure 9-5: Click the Custom tab to create a new color scheme.

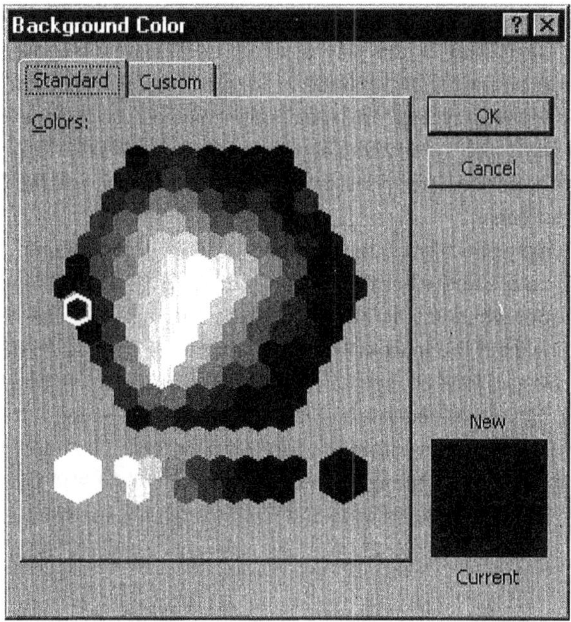

Figure 9-6: To choose a color, click a square.

Fast Track

After creating a custom scheme, click the Add As Standard Scheme button on the Custom tab to add the new scheme to the Standard tab, so you can easily apply it again in the future.

FYI: Working With "Masters"

A *master* is a slide or page whose contents and formatting affects all other slides or pages in a show. Every presentation has four masters:

- Slide master: Controls the appearance of all slides in the show.
- Title master: Controls the appearance of just the title slide, so it can differ from the rest of the show.
- Notes master: Controls the appearance of all notes pages in the show.
- Handout master: Controls the appearance of all handouts in the show.

A master establishes default formatting for the show, and can also include text or pictures than can appear on every slide (or page). In other words, any text, pictures, or formatting in the master affect everything else. You can even put a company logo or special background in a master, and it will automatically appear on all slides—except those you specifically change. Also, whenever you apply a new design template, the masters are changed automatically. To view or edit one of the masters, choose View|Master, and then choose the master you want from the Master submenu.

When you specifically change the background, color scheme, or other slide formatting, you break the bond between slide and master, and make that slide go its own way. But when you do not make these changes to a slide, the slide retains the formatting from the master. When you make any changes to the master of an existing show, all slides change to match the master—except any slides whose bond to the master you have broken with custom formatting.

In general, you don't have to think about the masters if you don't want to—you can just format slides as you wish. But when creating an especially long show and you want to have a consistent look and feel throughout, a master is a handy tool.

Changing Backgrounds

You can choose a background color by choosing or creating a new color scheme as described in the preceding section. However, there's more to backgrounds than color. Using the Background dialog, you can change not only the color, but also the *fill* of the background—a pattern, texture, or picture that dresses up the slide.

Begin by selecting the slides whose background you want to change (if you plan to change the background for the whole show, it doesn't matter which slides are selected). Choose Format | Background to open the Background dialog. In the dialog, the Background fill box shows the current background settings. Drop down the list in the Background fill box (see Figure 9-7) to reveal options for changing the background.

As Figure 9-7 shows, you can choose Automatic to have PowerPoint pick an appropriate background color for you, or click one of the squares beneath Automatic to choose any color in the current color scheme. If none of the colors is what you want, choose More Colors. A dialog just like Figure 9-6 (shown earlier under "Changing Color Schemes") appears. Choose a color from the dialog just as you would pick a color for a custom color scheme.

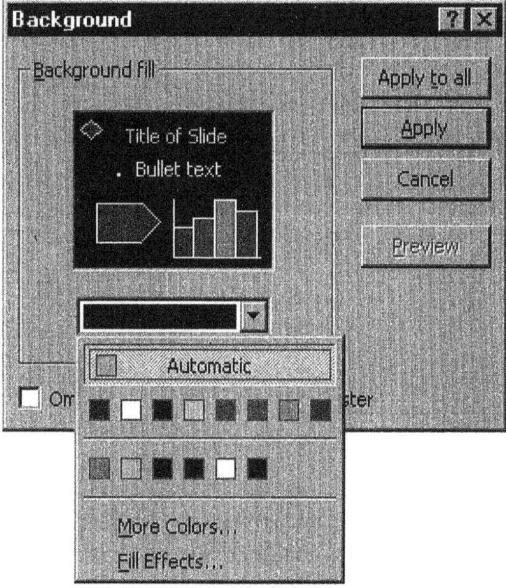

Figure 9-7: Choose Format | Background to change the slide background.

To change the fill pattern or texture, choose Fill Effects. A dialog opens like the one in Figure 9-8. The first three tabs—Gradient, Texture, and Pattern—offer a wide range of different fill effects you may select for your background. The fourth, Picture, opens a file dialog you can use to navigate to, and select, a picture file to use as the background. (To learn more about pictures, see Chapter 10, "Livening Up Your Presentations.") Make a selection on any tab, then click OK to return to the Background dialog.

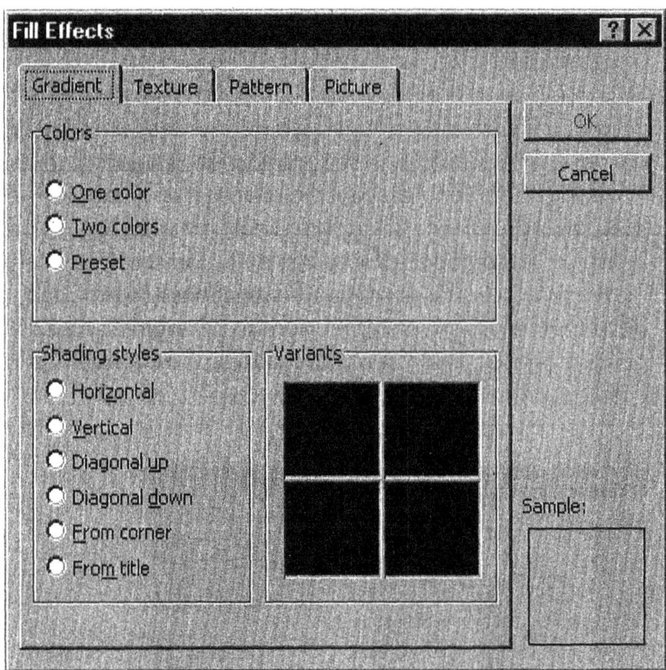

Figure 9-8: You can apply a background fill, *a color or pattern for the background.*

FYI: One Fill to a Customer

Throughout a presentation, you may apply as many different background fill effects as you like. However, any given slide can have only one of the four options in its background. In other words, a slide cannot have both a background picture and a pattern, or both a texture and a gradient. When using the Fill Effects dialog, complete one—and only one—tab to add a fill effect.

After choosing your background color and fill, click Apply to apply the background only to selected slides, or Apply to All to apply the background to the whole presentation.

Walk Through: Changing Slide Elements

1. Create a new presentation based on Marketing Plan.pot (in the Presentations tab).
2. Switch to Slide Sorter view.
3. Double-click Slide 6 to open it in Slide view, and click Slide Layout on the Standard toolbar.
4. On the Slide Layout dialog, choose the layout from the third row, first column (called Text & Clip Art).
5. Click Apply.

   The text placeholder containing the bullet items is squeezed into a left-hand column, and a placeholder for clip art appears to the right.
6. Choose Format|Background.
7. On the Background dialog, drop down the list in Background fill, and choose Fill Effects.
8. On the Gradient tab, click the upper-right square under Variants, then click OK.
9. On the background dialog, click Apply.

   A new gradient fill is applied to Slide 6.

Getting Expert Help

PowerPoint 97 includes all of the same help facilities featured throughout Office 97, including the Office Assistant, Help Contents and Index, What's This, and Microsoft on the Web (all available from the Help menu). But PowerPoint has its own, additional helper: PowerPoint Central.

PowerPoint Central (see Figure 9-9) is a PowerPoint show (.pps file) stored on your hard disk as part of the typical installation. Offered as a sort of "user magazine," the show includes PowerPoint-related news items, a few tips and tricks, plus links to "free stuff"—templates, sound clips, and so on—both on your Office 97 CD and on the Web. The show also includes articles in a Magazine section; in the issue included with Office 97, the Magazine features a primer in the famous Dale Carnegie presentation method ("The 'Four Ps' for Better Presenting").

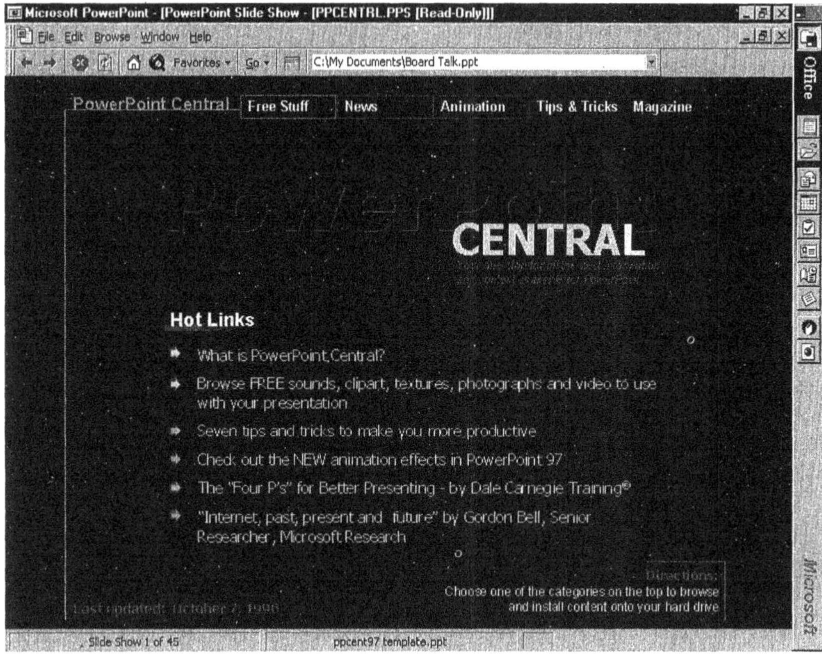

Figure 9-9: PowerPoint Central gives you access to online PowerPoint resources and also provides a tour of PowerPoint features.

Since PowerPoint Central is a PowerPoint show, you can open it as you would any other PowerPoint show by opening the file ppcentrl.pps (which you'll find in C:\Program Files\Microsoft Office\Office). But PowerPoint also provides access to PowerPoint Central through PowerPoint's menu bar. Just choose Tools | PowerPoint Central to start the show. While exploring PowerPoint Central, observe that the show not only offers quick access to resources but also serves as a terrific demonstration of the kind of interactive electronic presentations you can create using the techniques in Chapter 10.

You can move from page to page, in order, just as you can in any show displayed in Slide Show view—PgDn goes forward one slide, PgUp goes back one slide. However, PowerPoint Central is designed as a viewer-driven, interactive presentation that works very much like a Web page. When you point to different onscreen objects, the pointer becomes a hand with a pointing finger to indicate that the pointer is on a link that leads to another slide or activity. You click the link to jump where it leads. For example, point to any of the headings along the top of the slide—Free Stuff, News, Animation, and so on—to jump to a different section of PowerPoint Central.

Fast Track

To ask PowerPoint Central to show you a brief, painless overview of creating presentations, open PowerPoint Central, click the Free Stuff link to open the Free Stuff slide, then click the arrow labeled "Start" near the bottom of the slide.

Some of the links you'll see in PowerPoint Central don't lead to other slides. Instead, a link may lead to a file on your hard disk or your Office 97 CD, or a link may in fact be an Internet hyperlink—clicking the link directs Windows to connect to the Internet and navigate to a specific Web page.

Net-Savvy

After every three months passes, the next time you open PowerPoint Central it asks whether you want it updated. If you say yes, and you have a Web browser and Internet access installed in Windows, PowerPoint Central connects to the Web and downloads fresh news, articles, tips, and free stuff.

Walk Through: Opening a Presentation, Views

Follow the steps below to practice opening presentations and working with views.

1. Open PowerPoint from Windows's Start menu.
2. Choose File|Open.
3. In Look in, choose the hard disk on which Office 97 is installed (usually C:).
4. In the box beneath Look in, click the following folders as they appear: Program Files, Microsoft Office, Office.
   A list of folders and .ppt/.pps files in the Office folder opens; Ppcentral.pps appears at the bottom of the list.
5. Click Ppcentral.pps, and click Open.
   The PowerPoint Central presentation opens in Slide view.
6. Press PgDn to advance to Slide 2, and again to advance to Slide 3.
7. Switch to Outline view (click the Outline view button or choose View|Outline).
8. Switch to Slide Sorter view (click the Slide Sorter view button or choose View|Slide Sorter).
9. Double-click any slide to view it in Slide view.
10. Choose Slide Show|View Show.
    The show begins at Slide 1.
11. Under Hot Links, point to the action button (the arrow) to the left of the second item, "Browse FREE Sounds..." so that the pointer becomes a pointing finger, then click.
    Slide 2 opens.
12. Click the action button labeled Start at the bottom of Slide 2.
13. Enjoy the tutorial.
14. When finished with the tutorial, click the Exit action button on the tutorial.
15. Choose File|End Show to return to Slide view.
16. Choose File|Close to close Ppcentral.pps.

Creating Notes Pages & Handouts

Notes pages are printed pages, each of which shows one of your slides, plus any notes you've typed relating to that slide. You may want to create notes pages for either of two purposes:

- You may create notes pages for yourself—*speaker notes*—to use during the presentation as a guide to what you planned to say or do during the display of each slide. The notes beneath the slide image should include a more detailed outline of what you planned to say during the display of the slide.
- You can create notes pages for your audience, to provide your listeners with a picture of each slide as well as notes expanding upon that slide (or empty space to jot their own notes).

If you want to give your audience copies of slides—but no notes—you can also create *handouts*. While handouts cannot include notes, they can feature two, three, or six slides per page—enabling you to fit the slide images for a whole presentation in just a few handout pages.

Typing Slide Notes

To type the notes for a slide, open the slide in Slide view, or select the slide in Outline view or in the Slide Sorter. Then choose View | Notes Page. The notes page for the selected slide opens as shown in Figure 9-10.

The whole area beneath the slide image is a big text placeholder you use like any other. Click in it and type to add text. Format text as you wish by selecting the text and choosing buttons from the Formatting toolbar.

When the Notes Page view opens, it shows you the whole page by default. That's helpful, because you can see the slide you're writing about. However, you may have trouble seeing your typing when the whole page appears—your text will be too small. To see better without new glasses, click the Zoom box on the Standard toolbar and raise the Zoom percentage to 100% or so. When typing notes, scroll up the page whenever you need to refer back to the slide.

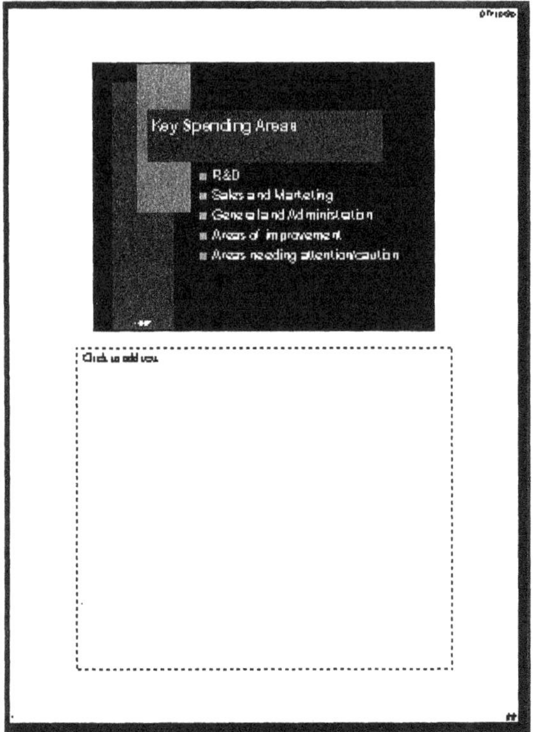

Figure 9-10: Type your speaker notes in Notes Page view.

Fast Track

You can also type the notes for a slide while working on that slide. Choose View | Speaker Notes and type notes for the current slide, which will show up on your Notes pages when you print them.

Printing Notes & Handouts

To print notes or handouts, begin by opening the presentation for which you want to print notes or handouts, then choose File | Print to open the Print dialog. Near the bottom of the dialog appears a list labeled Print what (see Figure 9-11).

- To print handouts, drop down the Print what list and choose one of the three Handouts options—two slides per page, three per page, or six per page—and click OK.
- To print notes pages, drop down the Print what list and choose Notes Pages, then click OK.

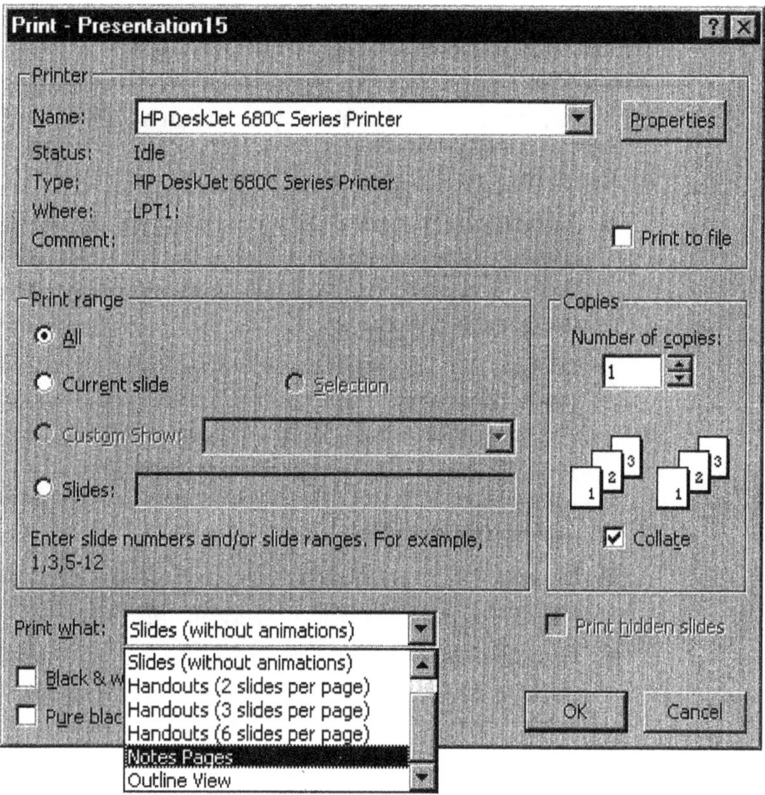

Figure 9-11: Choose from the Print what list to print notes or handouts from the Print dialog.

Choosing a Presentation Medium

As you begin creating your show, decide right up front how and where you will present your show. PowerPoint supports the full range of presentation media, from simple transparencies to animated, multimedia PC presentations, to Web pages. The great part is that the steps required to create your show are essentially the same, no matter where and how it will be shown. Of course, the one important difference is that, when you present your show on a PC, you can apply a family of multimedia features that obviously can't play a part on a slide or transparency.

Special content you may include in your PC-presented show—known as an *electronic presentation,* in PowerPoint's parlance—includes:

- **Animation.** PowerPoint's animations are easy-to-apply animation effects that reveal text in a slide, make fun transitions between slides, and more. Animations are the quickest, easiest way to add real sparkle to a show.
- **Sound.** You can attach sound effects or other sound clips to events within your show—such as slide transitions—or record and play slide narration for a self-running show. You can also instruct PowerPoint to play a CD in the background, or to dynamically compose and play an electronic soundtrack—automatically—to underscore the show.
- **Movies.** PC video files in standard formats (.AVI, .MOV) can be embedded in slides and played during your show.
- **Hyperlinks.** You can configure text on a slide as a link so that clicking on it opens something new. When clicked, a link can open a new slide, a Word document, or even a page on the Web.
- **Action buttons.** Action buttons are attractive, graphical buttons onscreen that can do all of the same things links do.

Also, when a presentation is destined for PC play, you have an extra set of options that customize the show for presentation in different venues and circumstances. Using these options, you can set up any show to play on a PC as:

- **A full-screen, speaker-driven presentation.** The slides take up the whole screen, hiding PowerPoint behind. The speaker controls the show, moving from slide to slide and activating any links or action buttons.

- **A windowed, viewer-driven presentation.** The slides appear in a Window with the Web toolbar along the top so that the viewer controls the presentation. (The Web toolbar is really just a set of buttons for moving around in the show; it's called "Web" not because it's used for Web presentations, but because it's used just the way the navigation tools on Web browsers are used, leveraging skills many viewers already possess.) This option provides individuals or small groups with self-training presentations or similar shows that viewers can view at their own pace.
- **A kiosk presentation.** A viewer-controlled show that appears full-screen (hiding PowerPoint). Unlike a speaker-driven full-screen show, in a kiosk show access to PowerPoint navigation and editing tools is completely cut off—the viewer can get around by clicking any links or access buttons in slides, but cannot otherwise control the show or access PowerPoint. Kiosk mode is designed to support kiosks at trade shows or other venues where an unsupervised viewer may approach the PC and explore the show on his or her own. See Figure 9-12.
- **A self-running presentation.** You can configure any of the preceding types of shows as a self-running show, one that moves from slide to slide all by itself, with no viewer or speaker control. You get to select the *timings* for self-running shows, the number of seconds PowerPoint displays each slide before proceeding to the next. While the most obvious place for a self-running show is a kiosk, some speakers prefer carefully timed and rehearsed self-running shows to advancing the slides manually.
- **An online presentation.** Finally, a PowerPoint presentation may be shown over a network, so that viewers in different cities—or countries—may take part. PowerPoint supports several ways to create online presentations, including saving shows in HTML (Web) format for universal support of Internet and intranet environments, and running a "Presentation Conference" in which multiple viewers in different cities can simultaneously view and participate in a single presentation. To learn more about online presentations, see Chapter 22, "Office 97 & the Internet."

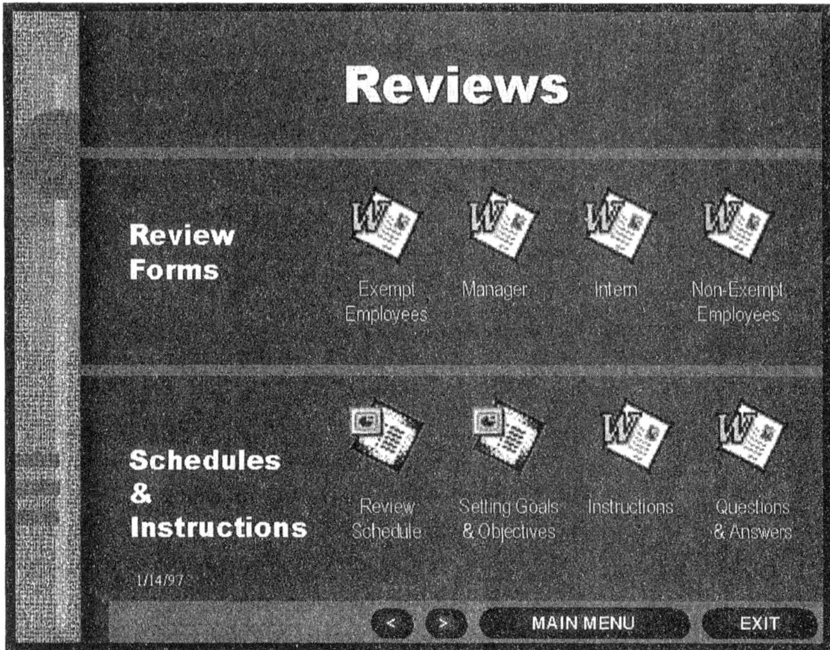

Figure 9-12: In a "kiosk" show, you can add onscreen buttons to enable the viewer to move from slide to slide.

Printing Transparencies

Printing overhead transparencies is as simple as printing a document from Word or from any Windows application. Open the presentation you want to print (don't worry about the view you start in; view doesn't affect printing), and click the Print button on the Standard toolbar (or choose File | Print). The Print dialog (see Figure 9-13) opens. To print all slides in the presentation using the default Windows printer and options, simply click OK.

Fast Track

If you don't want to make your own transparencies, or if you don't have access to a good color printer that accepts transparencies, you can order high-quality overhead transparencies from many of the same service bureaus that can create 35mm slides from your PowerPoint files. See "Making 35mm Slides," later in this chapter.

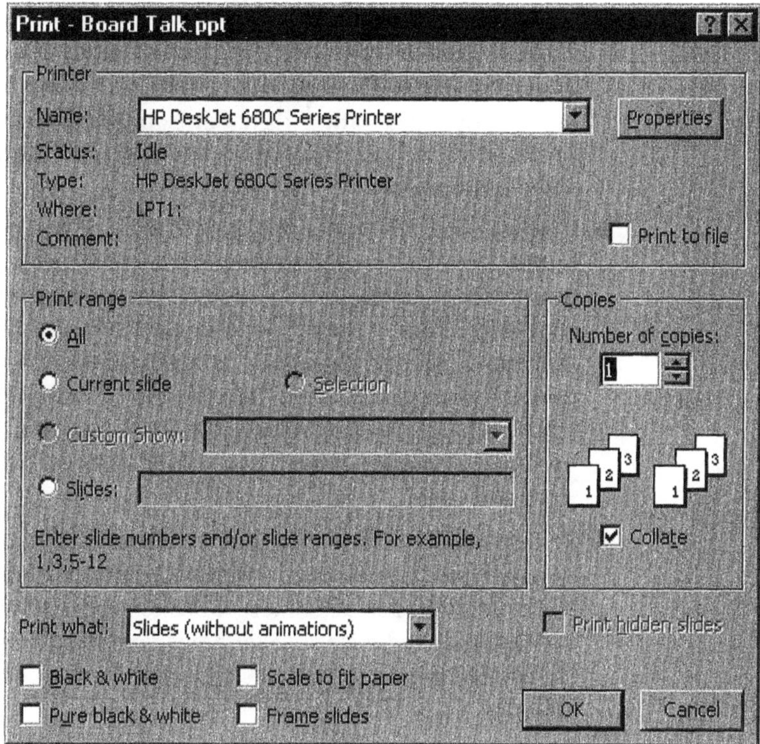

Figure 9-13: Printing transparencies is as easy as printing on paper.

Of course, before clicking OK on the Print dialog you may choose from a variety of options affecting the printout. The most important are:

- **Name box.** The printer listed in the Name box is your default Windows printer. To use a different printer connected to your PC or network, drop down the Name list and select it.
- **Properties button.** Click this button to open a dialog for configuring the printer shown in the name box. Most color printers have variable print-quality settings (from ink-stingy economy quality to ink-eating high quality), different paper trays you can select among, and more. By checking out and (if necessary) modifying the printer properties, you ensure that your printer produces the best-looking transparencies it can.
- **Print range.** By default, in the Print range box the radio button next to All is selected, so all slides in the current presentation print. But if you need to print only one or some of the slides (for example, if you corrected a single typo in a show you'd already printed), you can

save time, ink, and transparencies by choosing to print just the Current slide or by entering a group of slides to print in the Slides box. Separate individual slides with a comma, and indicate a range of slides with a dash. For example, the entry **4,7,11-14,20-** prints slides 4, 7, 11 through 14, and slide 20 through the last slide in the show.

- **Copies.** Enter a Number of copies to print. If you check the Collate button, your printer produces one copy of all selected slides at a time. (When you're printing the whole presentation, the result should be slides in the proper order, ready to go. However, note that many color printers stack printed pages face up, not face down. If your printer does that, you have to reshuffle each copy to collate it properly.) If you leave the check box blank, your printer produces all copies of the first selected slide, then all copies of the next, and so on.
- **Print what.** By default, the entry in this list is Slides. But note that you may use this list to print *handouts*—printed copies of your slides for audience reference—or *notes* pages—printed copies of slides annotated with speaker notes for your reference. (See "Creating Notes & Handouts," for more information on this subject.)

FYI: Plain Ol' Black & White—Making It Work

Color is so important to making an effective presentation that it's hard to imagine anyone wanting black and white output from PowerPoint. But some folks just don't have access to a color printer. And even when you print your slides in color, you may want to print handouts or notes pages in black and white. When you want to print in black and white, check either of the two check boxes in the lower-left corner of the Print dialog:

- Black and white optimizes the formatting of your color slides to make them look their best when printed on a good printer that's capable of producing a good range of gray levels.
- Pure black and white optimizes your slides for true monochrome printing: just black, no gray. Use this option when your printer (or paper stock) produces grays poorly.

If after trying these options you're still not happy with the look of your slides in black and white, you can edit the black-and-white appearance of your slides without making any change to their appearance in color. When formatting slides, click the Black and White View button on the Standard toolbar. In that view, PowerPoint shows you your slides as they'd appear when printed in black and white. Any changes you make to the slide formatting—such as removing background fills to make text easier to read—while in Black and White view have no effect on the color versions of your slides, but may dramatically improve the slides' look when printed in black and white.

Making 35mm Slides

To make 35mm color slides from a PowerPoint presentation, the file must be output to a device called a *film recorder*. Film recorders are cheaper than they used to be, so companies that make a lot of slides often have one somewhere in-house. If you have access to a company film recorder, the person who runs it will know how to make your slides. Typically, a film recorder is attached to a PC; the operator simply moves through your slide show in PowerPoint, a slide at a time, and clicks a button to record each image on 35mm film.

Lacking a film recorder of your own, you'll need to provide your presentation files to a *service bureau*, a company that records the slides on its own film recorder, develops them, and returns them to you, ready to pop into a projector. To find a service bureau near you, check the Yellow Pages under Computers-Graphics, Photofinishing, or Photographic Services. You may also ask your local copy/print shops if they make slides; many do. Note that some service bureaus can make not only slides from your PowerPoint files, but also high-quality overhead transparencies, posters, and who knows what else. (T-shirts? coffee mugs?)

When you've located the service bureau you intend to use, ask what you must supply to have your slides made. Typically, you send your .ppt or .pps file to the service bureau via modem, or use the Pack and Go option (described later in this chapter) to copy your show to diskettes that you can take to the service bureau.

Finally, there are high-volume service bureaus that can accept your files via modem or mail, make your slides, and send them back to you, often all within 24 hours. PowerPoint includes a Wizard that takes you through all of the steps required to send your files to Genigraphics (the largest slide service bureau, serving all of North America), along with payment information and return shipping instructions. If your PC has a modem and phone connection, you may use the Wizard to order slides in a jiffy. Keep in mind, however, that Genigraphics has no monopoly on making PowerPoint slides—you can use any service bureau you want to.

To use the Genigraphics Wizard, you must first make sure it is installed on your PC (it's not included in the Typical installation). In PowerPoint, choose File | Send to, and look at the bottom of the submenu that appears. If the Genigraphics item that appears there is grayed out, you need to install the Wizard from your Office 97 CD-ROM. You can learn how to add Office 97 programs in the Appendix to this book. When you run the procedure, you'll find the Genigraphics Wizard listed under the options for Microsoft PowerPoint.

Once the Wizard is installed, begin by opening the presentation you want to send. Then choose File | Send to | Genigraphics. The Wizard opens with a dialog explaining the steps you'll perform to place your order. Click Next to begin filling out your order instructions. A dialog like the one in Figure 9-14 opens, prompting you to select the type of output—slides, transparencies, and so on—you want made from your PowerPoint files. Note that this dialog contains a very important button—Display Pricing Information—that shows complete pricing information, not just for slides, but for costly extras such as Rush delivery.

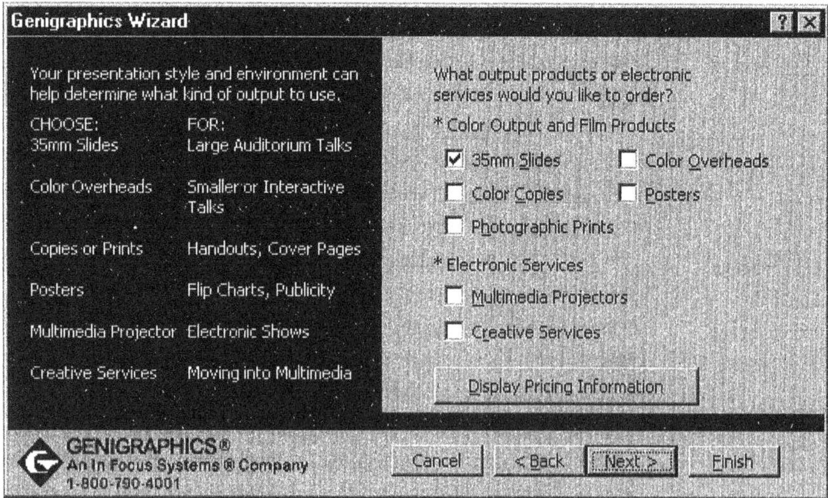

Figure 9-14: The Genigraphics Wizard prepares and sends your show files to a major service bureau to be printed on 35mm slides or transparencies.

Work your way through the Wizard's dialogs, completing each and clicking Next to move forward. If you fail to make any required selection, the Wizard displays a message when you click Next, telling you what you need to do. Note that Genigraphics' toll-free number appears in the lower-left corner of the Wizard, so you can call 'em if you run into any problems or have questions about pricing or policies.

Taking a Show on the Road

Frequent presenters these days often carry their PCs with them—as multimedia notebooks—so that they can run their shows from their own hardware, and that's a terrific advantage. If you're not so equipped, and you must present your show somewhere you can't take your own PC, you'll need to copy your show to disk and take it with you.

Also, you'll need to make sure that the PC you'll use to put on your show—let's call it the "presentation PC"—is equipped to display PowerPoint files. If the presentation PC has either Windows 95 or Windows NT and has PowerPoint installed, you're all set to go. If the PC has 95 or NT, but not PowerPoint, you'll need to bring along the PowerPoint viewer to teach the presentation PC how to show a PowerPoint file. And if the presentation PC has just Windows 3.1 and no PowerPoint, you're still okay—Office 97 includes a viewer program you can install on a Windows 3.1 PC to enable it to play PowerPoint 97 shows.

In the next few pages, you'll learn how to prepare and package everything you need to take it all with you.

Packing Up a Show

A short presentation's .ppt or .pps file will fit easily on a diskette—so in some cases, you can simply copy your .ppt or .pps file onto a diskette and take it with you. However, even when you can apply that approach—and often the size of a show prevents it anyway—I recommend a different way: PowerPoint's Pack and Go Wizard.

The Pack and Go Wizard solves three problems with taking a show on the road:

- It makes sure that you bring along all of the files a selected show needs. For example, when you pack up a show containing multimedia and links, you need to pack up not just the presentation file, but also linked files and multimedia files. Pack and Go can even ensure that the presentation PC has all the fonts your show needs.
- It automatically splits up the files as necessary to fit the whole show on one or more diskettes, and then includes a program on the first diskette that splices the files back together while copying them to the presentation PC.
- It adds to the diskettes (optionally) the Windows 95/NT PowerPoint Viewer, required to run your show on a PC that doesn't have PowerPoint.

To run Pack and Go, open the presentation in PowerPoint and choose File | Pack and Go. The Pack and Go Wizard opens. Work your way through the Wizard's dialogs, completing each dialog and following any additional instructions. Click Next to move forward to each new dialog, or Back to go back and change earlier entries. Note that an index appears on the left side of the Wizard; click a colored square in the index to jump directly to a specific dialog.

On the Pick files to pack dialog, you can simply instruct the Wizard to pack up the current presentation, or you can Browse to select another show to pack. In Choose destination, you select the disk drive on which the presentation will be packed.

Fast Track

While the main job of Pack and Go is to package a presentation on diskette, note that its Choose destination dialog enables you to package the presentation on any drive to which your PC has access. You can pack your presentation onto a shared network drive, for example, to make it accessible to others on your network who will view it from their own workstations.

The Links dialog (see Figure 9-15) includes two very important check boxes, both of which you should usually check, to be on the safe side.

- Check Include linked files to instruct the Wizard to include on the diskette any files pointed to by links (see Chapter 10, "Livening Up Your Presentations"). For example, if a link on a slide in the presentation opens a Word file, Pack and Go makes sure the Word file is copied to the diskettes along with the presentation.
- Check Embed TrueType fonts to include font definitions on the diskettes. When you format the text of your show, you can choose the font (typeface) for text. If the presentation PC doesn't have all of the same fonts installed on it that are on your PC, Windows automatically substitutes an available font when your show is presented—in which case your text will not look exactly as you intended it to. If you check this check box, PowerPoint embeds the font definitions—builds them into the document—so that your font formatting appears exactly as you intended it to, regardless of what fonts are stored on the presentation PC.

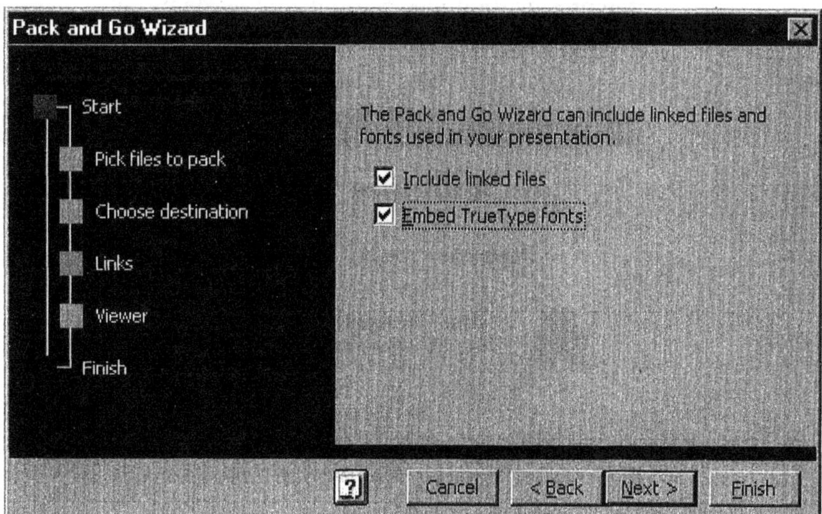

Figure 9-15: In general, always check both check boxes on Pack and Go's Links dialog.

Finally, on the Viewer dialog, you can choose to include the Windows 95/NT PowerPoint viewer on the diskettes. The viewer equips any Windows 95 or Windows NT PC to show your presentation, even if PowerPoint is not installed on that machine.

When you complete the Pack and Go dialogs, make sure you have inserted a blank, formatted diskette into the destination drive, and have a few more diskettes handy, in case you need them. Also, if you have chosen to include the viewer, insert your Office 97 CD in your CD-ROM drive (the Wizard copies the viewer from the CD). Click Finish. The Wizard prompts you through copying the files to the diskettes.

Setting Up & Running Your Road Show

To set up your show, insert the first (or only) diskette into the presentation PC. Open Windows Explorer, and open the file list for the drive in which you inserted the diskette (usually A:). In the list, find a file called Pngsetup, and double-click it. The setup program opens (see Figure 9-16), and prompts you for the name of the folder into which you want to copy the presentation files. Supply a folder name, and the setup program prompts you through the remaining steps.

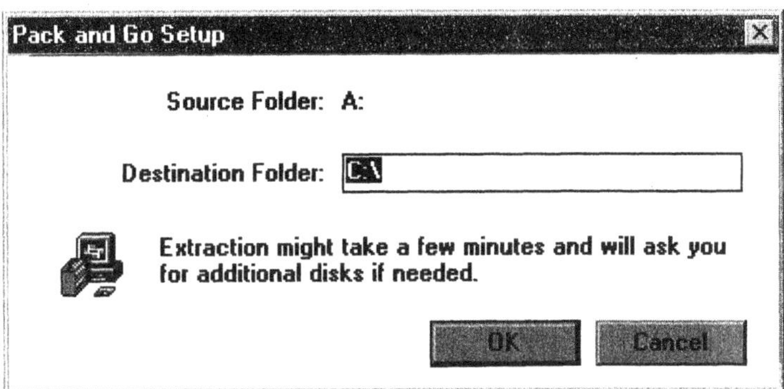

Figure 9-16: The Pngsetup program unpacks a show for presentation.

To run your presentation:

- **In PowerPoint (where available).** Open PowerPoint, open the presentation file, and choose Slide Show | View Show.

- **In the viewer.** Open the folder to which you copied your presentation files, and double-click the file Ppview32. Choose your presentation from the list that appears.

FYI: Running Your Show on Windows 3.1

Using the Windows 3.1 viewer, you can run your PowerPoint 97 presentation on a PC running Windows 3.1. Begin by using Pack and Go to pack up your show, but don't bother packing the Windows 95/NT viewer.

Instead, prepare a blank, formatted diskette (high-density—you need 1.32MB of space). Copy onto the diskette all of the files from the following folder on your Office 97 CD:

Valupack\Ppt4view

On the presentation PC, set up the presentation files on the hard disk as described earlier. When finished, insert the Windows 3.1 viewer diskette, open its file list in Windows Explorer, and double-click Vsetup.exe. Follow the prompts to install the viewer.

Moving On

In two chapters—8 and 9—you've discovered how to create and present elegant, professional-looking presentations, and to produce useful accessories—notes and handouts. That's a lot of presentation power for a little work.

However, at this point your slides contain just text. That's OK—90% of all presentations contain nothing more, and a well-organized text-based presentation is more effective than a dozen poorly organized light shows. Then again, smartly applied, a little flash never hurt a presentation. That's where Chapter 10, "Livening Up Your Presentations," comes in. There you'll learn not only how to add pictures to your show, but also how to create knockout effects with easy-to-apply animation effects, sound effects, recorded narration, video clips, and more.

10

Livening Up Your Presentations

Okay, it's no secret that a presentation with color makes a stronger impression than one without, and that a picture here and there helps spice up a show, keeping your audience attentive. But if that's true, how much *more* persuasive might the show be if charged up by animation, music, sound effects, and even movie clips?

In this chapter, you discover the exciting ways you can impact a presentation—sorry…give your presentation more *impact*—by adding to your PowerPoint slides the full thrust of Windows multimedia. Since most multimedia plants us squarely in the realm of electronic presentations, you'll also discover here the ins and outs of creating, configuring, and presenting electronic shows.

Note that although pictures can appear in slides whether the show is presented electronically or traditionally (on 35mm slides or transparencies), the steps for inserting pictures in slides logically belong in this chapter because those steps are essentially the same as those for inserting other media types—sound and movie clips.

So without further ado—on with the show!

Adding Multimedia to Slides

Adding multimedia to slides can be as simple or as complicated as you want it to be. As you discover throughout this chapter, PowerPoint offers a few quick, easy ways to add visual and aural interest to your show by choosing from among its own pre-made multimedia options and files from the Office 97 Clip Gallery. The more specific—and more personal—your multimedia needs, the more work you have to do, because you can't rely on PowerPoint to supply the media for you. Still, adding even custom multimedia is a pretty straightforward job.

Working Objects Into the Slide Layout

Just as the text on slides is contained within flexible placeholders, so are any other objects, including all types of media files, and even the speaker icon for a sound clip. Any time you add a new object to a slide, you add a placeholder. To fit the newly inserted element within the layout, you usually must reposition its placeholder, and sometimes edit the placeholder's size or shape, to make a good fit.

As you discover the ways to add multimedia, keep in mind that inserting the media is usually not the end of the job:

- After inserting any object, you usually must fiddle with its size, shape, and position to fit it attractively within the slide layout.
- By default, all objects on a slide appear when the slide does. But you can animate any object on a slide so that it materializes in the slide later—when you advance the show or after a preset number of seconds—in any of a wide range of fun, funky ways. See "Animating Objects," later in this chapter.

FYI: Other Stuff You Can Insert in Slides

Like its Office 97 sisters (brothers? cousins?), PowerPoint can use charts produced by Microsoft Chart and the many types of pictures you can create with the OfficeArt drawing tools. To learn more about OfficeArt and Chart, see Chapter 2, "Getting to Know the Office 97 Environment." To create and insert these objects from within PowerPoint, choose Insert|Chart (for a chart) or choose Insert|Picture and choose one of the drawing options.

Also, you can import a Word table or Excel worksheet right into a PowerPoint slide, where you can work it into the layout exactly as you would a picture. To learn about importing tables and worksheets, see Chapter 21, "Collaborating & Integrating With Office 97."

FYI: Working With Movies & Sound

As you do with pictures, charts, and tables, you must also work movie and sound clips into the layout. By default:

- A movie clip appears in the slide layout as a still image of the first frame of the video—it appears to be an ordinary picture, and you can size, shape, and position it just like a picture.
- A sound clip appears in the layout as a tiny speaker icon. You can size, shape, and position the icon.

During the presentation, the clips play when clicked. However, you can configure a clip's custom animation settings to enable it to play automatically, or to hide the icon or clip picture until the clip plays. See "Customizing Animations" later in this chapter.

Fast Track

When you use a template to create a new show, or apply one of PowerPoint's AutoLayouts to create the slide layout (see Chapter 9), some slides may have empty placeholders in them, in which instructions to "double-click" to add the object appear. When you double-click the empty placeholder, the dialog that opens is the one required for adding the particular type of object the placeholder wants. For example, if the note in the placeholder says "Double-click to add clip art," the Office 97 Clip Gallery opens.

Although the empty placeholder may be perfectly positioned within the layout, when you fill the placeholder with an object the placeholder's size and shape may change to conform to the object you inserted. So you still must fine tune the shape, size, and position of the placeholder, even when that placeholder was supplied by the template or AutoLayout.

In Chapter 9, "Designing Presentations," you learned how to manipulate the size, shape, and position of a placeholder by clicking and dragging on the placeholder's border and *handles*, the little squares that appear on each side of the border and at every corner.

Inserting Media From the Clip Gallery

The easiest and best way to add pictures, movies, and sounds to slides is to borrow them from Office 97's Clip Gallery. Not only is the Clip Art easy to use, but the pictures and movies in the Clip Gallery retain their appearance well after being worked into a slide layout. You can fire up PowerPoint's clever AutoClipArt facility to solicit PowerPoint's suggestions for clip art, or you can selectively browse the Clip Gallery for pictures to add to your slides.

Fast Track

You can use the Clip Gallery to insert art into any Office 97 document, and you can customize and add to the Clip Gallery. To learn more about the Clip Gallery, see Chapter 2, "Getting to Know the Office 97 Environment."

Asking PowerPoint to Choose Art for You

The AutoClipArt facility scans the text of your show, looking for keywords or phrases it can associate with files in the Clip Gallery. You can then review the suggestions and apply any with which you agree. AutoClipArt is a fast and easy way to dress up a show in a hurry.

To use AutoClipArt, open the presentation in Slide view, then choose Tools | AutoClipArt. PowerPoint analyzes the show, then presents the dialog shown in Figure 10-1. Two lists appear at the bottom of the dialog: The list on the left shows words in your show for which AutoClipArt has art suggestions. Because some words appear on more than one slide, the list on the right, On Slide, lists the slide numbers of all slides on which the selected word appears.

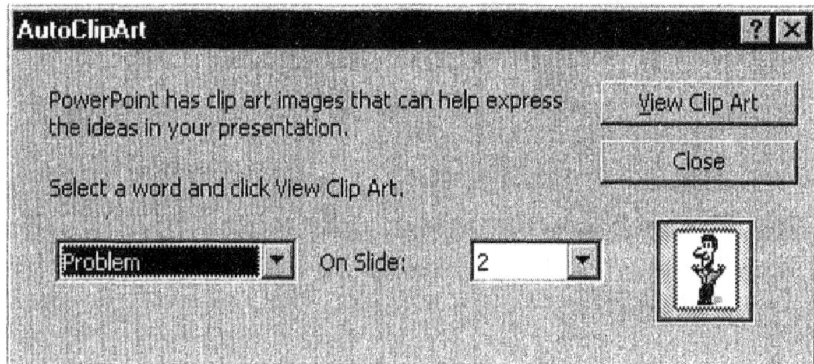

Figure 10-1: To ask PowerPoint to choose art based on your show's content, choose Tools | AutoClipArt.

To view, and accept or reject, a suggestion, choose a word from the list and a slide number. The slide whose number you selected appears in PowerPoint, behind the AutoClipArt dialog. Click the View Clip Art button. The Clip Gallery opens (see Figure 10-2), but on each of its four tabs—Clip Art, Pictures, Sounds, and Videos—the gallery shows just the items that AutoClipArt thinks may help to illustrate or support the word you selected on the AutoClipArt dialog.

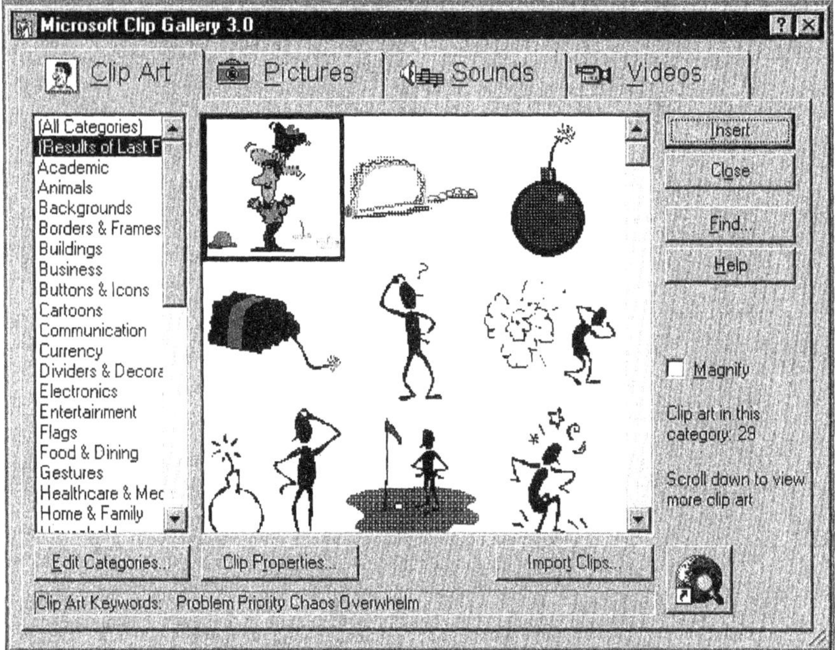

Figure 10-2: When AutoClipArt opens the Clip Gallery, only the suggested artwork appears.

To accept a suggestion, click it, then click Insert. The item is inserted into the current slide, and the AutoClipArt dialog returns so you can select another word or slide number. To close the Clip Gallery without accepting a suggestion and return to the AutoClipArt dialog, click Close on the Clip Gallery.

When finished with the suggestions, close the AutoClipArt dialog, then work through your show, fitting each new image into the layout of its slide.

Fast Track

Whenever you insert a picture—whether from the Clip Gallery or from a file—the Picture toolbar appears automatically (see Chapter 6, "Adding Pictures, Tables & Borders"). You can use the Picture toolbar to crop the picture or change its brightness, contrast, or other characteristics. To close the Picture toolbar, press Esc.

However, it's often wisest—especially when using professionally created artwork—to avoid manipulating the image with the Picture toolbar. The image has been designed to look its best already under a variety of circumstances, and any change might detract from its appearance.

Choosing Art From the Gallery

Instead of using AutoClipArt, you can go straight to the Clip Gallery to add any image or clip you like. Begin by opening in Slide view the slide for which you want to add art. Then click the Insert Clip Art button on the Standard toolbar (or choose Insert | Picture, Clip Art). From the tabs in the Clip Gallery, choose the art you want to use, then click Insert.

Note that you can add anything in the Clip Gallery—a clip art image, picture, sound, or video clip—this way. Instead of opening the gallery as described above, you can open it by choosing Insert | Movies and Sounds, then choosing Movie from Gallery or Sound from Gallery. But it really doesn't matter how you open the gallery—once you're there, you can choose any form of art from the gallery.

Placing Other Types of Media Objects

If the Clip Gallery doesn't have the media you want, you can insert many types of picture, sound, and movie files in PowerPoint slides. PowerPoint includes built-in support for popular sound, image, and video file formats, including:

- Pictures: .emf, .jpg, .png, .bmp, .rle, .dib, .wmf
- Sound clips: .mid, .rmi, .wav
- Movie (video) clips: .avi, .mov, .pic, .jpg

In addition to these file types, you may insert other types for which Office 97 *filters* have been installed. See the Appendix to learn how to install optional filters from your Office 97 CD.

To insert a media file, open in Slide view the slide in which you want to insert the media. Then choose from the menu:

- To insert a picture, choose Insert | Picture | From File.
- To insert a sound clip, choose Insert | Movies and Sounds | Sound from File.

- To insert a movie clip, choose Insert | Movies and Sounds | Movie from File.

No matter which file you choose, a dialog similar to the one in Figure 10-3 opens. (The dialog's name will be Insert Picture, Insert Sound, or Insert Movie, depending on what you're up to, but otherwise it'll look the same in all cases.) Use the Look in list to navigate to the folder containing the media file. For each folder you choose from Look in, the box beneath Look in shows all of the picture files in that folder. When you see the file you want, click it, then click OK.

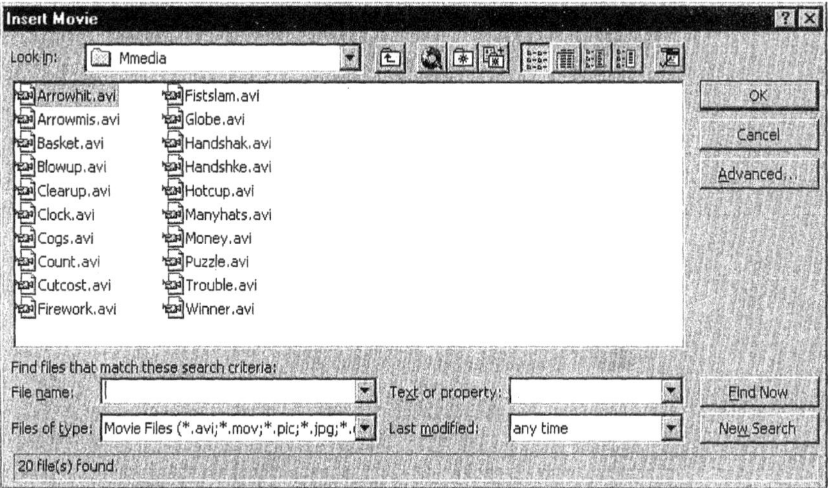

Figure 10-3: To insert a media file, navigate to the file and select it.

The picture, still movie clip, or sound file icon appears in the slide. If you inserted a picture file, the Picture toolbar appears—so if you want, you can fine tune the picture's appearance.

Walk-Through: Inserting Objects in Slides

Follow the steps below to practice inserting objects in slides.

1. Open or create a presentation (remain in Slide view).
2. Choose a slide on which there's room for a picture. If that slide contains some text besides the title, change the shape and position of the text placeholder to leave open a rough area into which you'll put a picture. (Be sure to deselect the text placeholder when you're finished.)
3. Make sure your Office 97 CD is in your CD-ROM drive.
4. Click the Insert Clip Art button on the Standard toolbar (or choose Insert|Picture|Clip Art).
5. Click the Clip Art tab, click any image you like, and click Insert.

   The clip art appears in the slide, its placeholder selected.
6. Point to the picture's placeholder border, click and drag the picture to position it in the area you set up for it.
7. Click and drag the placeholder's handles as necessary to make the picture's shape and size conform to the area allotted to it.
8. Press Esc to deselect the picture.
9. Click the New Slide button on the Standard toolbar (or choose Insert|New Slide).

   The New Slide dialog opens, showing the AutoLayouts.
10. Scroll down the list of AutoLayouts, choose one that contains a picture of a movie slate, and click OK.

    The slide layout changes, and a placeholder prompts you to "Double-click to add media clip."
11. Double-click as instructed.

    The Insert Movie dialog opens.
12. In Look in, select the drive letter of your CD-ROM drive.
13. Choose the ClipArt folder, then the Media folder.
14. Click Clock.avi, then click OK.

    A clock image—the frozen first frame of a clock movie—opens in the placeholder.
15. To test the clip, click the Slide Show view button, then click the clock.

Creating Your Own Sound for Presentations

When you want a sound that's truly personal or specific to the show, you need to record it yourself, then attach it to a slide. You can do that easily, all from within PowerPoint.

Recording New Sound Clips

In Slide view, open the slide in which you want to insert a recorded sound. Then choose Insert | Movies and Sounds | Record Sound. The Record Sound dialog opens, as shown in Figure 10-4. Click in the Name box, and enter a name for your new sound.

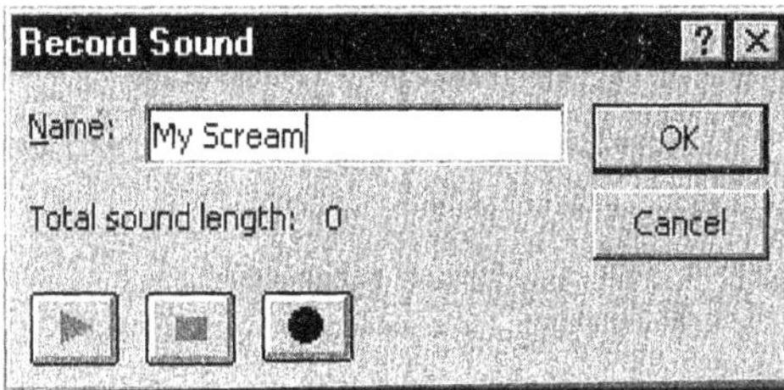

Figure 10-4: Choose Insert | Movies and Sounds | Record Sound to record a new sound clip.

FYI: Microphone Basics

In case you hadn't thought about it, note that recording a sound requires a microphone or other sound input (such as a line input from a tape player) attached to your PC's sound card. While many notebook PCs, and some desktop PCs, have built-in mics, these usually record unacceptable sound clips—the mic is so close to the PC that it picks up too much of the PC's fan noise. If you're recording from a microphone, attach an external one, and record as far away from the PC as practical. (Consider standing a few feet from the PC and having a partner work PowerPoint for you.)

On the dialog, the recording and play controls mimic those on a VCR or tape deck. The rightmost button—with a big red dot on it—is the Record button. When ready, click the Record button, then speak, whistle, play a tape, or otherwise make the sound you want to record. When finished, click the Stop button (the middle button with the square on it). Then do any of the following:

- To hear your new sound, click the Play button (the left button with an arrow on it).
- To record over the sound (in case you don't like your first try), click Record.
- To insert the sound clip in the slide, click OK.

Narrating Slides

You can record narration for a specific slide in the same way you would record any new sound. But if your plan is to record narration for an entire show, you're better off firing up PowerPoint's Record Narration dialog. Record Narration enables you to step through your slides—just as if you were presenting them—and narrate as you go, so you can record all of your slide narration in a single session. More importantly, with Record Narration you can automatically set the timings of slide changes for a self-running presentation (see "Setting Up & Running Electronic Shows," later in this chapter).

Before recording narration:

- Finish creating and editing the rest of the presentation, including adding any animation effects. You want to avoid making changes after recording narration that would affect the timing of the presentation.
- Script your narration, and rehearse it—while watching the slide show—until you can perform it smoothly.
- Connect a good external microphone to your PC's sound card.

When ready, open the presentation, and choose Slide Show | Record Narration. The Record Narration dialog opens (see Figure 10-5). On the dialog, the current settings for recording quality are shown.

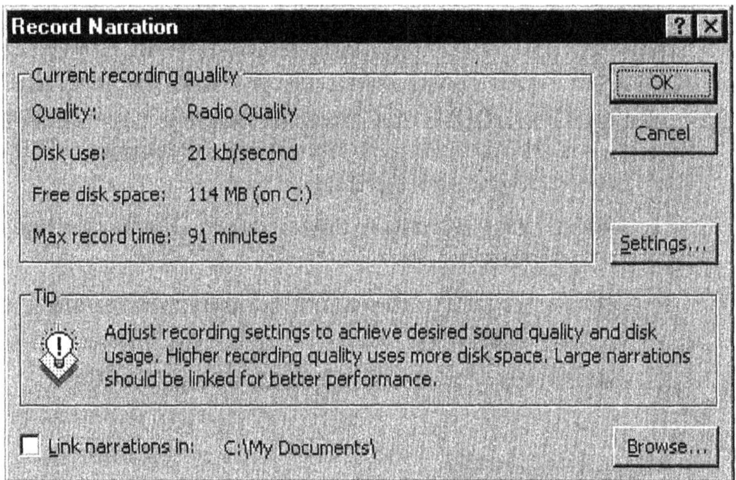

Figure 10-5: You can record narration slide-by-slide with the Record Narration dialog.

FYI: Sound Quality vs. Disk Space

Most sound cards can record at several different quality levels, from scratchy-sounding "telephone" quality, to serviceable "radio" quality, to "CD" quality, the highest-quality audio.

The higher the quality of the recording, the more disk space it takes up per minute. While you may be tempted to record your narration at CD quality, note that a mere 10 minutes of CD-quality narration requires over 100MB of disk space. At radio quality, you can fit around 80 minutes of narration in 100MB. (Obviously, even at radio quality, recording complete narration is practical only for relatively short shows.)

The Record Narration dialog shows how much hard disk space will be used for each second of narration at the current quality level (Disk use) and the maximum length of narration you can record based on the available disk space. If you want to change the recording quality, click the Settings button.

Note that the Record Narration dialog recommends linking narration to the presentation file by checking the Link narrations in check box. That's always a good idea. If you do link and later use Pack and Go (see Chapter 8, "Getting Started With PowerPoint") to pack up your show, be sure to use Pack and Go's Include linked files option to pack the narration file along with the presentation. (To learn more about linking, see Chapter 21, "Collaborating & Integrating With Office 97.")

When the settings on the Record Narration dialog are what you want them to be, you're ready to record. Take a deep, relaxing breath, then click OK. The Slide Show begins with Slide 1. Speak your narration for Slide 1, and when you finish, advance to Slide 2 and continue your narration.

Continue through the show until you reach the end, then press Esc. A dialog opens, informing you that the narrations have been saved, and asking whether you'd like PowerPoint to save slide timings (for a self-running show; see "Setting & Rehearsing Slide Timings," later in this chapter) based on the "performance" of the slide show you just gave. Click Yes to save the timings and close the slide show, or No to discard the timings.

Playing a CD in the Background

To accompany your show, you can play an audio CD from the presentation PC's CD-ROM drive. You can attach any track or cut from a CD to a slide, or you can start a CD from any slide and have it play continuously through successive slides.

Note that, for you to use this feature when presenting, the presentation PC must be equipped with a CD-ROM drive and speakers, and must be capable of playing an audio CD (not all CD-ROM drives can).

Begin by inserting the audio CD in your CD-ROM drive. In Slide view, open the slide on which you want the audio to play (or begin playing), and choose Insert | Movies and Sounds | Play CD Audio Track. The Play Options dialog opens (see Figure 10-6).

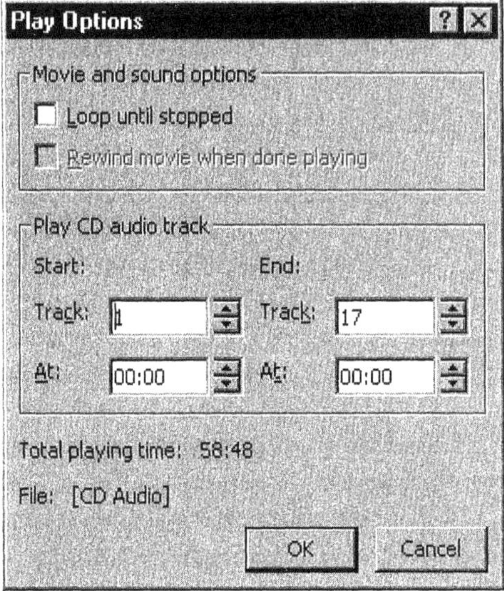

Figure 10-6: Play your favorite CD during a show.

On the dialog, choose the number of the Start and End track (by default, Start shows track 1 and End shows the number of the last track on the CD). To start or end at a particular moment within a track, enter the time index in the Start or End At lists. (Use the display on your CD player, or Windows's Media Player applet, to find the time index settings for the moment you want to start or end.) If you want the track to repeat itself if it finishes before the slide is advanced, click Loop until stopped. Click OK.

A CD icon appears on the slide. You may edit the CD icon's placeholder like any other to change its position, size, or shape. When you view the show, click the CD icon to play the CD track. If you advance the slide before the CD track finishes playing, play stops automatically.

To change the settings on the Play Options dialog later, right-click the CD icon and choose Edit Sound Object from the context menu.

Fast Track

To configure the CD audio to play automatically, or to play through multiple slides, change its Custom Animation settings (see "Customizing Animations" later in this chapter).

Adding Animation Effects

Animation effects are a great (and easy!) way to add the visual kick of motion—and often sound, too—to your show. Animation effects change the way an object in a slide makes its way onto the screen.

For example, without animation, a picture on a slide appears at the same time the slide does. If you animate that picture, the slide at first appears without the picture. Then, when you advance the presentation or when a selected number of seconds passes, the picture animates its way into the slide—it may slide in from the side, explode from nowhere, or materialize like it was transported from the starship *Enterprise*. Usually, the animation effect is accompanied by a sound effect which just makes it more fun.

You can animate anything that appears on a slide: the title, bullet text, pictures, charts, tables, or movies. More important, you can animate multiple objects on a slide. A slide can appear with nothing but a title—then, one by one, the words and pictures come in flying, wiggling, and sliding. In addition to animating objects in slides, you can animate the way the slide itself shows up. Animating a slide's arrival is called animating its *transition*.

In the next few pages, you learn how to animate any slide object, to customize the way the animation behaves, and to animate slide transitions.

Applying El Quicko Animations

The easiest way to animate is to apply one of PowerPoint's Preset animation effects. In Slide view, click the object you want to animate to select it. Choose Slide Show | Preset Animation. A list of animation options appears, as shown in Figure 10-7. (The list is too long for me to describe what each choice does—and besides, an animated picture is worth a thousand words. Try 'em and see what happens.)

After you select a preset animation, you return to Slide view. To see your selected animation in action, click the Slide Show View button; the current slide opens in Slide Show view. By default, a slide containing animation appears at first without any of the animated objects on it; advancing the show—by pressing PgDn or the Right arrow key—starts the animation to bring the object onto the slide.

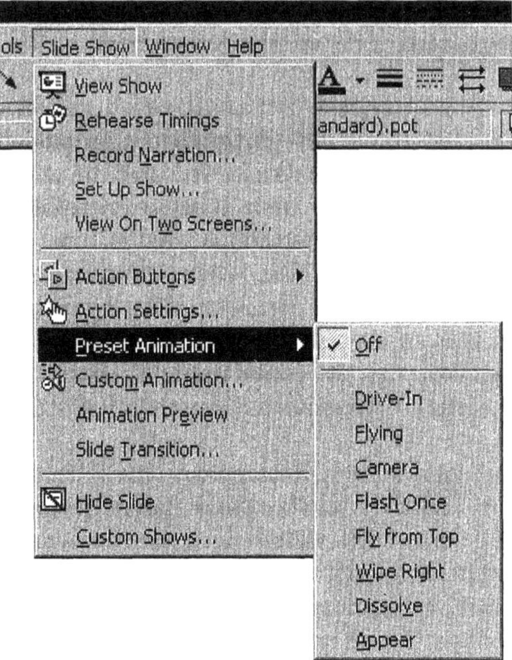

Figure 10-7: You add Preset Animation in a snap from a submenu.

Note that when you apply animation to a placeholder containing multiple paragraphs—such as a bulleted list—each item in the list is animated separately. In other words, when you advance, only the first paragraph or list item in the placeholder animates its way onscreen. When you advance again, the next item appears, and so on. (You can change this behavior; see "Customizing Animations," next.)

Also, you can animate multiple placeholders on a single slide. When you run the slide show, the objects appear one at a time—one object each time you advance. The objects appear in the same order in which you assigned preset animation to them. For example, if you apply animation to the title, then to a picture, the title appears the first time you advance, then the picture appears the second time you advance. You can change the animation order by re-applying the preset animation in a new order or by changing the order in the Custom Animation dialog.

Customizing Animations

The custom animation effects are not really different from the preset ones. What's different is the level of control Custom Animation gives you over the order of animations on a slide, the timing of their appearance,

and other aspects of slide animation. You can use the Custom Animation dialog to apply new animations, to change the behavior of existing ones (including preset animations you've applied), and to change the animated behavior of charts, movies, and sounds.

To apply or edit custom animation, open in Slide view the slide whose animation you want to customize (you need not select a placeholder). Choose Slide Show | Custom Animation to open the Custom Animation dialog (see Figure 10-8).

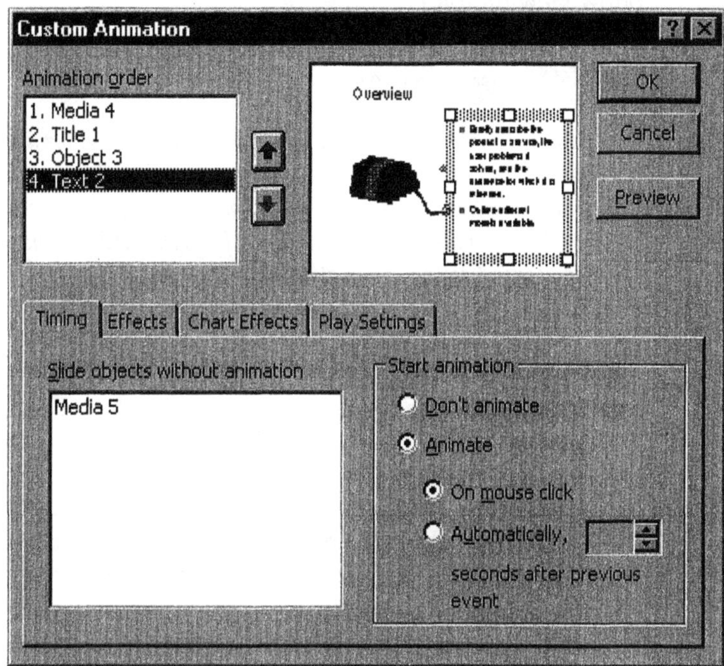

Figure 10-8: Choose the timing for animation on the Timing tab of the Custom Animation dialog.

On the dialog, the Animation order list shows any objects in the slide which are already animated and shows them in the order in which they'll make their appearances. To change an object's order, select it in the list (when you select, the Preview pane on the right shows the placeholder for the object you've chosen). Click one of the arrows to the right of the list: Up to make the object appear earlier in the animation order, Down to make it appear later.

The Timing tab lists any objects on the slide that are not currently animated. To animate any object listed, select it, then click the radio button for Animate. The object appears in the Animation order list; you may change its order and customize its animation just like the other animated objects.

To customize the animation of an object, select it in the Animation order list, then change the settings on the four tabs. After making any change, you may click the Preview button to see the effects in the Preview pane—with one important exception. The Preview pane automatically runs through all animations on the slide, without your having to advance the slide. (To better test the real-life appearance of an animated slide, click OK to close the Custom Animation dialog, then click the Slide Show view button.)

Fast Track

To go directly to changing the animation settings for a specific object, select that object in Slide view before opening the Custom Animation dialog. When the dialog opens, that object is preselected for customizing.

You can also do the same thing by right-clicking the object, then choosing Custom Animation from the context menu.

Important settings in the Custom Animation dialog include:

- **Timing tab (see Figure 10-8).** For animated objects, choose On mouse click to specify that the object appear only when you advance the slide (whether by mouse click, PgDn, or the Right arrow key). Choose Automatically, and a number of seconds, to enable the object to appear a few seconds after the previous event without any action from you. If the selected object is Number 1 in the animation order, it appears the set number of seconds after the slide appears. If it is Number 2 or later, it appears the set number of seconds after the preceding object in the animation order.
- **Effects tab (see Figure 10-9).** On this tab you can choose from lists to select an animation effect (from a much wider array of options than the Preset animations) and a sound effect to go with the animation (or No Sound). In After animation, choose how an object should appear when its animation is done and the next object appears. For example, if you open this list and click one of the color squares it offers, the selected object "dims" to that color when the next animated object arrives. This is a great way to help viewers focus on new ideas as they appear. For example, when a new item in a bullet list materializes, the preceding items dim.

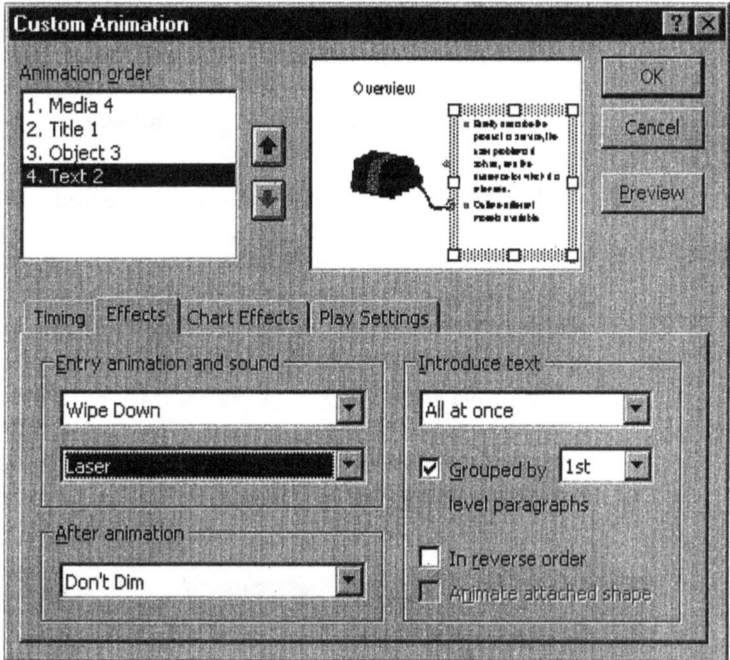

Figure 10-9: Change what the animation does on the Effects tab of the Custom Animation dialog.

When the selected object contains text, you can drop down the list under Introduce text to make each paragraph (or bullet item) animate its way onto the screen in a single block (All at once), or a word or letter at a time. By default, a checkmark appears in Grouped by, so that each paragraph in the placeholder is animated separately, requiring its own advance to appear. If you uncheck the check box, all text within the placeholder appears at once—bullet items don't materialize separately.

If you leave the checkmark in Grouped by, you can select how the various levels within nested lists (see Chapter 9, "Designing Presentations") appear. By default, lists are grouped by 1st-level items for animation. In other words, at each advance, one 1st-level bullet *plus* any bullets indented beneath it—2nd level, 3rd level, and so on—appears. If you change the Grouped by entry to 2nd level, at an advance one 1st-level item appears, but not any 2nd- or 3rd-level item beneath it. At the next advance, the first 2nd-level bullet (and any 3rd-level bullets beneath it) appears.

- **Chart Effects tab.** Here you can customize the effects for an animated chart, including selecting different effects for different elements of the chart, and After animation effects (see Effects tab). You can also animate a chart's grid and legend separately from the chart by checking the check box provided.
- **Play Settings tab (see Figure 10-10).** Here you customize the play of sound files, movie clips, or CD audio tracks you've inserted in the slide. The Play using animation order configures the object to play automatically at its spot in the Animation order list, instead of waiting for you to click it. If you check that check box, you can apply further options in the same part of the tab. For example, to configure a sound clip or CD audio track to continue playing even after the slide is advanced, choose Continue slide show, then choose After current slide and select the number of slides through which you want play to continue.

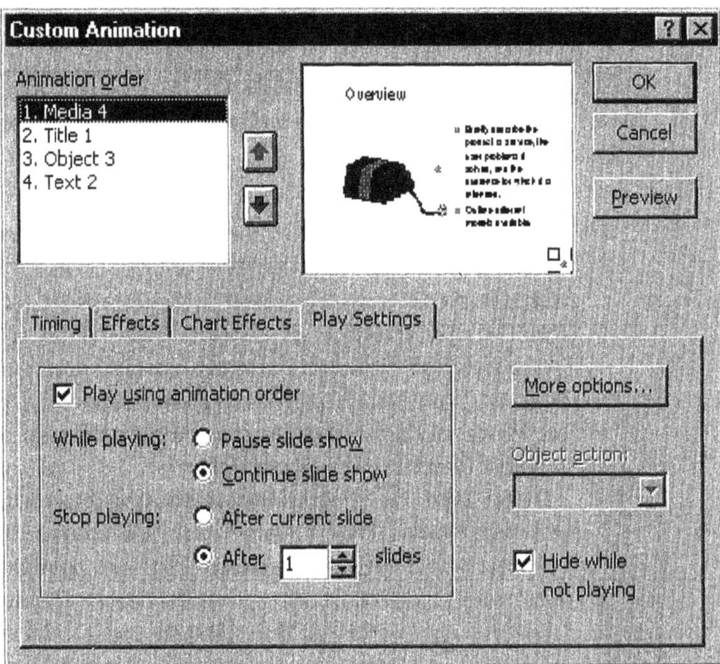

Figure 10-10: Control how sound, movies, and CD tracks play on the Custom Animation dialog's Play Settings tab.

Walk-Through: Animations

Follow the steps below to practice adding animation to slides.

1. In Slide view, open (or create) a slide containing a bulleted list and a picture.
2. Click the list to display its placeholder.
3. Choose Slide Show|Preset Animation|Drive-In.
4. Click the picture to display its placeholder.
5. Choose Slide Show|Preset Animation, Flying.
6. Click the Slide Show View button.
   The slide appears without the list or picture.
7. Advance the slide (press PgDn).
   The first list item "drives in" and makes a screeching sound.
8. Advance through the rest of the animations.
9. Return to the slide in Slide view.
10. Choose Slide Show|Custom Animation.
11. In Animation order, choose Text 2.
    The list will be selected in the Preview pane; if not, select a different Text entry in the list until you see the list highlighted in the preview.
12. Click the Effects tab.
13. Drop down the After animation list, and click a color square.
14. Click OK to save the custom animation.
15. Switch to Slide Show view, and advance through the animations.
    What's different?

Animating Slide Transitions

In addition to animating what's on a slide, you can animate the way the slide itself materializes on the screen—the *slide transition*. By default, all slide transitions are simple "cuts"—one slide vanishes, the next appears. To choose a more creative transition, open in Slide view the slide whose transition you want to change. (You'll be editing the way the selected slide makes its way onscreen, *not* they way the selected slide makes way for the next.)

Choose Slide Show | Slide Transition to open the Slide Transition dialog (see Figure 10-11). The little preview picture is not your show, but a two-slide example (a doggy and a key—make up your own story for it!) that automatically demonstrates any Effect you choose from the list beneath it. (The example also plays the selected transition any time you click it.) Choose an Effect from the list, and click a radio button to choose whether the animation of that effect should be Slow, Medium, or Fast. (To choose no effect, choose Cut, or No transition, from the list of effects.)

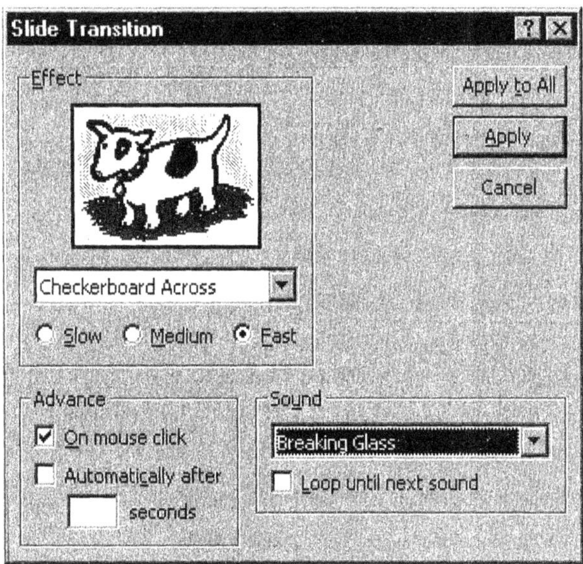

Figure 10-11: Choose Slide Show | Slide Transition to add an animated transition between slides.

Under Advance, choose On mouse click to display the transition effect only when you arrive at the slide. If you choose Automatically after and enter a number of seconds, while you view the slide the transition effect repeats itself every time the set number of seconds passes (the transition effect repeats automatically, but the show doesn't advance to the next slide).

Under Sound, select a sound to play accompanying the transition. If you check the check box next to Loop until next sound, the selected sound plays over and over until another sound plays.

When finished configuring the transition, click Apply to apply the transition to just the selected slide, or Apply to All to make this the transition for every slide in the show.

Fast Track

To preview the animation and transition for a slide without starting the show, open the slide in Slide view and choose Slide Show | Animation Preview. The slide miniature opens and shows the transition and all animation (without waiting for advances between animations, even if they are required). To see the animation again, click the miniature.

Adding Hyperlinks to Presentations

A *hyperlink* is anything in a slide—text, a picture, a chart, or table—that takes the presentation somewhere else when you click (or point to the link). A link can lead to another slide in the presentation or to a custom show, or it can even open a Word document, Excel spreadsheet, or other file. To make a hyperlink more obvious for the benefit of kiosk users and others who must run a show for themselves, PowerPoint includes an assortment of "action buttons," attractive buttons you can easily insert in any slide and then configure as hyperlinks.

During a show, when the pointer is over a hyperlink (whether text, an action button, or other type), the regular Windows pointer changes to a hand with a pointing finger, just as it does in a Windows-based Web browser when on an Internet link. When a viewer—rather than a presenter—controls the show, the pointing finger helps the viewer locate and activate the hyperlinks.

In the next few pages, you'll learn how to make any object in a slide into a hyperlink and to specify where each link leads. You'll also learn how to add action buttons to your slides and how to configure them.

Although hyperlinks and action buttons are obvious candidates for windowed and kiosk shows (see "Setting Up & Running Electronic Shows," later in this chapter), you may want to use them in your speaker-driven shows. For example, suppose a Word document is available that elaborates on or supports a bullet item on a slide. If that bullet is a link to the Word file, and someone in the audience asks you to expand upon the bullet, you can call up the Word file in a heartbeat—how's that for interactive?

Net-Savvy

In addition to pointing to local resources, a hyperlink in a slide can contain a Web page address. If the PC on which the show is run has a default Web browser and Internet access, clicking the link automatically opens the browser, connects to the Internet, and opens the specified Web page online. For more, see Chapter 22, "Office 97 & the Internet."

Creating a Hyperlink

To add a hyperlink, open the slide in Slide view, and begin by selecting the object you want to make into a link. If the object is a picture, simply clicking the picture to display its placeholder is enough to select it. If you want to make just some of the text within a placeholder or table into a link, select the text just as you do to edit it (see Chapter 9, "Designing Presentations"). For example, to configure one bullet item in a list as a link (but not the others), select the placeholder containing the text, then double-click to the right of the bullet item.

With the object or text selected, choose Slide Show | Action Settings. The Action Settings dialog opens (see Figure 10-12). The dialog has two tabs:

- **Mouse Click.** The action you specify on this tab happens when the link is clicked.
- **Mouse Over.** The action you specify on this tab happens when the pointer rests on the link for a moment; no click is necessary.

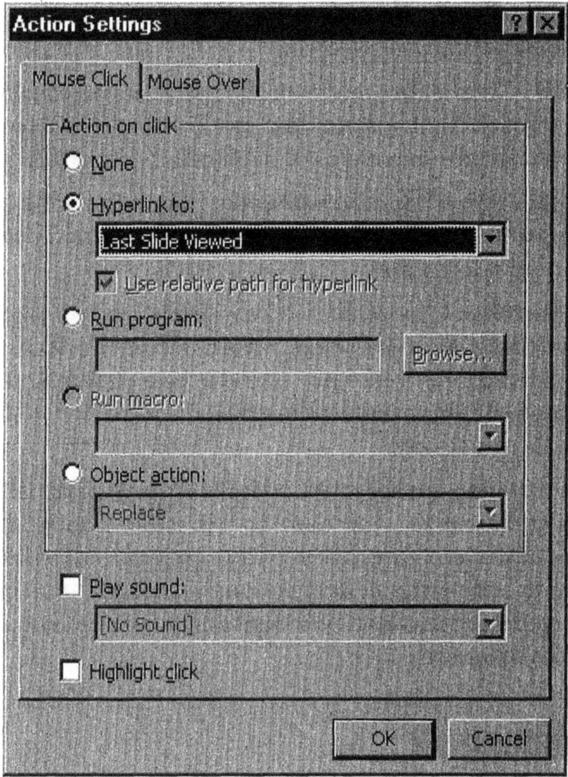

Figure 10-12: Use the Action Settings dialog to determine where a link leads.

You can specify an action on just one tab, or complete both tabs to assign two separate actions to one link: one action that happens when the pointer moves to the link (Mouse Over), another that happens when the link is clicked (Mouse Click).

To specify where the link leads, choose the tab for which you want to define the link, then click the radio button next to Hyperlink to. Drop down the Hyperlink to list, and choose one of the options. Note that choosing some options in the Hyperlink to list brings up another dialog so you can further define the action:

- **Custom Show.** Choose this, and a list of custom shows based on this presentation opens so you can select the one to which to link. (For more on custom shows, see "Setting & Rehearsing Slide Timings" later in this chapter.)

- **Slide.** Choose this, and a list of the slides in the current show opens so you can select one.
- **URL.** Choose this, and a dialog opens so you can enter the full Internet URL (Uniform Resource Locator); for example, http://www.microsoft.com (see Chapter 22, "Office 97 & the Internet").
- **Other PowerPoint Presentation.** Choose this, and a dialog very much like PowerPoint's Open dialog appears, so you can navigate to and select a file.
- **Other File.** Choose this, and a typical Open dialog appears so you can navigate to and select a Word document, Excel worksheet, or other file. The "other file" can also be a picture, sound clip, or video clip that you want to appear when a link is clicked instead of in the usual way.

After making your selection from the Hyperlink to list and completing any dialog that opens, you return to the Action Settings dialog. A description of the hyperlink's destination appears in the list box. Click OK to return to editing the slide. If you made the link from text, notice that the text in the presentation now appears underlined and in a different color from other text.

Fast Track

Near the bottom of the Action Settings dialog appears a check box called Play sound. If you check the check box and then choose a sound from the list, the selected sound plays whenever the link is used.

Creating an Action Button

An action button is no big deal: it's really just an extra-handy, button-shaped hunk of clip art whose mission in life is to be a hyperlink. While action buttons are attractive and convenient, you can insert any button-like images you want and use them as buttons, just by making them into hyperlinks. Action buttons, however, have one additional trick: when clicked, their borders change shading, creating a sort of 3-D imitation of a button being depressed. It's up to you whether you think that's cool or not.

To insert an action button, open the slide in which the button goes, in Slide view. Choose Slide Show | Action Buttons to open the Action Buttons submenu (see Figure 10-13). There are 12 buttons in the submenu; if you rest the pointer on one, a tooltip appears to describe that button's intended use. For example, a button whose picture looks like a movie camera is called Movie in the submenu.

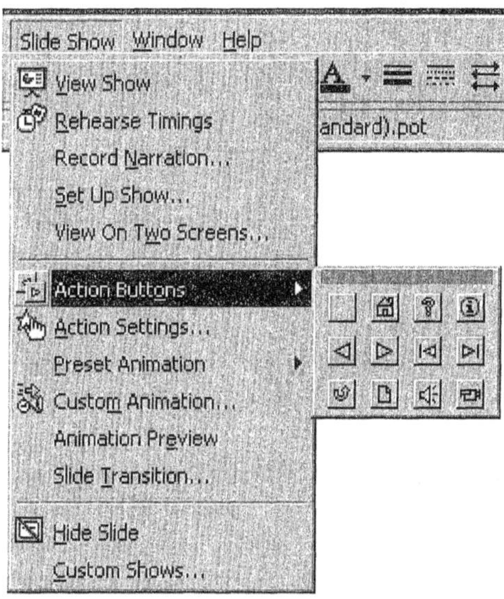

Figure 10-13: Choose an action button from the Action Buttons submenu.

Fast Track

The first button on the Action Buttons submenu, Custom, is a button backing to which you may add a picture to define your own, custom button.

In general, try to use the buttons for their designated purposes, since their designs match icons and buttons used for similar purposes in software and electronics. In a kiosk or windowed show, applying the buttons in their intended roles will help your viewers intuitively guess each button's purpose from its appearance. However, the buttons' actions are not predefined—you're free to assign any action to any button.

Click your chosen button, and the pointer changes to a big crosshair. The crosshair enables you to position and, optionally, size the button. To simply insert the button in the slide in its default size, point the crosshair pointer to the desired spot and click. To size and shape the button as you insert it, point the crosshair pointer to the area where you want to insert the button, click and hold, drag to form an outline of the size and shape you want, then release. (If you don't get the size, shape, or position just right, don't worry—you can edit the size, shape, and position of an action button like any other picture.)

When you insert the button, the Action Settings dialog opens automatically so you can define the button's hyperlink destination and sound.

Setting Up & Running Electronic Shows

Once *everything* else in your electronic show—the slides, the text, the pictures and multimedia, the hyperlinks and action buttons—is done, it's time to configure a few final options that control how your show operates when it's running. For example, you must select whether the show will be presented by a speaker, be browsed in a window, or be browsed at a kiosk—since each of these affects the options available during the running of the show.

Also, you may choose to configure the presentation as a *self-running* show, one that just keeps cranking through the slides with no input from you or the viewer. If you create a self-running show, you'll need to select *timings* for the show, the length of time between each slide change, or between animations.

In this section on PowerPoint, you discover how to configure your show for the precise venue and other circumstances in which it may appear.

Choosing the Presentation Type

On the Set Up Show dialog, you select how you want your electronic show presented. To open the dialog, choose Slide Show | Set Up Show (see Figure 10-14).

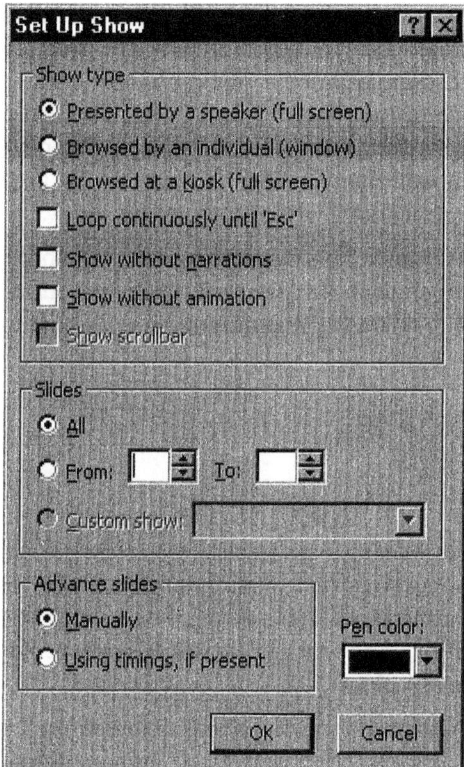

Figure 10-14: Use the Set Up Show dialog to control how your show will be presented.

Under Show type, choose from among options for how the show will appear when viewed in Slide Show view, when run by View Slide Show (on the Slide Show menu), or run in the PowerPoint viewer:

- **Presented by a speaker.** Select this type (the default, traditional show type) to present your show full-screen, hiding everything—PowerPoint (or the PowerPoint viewer), the Office 97 shortcut bar, and so on—but the slides. While the presentation appears to take over the PC, the speaker still has access to all of PowerPoint's editing features underneath, so the speaker can make changes in a pinch. The speaker may also access a number of mid-show tools, such as a pen for scribbling notes onscreen (see "Using Speaker Options in a Presentation," later in this chapter).

- **Browsed by an individual.** This type presents the show in a window, accompanied by navigation tools (the Web toolbar). This type is ideal for presentations the viewer will run him- or herself—such as internal computer-based training sessions. The viewer can advance slides and activate hyperlinks, and can even change the size and shape of the window. The viewer can also run other Windows applications while viewing the show.
- **Browsed at a kiosk.** This type takes over the whole screen—just like the top menu choice—but prevents the viewer from accessing PowerPoint or changing the presentation. Viewers can activate links.

FYI: Kiosk Behavior

A show presented in kiosk mode looks just like one in speaker mode but behaves differently in the following important ways. These differences—which are based on the assumption that the kiosk may include a mouse or other pointing device but does not include a keyboard—must be taken into account in the design, structure, and testing of a kiosk show:

- Slides can be advanced only by the actions of hyperlinks (or action buttons), or automatically advanced by timings (see "Setting & Rehearsing Slide Timings"). If you intend for the viewer to advance the slides or navigate the presentation, you must include on your slides all of the links required to get around. PgUp/PgDn and other advancing methods are disabled.
- The show can be stopped only by the Esc key. Until Esc is pressed, the show loops automatically—when the timings or the viewer advance past the last slide, the show starts over at Slide 1 automatically.
- When the show is not a self-running one, and five minutes pass during which the viewer does not click a link, the show automatically returns to the first slide (it assumes the previous viewer has left, and resets itself for a new viewer).

After you choose a Show type, everything else on the Set Up Show dialog is optional. But you'll find a number of options for fine tuning the behavior of the presentation, beginning with the check boxes in the Show type section. You can choose to show the presentation without animation (slides containing animation appear as if all animations have already been completed) or without narration, if you have recorded it. These options are useful for creating alternate, lower-tech versions of a multimedia-rich presentation when the right equipment may not be available for playing the show in its full glory.

In the Slides section, you can choose to present only a portion of a show by entering a slide number in From and another in To. When you next present the show, it will begin with the slide in From and end at the slide in To. To present a show made up of slides in the current presentation in any order you wish, choose one of your Custom shows.

Finally, in the Advance slides section, choose Manually to allow slides to be advanced at will by the presenter or viewer (except for Kiosk shows), or choose Using timings to make the show a self-running one in which slides advance automatically according to a schedule you set (see "Setting & Rehearsing Slide Timings," next in this chapter).

Fast Track

To prevent the PowerPoint window from appearing after the last slide in a show, choose Tools | Options, choose the View tab, and check the check box for End with black slide.

Setting & Rehearsing Slide Timings

The *timings* of a show are the fixed amounts of time PowerPoint holds on a slide, or between animations, before advancing automatically in a self-running show. If you record narration for your show, you can automatically apply the timing of your narration session to the show. Otherwise, you'll need to set the timings.

Fast Track

Some folks use timings not just for self-running shows, but to prepare very tightly timed speaker-driven presentations. By setting timings, you give yourself a sort of time budget, with a certain amount of time allotted to each slide, or topic. By rehearsing the show as a self-running presentation, you can tailor your own performance to fill precisely the amount of time you wish. When you present for real, you can use the timings or trust that your rehearsal has conditioned you to time the show precisely.

To set timings, first work through the presentation several times to develop a good sense of what the timing should be like. When you're ready, choose Slide Show | Rehearse Timings. The show begins at Slide 1, and the Rehearsal dialog appears (see Figure 10-15). In the dialog, two time scales appear: on the left, the total time of the presentation is tracked continuously; on the right, the total time spent on the current slide appears.

Figure 10-15: Use the Rehearsal dialog to set automated timings for slide advances.

The arrow button on the dialog advances to the next animation or slide. Wait the desired length of time between slides and animations, and click the arrow to advance. As you go, the timing is recorded. Each time you advance to a new slide, the slide time counter starts over at 00:00:00. If you need to stop or take a break along the way without affecting the timings, click the Pause button (the button marked by two vertical lines).

If you feel you've spent too long on a slide, click the Repeat button. Repeat resets the counters (total time goes back to the moment you advanced to the slide, slide time goes to zero) so you can try setting the timing for the current slide again.

When finished, press Esc. A message appears, asking whether you want to save the timings you just recorded. Click Yes to save them. A final dialog opens, asking if you want to review timings in Slide Sorter view. If you click Yes, the show opens in Slide Sorter view, showing the timings beneath each slide image.

Before running the show, open the Set Up Show dialog (Figure 10-14) and make sure the Use timings check box is checked.

FYI: Custom Shows

Sometimes, you may want to present a variation on an existing show. For example, if you have a long show you perform for different groups, you may want to shorten the show, or change the order of slides, to customize it for a particular group.

A great way to do that is to create a *custom show*, a new show constructed by reshuffling slides from an existing show. To create a custom show, open the show you want to customize, then choose Slide Show|Custom Shows. A dialog opens, from which you may select existing custom shows for editing. To create a new one, click New. The Define Custom Show dialog opens, showing a list of slides in the current presentation.

To create the custom show, select desired slides from the list, and click Add to copy them into a list of slides in the custom show. In the list of slides you create, you can change the order of the slides any way you like. Note that the slides bring along their animation, multimedia, and narration.

To present a custom show, choose it from the Set Up Show dialog (see Figure 10-14, earlier in this chapter).

Using Speaker Options in a Presentation

By now, you understand the basics of running your electronic show: Fire it up in PowerPoint (or the PowerPoint viewer), start the slide show (switch to Slide Show view or choose Slide Show | View Slide Show), and advance through the slides and animation by pressing PgDn or the Right arrow key. If that's all you want to do, you're all set.

But just in case you want to get fancy, you should be aware that you can do more during a slide show than just step through slides. You can jump directly to a selected slide, draw right on the slides as if they were transparencies, take notes during a meeting, and more. Here you learn how.

Note that the stuff you learn how to do on the next few pages is available only when:

- The Slide Setup dialog for the current presentation shows Presented by speaker as the Show type.
- The Slide Show is being presented in the PowerPoint viewer or in PowerPoint in Slide Show view.

During a show, you can call up a context menu of activities available in mid-show. The menu appears when you right-click anywhere on the display except on a hyperlink. Alternatively, as soon as you move the mouse while viewing any slide, a little control button appears in the lower-left corner of the slide; click the button to open the context menu (see Figure 10-16).

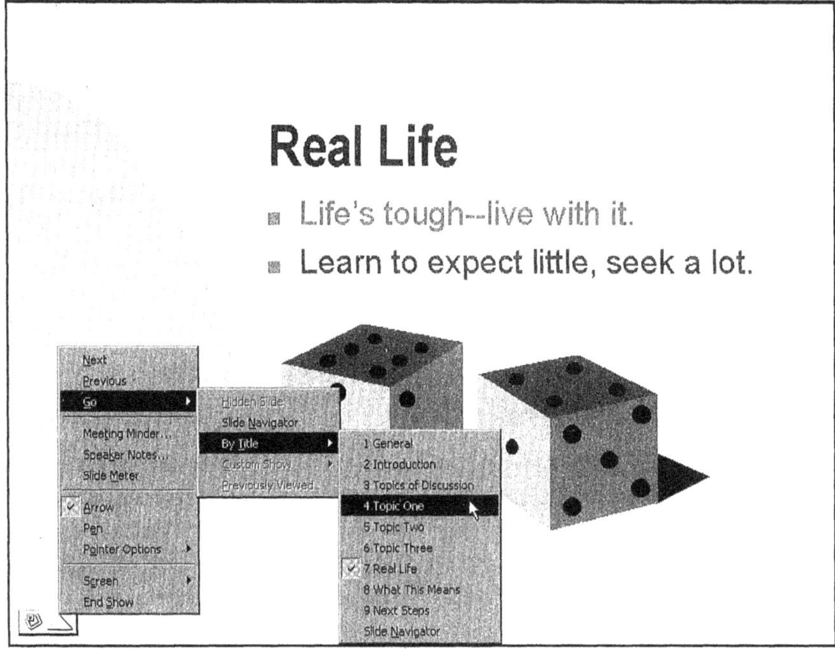

Figure 10-16: During a show, right-click a slide to choose from among display and navigation options.

Much of what's on this context menu is self-explanatory; for example, Next and Previous advance and move backward within the show, while Go opens further submenus for navigating in the presentation. Choose Go | By Title to jump to any slide by picking its title from the list that appears.

Meeting Minder (see Figure 10-17) opens an easy dialog on which you can make notes while presenting in a meeting or small conference. You can record the minutes of a meeting on the Meeting Minutes tab and build a list of "action items"—the stuff people promise in meetings they'll do later—on the Action Items tab.

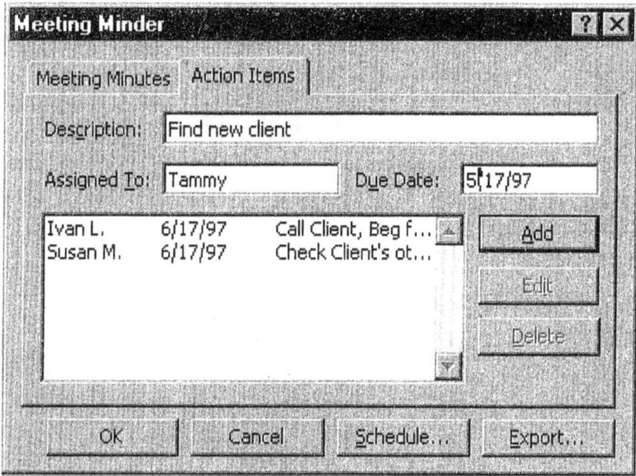

Figure 10-17: Use the Meeting Minder to keep notes during a meeting.

Fast Track

On the Meeting Minder dialog, a button called Schedule appears. Click this button to schedule a meeting in Microsoft Outlook. To learn more about Outlook, see Chapter 11, "Getting Started With Outlook."

The Pen item on the context menu changes the Windows pointer into a pen pointer (Figure 10-18). While the pointer is a pen, you can draw on the screen as you would on a blackboard—circling important items, checking off items in a list, crossing out items. To draw with the pen, point to where you want to begin drawing, click and hold the mouse button, draw your line, and release.

After you draw, the pointer stays a pen, in case you want to draw some more. To revert the pen back to the regular pointer, press Esc. (Be careful to press Esc only once, since pressing Esc twice would close the show.) To erase drawing on a slide, open the context menu and choose Screen | Erase Pen.

Finally, the Pointer Options item on the context menu opens a submenu on which you can choose to hide the windows pointer (so it doesn't distract in a show where it's not used) or choose a new Pen Color, in case the color of your onscreen drawings isn't showing up well.

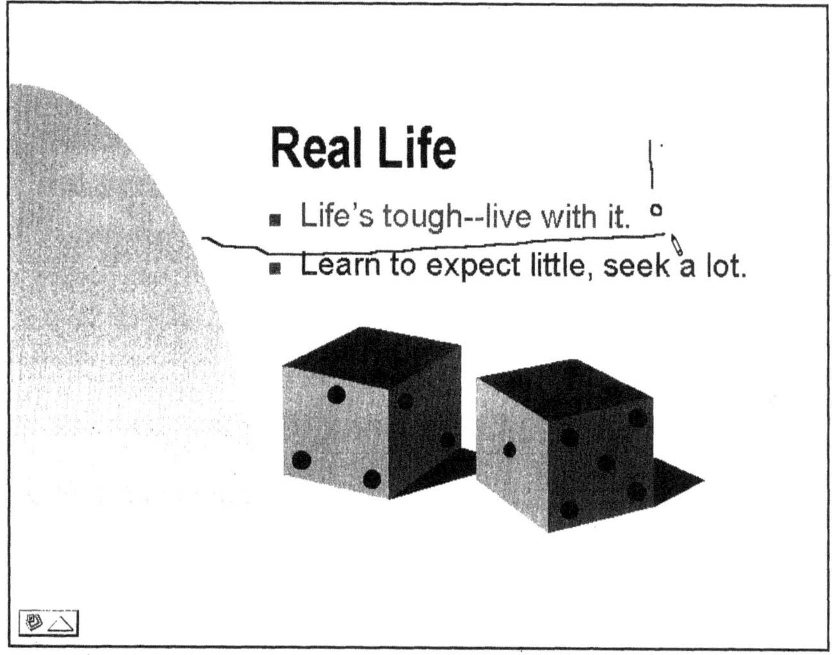

Figure 10-18: Using the Pen, you can draw on slides without getting dry-erase chalk on your cuffs.

Moving On

That's it for PowerPoint. If you want to explore further, and find new artwork or animation you can download for free, explore the PowerPoint resources available on the Web. Good places to start are PowerPoint Central (Tools | PowerPoint Central) or Microsoft's Free Stuff page (Help | Microsoft on the Web | Free Stuff).

Of course, if you've had your complete PowerPoint fill, check out Microsoft Outlook, Office 97's new Swiss Army knife: It's a personal time manager, a file manager, a contact manager, an e-mail program, and more. Move ahead to Chapter 11.

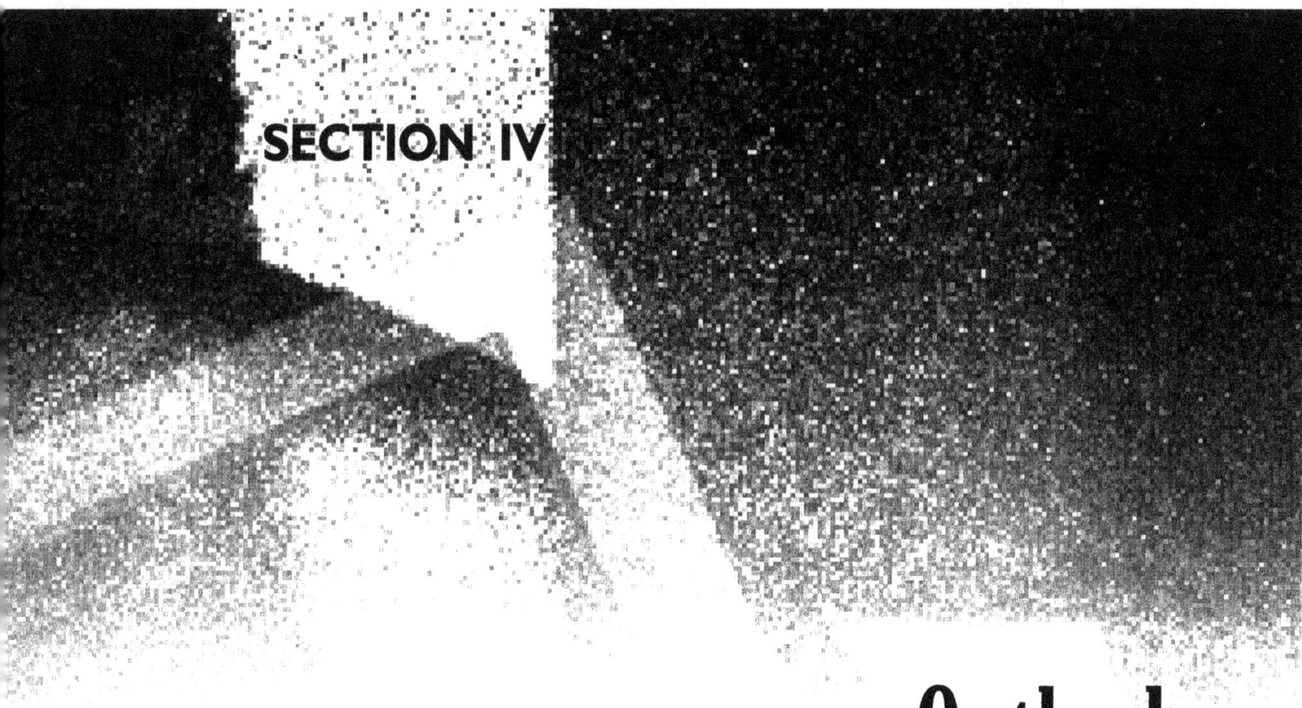

Outlook

11

Getting Started With Outlook

Outlook is an unusual animal, different from the other Office programs in its appearance and behavior. In the Office 97 combo, Outlook is Ringo.

The other Office 97 programs are mostly for creating something—a document, a presentation, a worksheet, a database, or a report. Outlook, honestly, is mostly for keeping track of the random, tangled threads of a life. When future archaeologists dig up the relics of our culture and try to learn what our lives were all about, they'll base whole theses on the contents of our Outlook files and maybe any copies of *TV Guide* that survive.

With one exception, you don't really *create* anything with Outlook—you *manage* stuff, like your list of business and personal contacts, your schedule and task list, your hopes and dreams, and so on. The exception, of course, is e-mail messages, which you can compose and send from within Outlook. Because Outlook serves as a repository for all of this information, it also supplies this information to other Office programs, upon request. For example, Word can use the contents of your Office Address Book to automatically address form letters or envelopes in a mail merge.

In this chapter, you learn the basics of Outlook, including jumping among its many different activities. If you already use a program that does any of the things Outlook does—another personal information manager (like old Office 95's Schedule+ program) or e-mail client—you'll discover here how to import your accumulated information from those programs into Outlook.

But most important, this chapter gets you up and running in Outlook's e-mail client—or, more accurately, its *universal messaging client*. Here you learn not only how to send and receive messages with Outlook but also how to configure Outlook for all the types of message communication you use.

By the way, while the toolbars you see in Outlook vary depending upon what you're doing, you almost always see the Standard toolbar (see Figure 11-1), from which you can perform many of the Activities in this chapter. If you don't see Outlook's Standard toolbar, choose View | Toolbars | Standard.

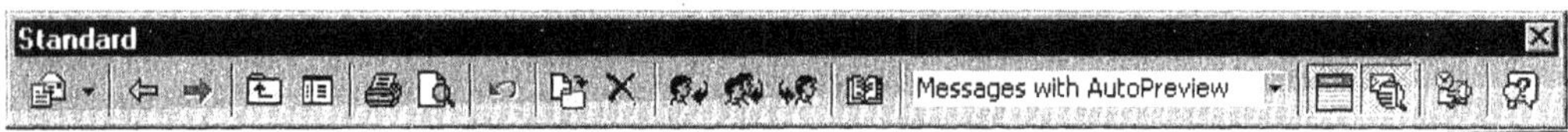

Figure 11-1: Outlook's Standard toolbar.

Opening Outlook

Like all Office 97 programs, Outlook opens from the Windows Start menu. Choose Programs | Microsoft Outlook, and Outlook drags itself lugubriously to life. Note that unless you have a surprisingly fast PC and hard disk, Outlook opens *very* slowly; don't be surprised to wait several seconds before anything at all happens on your display, and many more until Outlook is open and ready for work.

Outlook opens in another way—sort of. In its default configuration, the Office Shortcut bar has *six* buttons—count 'em!—that open a piece of Outlook (see Figure 11-2). Each button opens an Outlook dialog for adding the particular item the button describes, so you can get right to work:

- **New Message.** Compose an e-mail message or fax.
- **New Appointment.** Add an appointment to your calendar.
- **New Task.** Add a task to your to-do list. (Like you need one more!)
- **New Contact.** Add a new *contact*—a person's name, address, phone, and other descriptive information—to your file of personal and professional contacts.

- **New Journal Entry.** Add an entry to an Outlook journal that records your daily activities (some automatically, some upon request).
- **New Note.** Add an electronic sticky-note wherever you need one.

Figure 11-2: Office Shortcut bar buttons that open Outlook activities.

While the Office Shortcut bar buttons offer quick access to these dialogs, they do not open the rest of Outlook, where you could work with existing information, print stuff, and so on. That's not a limitation—that's an advantage. Often, you may want to jot a quick note or add a new contact, then get back to some other, Outlook-free work. The Shortcut bar buttons enable you to quickly open a dialog, add something, and quit. Again, you could microwave a cup of soup in the time it takes the whole Outlook program to open on most PCs, so when all you need to do is make a quick entry, it's nice to be able to keep the rest of Outlook *closed*.

Getting Around in Outlook

To understand how Outlook helps you manage information, it helps to understand three basic Outlook terms:

- Item—Each useful chunk of information you may work with in Outlook is called an "item." An e-mail message is one item. One appointment in your calendar is an item, as is one task, one contact, one journal entry, or one note.

- Folder—Each type of item is stored in a different Outlook *folder*. There's a folder for appointments (Calendar), one for tasks (Tasks), and so on. (These Office folders are not *bona fide* Windows folders; they're a special way of organizing data that's unique to Outlook. You won't find these folders in My Computer or Windows Explorer.) Within Outlook's folders, you may create new *subfolders* for organizing the type of items the folder manages. Note that Outlook offers just one folder for each type of item, except for mail items, which you manage in four folders: Inbox, Outbox, Sent Items, and Deleted Items.
- View—Each Outlook folder has a different *view*, a method of showing and organizing its items and also the set of menu options and toolbar buttons available. After all, you need to see and work with contacts in a very different way from appointments, so when you switch from the Contacts folder to the Calendar, you see a whole new view—almost as if you had switched to a different program. In any folder, you can use options on the View menu to customize the view so that Outlook presents items, menus, and toolbars in a way you find useful for managing the type of item the folder presents.

Folder-Hopping With the Outlook Bar

The main way you move among your principal Outlook folders is by clicking the shortcut icons on the Outlook Bar (see Figure 11-3), which runs vertically along the left side of the Outlook window. Each shortcut's name is the same as the folder it opens, and the shortcut's icon represents the type of item the folder contains (a Rolodex for Contacts, a Calendar for Calendar, and so on).

Figure 11-3: The Outlook Bar.

Fast Track

On the Outlook Bar, a number always appears next to the Inbox shortcut. That number reports the number of unread messages *in your Inbox folder, mail messages you have received but not looked at yet.*

The Outlook Bar is really three different bars in one. In addition to the shortcuts you see on the bar, observe that the bar holds three buttons that appear at the very top or bottom of the bar: Outlook, Mail, and Other. Clicking a button changes the contents of the Outlook bar:

- Click Outlook to show shortcuts for the main Outlook folders: Inbox, Calendar, Contacts, and so on.
- Click Mail to show just the four folders used for working with mail items: Inbox, Sent Items, Outbox, and Deleted Items.
- Click Other to access your regular Windows folders through the My Computer icon and other selected Windows folders. (By default, the My Documents folder appears here, so you can quickly navigate to Office documents.)

FYI: Don't Be Fooled by "Move to Folder"

The Standard toolbar features a button called Move to Folder, but that button does not move you among folders, as you might mistakenly guess.

The Move to Folder button moves information from one folder and item type to another. For example, Move to Folder can copy information from a message in the Inbox folder to the Contacts folder to fill in a new Contact. You'll learn how to move information among items in Chapter 12, "Organizing Yourself & Others."

Other Ways to Get Around

While working in any folder and view, you can display a list of all Outlook folders, the *Folder list* (see Figure 11-4). To display the Folder list, click the Folder List button on the Standard toolbar, or choose View | Folder List. Also, in most views, the name of the folder appears in huge letters—the biggest on the screen—above the items. That big folder name is actually a button; click it and the Folder list drops down from it.

Figure 11-4: The Folder list.

The Folder list looks a lot like a folder tree in Windows Explorer, and it works the same way: Just click a folder in the list to open it in Outlook. When a plus sign (+) precedes a folder name, there are further subfolders within that folder. Click the plus sign to display the names of the subfolders.

FYI: Adding to the Outlook Bar & Folder List

At first, the Outlook Bar and the Folder list appear to contain an almost identical list of options, leading to the inevitable question, "Why have both?"

Well, within each main Outlook folder, you may add subfolders to group your items. To the extent that you do that, your Folder list evolves away from your Outlook Bar. Also, you may add new shortcuts to the Outlook Bar, as needed.

- To add to the Folder list, choose File|Folder, Create Subfolder to open the Create New Folder dialog. Give the subfolder a Name, choose the type of item—mail, contacts, and so on—it will hold, and choose the main folder in which the subfolder will live. (At the bottom of the dialog, you can check a check box to automatically add a shortcut for the subfolder to the Outlook Bar.)
- To add to the Outlook Bar, choose File|Add to Outlook Bar, then select a folder or subfolder.

Other than the Outlook Bar and Folder list, you have a few more ways to navigate within Outlook:

- On the Standard toolbar, clicking the Back button takes you to the folder you used before the one you're on. Click Back several times in a row to move progressively back through folders you've visited in the current Outlook session. After using Back, you can click the Forward button to move forward again.
- From the menu bar, choose Go, and choose a folder from the list on the Go menu. If the folder you want doesn't appear on the list, choose the Go to folder item on the Go menu to display a dialog that shows the whole Folder list, then choose a folder from the dialog.

Walk-Through: Getting Around

1. From the Windows Start menu, choose Programs|Microsoft Outlook.
   Do a crossword puzzle or eat a doughnut to kill time while waiting for Outlook to open.
2. On the Outlook Bar, click the Outlook button, to make sure you see the standard Outlook folder shortcuts.
3. Beginning with the top shortcut, Inbox, click each of the shortcuts on the Outlook Bar to take a tour of the main folders and their views.
   In each folder, observe how the view changes, including the toolbars and menu bar.
4. After visiting all of the folders, click the Back button (on the Standard toolbar) a few times to move back through the folders you've seen.
5. On the Outlook Bar, click the Mail button, to make sure you see just the mail folder shortcuts.
6. Click shortcuts on the Outlook Bar to visit the folders you haven't seen yet: Outbox and Sent Items.
   Observe that all four mail folders use essentially the same view.
7. Click the Folder List button on the Standard toolbar.
8. In the Folder List, click any folder under Personal Folders.
   The folder opens.
9. Click the Folder List button again to close the Folder list.

Printing From Outlook

To print the stuff you manage in Outlook, begin by switching to the folder that contains the item or items you want to print and select the items to print. Then choose File | Print to open the Print dialog (see Figure 11-5).

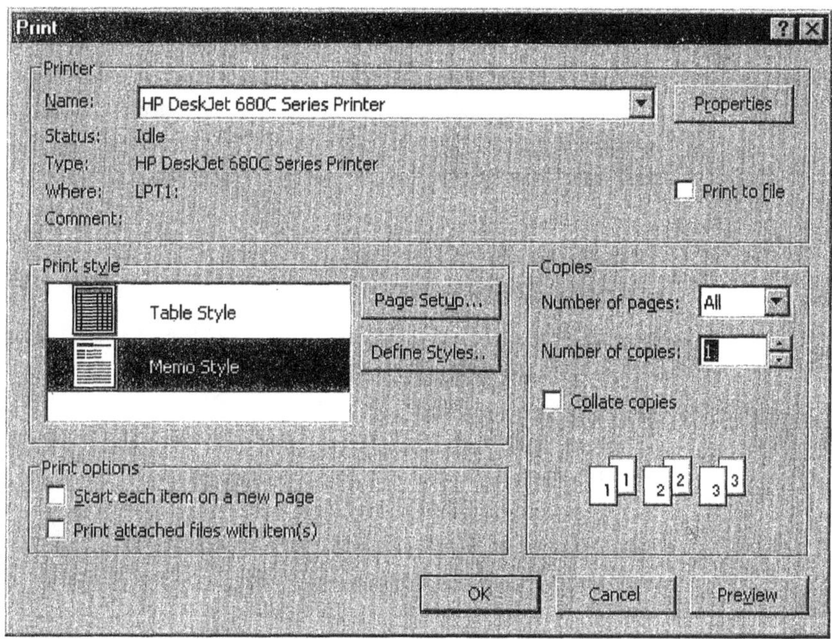

Figure 11-5: The Print dialog (as it appears when opened from a mail folder).

Outlook's Print dialog is a little different from other Print dialogs in Office 97. On the dialog, you select a Print style from a list of options that differs from folder to folder. For example, when printing from a folder that contains mail items, you can choose between two styles: Memo Style (print the contents of selected messages) or Table Style (print the message list entries for selected messages, but not the message contents). When printing from the Calendar folder, you can select from among four different Print styles, each a different calendar format: Daily, Weekly, Monthly, Tri-fold.

From the Print style options presented, choose one, and choose from other options on the dialog for ranges of dates, items, or other criteria that vary by folder. (If you're not sure of your choices, click the Preview button to see a Print Preview, then change your choices on the Print dialog as necessary.) After choosing a style and other options, click OK to print.

Importing Information Into Outlook

If you've been using another program that does something Outlook does, you may be able to transfer information—*import data*—from the other program into Outlook so you can continue working with that information without having to re-create it in Outlook.

Importing From Exchange (Inbox)

Windows's built-in messaging client is called Microsoft Exchange, although lots of folks call it "Inbox" because that's the name of the desktop shortcut that opens Exchange.

If you installed Outlook on the same PC where you were using Exchange, you do not need to import anything. Outlook automatically replaces Exchange (it doesn't delete Exchange from your PC, but it takes over Exchange's job), and it also automatically locates and uses your existing Exchange mail folder and files. All of your stored message files are available in Outlook's mail folders.

Importing Your Schedule From Schedule+

Outlook replaces Office 95's personal scheduling program, Schedule+. If you used Schedule+, you can import your Schedule+ data—including appointments, tasks, and contacts—into Outlook.

The Import and Export Wizard leads you through the steps required to import your Schedule+ data. To run the Wizard, open Outlook. From within any folder (it doesn't matter which), choose File | Import and Export. The Wizard opens, as shown in Figure 11-6. Click Import from Schedule+ or another Program or File, then click Next. From the list in the dialog that appears, choose your version of Schedule+ (Schedule+ 1.0 or Schedule+ 7.0), and click Next.

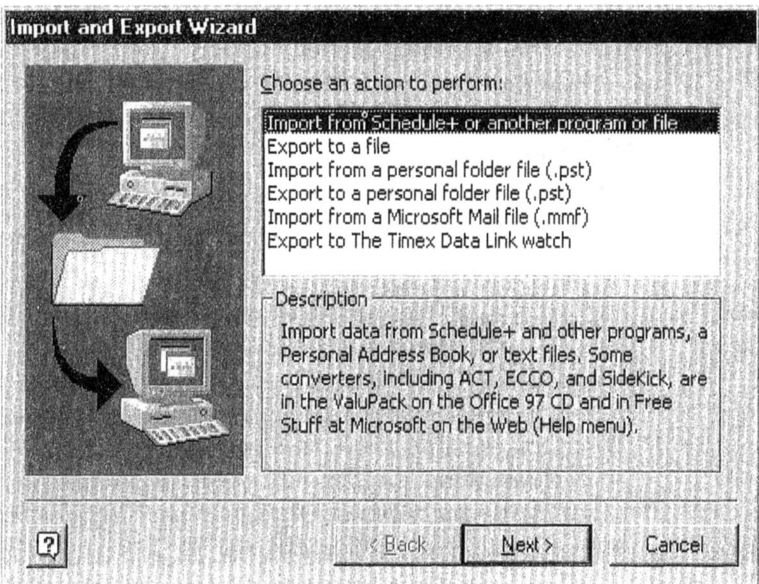

Figure 11-6: The Import and Export Wizard.

Continue to follow the Wizard's prompts until the Wizard reports that you have successfully imported your Schedule+ data.

Importing From Other Mail and Scheduling Programs

As you can see in Figure 11-6, the Import and Export Wizard can import data from many different programs. However, Outlook does not come pre-equipped to import all of these. To enable Outlook to import information from the broadest range of sources, you must install the optional converters included in the Valupack on the Office 97 CD.

Net-Savvy

If you don't have an Office 97 CD, you can pick up converters from the Office 97 Free Stuff Web page. In Outlook, choose Help | Microsoft on the Web | Free Stuff.

To install the converters, insert your Office 97 CD in your CD-ROM drive. Open Windows My Computer icon, and click the icon for your CD-ROM drive to display its contents. Click the Valupack folder, then the Convert folder, then the Outlook folder. In that Outlook folder, you'll see two programs:

- Outcvt.exe—Installs the converters for Windows 95.
- Outcvtnt.exe—Installs the converters for Windows NT.

Double-click the appropriate icon for your system, and follow the prompts. After the converters have been installed, return to Outlook and choose Help | Contents and Index. In the Contents tab, choose Key Information. A list of Help items appears, each detailing the precise choices you must make in the Import and Export Wizard—plus any other steps you must take—to import information from Lotus Notes, SideKick, and other programs. Read the Help for the program you want to import from, and then run the Import and Export Wizard as instructed (choose File | Import and Export to begin).

Exchanging E-mail

Outlook consolidates all of your message-type activity—company e-mail, Internet mail, even PC faxing—into one facility. Instead of using a separate program for each type of message, you use one program for all messages, regardless of their source, or *information service*. This consolidation makes keeping up with your communication simpler, and also offers a few great time-savers, such as the ability to send one message to multiple recipients, each of whom may be on a different information service.

FYI: There's More to Mail...

In the remainder of this chapter, you learn about sending and receiving messages. As you work, however, keep in mind that messages are Outlook items, and as with all items you have myriad ways of dealing with them. In Chapter 12, "Organizing Yourself & Others," you'll learn how to perform more activities with items (mail items included), including deleting (and restoring) items, and *archiving* items—packing them away in storage when they're out of date.

Configuring Outlook to Exchange Mail

Before you can begin using Outlook for messaging, you must set it up for each information service through which you plan to send or receive messages. For example, if you use a corporate e-mail system, that's one service. If you also use a separate Internet e-mail account from the same PC, Internet mail is another service. If you receive faxes through Microsoft Fax, it too, is a service. You select and configure each of your services in your *user profile*, your personal configuration file in Outlook.

Because Outlook automatically picks up services that were installed in Exchange before you installed Outlook, you may already have some services set up and ready to go. To see what's already set up, choose Tools | Services to open the Services dialog (see Figure 11-7). If the list on the Services tab does not show all the services you want to use in Outlook, you must add each one. If a service appears in the dialog, but you've been unable to access it from Outlook, you may have to edit its configuration, or *Properties*. In the next few pages, you learn how to add and configure services in Outlook.

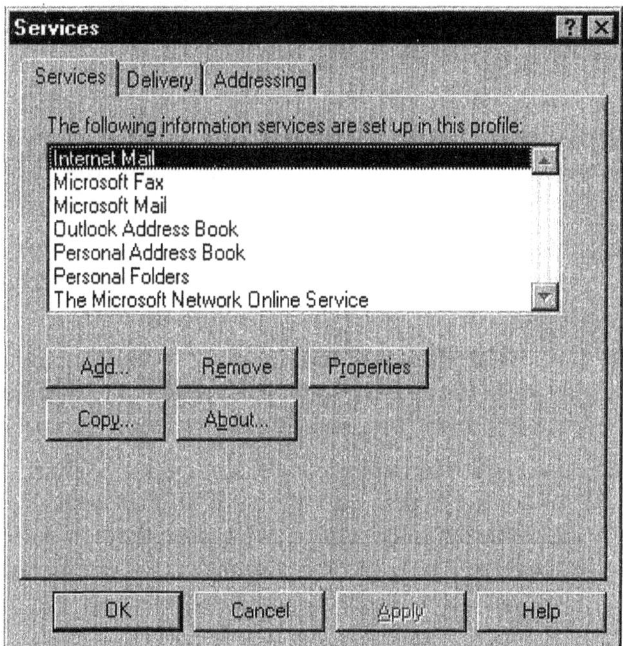

Figure 11-7: The Services dialog.

Adding a New Service

To add a service, click the Add button on the Services dialog. The Add Service to Profile dialog opens, as shown in Figure 11-8. The dialog lists all of the services for which Outlook includes a pre-built configuration file. If the list includes the service you want to add, select it, then click OK. (If the service you want to add does not appear in the list, you need to obtain a disk of driver files for that service; contact the seller or administrator of the service. When you have the required files, click the Have Disk button on the Add Service to Profile dialog.)

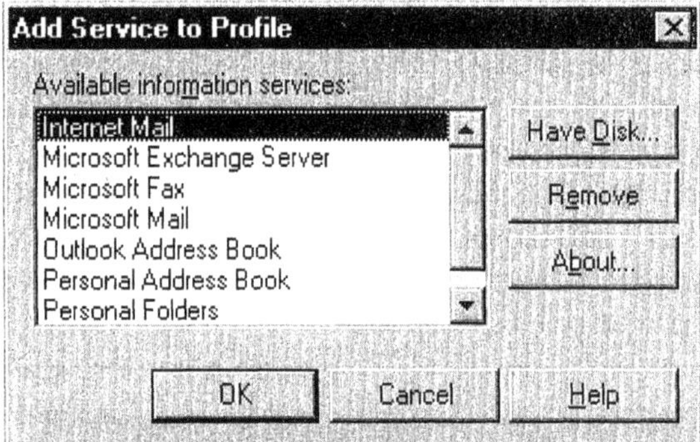

Figure 11-8: The Add Service to Profile dialog.

Each service requires different information to complete its setup. After you click OK to add a new service, one or more dialogs opens to request any additional information required to set up the service. For example:

- If you add Microsoft Fax as a new service, a dialog prompts you to enter your name and return fax number and to select the modem through which you will send and receive faxes.
- If you add Microsoft Mail as a new service, a dialog containing several tabs opens, so you can supply the location of your Microsoft Mail Post Office and other required information.
- If you add Internet Mail, a dialog opens on which you can indicate that you connect to the Internet through the local network, or select the Dial-Up Networking connection you use. On the same dialog you'll also specify the address of your Internet mail server, your username, and your e-mail password.

Fast Track

If you don't know all of the information the service dialogs demand, open the program you used for the service before you installed Outlook, and examine the menus for an item that displays your configuration settings.

For example, you can open your previous Internet e-mail program and find its configuration dialog to learn most of the information you'll need to set up the Internet mail service—with one exception. For security purposes, most Windows communication programs hide passwords by displaying them as asterisks (****). If you've forgotten a password you need to set up a service, contact the service's administrator.

When you finish adding all of your services, restart Windows to make your changes effective. (Restarting is not always required, but it can't hurt, and any changes to Windows communications facilities may not behave properly until after a restart, even when Windows does not prompt you to do so.)

FYI: Add a Service, Add a Menu Item...

Often when you add a service, new toolbar buttons or menu items are added automatically to Outlook to support the service. For example, if you add Microsoft Mail, a new item—Microsoft Mail Help Topics—is added automatically to Outlook's Help menu. Another item, Microsoft Mail Tools, is added to the Tools menu and leads to a submenu of items for working with MS Mail.

After adding services, it's a good idea to tour Outlook's menus to find any helpful items the service may have deposited there.

Changing a Service's Configuration

When you add a service, you're automatically prompted for all required configuration information. Still, if a service is not working properly—or if you want to change a service's setup, as you would if you switched Internet suppliers or your Microsoft Mail post office—you can edit the service's Properties sheet.

To edit a service's Properties, open the Services dialog (Tools | Services) shown in Figure 11-7, select the service whose properties you want to edit, and click the Properties button. The Properties sheet (Figure 11-9) for the selected service appears (it will be different for each service), showing the same information you were required to supply when you added the service. Make your changes, and click OK when finished. Before using the service, restart Windows to ensure that your changes have taken effect.

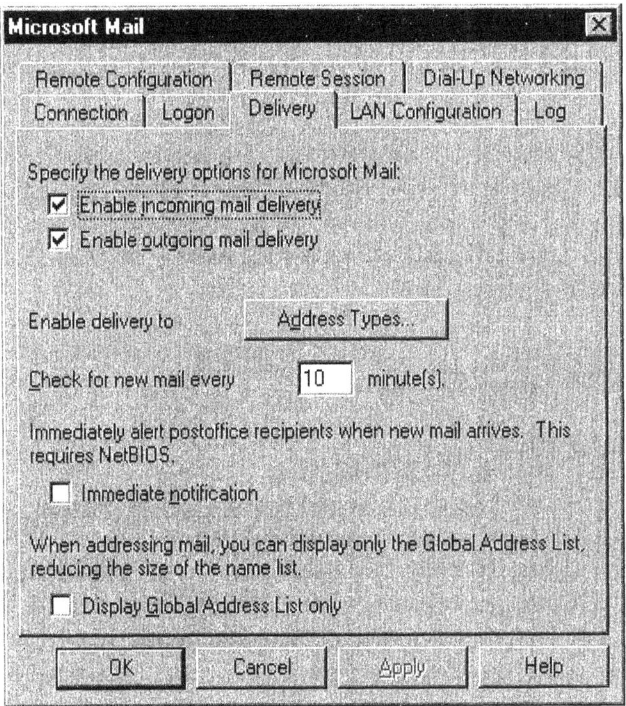

Figure 11-9: Editing a service's Properties sheet.

Retrieving E-mail

What you have to do to retrieve your mail depends largely upon the service and its configuration. With most internal company e-mail systems (such as Microsoft Mail), retrieval is automatic and transparent. Messages arrive in your Inbox folder whenever received from the server. These might be described as *online* mail systems.

With *offline* or *remote* mail services—those you connect to as needed, such as the Microsoft Network or a dial-up Internet account—you have two choices for checking and retrieving new e-mail:

- **Automatically, by schedule.** Outlook automatically checks for new messages when you first open Outlook, and checks again every time a selected number of minutes passes. If, when attempting to check mail, you are not already connected to the service, Outlook attempts to connect for you. For example, if Outlook attempts to check your Internet mail and discovers that you're not online, it automatically opens your Internet Dial-Up Networking connection.
- **On-demand.** Outlook checks your incoming mail—and sends any outgoing mail waiting in your Outbox folder—only when you instruct it to.

You choose between these two types of mail handling on a service's Properties sheet. The exact wording and options differ depending upon the service, but Internet Mail's Properties sheet (see Figure 11-10) provides a good example.

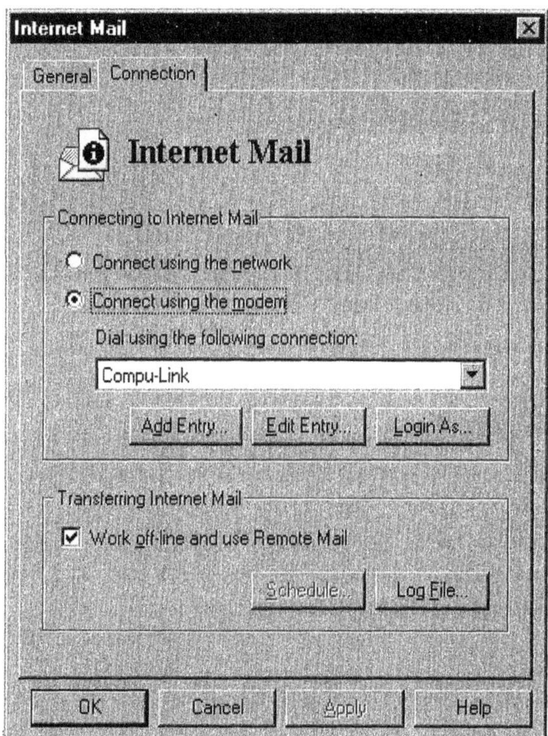

Figure 11-10: Configuring for remote mail.

Near the bottom of the Connection tab appears a check box, Work offline and use Remote Mail. If you check that check box, Outlook does not check automatically for mail. If you clear the check box, Outlook connects to the Internet (if you're not already connected) as soon as you open Outlook, and retrieves any new messages. It also checks the mail again, automatically, according to a schedule you choose by clicking the Schedule button at the bottom of the Connection tab.

After you've configured a service for on-demand mail, or "remote mail," you can usually retrieve your mail in two different ways from any of Outlook's mail folders:

- **Choose Tools | Check for New Mail.** Outlook checks for new mail on all of your services, connecting to (and disconnecting from) offline services as necessary.
- **Choose Tools | Check for New Mail On.** Outlook opens a dialog listing your mail services (see Figure 11-11). Check the check box next to any service for which you want to retrieve mail, then click OK. Outlook checks for new mail on the selected service(s), connecting to (and disconnecting from) each service as necessary.

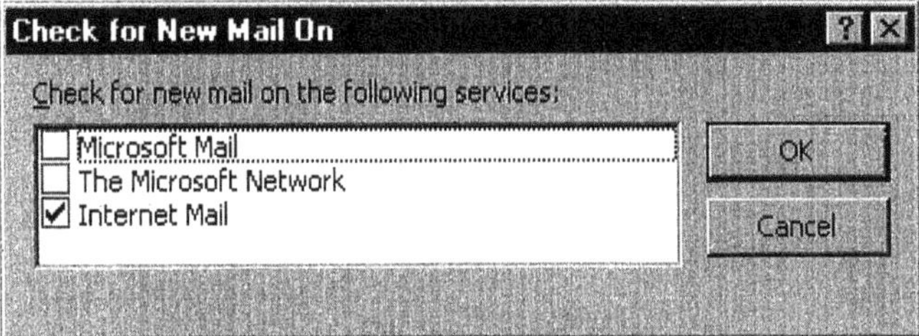

Figure 11-11: Choosing services to check for new mail.

Fast Track

For some offline services you can use true "remote mail" by opening the Remote Connection Wizard (choose Tools | Remote Mail | Connect). With true remote mail, Outlook doesn't retrieve whole messages. Instead, for all new mail, it retrieves only the message header, the name (or address) of the sender, and the subject of the message.

After retrieving headers, you switch to the Inbox folder, where the headers are listed. Select the entry for any message you want to retrieve, then mark it for retrieval by choosing Tools | Remote Mail | Mark to Retrieve. The next time you check mail, the marked items will be retrieved in full.

Remote mail is a handy way to go when you often receive long messages that you may not want to retrieve right away—or at all.

Reading E-mail

Messages you've received appear listed in the Inbox folder (see Figure 11-12). By default, the listings for messages you have never opened—*unread* messages—appear in bold, and beneath each unread listing appears the *AutoPreview,* the first few lines of the message. The AutoPreview helps you determine what a message is about before reading it.

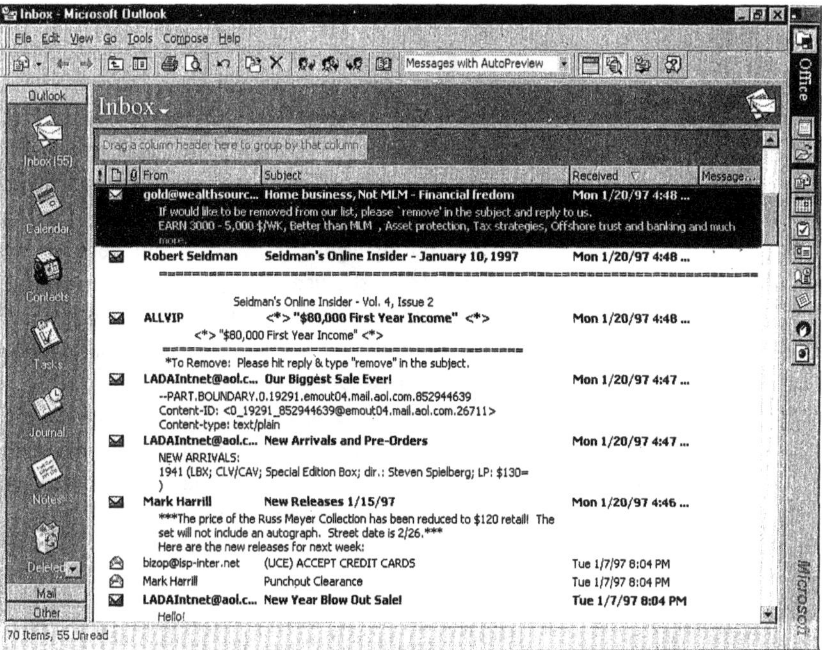

Figure 11-12: Messages in the Inbox folder.

To read a message, double-click it in the list. The full message opens in a new window, a *message window*, where you can read it, and also work with it in other ways, such as deleting it or composing a reply. When finished reading a message, close the message window by clicking the close corner (the X in the upper-right corner of the window) or by choosing File | Close.

When the Inbox folder reappears, the listing for the message you just opened is no longer bold, and the AutoPreview no longer appears—the message is now a *read* message (because you opened it—Outlook doesn't know whether you actually read it or not). You can still read the message again, at any time, by double-clicking its listing in Inbox.

FYI: Using Word to Write E-mail

Depending upon how Office was set up on your PC, Word may be configured as your default e-mail editor. If so, when you choose to read or create a new message in Outlook, Word opens instead—although it's in its "WordMail" mode, and it looks a lot like the Outlook message window. The steps for creating messages in WordMail are generally the same as those used in the Outlook message window, and when you close WordMail, you return to Outlook.

What's the point of this charade? Well, there are a number of advantages to using Word as your e-mail editor. First, you have access to all of Word's powerful spell-checking, grammar checking, and thesaurus facilities when composing new mail. Second, you have access to a richer set of options for formatting text—including adding colored highlights. (However, your recipient will only see the advanced formatting if he or she uses WordMail to view your message.)

There's a tradeoff, too. WordMail opens considerably more slowly than Outlook's message window. If you're in a hurry, and don't need Word's features, using Word as your e-mail editor is a pain.

To choose whether Word is your e-mail editor, open Outlook and choose Tools|Options. Near the bottom of the E-mail tab, find the check box for Use Microsoft Word as the e-mail editor. Check the check box to use Word, or clear the box to use the Outlook message window.

Building Your Address Book

By design, Outlook wants you to address all of your messages by using names from your *Address Book* (in fact, it makes doing otherwise somewhat difficult). Your Address Book is a listing of names for which Outlook knows an e-mail address (or fax number, if Microsoft Fax is one of your services).

Your Address Book is divided up into a few separate lists. The most important of these is Contacts, an address list created automatically by Outlook out of all items in your Contacts folder that include e-mail addresses. Any time you add a new contact (see Chapter 12, "Organizing Yourself & Others") and supply an e-mail address for it, the contact becomes accessible from the Address Book.

If you're on a local network, another list, sometimes called Global, appears. This list is created and maintained by your network administrator and includes a list of others on the network with whom you may exchange mail. Finally, some services, such as the Microsoft Network, may add their own lists.

The best way to build your Address Book is to build your Contacts list. However, if you want to build an Address Book separately from your contacts, you must first add a new service, a Personal Address Book, using the steps shown earlier in this chapter for adding services.

Once your Personal Address Book has been added, you may add new names or addresses to it by clicking the Address Book button on the Standard toolbar, then clicking the New Entry button on the Address Book dialog's toolbar. A dialog opens in which you select the service that messages to the new entry will be sent through (see Figure 11-13). That dialog is followed by one where you supply the name and e-mail address (or fax number) for the new entry (see Figure 11-14). Note that the required address information will differ, depending on the service you select.

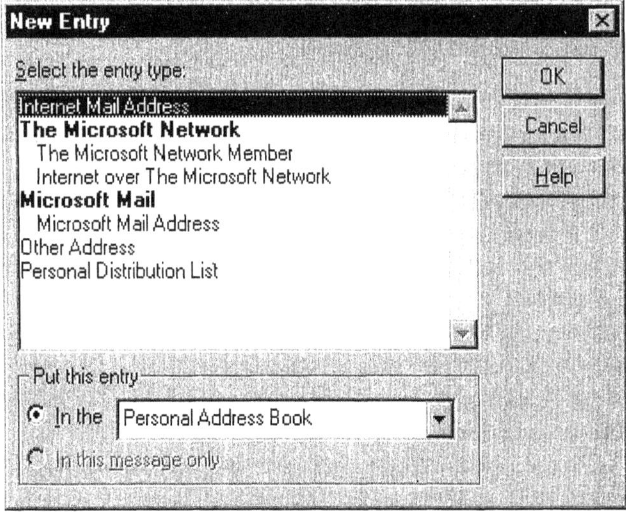

Figure 11-13: Adding a new entry to your Personal Address Book.

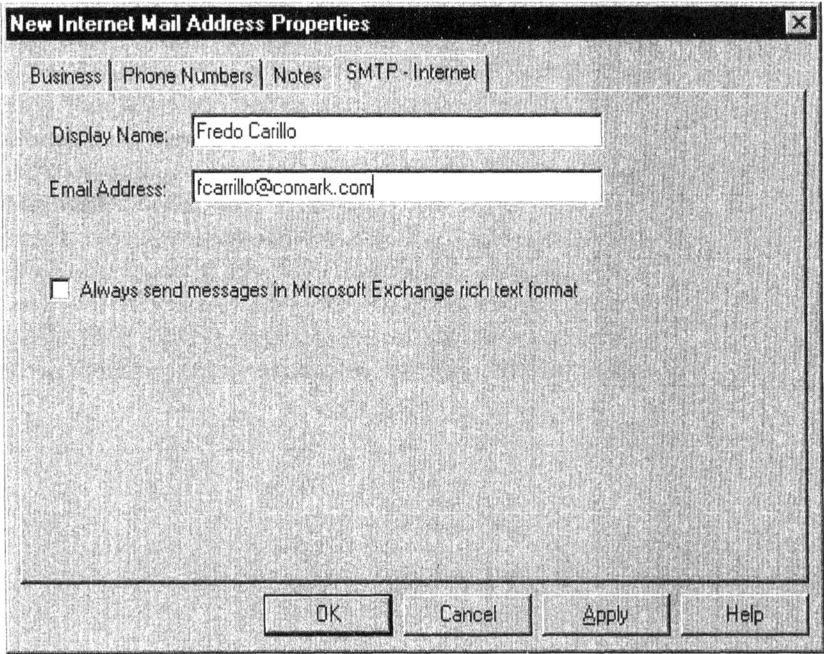

Figure 11-14: Completing the address information for a new Address Book entry.

Composing & Sending E-mail

To create a new message, click the New Mail Message button on the Standard toolbar, or choose File | New | Mail Message. The message window opens, as shown in Figure 11-15. This message window has two tabs: Message, on which you address and compose the message, and Options, where you may choose from a variety of available options, such as assigning an Importance level (Low, Normal, or High) to the message.

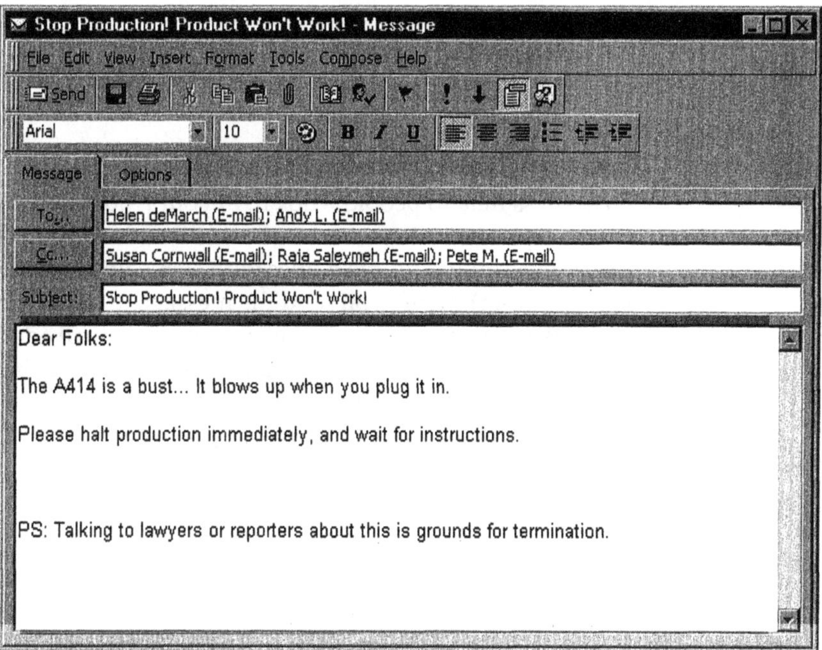

Figure 11-15: Composing a new message.

The first step in composing a new message is to complete the *header* of the message by supplying entries in the three boxes at the top of the Message tab:

- To—The principle recipient(s), to whom the message is directly addressed.
- Cc— Optionally "Carbon-copy" recipient(s), to whom the message is not directly addressed but who should see a copy anyway.
- Subject—A brief description of the subject of the message.

The Subject is the simplest part—click in the box and type what you want (keep it short and meaningful). In the To and Cc lines, you must supply names of people in your Address Book (as described next). Observe that you can enter as many different names in the To and Cc lines as you wish, to send one message to multiple recipients. When using multiple names, separate names with a semicolon (;).

Fast Track

While in Outlook's Contacts folder, you can drag any contact and drop it on the Outlook bar's Inbox icon to open the message window and compose a message that's pre-addressed to that contact.

Choosing Addresses From the Address Book

To address mail to people who are in your Address Book, just type their names—yes, their *names*, not their e-mail addresses—in the To or Cc lines, separating multiple names with semicolons (see Figure 11-15, shown earlier). When you send the message (as described shortly), Outlook automatically finds the appropriate e-mail address for each name by checking the names you type against names in your Address Book. Outlook supplies the correct addresses behind the scenes—all you ever see in the To and Cc lines are the names.

FYI: One Message Can Go Through Many Services

Note that you can mix and match types of recipients you communicate with through different services. For example, the To line could contain three names: one you reach through Internet Mail, another through internal e-mail, and another by fax. Outlook will send the message to each through the three services.

Alternatively, you can display a list of names in your Address Book and selectively copy them into the To or Cc lines. This method is especially useful when you must send one message to many people. To select names from your Address Book, open the Select Names dialog (see

Figure 11-16) by clicking any of three buttons in the message window: the Address Book button on the toolbar, or the To or Cc button in the Message tab. At the top of the dialog, choose the list from which you want to select names.

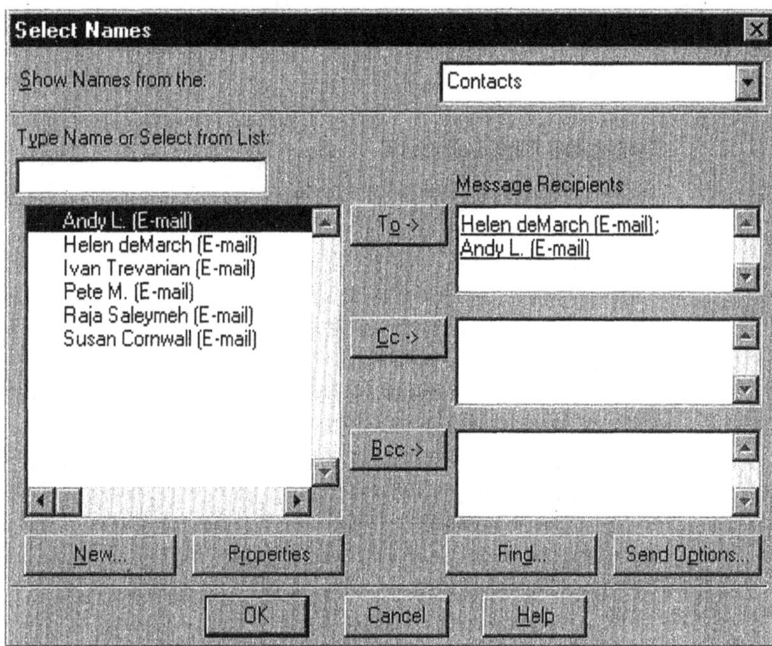

Figure 11-16: Selecting names from an Address Book list.

The names in the selected list appear in the box on the left side of the dialog. In the box, click a name to select it, then click the To button to copy the name into the To line, or Cc to copy the name to the Cc line. You may select as many names as you want to build lists of message recipients. When finished selecting names, click OK.

Fast Track

When in a hurry, you can address a message to someone who's not in your Address Book. The easiest way to do that is to enter the person's name in the To or Cc line. When you click Send, the Check Names dialog opens to tell you it doesn't know who that person is.

On the dialog, click the radio button for Create a new address. The New Entry dialog opens (see Figure 11-13, earlier in this chapter) so you can add a new Address Book entry.

When you complete the new entry, if you have created a Personal Address Book, the new entry is added there automatically. If not, a radio button appears that you can click to use the address for just this one message (the address is not saved in any address book).

Typing the Message Body

After completing the message header, click in the main pane of the message window, and type your message.

Observe that a Formatting toolbar—similar to Word's and PowerPoint's Formatting toolbars—appears on the message window. You may apply various types of text formatting—including fonts and font sizes, color, attributes (bold, italic, underline), and list formatting—by selecting the message text you want to format, then clicking the desired button on the Formatting toolbar.

However, keep in mind that text formatting like fonts and colors requires both the sender *and* the receiver to have an e-mail program that is compatible with the *MIME* (Multipurpose Internet Mail Extensions) standard, such as Outlook. Recipients who use e-mail clients that are not MIME-compliant will see just plain text, with no special formatting.

If you apply a lot of fancy formatting, you may inadvertently build your message in such a way that the formatting carries part of the meaning; for example, an important word may be emphasized with a special color. In such cases, non-MIME recipients may not take the meaning of your message exactly as you intend. Unless you're sure all of your recipients have MIME-compliant e-mail programs, resist the formatting buttons.

Sending the Message

When finished addressing and formatting your message, click the Send button on the message window. Outlook first checks the names you've supplied in To and Cc against the Address Book. If any name does not match an Address Book entry, the Check Names dialog opens, reporting the unrecognized name and giving you a three-way choice: Choose a different list to check the name against, choose another name from the Address Book list, or create a new Address Book entry for the name.

Once Outlook knows what to do with all the names you've entered on the To and Cc lines, what happens next depends on the recipient.

- To recipients with whom you communicate through online services, the message is sent immediately.
- To recipients with whom you communicate through offline services, the message waits in the Outbox folder until the next time you retrieve mail, when it is sent automatically. While the message is still waiting in your Outbox, you can open it (by double-clicking it) and edit it.

After the message has been sent, a copy of it appears in your Sent Items folder.

Fast Track

While viewing or composing a message in the message window, click the Message Flag button to add a flag to it. A flag marks a message as one requiring follow-up. When you add a flag, a dialog opens on which you can specify the type of follow-up required (or another reason for the flag) and choose a date by which the follow-up must be performed.

When you add a flag to a message you've received, a flag icon appears next to the message's entry in the Inbox folder, to remind you to act upon it. When you add a flag to a message you send, the reason for the flag and the due date appear at the top of the message when your recipient views it.

Replying to & Forwarding E-mail

It's not called "exchanging" e-mail for nothing. A big part of e-mail is responding to messages you've received (replying), or sending a copy of a received message to someone else who may want to see it (forwarding). Outlook makes replying and forwarding easy by doing most of the work for you.

For example, Outlook automatically *quotes* the entire original message in the body of your reply or forward (see Figure 11-17). It also creates the subject line of the message header by using the subject line of the original message and adding Re: (Reply to) or Fw: (Forward) in front of it.

To reply to or forward a message, open the message and choose one of the following buttons:

- **Reply.** Pre-addresses the message back to the sender of the message.
- **Reply to All.** Pre-addresses a message back to the sender and all other recipients of the message (everyone the sender entered in To and Cc).
- **Forward.** Opens a new message quoting the original message, but leaving the To and Cc lines empty.

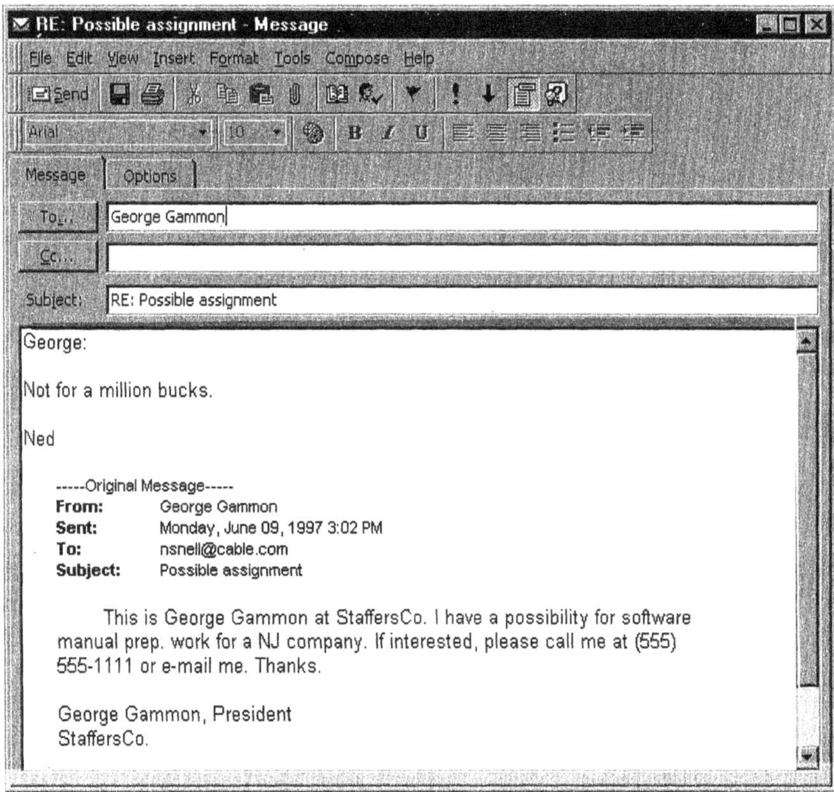

Figure 11-17: Replying to a message.

To complete a reply, type your reply above the quote. Alternatively, you may edit the quote, cutting it down to just the portion to which you're replying, or you may insert your comments anywhere within the

quote to respond to particular passages within. (Note that when you reply, you needn't worry about whether the recipients of your reply are in your Address Book. In this one case, Outlook simply copies the addresses from the header of the original message and doesn't worry about the Address Book.)

To complete a forward, use the To line (and optionally the Cc line) to address the message to anyone who should see it, using Address Book names as you would for a new message. You may add a comment at the top of the message (over the quote), perhaps explaining to recipients why you are forwarding the message. You may also edit the message itself, cutting it down to relevant points. Take care, though, not to edit the header at the top of the quote; that quoted message header tells your recipients who sent you the message in the first place.

When finished creating your reply or forward, click Send to send the message. After the message is sent, a copy appears in your Sent Items folder.

Fast Track

File attachments *are a great way to send longer documents, programs, or anything that can go in a file to anyone with whom you exchange e-mail.*

To attach a file to a message, address and compose the message. An icon will appear in the message to represent the file, so position the edit cursor at the spot in the message where you want the icon to appear. Then click the Insert File button on the message window (or choose Insert | File). A dialog opens on which you can navigate to and select the file.

Organizing E-mail Folders

Because you can customize the view of any Outlook folder, you have myriad (and, frankly, overwhelming) options for changing the way messages are grouped and sorted in the four mail folders—Inbox, Sent Items, Outbox, and Deleted Items.

The quickest way to rearrange a folder is to choose a new option from the list of prebuilt views. Choose View | Current View, and a submenu of optional views for the current folder appears (the list differs from folder to folder). The list that appears for the mail folders (see Figure 11-18) allows you to show the message list without the AutoPreview (Messages), or to sort the messages by sender, topic, and other criteria. It also enables you to limit the list to show only certain groups of messages; for example, the list may display only messages from the "Last Seven Days" or only "Unread Messages."

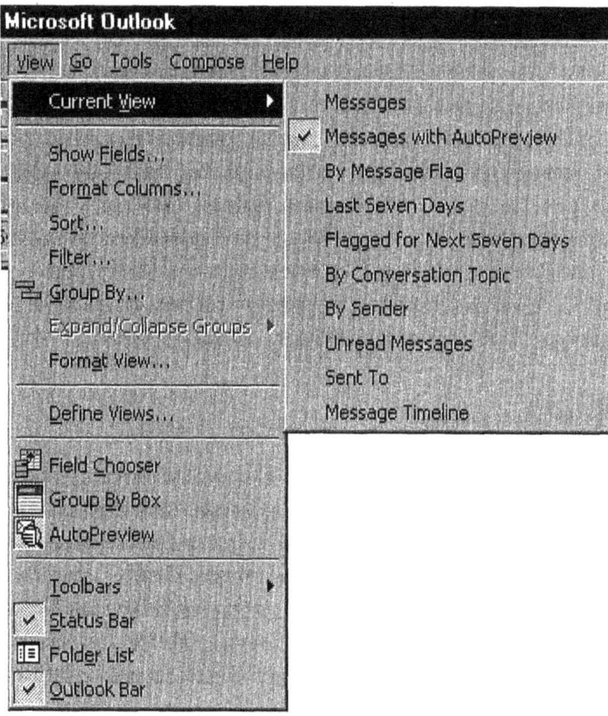

Figure 11-18: View options for a mail folder.

Another way to organize your messages is to fiddle with the message list column headings (From, Subject, etc.) Each of these is actually a button. You may use the buttons in the following ways:

- **Double-click a button to sort the message list by that column heading.** For example, to sort the messages alphabetically by subject, double-click the Subject heading.
- **Click a button to switch between *ascending* and *descending* order.** For example, if messages are sorted by date received and are listed in descending order (newest down to oldest), click the Received column heading to sort in ascending order (oldest down to newest).

- **Drag and drop a button to change the order of the columns.** For example, if Subject is the second column, you can drag its column heading and drop it near the left side of the list to make it the first column.
- **Right-click a button to choose from among a variety of sorting and positioning options for that column.**

Walk-Through: Exchanging Mail

This walk-through requires that you have at least one e-mail service set up in Outlook and that you have some names in your Address Book.

1. Open any of the mail folders.
2. Click the New Mail Message button on the standard toolbar.
3. In the message window, click the To button.
4. If you don't see a list of names in the box on the left of the Select Names dialog, drop down the list at the top of the dialog and choose a list from which to show names.
5. In the list of names on the left, click a name (preferably a friend, your network or e-mail administrator, or both) to select it.
6. Click the To button.

   The name appears in the Message Recipients list, on the right.
7. Click OK to close the Select Names dialog.
8. In the message window, click in the Subject line and type:

   Test: Please ignore or reply, if desired.
9. Click in the large empty pane (the message body), and type a brief message.
10. Click Send.
11. Switch to the Outbox.

    If the message is listed in the Outbox, the recipient you selected is on an offline service. Choose Tools|Check for New Mail.

Moving On

You know how to get into Outlook, get around within it, and exchange messages. What's left? For lack of a better word, I'll say that what's left is "personal information management," the side of Outlook that enables you to manage your calendar, contacts, and more.

If you think personal information management means just typing in your appointments and contacts and then retrieving them when they're needed, you're not seeing the "big picture." Outlook doesn't just collect and store all this stuff—it helps you use the information productively. In the chapter you just finished, you already saw how your contacts automatically show up in your Address Book, for easy e-mail addressing. Other examples of Outlook built-in productivity-enhancers include the Plan a Meeting facility, which helps you schedule a meeting and get the word out to everybody who's supposed to be there.

Turn now to Chapter 12, and learn how to organize yourself and others with Outlook.

12

Organizing Yourself & Others

I use four different paper address books. One my wife and I started 12 years ago when we got married, so it contains addresses of people we knew then but may not know any longer. I consult that book when I need an address I've not used for years—I'm careful not to use it for more recent contacts, since that book also includes addresses of people who have since moved, divorced, or died. We started another book about six years ago, and it has more recent contacts in it—we never copied the older contacts from the first book, so we need both. A third book contains my business contacts—I'd use it often, but I can't find it (I may have left it in New Jersey). Finally, my wife carries a tiny, inch-high address book in her purse which sometimes yields an address when the other three books fail.

What's my point? Well, partly I want my friends to understand why I never call. I also want you to understand that Outlook does a great job of helping you manage your contacts, daily tasks, calendar, and other organizational info—but only after you've made the initial effort to enter all of this stuff. If you don't update the information in Outlook regularly, it quickly becomes as useless as my 12-year-old address book. Outlook helps, but you have to do your part. Do it, and you'll be impressed at how much Outlook can do with the information you give it. Your input and update efforts are rewarded threefold in a better organized life. (And who doesn't need that?)

In this chapter, you learn how to enter and edit information in your contacts list, calendar, task list and journal, and also how to add notes. You also learn how to use all this information in productive, surprising ways once Outlook has it on file. Finally, you learn how to perform a number of handy housekeeping tasks for making your Outlook data more manageable, such as deleting outdated items.

What kind of information should you enter first? Well, that's really up to you. In this chapter, I start you off with a general discussion of the many ways you can open dialogs to add information in Outlook. Then you begin adding information with contacts, for a few reasons. First, entering your contacts is likely to be the most time-consuming, tedious part of getting yourself Outlooked, so you might as well get it over with. Second, your contacts are immediately useful in other folders—you can use them to address e-mail or envelopes, plan a meeting, and more.

So pull out your address book (or books), clear the papers and doughnuts from your desktop calendar, and get started on getting organized.

FYI: Using Outlook Together

When Outlook is used on a local network with Microsoft Exchange Server, Outlook folders can be *shared*, so that some or all of a user's Outlook files can be seen by others.

Shared Outlook folders enable a variety of powerful workgroup features. For example, a supervisor may be given access to the Tasks and Calendar folders of his or her subordinates. The supervisor can keep track of workloads and schedules, and can use the Meeting Planner to pick a meeting time when all attendees have no conflicting commitments, according to their calendars.

For a workgroup to share Outlook folders, the administrator must set up the folders on the server and issue the necessary permissions to those who must access others' private Outlook folders. If you believe your workgroup can benefit from sharing Outlook folders, talk to your administrator.

Opening Dialogs to Add Items

The problem with Outlook is that it tries too hard. In an effort to be flexible and helpful, Outlook gives you multiple ways to do most things—particularly opening the dialogs you use to add information to Outlook. You open a different dialog for adding or editing each type of

item; there's a contact dialog for adding or editing a contact, a task dialog for adding or editing a task, and so on.

On the extreme left side of Outlook's Standard toolbar appears a very strange button. I can't give you an exact name for it, since its name changes every time you change folders, as does its appearance. Clicking that button always adds a new item of the type managed in the current folder. For example, when you're in the Contacts folder, if you point to that button, the tooltip that appears says "New Contact," and clicking the button opens a contact dialog so you can add a contact. In the Inbox folder, the tooltip says "New Message," and clicking the button opens the message window. Since the button always creates a new item, and its tooltip—in any folder—always begins with the word "New," I'll call it the New button, hereafter.

A tiny arrow appears to the right of the New button. Click that arrow, and a list drops down from which you may choose to add any type of item (see Figure 12-1). Thus the New button enables you to create a new item of any type, from within any folder.

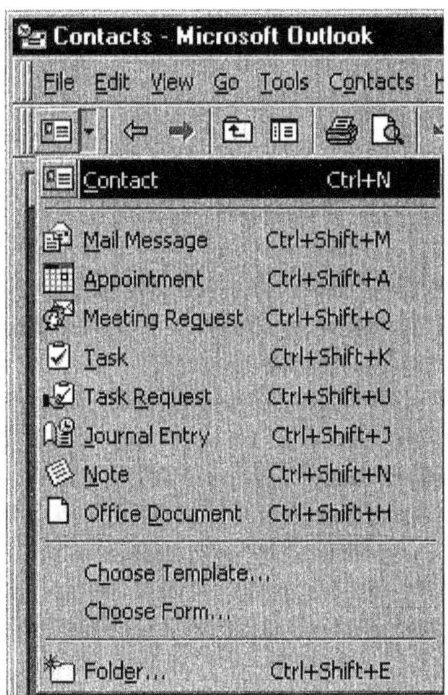

Figure 12-1: The New button on the Standard toolbar opens a dialog for creating the type of item the current folder holds.

But that's not good enough for Outlook. Outlook also gives you at least four more ways (and for some items, as many as six) to open each of the dialogs that creates a new item. For example, consider the ways you can open a contact dialog to add a new contact. You can switch to the Contacts folder and click the New button, or from within any Outlook folder you can drop down the list from the New button and choose Contact. You can also open the same dialog four more ways:

- In any folder, choose File | New | Contact.
- Switch to the Contacts folder, and choose Contacts | New Contact.
- Click the New Contact button on the Office Shortcut bar.
- While working with a contact in a contact dialog, choose Contact | New Contact to open a second dialog.

Now that you know how all of this works, as you work through this chapter, I won't make you nuts by repeating all the ways you can open each dialog. Instead, in each case, I'll tell you to start off by switching to the folder containing the type of item you want to create, then click the New button—after all, that's usually easiest. Just keep in mind that you have all of these other options, and if you want to go another way, hey...knock yourself out.

Keeping Up With Names & Addresses (Contacts)

Your Contacts list is your Rolodex, the place you keep up with names and addresses—including mailing addresses, e-mail addresses, phone, fax, pager, personal Web page, carrier pigeon....

Actually, Contacts is about more than just recording names and addresses. For any name in your contact list, you can record all sorts of related information: business and personal profile information, a journal of interaction with that person, and more. Most importantly, once a person is saved in your Contacts folder as a contact item, you may use that item in many different, time-saving ways. For example, you can use it to address a message, assign a task, plan a meeting, and dial the phone.

Adding & Editing Contacts

To create a new contact, open a new contact dialog by switching to the Contacts folder and clicking the New button. Fill in any information you wish on the four tabs of the contact dialog. The details of each tab are described over the next several pages for your reference, but most of what you'll find there is pretty self-explanatory.

Although the four tabs collect a lot of information, you do not have to use every tab or fill in every box. The only required entry in the whole dialog is Full Name, at the top of the General tab. If you're like most people, you'll record everything you need to know about most contacts just by completing some of the boxes in the General tab—Full Name, Address, E-mail, and Phone numbers. But when you need to record more detailed information about a contact, the other tabs are there to receive it. Note, too, that you can vary the level of information you supply, contact by contact—you're free to record only a little information about some contacts, and a lot about others.

After supplying as much information about a contact as you wish, finish by making a choice from the toolbar on the contact dialog or from the contact dialog's menu bar:

- Click the Save and Close button—or choose File | Save, then File | Close—to save the contact and close the contact dialog.
- Click the Save and New button—or choose File | Save and New—to save the contact and then present a new, empty contact dialog so you can immediately add another new contact.

To edit an existing contact, simply double-click the contact in the Contact list. The contact dialog opens, showing all of the current information recorded for the contact. Change what you wish, then click Save and Close or Save and New.

Fast Track

If you've received e-mail from a person you want to create a contact item for, you can easily give yourself a head-start on the job. In the Inbox folder, click and hold on the message, drag it to the Outlook Bar, and drop it on the Contacts shortcut. (Alternatively, you can click the message to select it, then click the Move to Folder button and choose Contacts.)

A new contact dialog opens, with the contact's name and e-mail address already filled in with information from the e-mail message. You can edit and expand upon that information, or just click Save and Close to record the new contact.

General Tab

The General tab (see Figure 12-2) is the meat and potatoes of contacts, the place where you enter the essentials: full name, mailing address, phone, and so on.

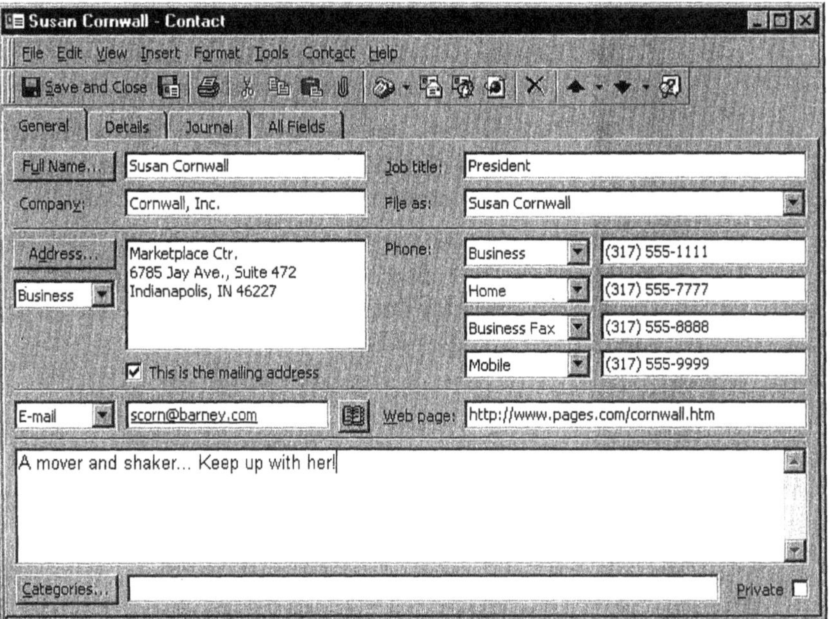

Figure 12-2: On the contact dialog's General tab, type the basic name and address information for the contact.

While you can type the full name and address in the boxes provided, you may do a better job supplying complete information, in the right order, by clicking the Full Name or Address button. Each opens a small dialog in which you enter the information piece by piece. For example, if you click the Full Name button, the dialog that opens has separate boxes for Title (Dr., Miss, Mr., Ms., and so on), First, Middle, Last, and Suffix (Jr., Sr., III).

For many types of information on the tab, including address, e-mail, and the four phone boxes, a drop-down list enables you to make multiple entries for that box. For example, drop down the list under the Address button and choose Home to type a home address for this contact. Then drop down the list again and choose Business to record a business address for the same contact.

As you work, follow these simple rules for filling in the boxes (see Figure 12-2 for examples):

- **Full Name.** Type the name straight out, as you do on an envelope.
- **Address.** Again, type as you do on an envelope, typing each part of the address on a separate line.
- **E-mail.** Type the complete e-mail address as you do when addressing a message in your e-mail program.
- **Phone.** Type the area code and number using no punctuation. When you move on to another box on the dialog, Outlook automatically formats the number for you, like this: (555) 666-7777. If the number is an international number, type a plus sign (+) before the country code, and enclose the area code in parentheses to help Outlook format the number.
- **Web page.** Enter the full URL (Uniform Resource Locator); for example http://www.mypage.com/mypage.htm.

The large box at the bottom of the dialog is a free-form notes area where you can jot any general information regarding the contact: gift ideas, grudges or vendettas, and so on. Note that the box expands to accept as much information as you care to type.

Details Tab

In the Details tab (see Figure 12-3), you record business and personal details about the contact, including the contact's department, manager, and more. You may also enter the contact's birthday and wedding anniversary; these dates are automatically added as events to your calendar (see "Managing Your Calendar" later in this chapter).

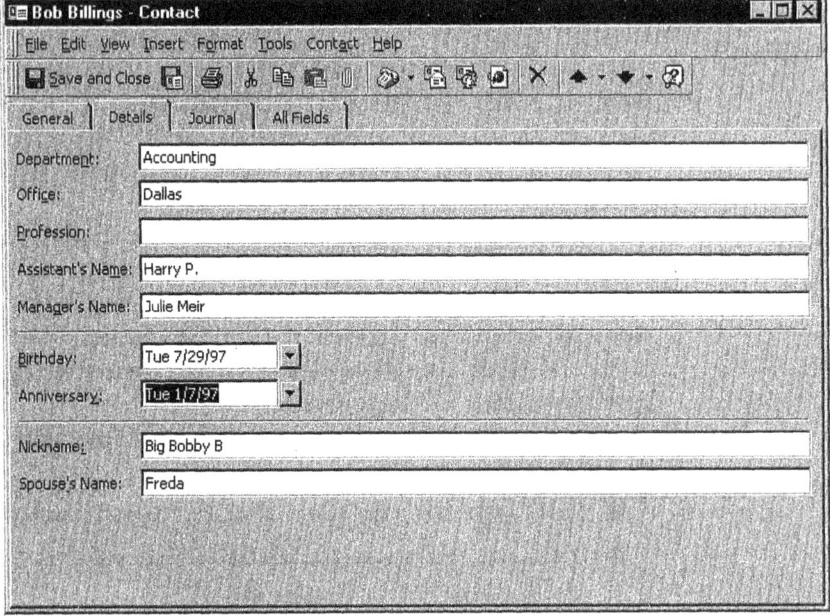

Figure 12-3: On the contact dialog's Details tab, add business and personal profile info about the contact.

Journal Tab

The Journal tab shows Journal entries related to the contact (see "Keeping Your Journal" later in this chapter). You can click the New Journal Entry button to add a new entry. To instruct Outlook to keep a journal for this contact, check the check box next to Automatically record journal entries for this contact.

Fast Track

After entering a contact from a particular company, you can save yourself some work when creating a new contact item for another person in the same company.

Open the contact you've already created, then choose Contact | New Contact from Same Company. A new contact dialog opens, with all of the business-related entries—company, business address, business phone, and so on—already filled in with the entries from the other contact. Supply a full name for the contact, edit and expand the other information as necessary, and click Save and Close.

All Fields

The All Fields tab provides you with a tab on which you can record and view even more detailed information than that collected by the other tabs. You select a table of *fields* (types of data to display) from the list at the top of the dialog. A table of data appears, showing Names (the name of each field) and Values (the data for this contact). Information you have already supplied for this contact appears in the Values column.

To enter expanded information for this contact, select a list of fields that contains the Name entries you want, then type the values. To create your own custom fields, click the New button.

Fast Track

In the contact dialog's General tab, the File as entry shows the name by which this contact will be shown (and alphabetized) in the Contact list. By default, the File as entry matches the Full Name entry. You can, however, change the File as entry to show a contact under a different heading in the list.

You may drop down the File as list to choose a different presentation of the full name; for example, you may choose to file your contacts in last-name-first format (Corleone, Fredo) so that they'll appear in the contact list alphabetized by last name. You may instead type an entry in File as to file a contact under a completely different name. For example, if the contact is your dentist, you may want to enter Dentist in File as. For casual contacts, enter a nickname, or just a first name, in File as.

Saving Time & Typing With Your Contacts

The default view for the Contacts folder is the Address Cards view, in which each contact appears as a simple card (see Figure 12-4) showing name, phone numbers, and e-mail addresses. Address Cards view is convenient, because you'll see many contacts at one time, and because the phone numbers are easy to see. Other valuable views include:

- **Detailed Address Cards.** Shows complete information for each contact: name, company, address, phone, and so on.
- **Phone List.** Formats all of your contacts in a table and shows just names and phone numbers.

You can choose these views and others by dropping down the Current View list from the toolbar or by choosing View | Current View.

In any view, you can open the full contact dialog to see all of the information for the contact by double-clicking the contact in the Contact list.

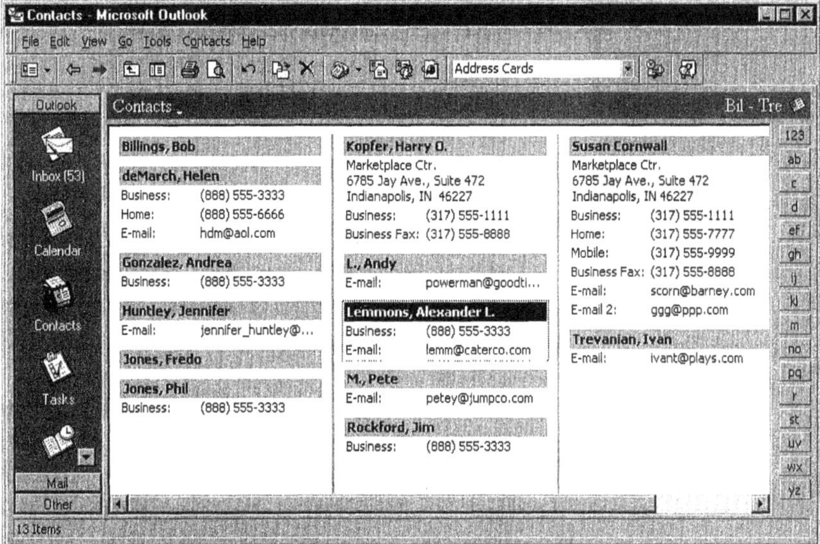

Figure 12-4: The default view in the Contacts folder, Address Cards, shows just the basics for each contact.

Net-Savvy

If you've supplied a Web page entry on the General tab for a contact, and if Windows is configured for Internet access, you can access the Web page by opening the contact and clicking the Explore Web page button. When you click the button, your default Web browser opens, Windows establishes the Internet connection, and the page appears.

Addressing a Message

When sending e-mail to your contacts, you can open a new message window pre-addressed to one or more of your contacts, saving you the step of choosing a contact from the Address Book (see Chapter 11, "Getting Started With Outlook").

As with most other things, Outlook gives you too many ways to do this (the results are identical, no matter which way you do it). While the contact is open, or when it is selected in the Contact list, click the New Message to Contact button or choose Contact | New Message to Contact. Also, you can drag a contact from the Contact list and drop it on the Inbox shortcut icon in the Outlook Bar. Finally, you can select the contact in the Contact list, click the Move to Folder button on the toolbar, and choose Inbox.

A new message window opens, pre-addressed to the contact. (See Chapter 11 to learn how to complete and send the message.)

Fast Track

To quickly address a paper letter to a contact, select the contact in the list and choose Contacts | New Letter to Contact. Word opens, and in Word the Letter Wizard opens to take you quickly through the steps for setting up the letter. When you finish with the Letter Wizard, you'll have a formatted letter pre-addressed to the contact and also an envelope ready to print. All you have to do is type the body of the letter, and you're finished.

Telephoning a Contact

If your PC modem is connected to the same phone line you use to make voice calls from your telephone, you can ask Outlook to dial voice calls to your contacts.

In the Contacts folder, select the contact you want to call. On the toolbar, click the AutoDialer button to open the New Call dialog (see Figure 12-5). If the contact has only one telephone number, click Start Call. If you've entered multiple numbers for the contact, drop down the Number list on the dialog, choose a number, then click Start Call.

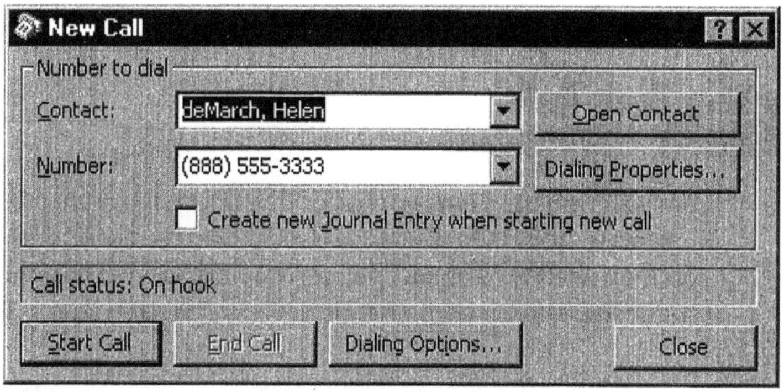

Figure 12-5: Select a contact and click the AutoDialer button to make a phone call.

Walk-Through: Adding a Contact

Follow the steps below to practice adding a contact to your contacts list.

1. Think of someone who you'd like to add to your contacts list (or invent someone—an imaginary friend), and assemble any notes or papers you need to recall the person's address, phone number, and other information.
2. Open the Contacts folder.
3. Click the New button.
4. On the General tab, click the Full Name button.
5. Fill in the boxes on the Check Full Name dialog, and click OK.
6. Click the Address button.
7. Type the contact's business address in the Check Address dialog, and click OK.
8. Drop down the list beneath the Address button, and choose Home.
9. Click the Address Button, type the contact's home address in the Check Address dialog, and click OK.
10. Click in the Business phone box, type a complete number (area code first, no spaces or punctuation; for example 5556667777). When finished, click in the Home phone number box.

    The business number you supplied is reformatted with standard spacing and punctuation; for example, (555) 666-7777.
11. Using other boxes on the General and Details tabs, supply any other information you want to record for this contact.
12. Click Save and Close on the contact dialog's toolbar.

    The new contact appears in your Contacts list.

Tackling Daily Tasks

Your *tasks* are the items you enter in a to-do list, both short-term and long-term projects that you need to remember to do and whose progress you may need to keep an eye on. You add to your to-do list—or *task list*—by describing each of your tasks in the task dialog. To review your task list and keep up with what you're supposed to be doing, you can open the Tasks folder, or you can open the Calendar folder and review the TaskPad (see "Managing Your Calendar" later in this chapter).

Adding or Editing a Task

To create a new task, open the Task dialog (see Figure 12-6) by switching to the Tasks folder and clicking the New button. On the dialog's two tabs, enter any information relevant to the task at hand. To edit an existing task, open the Tasks folder and double-click the task in the task list.

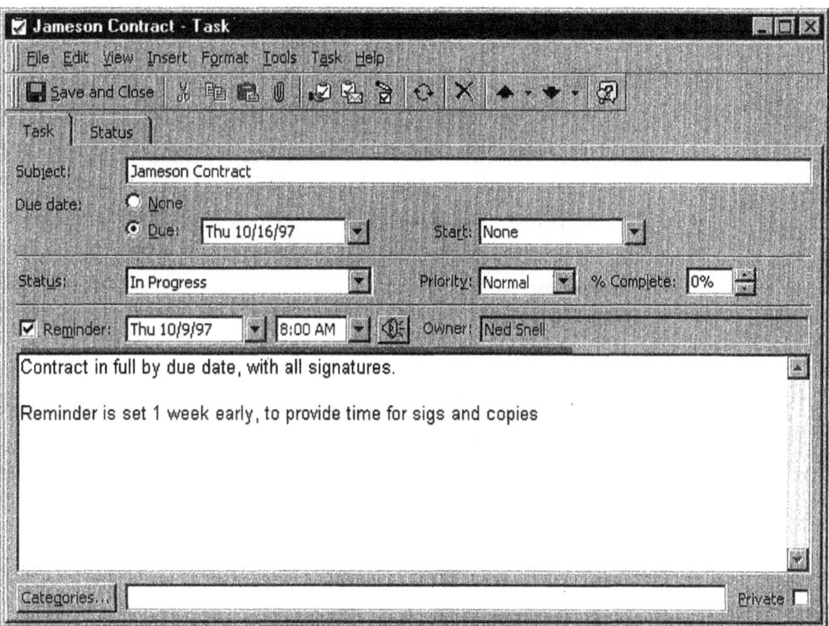

Figure 12-6: Use the Task dialog's Task tab to describe a new task.

In the Task dialog, the only required entry is the Subject box on the Task tab, where you describe the task. Take care to phrase the subject in a way that meaningfully describes the task; the subject is what will represent this task in the task list.

Fast Track

You can create a new task from an e-mail message. From any mail folder, drag the message and drop it on the Office Bar's Tasks button. (Alternatively, you may select the message, click the Move to Folder button on the toolbar, and choose Tasks.)

A task dialog opens, with some boxes automatically filled in with information from the message. For example, the Subject box on the Task tab shows the message's subject. The text box at the bottom of the Task tab shows the complete text of the message. You may add to or change the information on the task any way you like.

Task Tab

In addition to entering the task's subject, you may use the Task tab to assign a due date and start date for the task. The easiest way to select dates is to click the Down arrow keys on the Due date or Start date entry boxes. When you do, a little calendar drops down (see Figure 12-7). On the miniature calendar, click a date, or click the Today or None button. To change the month shown by the calendar, click one of the arrows on either side of the month name at the top of the calendar.

Figure 12-7: Dropping down most date list boxes in Outlook displays a miniature calendar, from which you choose the date.

To further describe the task's status and importance, the following fields have drop-down lists for assigning various labels to the information.

- **Status.** A description of the current status of the task, which you may update later as the task's status changes.
- **Priority.** You can assign Low, Normal, or High priority to any task. In some Tasks folder views, a priority column appears. The column is empty next to a task with Normal priority, but shows an exclamation point next to a high-priority task, and a down arrow next to a low-priority task.
- **Percent Complete.** Your estimate of the percentage of the task already finished.

Check the Reminder check box to ask Outlook to display a reminder regarding this task at a date and time you choose from the drop-down lists provided. At the selected date and time, a little pop-up message appears on your screen—on top of any Windows application you may be using at the time—reminding you about the task. (If Outlook is closed when the time for the reminder comes, the reminder appears the next time you open Outlook.) Click the speaker button to instruct Outlook to play a sound clip when displaying the reminder, just to help bring your attention to the reminder.

At the bottom of the Task tab, a free-form text box appears, in which you can enter as much information as you like to further describe the task.

Status Tab

On the task dialog's Status tab, enter amounts of time (hours, days, weeks, etc.) in Total work and Actual work to describe the status of the project. For example, if a task is expected to require 80 hours to complete, enter **80 hours** in Total work. If some work has already been completed on this task, enter the number of hours already spent in Actual work. As the days pass, Outlook automatically adds eight hours a day to Actual work until you mark the task completed. If you did not actually spend eight hours a day on the project, you can edit the Status tab to record the actual time worked on the task.

The remaining boxes on the Status tab provide a place for you to record miscellaneous information related to the task, such as mileage, billing information, and so on.

FYI: Outlook Knows What "Tomorrow" Means

Outlook is smart about dates and times. In any of the boxes where you may enter a date or time, Outlook accepts an English description of a date or time and figures out the correct entry on its own.

For example, in any box requiring a date, you may type a date properly, in the form month/date/year (for example 9/11/97). However, you may instead enter a description of a date, such as **this Friday** or **four days from now**. Outlook automatically determines the date you're describing and replaces your entry with the date. In a box requiring a time, you may enter **noon**, and Outlook replaces your entry with 12:00 PM. Other types of descriptions Outlook can decipher include:

- Midnight
- 10 hours from now
- Two days ago, three months ago
- Four months from yesterday
- Last Wednesday

Outlook also accepts the names of well-known holidays that occur on the same date every year. For example, Outlook automatically converts "Christmas" to 12/25, but can't figure out "Easter," because that holiday moves. Frankly, you may as well just type the date. After all, what's easier: typing Feb 14 or 2/14, or typing Valentine's Day?

Working With Tasks

Once your tasks are recorded, you may review them in the list that appears in the Tasks folder or in the Calendar folder (when its view includes the TaskPad). Note that the Subject and other information shown in the task list differs depending upon the status of the task:

- Current tasks are shown in regular black text.
- Overdue tasks (as determined by the due date you entered in the Task tab) are shown in red letters, to remind you of their urgency. (If *all* of your tasks are red, hide.)

- Completed tasks are shown in gray letters, ~~struck through~~. Even though you've marked them as complete (see "Marking a Task Complete" next), they remain in the task list in this crossed-out form until you delete them (see "Archiving & Deleting Items" later in this chapter).

The default view in the Tasks folder is Simple List, which shows just subjects and due dates. To see the details of any task, double-click the task to open it in the Task dialog. To see more detail in the Tasks list itself, drop down the Current View list on the toolbar (or choose View | Current View) and choose Detailed List, which shows most of the same stuff Simple List shows, plus priority, percentage complete, and other status information.

Marking a Task Complete

In the Tasks folder's Simple List view, and in the TaskPad, the heading for the second column from the right is a checked checkbox—that's the Completed column. To mark any task as completed, click in the Completed column in the row occupied by that task. A checkmark appears in the Completed column for the task, and the task's entry in the list turns gray and appears crossed out. The task remains in the list until you delete it or archive it (see "Archiving & Deleting Items" later in this chapter).

Creating a Status Report

You can quickly create and send a status report summarizing any task. This feature is great for keeping supervisors or others updated on the status of a project.

To create and send the report, open the task, then choose Task | Send Status Report. A new message window opens (Figure 12-8). In the body of the message, a summary of information from the task dialog appears, including the task's subject, priority, due date, percent complete, and other status information. You may type in the message body to add your own comments, explanations or excuses, and address and send the message as you might any other (see Chapter 11, "Getting Started With Outlook").

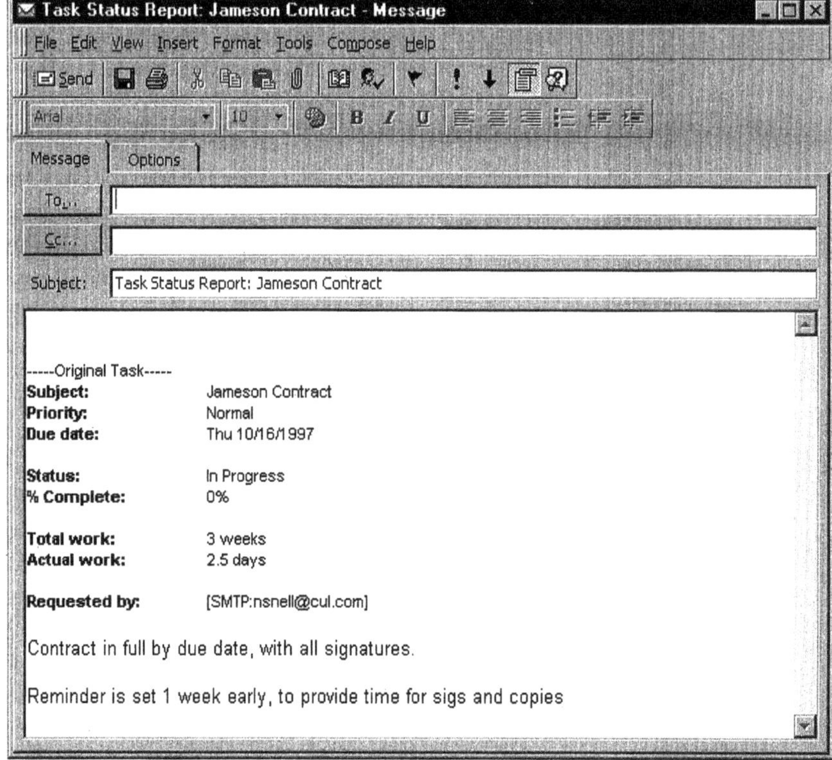

Figure 12-8: To send a Status Report, open the task and choose Task | Send Status Report.

Assigning a Task to Someone Else

Call it "management," or call it "passing the buck," there are times when you may want to create a task, then throw it into some poor soul's inbox. You can assign a task to anyone in your Contacts list who uses Outlook. When you assign a task, you send a *task request* to the contact. That contact responds by sending you a *task response*.

The best way to assign a task is to create the task first as you might any other, then create the task request by opening the task in its task dialog and choosing Task | Assign Task. A To line is added to the Task tab, and a Send button replaces the Save button on the dialog's toolbar. Type the name of the contact in the To line, or click the To button and choose from the list that appears (Figure 12-9).

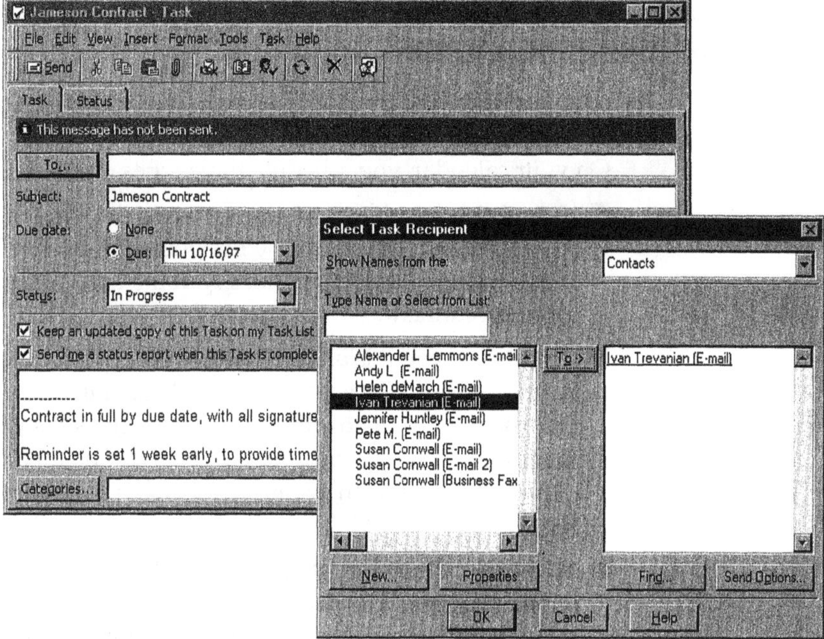

Figure 12-9: Choose Task | Assign Task to hand off a task to another person.

Above the text box at the bottom of the Task tab, observe two check boxes you may use to help keep track of the task after it leaves your hands:

- **Keep an updated copy of this task on my task list**. Check this check box to keep a copy of the assigned task in your own task list.
- **Send me a status report when this task is complete**. When you check this check box, a status report is automatically generated and sent to you from the contact's PC when he or she marks the task completed.

Click the Send button on the task dialog's toolbar to send the task request. When the contact opens the message in Inbox, the message features two buttons: Accept and Reject. When the contact clicks Accept, Outlook automatically generates and sends the task response to inform you that the contact has accepted the task. Note that, even if you keep a copy of the task in your task list, the contact is now the "owner" of the task and is the only person who can make changes to it.

Managing Your Calendar

The *Calendar* is Outlook's replacement for your desktop calendar—your daily, weekly, and monthly time planner.

On your calendar, you schedule three types of time-takers:

- **Appointments.** Blocks of time set aside in a day for any purpose. Appointments appear at their appointed times in the Day pane, as a blue-bordered box that blocks out the time you have allotted to the appointment.
- **Events.** An event is an activity that takes one or more full days, such as a conference. Events are indicated in a box at the top of the Day pane (right below the date) for the days they take place. Because you may have appointments during an event, on some days you may see an event at the top of the day, and appointments below.
- **Meetings.** A meeting is an appointment that requires the presence of other people. You can put a meeting on your calendar as a regular appointment. But Calendar offers special meeting planning tools that may help get the meeting organized.

The default view in the Calendar folder is Day/Week/Month (see Figure 12-10), and it's certainly the most useful view. In Day/Week/Month view, your schedule for one day appears in a large pane on the left of the screen; you can move around in the day by scrolling up or down. At upper right, two months appear. You choose the day shown in the Day pane by clicking any day in the month. To change the months shown, click the arrows that appear to the left and right of the month names. Below the Month pane appears the TaskPad, which lists your current tasks from your Tasks folder. (In fact, if you double-click a task in the TaskPad, the Task dialog opens to show you the details.)

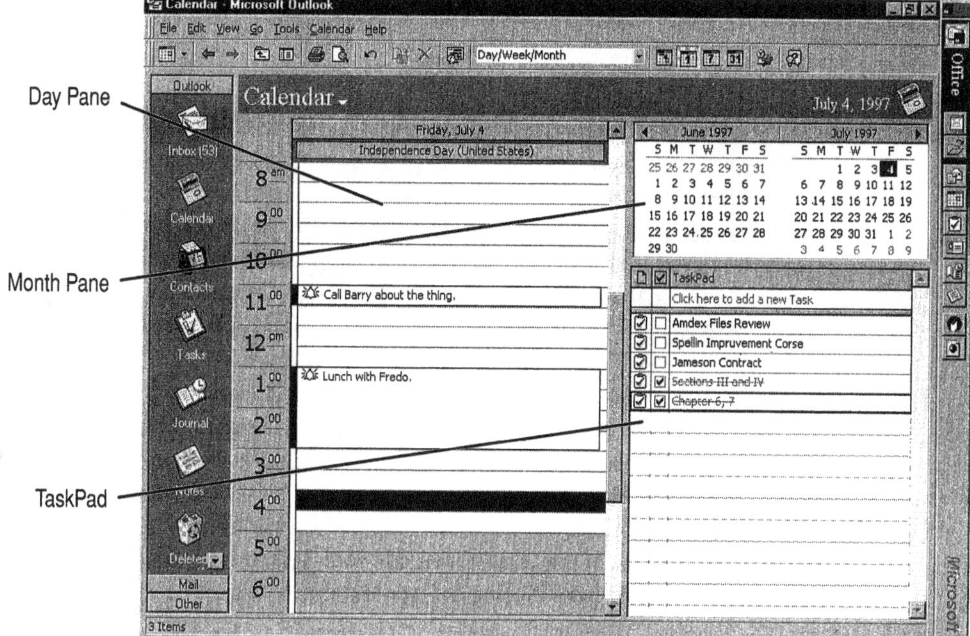

Figure 12-10: The default view in the Calendar folder—Day/Week/Month—shows a full day's appointments, two months, and your current tasks.

Adding Holidays

Just to get yourself started, you may want to add holidays to your calendar. Outlook can automatically add to the appropriate calendar dates all the holidays commonly observed in one or more countries. On its day, each holiday appears as an all-day event.

To add holidays, choose Tools | Options from within any Outlook folder, and click the Calendar tab of the Options dialog. Click the Add Holidays button that appears near the bottom of the tab. The Add Holidays to Calendar dialog appears, listing countries for which Outlook has a file of holidays. Click the check box next to one or more countries, then click OK.

FYI: What if Your *Country's* Holidays Aren't *Your* Holidays?

The holidays Outlook supplies for each country generally include national and secular holidays, plus only those religious holidays that are also popularly observed as secular holidays. For example, Outlook's file of U.S. holidays includes national holidays (Independence Day and the assorted Monday holidays) and major secularized Christian holidays such as Easter and Christmas, but no Jewish or Islamic holidays, and none of the less secularized Christian holidays, such as Good Friday. (St. Patrick's Day, however, is included—go figure.)

However, if you look carefully at the list in the Add Holidays to Calendar dialog, you'll see three entries that are not countries: Christian Religious Holidays, Islamic Religious Holidays, and Jewish Religious Holidays. By checking the check box next to one or more of these options in addition to the check box for your country, you may add to your calendar all of the holidays that matter to you. If you observe a faith that is not one of the three above, add your holidays to your calendar, one at a time, as new events (see "Adding an Appointment or Event" next).

Adding an Appointment or Event

You can quickly jot an appointment in your calendar without recording a lot of detail about it. To do that, switch to the Calendar folder, and use the Month pane to choose the day on which the appointment will take place. The day opens in the Day pane, which also shows any event or appointments already planned for that day. Single-click the time for the appointment, and type the text you want to appear.

To set up a more detailed appointment listing or meeting, double-click the Day pane at the time the appointment or meeting will begin. The appointment dialog opens (see Figure 12-11), and shows two tabs: Appointment and Meeting Planner. On the Appointment tab, fill in the boxes to describe the appointment or event. Type a subject to name the appointment (be descriptive—the subject appears in the Day box to describe the appointment). If you need to remember a particular location for the appointment, supply one.

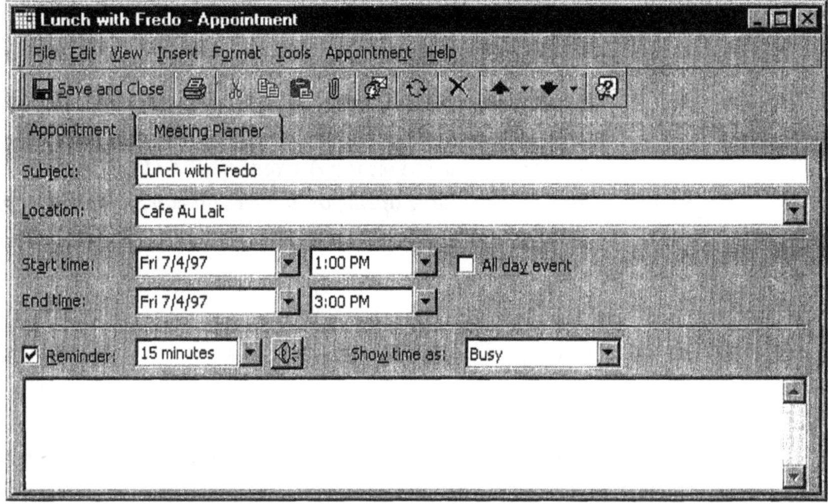

Figure 12-11: Fill in the appointment dialog to create a detailed appointment description or plan a meeting.

If you're adding an event, check the All day event check box. For an appointment, use the drop-down lists to choose a Start time and End time. Note that the date portion of the Start and End times, and the Start time, are already filled in with the date and time you double-clicked in the Day pane to open the dialog. However, you may change the dates and times. Also, if an event will take more than one day, change the date box for End time to the final day of the event.

Fast Track

To schedule an appointment at which you will work on a task from your task list, display the day of the appointment in the Day pane. In the TaskPad, click and hold on the task, drag it to the Day pane, and drop it on the time you want the appointment to begin. The Appointment dialog opens, showing the task's subject as the appointment's. Edit or expand the appointment however you want to.

Fast Track

If the appointment or event is one that may be repeated at regular intervals—for example, a regular weekly or monthly meeting—click the Recurrence button on the Appointment dialog's toolbar. The Appointment Recurrence dialog opens, on which you can set up the appointment to show up automatically on your Calendar at regular intervals.

Check the Reminder check box to ask Outlook to remind you of the appointment. Next to the Reminder check box, drop down the list to choose how long ahead of the appointment you want the reminder to appear. For example, choose 1 hour from the list, and a reminder pops up (if Outlook is running) 1 hour before the appointment time. Click the speaker icon to request that a sound clip play when the reminder appears, just in case you're not looking at your screen at the time. (When an appointment is configured for a reminder, a bell appears next to the appointment in the Day pane, to remind you that Outlook will alert you.)

When finished setting up your appointment, click the Save and Close button. If you just added an event, it appears in a gray box at the top of its day. If you added an appointment, it appears at its scheduled time on the Day box. Also, any date for which you have an appointment scheduled appears in bold when its month appears in the Month box.

Fast Track

For an appointment, you can save yourself some work on that dialog by first selecting the block of time for the appointment. In the Day box, click and hold at the time the appointment will begin, then drag downward to highlight the portion of the day the appointment will require. Release the button, then double-click on the selection.

Planning a Meeting

To plan a meeting, set up an appointment for the meeting time, then switch to the Meeting Planner tab of the appointment dialog.

Your name appears automatically in the list of Attendees along the left side of the tab (see Figure 12-12). In the calendar grid on the tab, a column is blocked to show the time for the meeting. The time is the same as for the appointment you just created, and it is also shown in the Meeting start time and Meeting end time boxes at the bottom of the dialog.

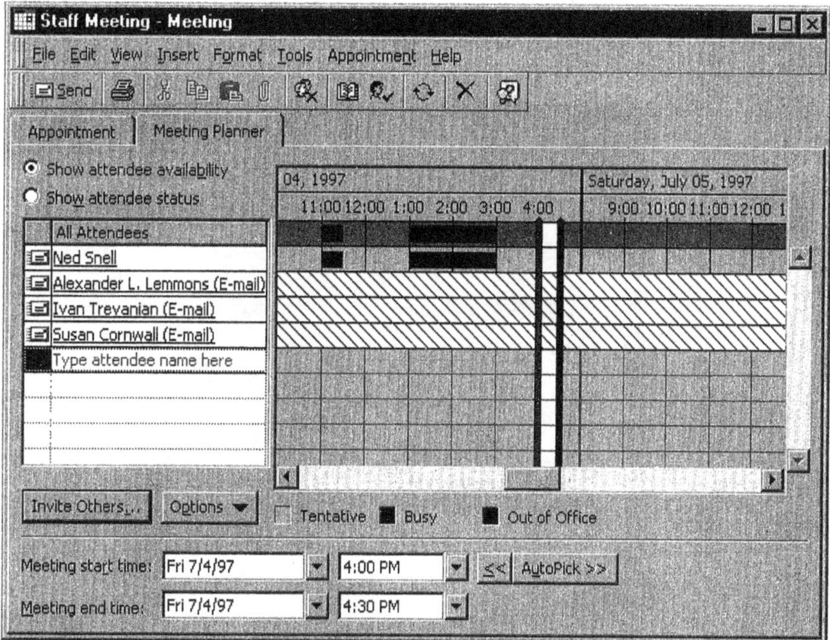

Figure 12-12: Use the Meeting Planner tab to choose a time, pick attendees, and automatically send out invitations.

Fast Track

Instead of filling in the Meeting Planner tab of the appointment dialog, you can plan a meeting from scratch. From the Calendar folder, click the Plan a Meeting button on the toolbar. The Plan a Meeting dialog opens, and it is nearly identical to the Meeting Planner tab. Plan the meeting (including its day and time) exactly as you would in the Meeting Planner tab, then click the dialog's Make Meeting button.

To choose who will attend the meeting, you may simply type names in the attendee list. However, if you want invitations sent automatically to the attendees, click the Invite Others button under the Attendees list. A dialog like the one in Figure 12-13 appears, showing names from your Contact list. For each person you want to invite, select the name in the list, and click the Required button (to send a message requiring the contact's presence) or the Optional button (to send a message that requests the contact's presence).

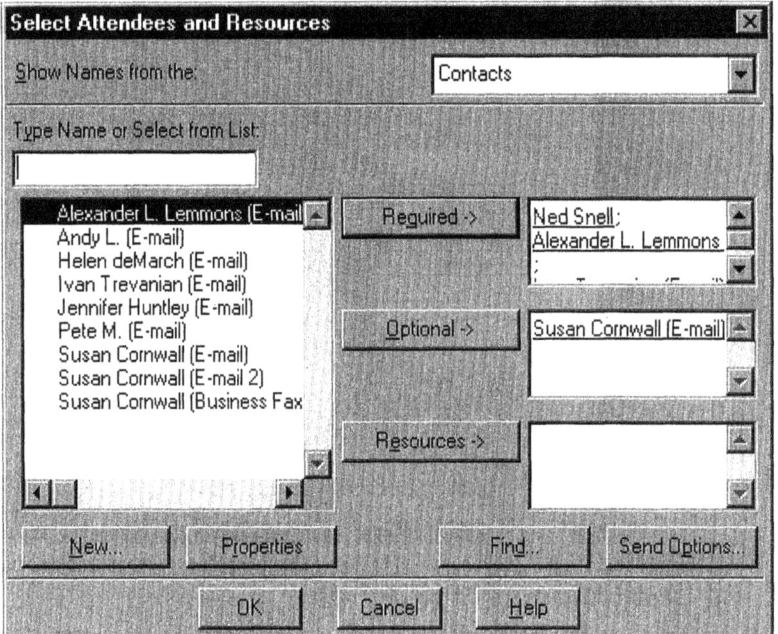

Figure 12-13: When choosing attendees to invite to a meeting, some may be Required, others are Optional.

When finished choosing attendees, click OK to return to the Meeting Planner tab. Verify that the attendees, times, and other options on the tab are what you want, then click Save and Close. The meeting appears in your calendar at its scheduled day and time, and invitations are sent automatically to all attendees. You may open and edit the meeting later. If you do, when you Save and Close, Outlook asks whether you want to send updated invitations to the attendees.

Fast Track

If your network uses Microsoft Exchange Server and your administrator has given you permission to share your contacts' private Outlook folders, the Meeting Planner can read each contact's Outlook files to determine when each is tied up with appointments on a selected day. For each attendee you select, the attendee's busy and free time is indicated on the calendar grid that appears to the right of the attendee list.

After choosing all of your attendees, you can review the calendar grid to select a meeting time when no one has a conflict. To solicit Outlook's help with picking a good meeting time, click the AutoPick button at the bottom of the Meeting Planner.

Rescheduling an Appointment or Meeting

When plans change (and they always do), you can double-click the appointment in the Day pane to open the Appointment dialog, then change the day, or the Start and End time. But there's an easier way, using the Day/Week/Month view and drag and drop.

- To change the appointment time, point to the left edge of the appointment in the Day pane, so that the pointer becomes a four-pointed arrow. Click and hold, drag the appointment to its new time, and drop.
- To change the appointment length, point to the top or bottom border of the appointment, so that the pointer becomes a two-pointed arrow. Click and hold, drag the border to lengthen or shorten the appointment, and release.
- To change the appointment day, display the appointment's current day in the Day pane, then display in the Month pane the month in which the appointment will take place. Click and hold on the appointment, drag it to the Month pane, and drop it on the desired day. The Day pane switches to the day you dropped on, and shows the appointment on the new day but at its old time. Change the time and length if necessary.

Walk-Through: Setting Up an Appointment

Follow the steps below to practice scheduling an appointment.

1. Open your Calendar in Day/Week/Month view.
2. In the Month pane, click a day on which you want to schedule an appointment.
   The selected day opens in the Day pane.
3. Point to an hour in the day, and click.
   A half-hour block is highlighted.
4. Type an appointment subject; for example, **Fire Lenny**.
   A half-hour appointment is scheduled.
5. Point to the bottom border of the appointment, so that the pointer becomes a two-pointed arrow.
6. Click and drag the border downward until the appointment takes up two hours, then release.
7. Point to the appointment and double-click.
   The appointment opens in the Appointment dialog.
8. In Location, type **Murphy's Tavern**.
9. Check the Reminder check box.
10. Drop down the reminder list, and choose 30 minutes.
11. Click Save and Close.
    On the selected day, one half-hour before it's time to fire Lenny, you'll be reminded that you planned to fire Lenny at Murphy's Tavern.

Keeping Your Journal

Just as your task list and calendar record what you *plan* to do, your journal keeps track of what you *really* do. Your journal records many activities—*journal entries*—automatically by monitoring your activity in Outlook and other Office applications. You can supplement the journal with entries you create yourself.

Automatically, the journal can record anything you do in Office, including:

- **Documents.** Each time you create, open, or edit a file in Word, PowerPoint, Excel, Access, or another program that's part of the Office family, a journal entry records the date and time, file name, and amount of time you spent on it.
- **Messages.** Every time you send or receive any type of message—e-mail messages, meeting requests and responses, and task requests and responses—a journal entry records it.

Not only can it record these events, but the journal also keeps track of which contacts were involved in any message activities. You can customize the journal so that it records entries for messages to or from some contacts, but not others.

In the default view (By Type), the Journal folder groups its accumulated entries by the type of activity recorded (see Figure 12-14). To see the entries, click the plus sign (+) that appears to the left of each type. A dateline appears along the top of the view, and the journal entries appear beneath the date on which the activity took place. To view later or earlier journal entries, click the month name on the dateline to drop down a small calendar. Click a date on the month, or click Today. To change the month, click one of the arrows that appears to the right and left of the month name on the calendar.

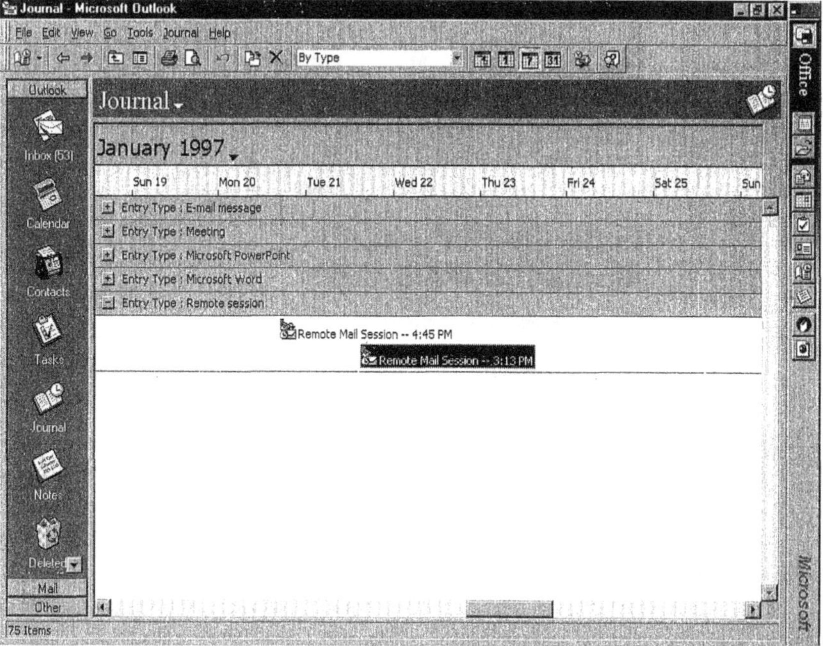

Figure 12-14: The Journal folder groups your journal entries by type and indicates the date of each entry by showing them along a horizontal dateline.

To see the details for any journal entry, double-click it. A summary appears (see Figure 12-15). If the entry refers to a file, a file icon appears in the summary. Double-clicking the icon opens the file in its application.

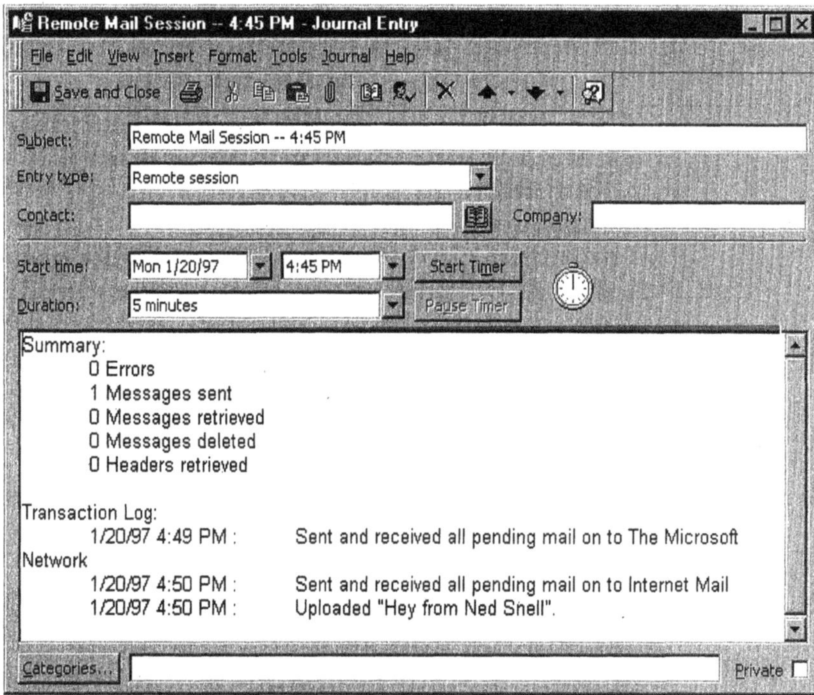

Figure 12-15: Double-click a journal entry to see the details.

Customizing the Journal

To choose what types of activity the journal records automatically (and what it ignores), choose Tools | Options in any Outlook folder, then click the Journal tab in the Options dialog (see Figure 12-16). Check check boxes next to the types of messages you want recorded and next to the contacts for whom you want to record these messages. (If a check box does not appear next to a name, messages to and from that contact will not be recorded.)

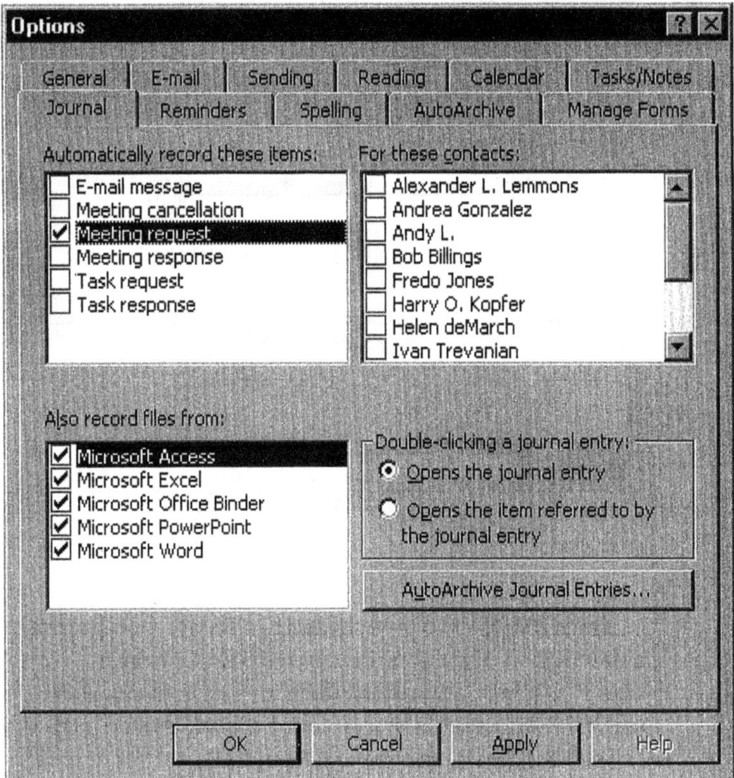

Figure 12-16: Choose Tools | Options | Journal to choose what activities the Journal records automatically.

In the bottom half of the Journal tab, choose the Office applications for which you want file activity recorded in the journal.

Adding Journal Entries

To create a journal entry to record an activity that's not recorded automatically, switch to the Journal folder and click the New button. The journal entry dialog appears (Figure 12-17), on which you can record any information you want.

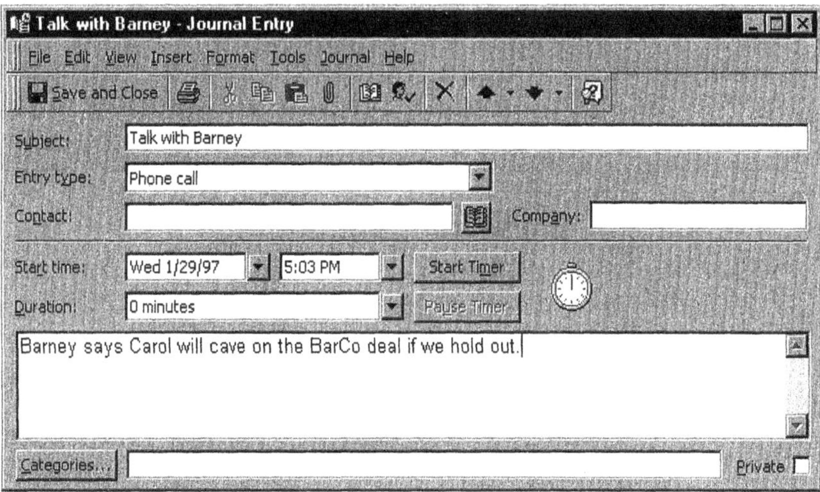

Figure 12-17: In the Journal folder, click the New button to add a new entry of your own.

Enter a subject to give the entry a name, then choose an entry type—a description of the type of activity you're recording—from the list provided. You may also record the names of contacts involved in the activity (click the Address Book icon in the dialog to open a dialog from which you can select names), and the length of time you spent on the activity.

In the large box at the bottom of the dialog, type a description of the activity, or add any other information that belongs in the entry. When finished making your entry, click the Save and Close button.

Jotting Notes

Quick Quiz: If you have a piece of information you need to record, and it's not a message, contact, appointment, task, or journal entry, what is it? It's a *note*. Notes are Microsoft's way of saying, "We've pretty much covered all the important types of information in the other item types and folders, but you never know what someone's going to want to record, so let's give 'em a free-form, no-rules type of item where they can jot down whatever they want."

While a note is a pretty simple animal, you can use it in myriad ways, just like the more sophisticated item types. For example, drag a note and drop it on the Office Bar's Inbox shortcut. A new message opens, showing the complete text of the note as the message body and the name of the note as the message subject. Notes give you a place to jot information that you may use later in a more formal way, as in a message or task, which you can then easily copy into other formats.

To create a note, switch to the Notes folder and click the New button. A note box opens—type away (Figure 12-18). When you're finished, press Esc to close the note. The note appears in the folder as a note icon, with a name created automatically out of the first few words of the note text.

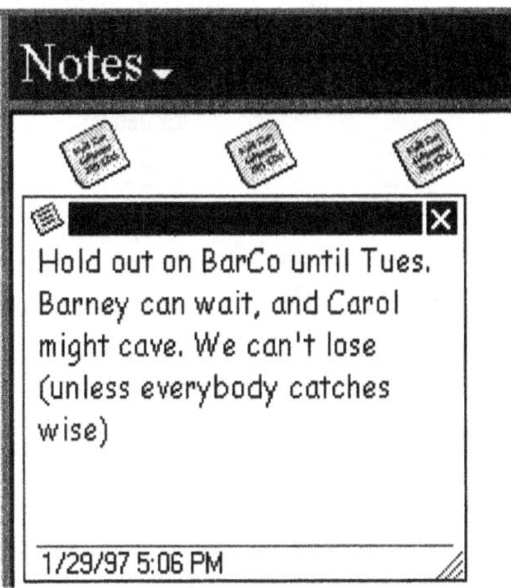

Figure 12-18: A note is a note—type what you want.

Managing Outlook Items

Almost everything you've learned to do in Outlook up to this point involves creating items, or just accumulating them (as you do when you receive messages or allow the journal to record your life). After some time, your folders have so many items in them that they become unmanageable. That's where this final bit about Outlook comes in.

On the next few pages, you'll learn how to use Outlook's powerful Find facility to locate any item and how to group items to help you manage them better. You'll also discover how to remove items when you no longer need them, either by *archiving* them or by deleting them.

Finding Items

Outlook's built-in Find facility works very much like Windows's Find dialog, only better. To use Find, begin in any Outlook folder. Click the Find Items button on the toolbar, or choose Tools | Find Items. Outlook's Find dialog opens, as shown in Figure 12-19.

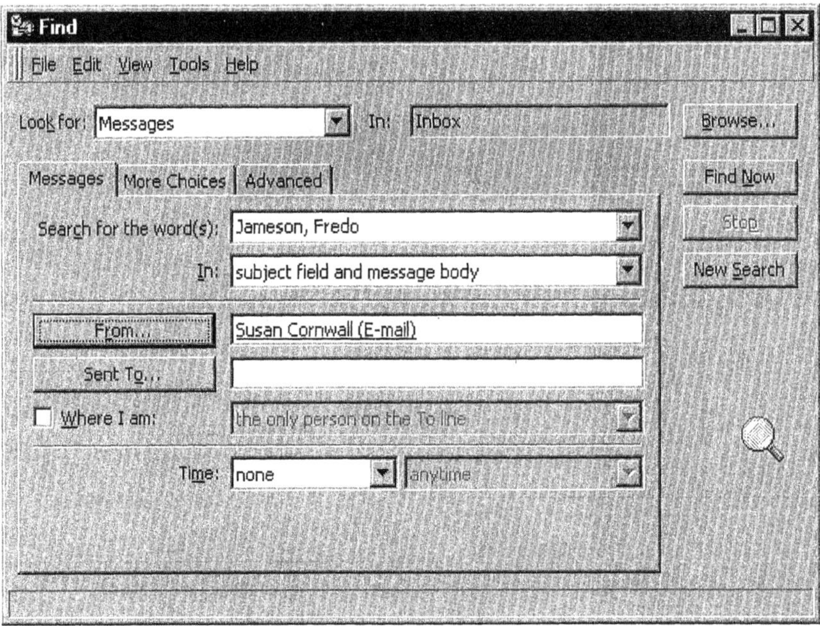

Figure 12-19: Fill in search criteria in the Find dialog to locate items and files.

Before doing anything else with Find, drop down the Look for list at the top of the dialog and select the type of item for which you're looking. The Look for list includes not only the separate types of Outlook items (Appointments, Tasks, and so on), but a choice to find "Any type of Outlook item," or to search for Windows files (the "Files" choice) beyond Outlook. The reason you must choose from Look in first is that the first tab in the dialog—and the options within it—changes, depending upon what you select.

After making your Look for choice, use the first tab (its name will match the Look for choice you made) to enter the search criteria. For example, when the Look for choice is Messages, the Messages tab shows a Search for the word(s) box. Enter a word or words in the box, and Find will locate only messages containing those words. Also on the Message tab, you may choose to find messages from specific senders or to specific recipients. If the first tab does not provide you with enough options to limit the search to exactly the files you seek, narrow the search using the More Choices and Advanced tabs.

After entering your search criteria, click Find Now. A list drops down from the bottom of the Find dialog; as Find locates items or files matching your search criteria, it lists them in the box. To view or edit any file or item in the list, double-click it.

Grouping Items by Category

When you create or edit any item, you can assign it to a *category*; for example, you may choose to categorize some items as business-related, others as personal. If you assign such categories, you can easily change the view of any folder so that it groups items by category. The grouping may help you better manage your items, especially when you must juggle many.

At the bottom of each of the dialogs on which you create or edit items, a Categories button appears. Click that button to open the Categories dialog (see Figure 12-20), and then assign the item to as many categories as you wish by checking check boxes in the dialog.

To group items in a Folder view by category, choose View | Current View | By Category.

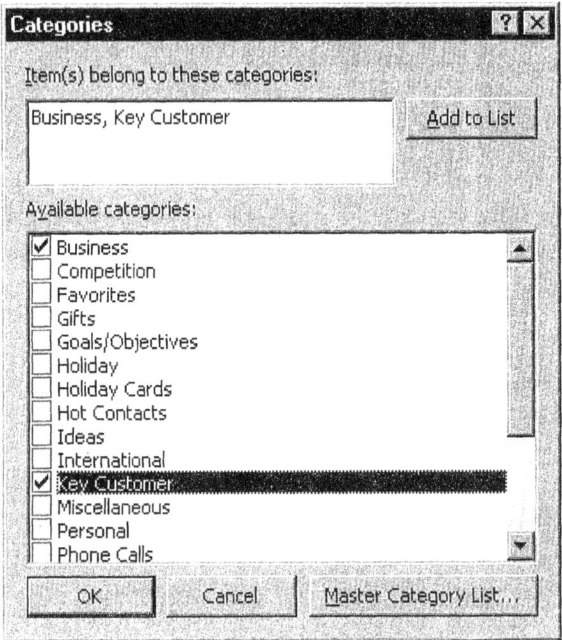

Figure 12-20: You can assign any item to one or more categories, then group the folder by category, for better organization.

Archiving & Deleting Items

Outlook piles up old e-mail messages, journal entries, and other accumulated crud faster than a storm drain gathers leaves. Eventually, you'll have a lot of old stuff on file in Outlook that you really don't need anymore. When that happens, you have two ways to clear out the clutter:

- **Archiving.** Moving old items out of your folders into a separate archive file. You can still open and view the old items in the archive file, if you suddenly discover a need for old information. But in the meantime, the old stuff is removed from the folders you work with every day.

- **Deleting.** Wiping the items out for good. When you delete items in Outlook, they're not deleted right away—they're moved to the Deleted Items folder, which works like Windows Recycle Bin, holding items until you confirm that you really want them deleted.

Archiving Items

Archiving is handled automatically by Outlook's AutoArchive facility. After a specified number of days passes (14 days, by default), AutoArchive goes into action when you start Outlook. AutoArchive checks for "expired" items and moves the expired items to the archive file. To control what AutoArchive moves, you must choose, folder by folder, when you want items in that folder considered "expired," by setting AutoArchive options. Note that you cannot AutoArchive Contacts.

You choose AutoArchive options separately for each folder, which makes sense. You may want to keep a message item for years, while you may want to clear out old journal entries after only a month or two. By default, the following folders are already set up for AutoArchive:

- **Calendar, Tasks, and Journal.** Items in these folders expire after six months. Appointments expire six months after the appointment date, tasks expire six months after the date they are marked completed (tasks not completed are not archived).
- **Sent Items, Deleted Items.** Items in these folders expire after two months.

The Inbox, Notes, and Contacts folders are not set up by default to AutoArchive; their items remain in the folders until you delete them, or until you configure AutoArchive options for each folder (except for Contacts, which cannot be AutoArchived).

To set up or change the AutoArchive options for a folder, open that folder in Outlook, then choose File | Folder | Properties. Choose the AutoArchive tab on the folder's Properties sheet (see Figure 12-21). To enable AutoArchive for the folder, check the check box next to Clean out items older than, and use the lists provided to choose a number of days, weeks, or months to hold onto an item before marking it "expired."

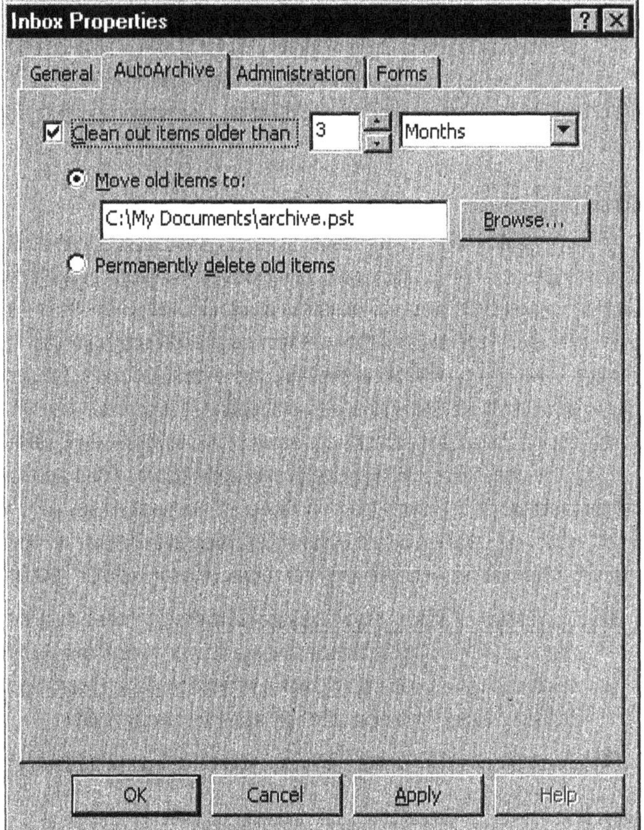

Figure 12-21: Choose AutoArchive options separately for each folder to control how and when items in the folder are AutoArchived.

Also on the AutoArchive tab, you'll find two very important radio buttons:

- **Move old items to.** When this button is checked, expired items are copied into the archive folder specified.
- **Permanently delete old items.** When this button is checked, AutoArchive won't archive expired items—it deletes them instead.

To change general options for AutoArchive—settings that affect all folders—choose Tools | Options, then click the AutoArchive tab. On that tab, you can choose such options as the number of days AutoArchive waits before each time it archives your expired items.

Retrieving Archived Items

Ideally, you should configure the AutoArchive options for each folder so that you never archive something you're likely to need later. However, there may be times when you need to refer to an old e-mail message or appointment, and when that happens, you need to see your archived items.

Before you can see them, you must configure the archive file as a service in Outlook. Following the steps in Chapter 11 for adding a service, choose Add on the Services dialog, then choose Personal Folders from the Add Service to Profile dialog. A dialog opens in which you can navigate to and select the archive file (by default, it's C:\My Documents\archive.pst).

After you create the service, open your Folder list in Outlook. You'll see a new Personal Folders folder above your regular Outlook folders. Click the plus sign on Personal Folders, and subfolders appear, each containing items you've archived. To view archived items, choose a subfolder. To restore an item (move it back into an active Outlook folder), drag it from the subfolder to the Outlook Bar and drop it on the desired shortcut.

Deleting Items

To delete items as needed, just select them in their folders and press your Del key (or click the Delete button on the toolbar). Deleted items are moved to the Deleted Items folder, and remain there until you deal with them, or until the Deleted items folder is archived.

To permanently delete items in your Deleted Items folder, select them and press your Del key (or click the Delete button). A message appears, asking whether you want the items permanently deleted. Click Yes to delete them. Note that when you delete items from your Deleted Items folder, they're really and finally deleted—they do not go on to the Windows Recycle Bin. To permanently delete all of the items in your Deleted Items folder at once, choose Tools | Empty "Deleted Items" Folder.

To restore a deleted item (move it back to an active folder), select it in the Deleted Items folder, click the Move to Folder button on the toolbar, and choose the folder to which you want to move the item.

Moving On

That's it for Outlook—the rest is up to you. As I told you before, keep up with Outlook, and it will keep up with you. Now, before moving on, go back and finish adding all of your current contacts, tasks, and appointments, so you can begin to reap Outlook's benefits. (Don't ask me how I know you didn't already do it—I just know.)

If you're ready to move ahead, you're about to discover Excel—an amazing, fun, powerful, frustrating, rewarding bag of buttons and baubles. It falls into the very oldest category of PC software—"spreadsheet programs." But truly, the category has fallen out of date. Sure, you can still total up columns of numbers in Excel, as in a PC spreadsheet of 20 years ago or a paper one from the 19th century. (Bob Cratchit used a parchment spreadsheet to do Scrooge's taxes.) But you can also use Excel to compose attractive documents; manage data; feed slick-looking tables to Word documents, PowerPoint shows, and Web pages; and much more. Turn the page slowly, as you repeat over and over, "It's not just a spreadsheet... It's not just a spreadsheet...."

appendix

Installing & Configuring Office 97

This appendix offers complete instructions for installing Office 97, and for adding and removing Office 97 programs and accessories after installation.

Note: Network Installations

The instructions in this appendix are for installing Office 97 on a stand-alone PC. To learn how to install Office on a network, consult the file Netwrk8.txt. You can find this file in the root directory of the Office 97 CD or on the first disk of the diskette-based version of Office.

System Requirements

- **PC.** A PC with a 486 or Pentium processor (Pentium recommended).
- **Operating System.** Windows 95, or Windows NT 3.51 with Service Pack 5, or Windows NT 4.0 (Service Pack 2 recommended with NT 4.0).

- **Memory.** To run Office 97, your PC must be equipped with the following memory:
    - For Windows 95, 8MB (12MB for using Access).
    - For Windows NT Workstation, 16MB.

  While meeting these minimums will enable you to run Office programs, performance may be slow, and you may not be able to run multiple Office programs simultaneously. For best all-around performance, the recommended minimum is 16MB for Windows 95, 24MB for Windows NT.
- **Peripherals.** A CD-ROM drive is required for installing Office from the CD-ROM. A mouse or other pointing device is not required, but is highly recommended. A sound card and modem are not required for running Office but will enable you to take advantage of sound and communications features in some programs.

Note: From a coupon included in all Office packages, you may order the Office 97 Standard Edition on diskettes; if you order the diskettes, a CD-ROM drive is not required for using the Office 97 Standard Edition programs (Word, Excel, PowerPoint, Outlook), but is still highly recommended. Note that the diskettes do not include many additional files that are included on the CD, such as Internet Explorer, a clip art library, and sound clips.

Preparing for Windows 95 Installation

While the following steps are not required, they will help ensure a smooth installation and the best possible performance of Office 97 programs after installation.

These steps are unnecessary on Windows NT PCs, where the hard disk is checked for errors and defragmented automatically at startup.

Run ScanDisk to Find & Repair Disk Faults

1. Close all programs except Windows 95.
2. Click the Start button and choose Programs | Accessories | System Tools | ScanDisk.

3. Click the radio button next to Thorough.
4. Click the Start button on the ScanDisk dialog and follow any prompts from ScanDisk. Note that the scan may take an hour or more, depending on the size of your hard disk.

Run the Disk Defragmenter to Consolidate Free Disk Space

Only *after* running ScanDisk:

1. Close all programs except Windows 95.
2. Click the Start button and choose Programs | Accessories | System Tools | Disk Defragmenter.
3. Choose the letter of the drive on which you will install Office 97, then click OK.
4. On the dialog that appears, click the Advanced button. (Note that the dialog that appears may say that your disk does not need to be defragmented. Proceed with the defragmentation anyway.)
5. On the dialog that appears, choose Full Defragmentation, and clear the checkbox for Check drive for errors.
6. Click the Start button on the Disk Defragmenter dialog and follow any prompts. The defragmentation may take an hour or more, depending on the size of your hard disk.
7. After defragmentation is complete, restart your PC before installing Office 97.

Installing Office 97

To install Office 97, follow these steps. The process typically requires from 5 to 20 minutes. Before beginning, have your Office 97 CD or diskettes and the Office 97 packaging handy. (In Step 9, you will need the CD key printed on a label at the back of the CD case.)

Installing From Diskettes

If you are installing the Office 97 Standard Edition from diskettes, the installation steps are generally the same as for the CD, except for Steps 3, 4, and 5. To install from diskettes:

Step 3: Insert the first diskette in your diskette drive.

Step 4: Click the Start button, and choose Run.

Step 5: Type the drive letter of your diskette drive, followed by a colon (:) and the word setup (for example, a:setup), then press Enter.

Throughout the installation, Office Setup will prompt you for each new diskette, as needed.

1. Start Windows.
2. Make sure no programs are running, other than Windows itself (including any virus-protection programs).
3. Insert your Office 97 CD in your CD-ROM drive.

   If a feature called AutoPlay is enabled on your PC, the Office Setup Program starts automatically and displays its Welcome dialog after a few moments; skip to Step 6.

   If after a few moments the Office Setup program does not begin, move on to Step 4.
4. Click the Windows Start button and choose Run.
5. Type the drive letter of your CD-ROM drive (on most PCs, it's d), followed by a colon (:) and the word setup (for example, d:setup), then press Enter.
6. After a few moments, the Office Setup program's Welcome dialog opens. Click Continue.
7. Type your Name and (optionally) a company or other Organization name, then click OK.

8. A dialog displays the entries you made in Step 7. Click OK to confirm them or click Change to go back to Step 7.
9. Type the CD key (you'll find it on a label on the back of the CD case) and click OK.
10. A dialog displays your product identification number. Jot it down and put it away where you can find it if you need to speak with a Microsoft technical support representative. Click OK.
11. A dialog displays the name of the folder in which Office will be stored. To accept the folder, click OK. To change the folder, click Change.
12. A dialog appears, offering you the three different Office 97 installation options (see Figure A-1). Click the option that best matches your current needs. Note that you can add or delete Office programs and files at any time after installation if you discover that the setup you choose now does not match your needs. (See "Adding & Removing Office 97 Programs," later in this Appendix.)

    - **Typical.** Includes all Office applications and most popular options. Choose Typical for a good, general-purpose Office installation.
    - **Custom.** Offers you dialogs from which you may select to install or ignore any Office application or accessory. Choose Custom installation when you want to leave out one or more Office applications you don't plan to use, or to ensure that particular Office support files are included.
    - **Run from CD-ROM.** Installs the bare minimum files on your hard disk, and requires that the Office 97 CD be in your CD-ROM drive at all times when you use Office. This option may serve temporarily (while you're shopping for a new PC or hard disk), but is not recommended for general Office use.

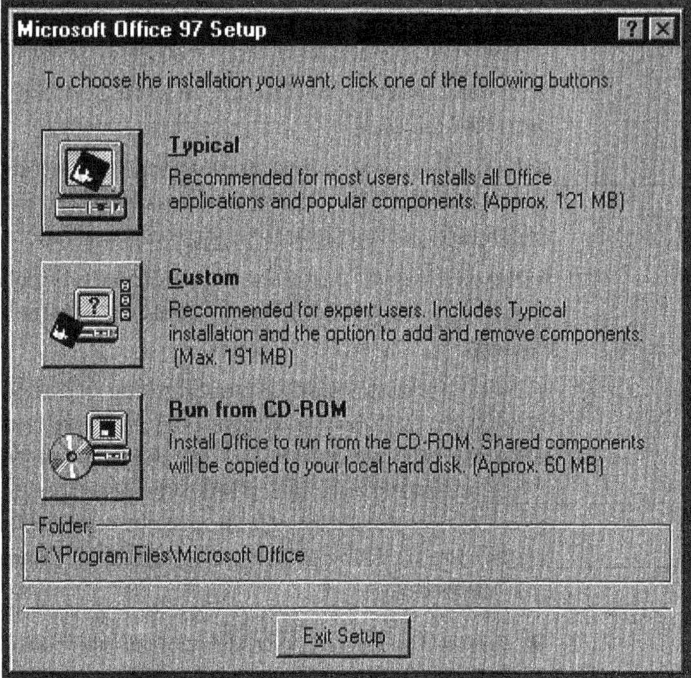

Figure A-1: Click a PC picture next to your desired installation option.

If you choose Typical, move ahead to Step 13.

If you choose Custom, a dialog opens on which you may check check boxes to customize your Office setup. When you arrive at this dialog, the items already checked are those that Office would include in the Typical installation. You add or remove the checkmark from any option to configure your custom installation. (To learn more about using checkmarks to choose options, review Steps 2-4 of the procedure for "Adding & Removing Office 97 Programs.") When finished choosing options, skip to Step 15.

13. A dialog listing optional Office components appears (see Figure A-2). To add any option to the installation, click its check box so that a checkmark appears there. To ignore any option, leave its check box empty (or click its check box to remove the checkmark, if the box is already checked). Note that you can add or remove any of these options later.
14. Click Continue.

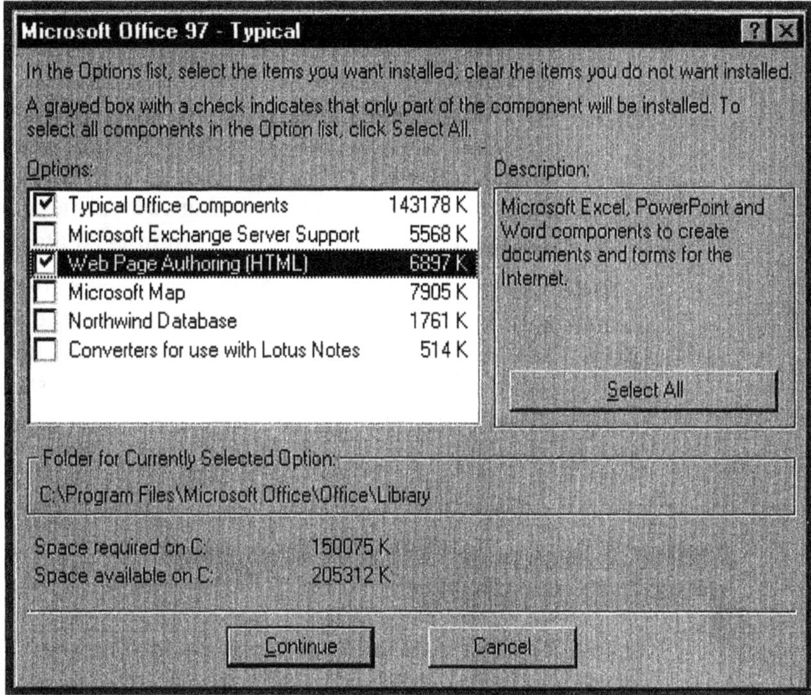

Figure A-2: In the Typical installation, check the check box of any optional component you want installed.

15. Office searches your PC for files and programs from earlier Office versions. If it locates any, a dialog appears asking whether you want old Office files removed. You may click Yes to remove the old Office files, or No to keep them. Note that keeping your old Office files has no adverse effect on Office 97. Note too that, if you remove your old Office files, only the program and support files are removed—the files and documents you created in those programs are not deleted.

    After you choose what you want done with your old Office files, the rest of the installation is automatic. Office Setup removes your old files (if you asked it to), then moves ahead to copying all of the selected Office programs and files to your hard disk.

16. When Office Setup finishes copying files and updating your Windows configuration for Office 97, it displays a message reporting that installation was completed successfully. The message includes a button you may click to register Office 97 online if you have a modem, although doing so is not required. Click the Online Registration button, or click OK to exit the Setup program.

17. You may remove your Office 97 CD (or final diskette) from your PC. Unless you selected the Run from CD-ROM option in Step 12, you do not need to have the Office CD in your CD-ROM drive while using Office. However, when performing certain activities—such as using the Office 97 Clip Gallery—you may need to insert the CD to take advantage of support files that are stored there. Whenever inserting your CD is beneficial or required for an activity, Office prompts you to do so.

Note: You may be prompted to restart Windows after you complete the installation. Even if you are not prompted to do so, it's always a good idea to restart Windows after installing the software and before beginning to use the Office programs. Until Windows is restarted, some Office configuration options may not be enabled, and thus won't function as they should.

Adding & Removing Office 97 Programs

At any time after installation, you may decide you want to add an Office component that you did not install originally. Or you may find that you don't use a particular Office program or accessory, and decide to remove it from your hard disk to reclaim some disk space. You can accomplish either with the steps below.

Throughout this book, you are alerted to some useful components which are not included in the Typical installation. In particular, you may want to run the Add/Remove Programs procedure to add:

- **Converters and Filters, and Web page authoring.** You'll find these options in the list on the first Maintenance dialog.
- **Office Shortcut Bar, Clip Gallery, and Clip Art Library**. You'll find these optional components under the Office Tools option in the first Maintenance dialog.

To add and remove Office 97 components:

1. Repeat Steps 1 through 5 of the Office installation procedure, as described earlier in this appendix.

When you complete Step 5, Office Setup searches your system, determines that Office 97 has already been installed, and displays a Welcome dialog with five buttons. In addition to adding and removing programs, you may use this dialog to reinstall Office 97, remove Office 97 from your PC, or register Office through your modem.

2. Click the Add/Remove button. The Maintenance dialog appears, as shown in Figure A-3. In the dialog, the Options list shows each of the major Office applications or groups of accessories. Next to each option in the list:
   - A black checkmark indicates that the option is already installed on your PC.
   - An empty check box indicates that the option is not installed on your PC.
   - A gray checkmark indicates that some components of the option have been installed, while other components have not been. You can see which parts of an option have or haven't been installed by clicking the option to highlight it, then clicking the Change Option button.

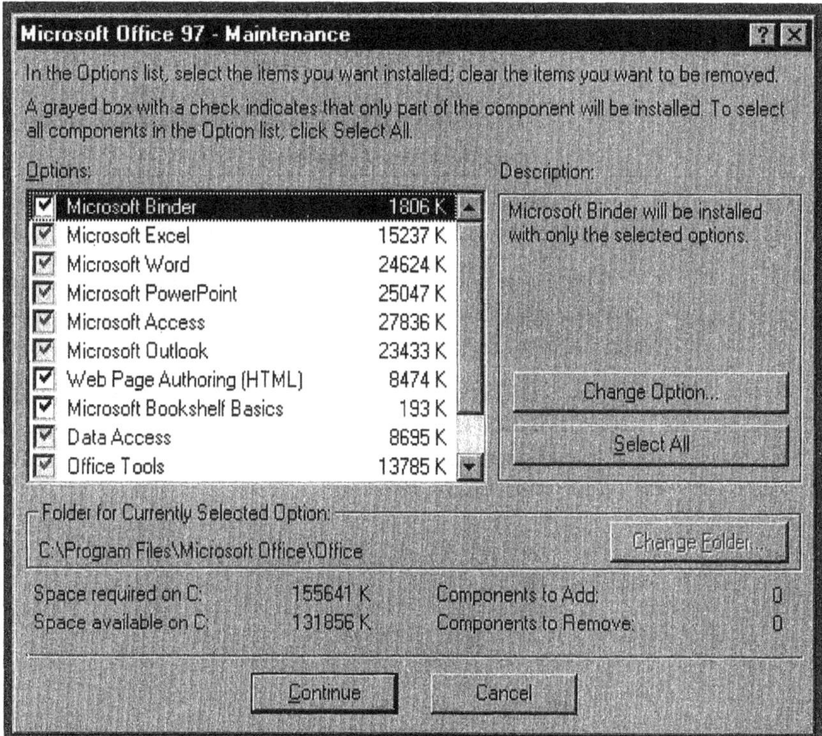

Figure A-3: Check and uncheck check boxes to specify which Office components you want on your PC.

3. By clicking a check box, you add or remove the checkmark there. Adding a checkmark next to an option instructs Setup to install that option on your PC. Removing a checkmark instructs Setup to delete that option. As you go, note that:
   - If you click an option's name to highlight it, a Description of the option appears on the right side of the dialog.
   - For most options, you may install or remove the whole option or just selected components of it. For example, click Office Tools to highlight it, then click the Change Option button to display a list of the separate components in Office Tools (see Figure A-4). In that list, check the check box for any components you want, then click OK to go back to the first Maintenance dialog. Note that, in some cases, you'll find options within options within options.
   - With each change you make on the Maintenance dialog, the bottom of the dialog keeps a running tally of the hard disk space the checked options will require (Space required) and the current free space on your hard disk (Space available). You can use these values to determine whether you need to uncheck some options.
   - To automatically check or uncheck all options listed in any Maintenance dialog, click the Select All button.

When you finish checking and unchecking check boxes, the pattern of checkmarks shows exactly which parts of Office will be on your PC after you perform Step 4.

4. Click OK on the main Maintenance dialog. Office Setup goes to work. Any checked components not already on your PC are copied to your hard disk, and any unchecked options that are on your PC are deleted.

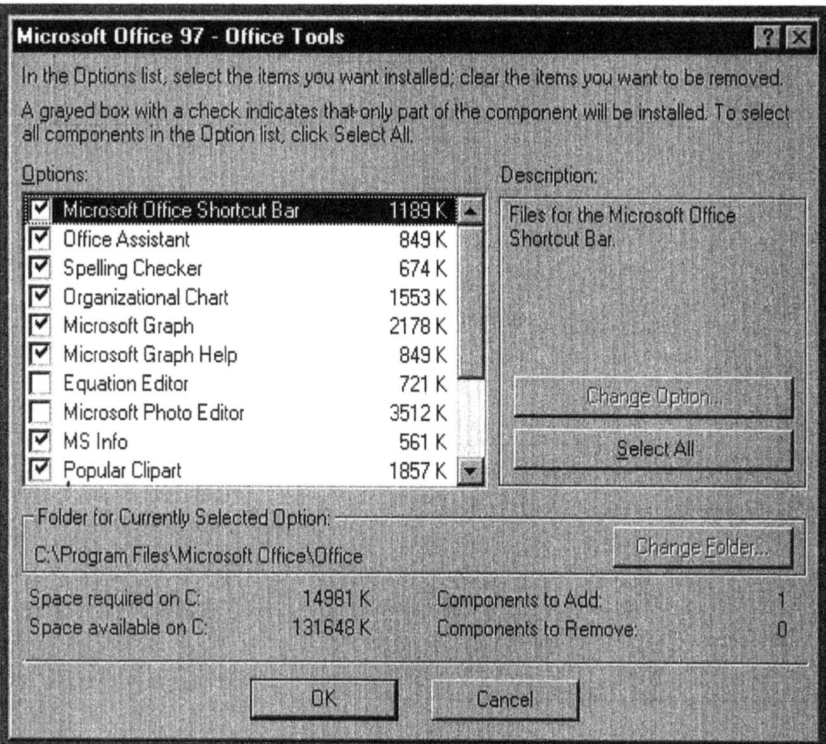

Figure A-4: Some options have multiple components you can choose individually. For example, in the previous figure (A-3), if you highlight the Office Tools option and then click the Change Option button, you see this list on which you individually check or uncheck each component of Office Tools.

When Office Setup finishes copying and deleting files and updating your Windows configuration, it displays a message reporting that the setup was completed successfully. You may remove your Office 97 CD (or diskette) from your PC.

You may be prompted to restart Windows after you complete the installation. Even if you are not prompted to do so, it's always a good idea to restart Windows after adding or removing Office programs.

Glossary

address 1. A set of instructions that describes the precise location of a file or other resource, such as a Web page address, or the path to a file on a network. 2. The precise row/column location of a cell or range in an Excel worksheet.

Address Book A file of name and address information used for conveniently addressing e-mail messages, envelopes, and letters.

alignment The relative position of text or data within a document page or in a cell. An object can have both horizontal alignment (left, center, right, justified) and vertical alignment (top, bottom, center, justified).

application A term generally applied to a computer program (or, more often, set of programs) used to accomplish a specific task. Each major part of Office 97—Word, Excel, and so on—is an application, though each may also informally be called a program.

attribute A type of formatting applied to text that does not change the font of the text, but still changes its appearance. Attributes include bold, italic, underline, and color.

background A color, pattern, or picture that appears in a file behind any other content in the document, including text, data, and pictures.

Binder An Office program that combines multiple files from different programs so you can edit and print them as a single project.

browser (see Web browser)

bulleted list A list of items in which each new item is preceded by a bullet character.

button A graphic on a toolbar or a rectangular button on a dialog that performs a function when the user points to it and clicks. Buttons in dialogs have labels on them which describe their function; the function of a toolbar button is suggested by its appearance, and also by the tooltip which appears when you point to a toolbar button. (See also radio button.)

cell One box within a grid created by the intersection of rows and columns. Text and data are entered within cells in Excel worksheets, Word tables, and Access tables.

cell range (see range)

check box A small square box on a dialog used to enable or disable an option. Each time you point to a check box and click, a checkmark is inserted or removed there. When the checkmark appears in the check box, the option is enabled.

client (see server)

clip art A general term describing a collection of picture files (and sometimes also multimedia) you may use freely in your documents.

Clip Gallery An optional Office facility that organizes a library of pictures, sound clips, and video clips by subject, and helps you insert those files into Office documents.

comment Text entered into a file, like a sticky note, to comment on the file, but not intended to be displayed or printed with the file in its final form.

copy and paste (see cut and paste)

cut and paste A Windows feature, supported by Office, which enables you to move information from one file or program to another (or from place to place within a file) by cutting it from one spot and then pasting it in another. A similar feature, copy and paste, copies information among locations, files, or programs.

data Information in a file. Data may take many forms: text, numbers, pictures, logical values, and so on.

database A collection of data organized into records so it can be manipulated by database operations such as filtering and sorting.

default A setting or action used automatically by a program when you do not indicate an alternative.

default Web browser A Web browser configured in Windows to open automatically any time an action requiring a Web browser is initiated. For example, if a hyperlink in an Office document leads to a Web page, clicking that hyperlink opens the default Web browser.

desktop The open area of the screen in Windows when not covered by programs or open files and folders. Folder, file, and program icons may be stored on the desktop, and certain icons—such as My Computer, Recycle Bin, and Network Neighborhood—may reside only on the desktop.

dialog Within a program, a pop-up window on which you select options that control how a particular action will be carried out.

drag and drop Dragging means pointing to an object onscreen, clicking and holding the mouse button, and moving the pointer to move the object. Dragging and dropping means dragging an object to a specific location—such as a folder—then releasing the mouse button to "drop" the object.

drawing object A simple line drawing created with the Drawing toolbar available in most Office programs.

drop-down list A list of options in a dialog (and occasionally in a toolbar) from which you may choose an item. An arrow appears at the right end of all drop-down lists; you click the arrow to drop down (open) the list so you may see the options and select one.

edit cursor A tall, flashing vertical bar that appears within text onscreen, indicating the spot at which whatever you type will appear within the text.

e-mail 1. Electronic mail, a system for exchanging messages through a computer network. 2. The messages exchanged through electronic mail.

extension (see file extension, filename)

file extension The three-letter suffix at the end of a filename, always preceded by a period (.) and usually phrased to indicate the type of file. For example, Word files generally use the extension .DOC, while Excel files generally use the extension .XLS.

fill 1. A patterned background for a cell, table, or document. 2. In Excel, data entered automatically in a worksheet when you drag the fill handle of a cell containing data.

filter In Excel and Access, a setting that restricts the display of data in a database to only a selected subset of the available data.

field A location in a form or database where a single piece of data resides.

fieldname A name used to identify a column of related fields in a database.

field code In a document, a code that accesses and displays information from another source, so that the information—not the field code—appears when the document is printed. Common field codes are DATE, TIME, and PAGE NUMBER.

filename The name by which a particular file is identified in Windows. A filename has three parts: A descriptive name, a period, and a three- or four-letter suffix called an extension. For example, My Word File.doc.

font A particular typeface in which text is set to control its appearance.

font size The precise size of text, measured in points (1/72 of an inch).

footer In a document, text repeated automatically across the bottom of multiple pages.

form A printed or online document designed to collect data. A typical form is made up of instructions for completing the form and fields in which the user will enter the data.

formula In Excel, an equation stored in a cell to perform mathematical operations.

function In Excel, a special operator used within a formula to perform complex equations and logical operations.

function keys The row of "F" keys on all PC keyboards, usually including F1 through F12. Each key has a specific use within a program, and some keys play the same role in multiple programs. For example, F1 opens some form of Help in all Windows programs; it opens the Office Assistant helper in all Office programs.

handle A small white or black square that appears along the boundaries of a selected object in a document. Clicking handles and dragging them alters the size and shape of the object within the layout of the document.

header In a document, text that's repeated across the tops of multiple pages.

HTML (see HyperText Markup Language)

hyperlink Text or a picture to which an unseen file address is attached. When viewing a document online, clicking a hyperlink opens the file to which the hyperlink points. Hyperlinks are often described casually as links.

HyperText Markup Language (HTML) The standard file format for publishing pages on the Web.

Internet Explorer A graphical Web browser from Microsoft, included with Office 97.

Internet account An account with an online service or Internet service provider through which you may access the Internet.

intranet An internal company network based on Web technology.

link The set of instructions that connects a linked object to a location within a document. (See also hyperlink.)

linked object A block of text, cells, a picture, or other data that is connected by a Windows link to a document in which it appears. Although the object appears in the document, it remains technically separate from the document file.

local network (see network)

mail merge A system for automatically generating pre-addressed form letters, envelopes, or labels by combining a database of names and addresses with a document containing field codes. Office supports mail merge by combining Word documents with Outlook's Address books.

Microsoft Network An international Internet service owned and operated by Microsoft.

MIME (see Multipurpose Internet Mail Extensions)

multimedia A general description for the creation and use of the various kinds of media files: pictures, sound clips, video clips, and animation.

Multipurpose Internet Mail Extensions (MIME) A standard that supports special features—such as fonts and colors—in e-mail messages exchanged between MIME-supporting e-mail programs.

network A group of computers interconnected so that they may share information. A network may be made up of computers all in one office or building (a *local network* or *local area network*), spread out to multiple cities (a *wide-area network*), or made up of computers and interconnected networks—*internetworks*—across the world, as is the Internet.

nonprinting characters Characters you type that affect the appearance of a document, such as tabs and paragraph breaks, that do not themselves appear in the printed document.

number format In Excel, a special formatting characteristic applied to data in cells to determine whether Excel is to treat the data as text, a number that can be used in an equation, a date, a time, or another format.

OfficeArt In Office 97, a set of tools for creating and conveniently inserting pictures in documents.

Office Assistant In Office 97, a new, animated cartoon help facility that monitors your actions, offers tips, and responds to your questions.

Office Shortcut bar (see Shortcut bar)

password A secret word that the user must type to enable a selected feature or open a protected file.

picture file A file in any of the many graphics file formats supported by Office programs. You can insert picture files in documents and format them there.

placeholder In PowerPoint, an invisible box that holds one element in the layout of a slide: a list, a title, a picture, and so on. Placeholders have handles so you can control their size and shape.

pointer The onscreen icon that moves when you move your mouse or other pointing device. You move the pointer to onscreen objects and then click the mouse button to perform an action on the object. The pointer usually appears as a white arrow, but you can customize it, and its appearance changes automatically under some circumstances.

query In Access, a set of database operations that together extract and display requested data from one or more databases.

radio button A small circle on a dialog used to enable or disable an option. Each time you point to a radio button and click, you select it (fill it in, black) or deselect it (make it empty, white). When the radio button is black, the option is enabled.

range In Excel, a specific rectangular block of cells described by an address or by a name you assign to the range.

right-click To point to an object and click the right mouse button, displaying a menu of actions you can perform related to that object.

select To highlight a block of text, group of cells, group of list items, a picture, or other object so that the next action you take affects everything that's selected. Selection is usually accomplished by clicking an object or by dragging across objects.

server A computer that stores files and programs for the use of other computers that are connected to it through a network. Computers that connect to a server and retrieve information from it (and the software on those computers that controls the exchange) are called *clients*.

Shortcut bar An optional Office 97 toolbar that resides (usually) along the right edge of the Windows desktop and provides quick access to some Office features.

shortcut key A combination of keyboard keys you can press to duplicate the action of a menu item or button in a program. Typically, you perform an action by pressing and holding Ctrl (or Alt), pressing another specific key, then releasing both keys.

Standard toolbar A toolbar that appears in all Office programs, containing buttons for basic operations such as creating, opening, and saving files. While all Office programs have a Standard toolbar, each program's Standard toolbar is different.

Start button A large button labeled Start that appears at the far left end of the Windows taskbar. Clicking the Start button opens the Start menu, from which all Office programs may be opened.

table Text or other data organized in rows and columns. Word, PowerPoint, Excel, and Access each create a different kind of table.

taskbar In Windows 95 and Windows NT version 4, a bar positioned (usually) along the bottom of the screen when Windows is running. The taskbar contains the Start button, and also has a button for each program or file that is currently open in Windows.

template In Word, PowerPoint, Excel, and Access, a special preformatted file used as a shortcut in creating a file of your own, or to impose formatting consistency among a group of related documents.

toolbar A row of graphical buttons appearing near the top of most program windows. You may click the buttons to perform common tasks quickly.

tooltip The name of a toolbar button, which appears momentarily when you point to the button and allow the pointer to rest on it for a moment. Tooltips are used to locate and identify the buttons on a toolbar.

Uniform Resource Locator (URL) A name for the address format generally used in Web browsers to identify resources on the Internet, such as Web pages.

URL (see Uniform Resource Locator)

view A display configuration that shows the data within a program window (and the Window itself) in a particular way. Most Office programs allow you to switch among various views, each suited to a different type of work.

Web Short for the World Wide Web (also known as WWW), a group of server computers that store Web pages and other resources that can be accessed through the Internet and displayed in a Web browser.

Web browser A program for interpreting HTML files to download and display Web pages stored on the Web or an intranet server. Netscape Navigator and Microsoft's Internet Explorer are two of the most popular browsers.

Web page A document written and stored in HTML file format. A Web page is designed to be viewed through a Web browser.

Web site A name used casually to refer variously to a Web page, a server on which a particular group of Web pages may be found, or a set of Web pages that together make up a multi-page document.

window The box within which a program or file appears in Windows.

Wizard A Windows program that helps you perform a complex task (usually within another program) by leading you through it, step-by-step.

workbook In Excel, a single Excel file made up of one or more worksheets.

worksheet In Excel, a single grid of cells within which you create tables and other Excel objects.

zoom The magnification level at which the program displays the text or data in a file. Office programs allow you to increase or decrease the zoom to fit the type of work you're doing.

Index

A

B

C

D

E

F

G

H

I

J

K

L

M

N

O

P

Q

R

S

T

U

V

W

X

Y

Z

www.ingramcontent.com/pod-product-compliance
Lightning Source LLC
Chambersburg PA
CBHW081455050326
40690CB00015B/2808

* 9 7 8 1 5 8 3 4 8 2 2 0 9 *